Changing War

Birmingham War Studies

Birmingham War Studies (BWS) is a series of works of original historical research in the area of History and War Studies. The works cover all aspects of war in the nineteenth and twentieth centuries, with the focus primarily, but not exclusively, on the British experience.

Series Editors:

Gary Sheffield, Chair of War Studies and Director of Military History and Jonathan Boff, Lecturer, both University of Birmingham, UK

Series Associate Editor:

Dan Todman, Senior Lecturer in History, Queen Mary, University of London, UK

Also in the series:

British Army Communications in the Second World War, Simon Godfrey

The British Army in Battle and its Image 1914–18, Stephen Badsey

The Human Face of War, Jim Storr

The Leadership, Direction and Legitimacy of the RAF Bomber Offensive from Inception to 1945, Peter Gray

Red Coat, Green Machine, Charles Kirke

Changing War

The British Army, the Hundred Days Campaign and the Birth of the Royal Air Force, 1918

Edited by
Gary Sheffield and Peter Gray

Bloomsbury T&T Clark
An Imprint of Bloomsbury Publishing Plc

B L O O M S B U R Y
LONDON · NEW DELHI · NEW YORK · SYDNEY

Bloomsbury T&T Clark
An imprint of Bloomsbury Publishing Plc

Imprint previously known as T&T Clark

50 Bedford Square	1385 Broadway
London	New York
WC1B 3DP	NY 10018
UK	USA

www.bloomsbury.com

BLOOMSBURY, T&T CLARK and the Diana logo are trademarks of Bloomsbury Publishing Plc

First published 2013
Paperback edition published 2015

© Gary Sheffield and Peter Gray, 2013

Individual chapters © the contributors

Gary Sheffield and Peter Gray have asserted their rights under the Copyright, Designs and Patents Act, 1988, to be identified as Author of this work.

All rights reserved. No part of this publication may be reproduced or transmitted in any form or by any means, electronic or mechanical, including photocopying, recording, or any information storage or retrieval system, without prior permission in writing from the publishers.

No responsibility for loss caused to any individual or organization acting on or refraining from action as a result of the material in this publication can be accepted by Bloomsbury or the author.

British Library Cataloguing-in-Publication Data
A catalogue record for this book is available from the British Library.

ISBN: HB: 978-1-441-15633-4
PB: 978-1-474-23297-5
ePDF: 978-1-4411-0125-9
ePUB: 978-1-4411-9952-2

Library of Congress Cataloging-in-Publication Data
A catalog record for this book is available from the Library of Congress

Typeset by Newgen Knowledge Works (P) Ltd., Chennai, India

Contents

Acknowledgements	vii
Series Editors' Introduction	viii
Editors' Biographies	x
Contributors' Biographies	xi
Introduction *Peter Gray*, *Ross Mahoney* and *Gary Sheffield*	1
1 Command Culture and Complexity: Third Army during the Hundred Days, August–November 1918 *Jonathan Boff*	19
2 'Delivering the Goods'. Operation *Landovery Castle*: A Logistical and Administrative Analysis of Canadian Corps Preparations for the Battle of Amiens 8–11 August, 1918 *Rob Thompson*	37
3 'After Amiens': Technology and Tactics in the British Expeditionary Force during the Advance to Victory, August–November 1918 *Bryn Hammond*	55
4 The Last Battle of the BEF: The Crossing of the Sambre-Oise Canal, 4 November 1918 *Niall Barr*	73
5 War of Liberation: British Second Army and Coalition Warfare in Flanders in the Hundred Days *Dennis Williams*	93
6 Behind the Lines: Sir Douglas Haig and the Cavalry Corps, September–October 1918 *Simon M. Justice*	111
7 The Air Ministry and the Formation of the Royal Air Force *Peter Gray*	135
8 The Smuts Report: Interpreting and Misinterpreting the Promise of Air Power *Christopher Luck*	149
9 The Genesis of Modern Warfare: The Contribution of Aviation Logistics *Peter Dye*	171
10 The Genesis of Modern Air Power: The RAF in 1918 *David Jordan*	191

11	The Battle of Amiens: Air-Ground Co-operation and its Implications for Imperial Policing *Simon Coningham*	207
12	The Battle of Amiens and the Development of British Air-Land Battle, 1918–45 *Alistair McCluskey*	231

Bibliography	249
Index	263

Acknowledgements

The editors would like to thank Ross Mahoney, a doctoral student of air power at the University of Birmingham, for his help with the donkey work of putting this book together and for stepping in at the eleventh hour to contribute to the Introduction. We would also like to thank the various University of Birmingham War Studies postgraduates who helped with the original conference, and also Mrs Carolyn Sweet and Dr John Bourne. Gary Sheffield would like to thank Dr James Pugh for some helpful steers on pre-1914 British military aviation. We have benefitted from an exemplary editor, Rhodri Mogford, who has also been very patient.

Thanks to the National Library of Scotland for permission to quote from Haldane's papers. Regarding the unpublished papers and diary of Major-General Sir Cecil Lothian Nicholson, IWM 01/14/1 (GB62) (World War One), every effort was made to contact the copyright holder who was unfortunately untraceable. Every effort has been made to contact copyright holders of all other material quoted in this volume. In cases where this has not been possible, the editors would appreciate any information which might help them do so.

Thanks to the Imperial War Museum, the Tank Museum and the Special Collections department at the Brotherton Library, University of Leeds, UK, for their kind permission to quote material used in Bryn Hammond's chapter.

Gary Sheffield and Peter Gray
University of Birmingham
January 2013

Series Editors' Introduction

War Studies is an influential, popular and intellectually exciting discipline, characterized by the broad range of approaches it employs to understand a fundamental human activity. It has the history of war at its heart, but goes beyond operational military studies to draw on political, cultural and social history as well as strategy, literature, law, political theory, economics and social science. *Birmingham War Studies* celebrates this diversity by publishing examples of the discipline at its best, bringing the best academic scholarship on war to a wide audience. The remit of the series is deliberately ambitiously wide, ranging across subjects, methodologies and geographic regions. In this, it takes its cue from the treatment of the subject by the Centre for War Studies (CWS) within the Department of History at the University of Birmingham. The launch of the series in 2008 as a joint venture between Continuum and CWS marked the latter's emergence as a major force in the field, both in the United Kingdom and internationally.

'Traditional' military history certainly has its place in *Birmingham War Studies*, but the series' scope is very broad. The high quality of research, analysis and expression will make these books required reading for all those interested in the study of war in general as well as in the topic covered by each volume. In each case, the methodologies used in these specific studies will drive forward the field as a whole.

In the last few years the reputation of the British Expeditionary Force (BEF) in the First World War has been significantly refurbished. This has gone hand-in-hand with a recognition of the importance of airpower in transforming the conduct of warfare. Scholarship on the British army and the Royal Air Force (RAF) and its predecessors, the Royal Flying Corps and the Royal Naval Air Service, has similarly been revolutionized. One need only compare the state of the field of study at ten year intervals – in 1980, 1990, 2000 and today – to see how scholarship has developed. Particularly for the Army, there is now a rich and nuanced literature. That is less true for the air dimension, but after many years of comparative neglect, historians are addressing this gap in the scholarly record.

This volume, based on the proceedings of a 2008 conference held to mark the ninetieth anniversary of the Hundred Days campaign and the formation of the RAF explores diverse aspects of both land and air warfare, and indeed the interface between the two in the critical year of 1918. It testifies to the continuing dynamism of the subject. In spite of some intensive study historians are still finding new things to say, whether by exploring under-researched fields or revising existing interpretations. It also performs a service by bringing together historians of land and air power in the First World War. Too often the two groups operate separately, whereas there is much mutual benefit in cooperation.

The year 2014 will mark the centenary of the outbreak of the First World War, and already we are hearing much comment in the media about this pivotal conflict. Sadly, although utterly predictably, much of this comment is ill-informed. Real historians are likely to struggle to have their voices heard over the centenary period, so it is good to be reminded how much excellent research on the war is going on, being undertaken by scholars who are carrying out the patient and unglamorous spade work in the archives.

Gary Sheffield, Editor, *Birmingham War Studies*
Dan Todman, Associate Editor, *Birmingham War Studies*

Editors' Biographies

Gary Sheffield is Chair of War Studies and Director of Military History at the Centre for War Studies, University of Birmingham. He was formerly Professor of Modern History and Land Warfare Historian on the Higher Command and Staff Course in the Defence Studies Department, King's College London based at the Joint Services Command and Staff College, Shrivenham. His most recent publication is *The Chief: Douglas Haig and the British Army* (London, Aurum, 2011). With John Bourne, he is currently editing the wartime papers and diaries of General Sir Henry Rawlinson.

Peter Gray is the Royal Aeronautical Society's Senior Research Fellow in Air Power Studies and Director of War Studies at the Centre for War Studies, University of Birmingham. His most recent publication is *The Leadership, Direction and Legitimacy of the RAF Bomber Offensive from Inception to 1945* (London, Continuum, 2012). He retired from the RAF in 2008 as an Air Commodore. His final appointment was as Director of the Defence Leadership and Management Centre.

Contributors' Biographies

Niall Barr is Reader in Military History at the Defence Studies Department, King's College London, based at the Joint Services Command and Staff College. His main research interest concerns the fighting methods of the British Army in the twentieth century but he also has an enduring interest in the Scottish military tradition. He has published extensively on British military history including *Pendulum of War: The Three Battles of El Alamein* (London, Jonathan Cape, 2004) and *The Lion and the Poppy: Veterans Politics and Society 1921–1939* (Westport, CT, Greenwood, 2005).

Jonathan Boff is Lecturer in the Centre for War Studies, Department of History at the University of Birmingham. His most recent publication is *Winning and Losing on the Western Front: The British Third Army and the Defeat of Germany in 1918* (Cambridge, Cambridge University Press, 2012) that emerged from his 2010 PhD from King's College London. He is currently working on a military biography of Crown Prince Rupprecht of Bavaria.

Simon Coningham is a PhD Candidate at the Department of War Studies, King's College London where he is researching RAF air/ground cooperation in Imperial Policing operations during the interwar period. Prior to retirement Simon worked in magazine publishing. His most recent publication is 'Chandragupta: Creator of the Mauryan Empire in India' in Jeremy Black (ed.), *Great Military Leaders and their Campaigns* (London, Thames & Hudson, 2008).

Peter Dye is Director General of the Royal Air Force Museum. He spent more than 35 years in the RAF, retiring as an Air Vice-Marshal. He has written widely about the support arrangements for air forces and is currently completing a PhD at the Centre for War Studies, University of Birmingham assessing the performance of the Royal Flying Corps' Logistic Organisation on the Western Front.

Bryn Hammond is Head of Collections at the Imperial War Museums. His interests lie in operational analysis and the study of tactical development in the two world wars. He is a member of the British Commission for Military History and the Western Front and Gallipoli Associations. His publications include

Cambrai 1917: The Myth of the First Great Tank Battle (London, Weidenfeld and Nicolson, 2008) and *El Alamein: The Battle that Turned the Tide of the Second World War* (Oxford, Osprey, 2012).

David Jordan is Senior Lecturer in the Defence Studies Department, King's College London based at the Joint Services Command and Staff College, Shrivenham. He is the academic lead for the air power aspects of the Advanced Command and Staff Course. He is a member of the Chief of the Air Staff's Air Power workshop and the RAF Air Power Review editorial board. He has written a variety of books and articles, most recently as co-author with James D. Kiras, David J. Lonsdale, Ian Speller, Christopher Tuck and C. Dale Walton of *Understanding Modern Warfare* (Cambridge, Cambridge University Press, 2008).

Simon M. Justice is a PhD candidate at the Centre for War Studies, University of Birmingham. His research, under the supervision of Professors Gary Sheffield and Peter Simkins, is an examination of the British Armies in France in 1917–18 and their defence against the German spring offensives in the final year of the First World War. His association with Birmingham's Centre for War Studies began in 2007, when he commenced an MA programme in British First World War Studies, from which he graduated in 2009.

Christopher Luck is an RAF helicopter pilot and instructor. He has extensive operational and staff experience and currently commands RAF Shawbury. He has an MA in Military Operational Art and an MA in Strategic Air Power from the USAF School of Advanced Air and Space Studies. He is a Portal Fellow at the University of Reading where he is a PhD candidate. His latest publication was 'Air Power and the Contemporary Army', *RAF Air Power Review* (Autumn 2009), pp. 65–76.

Alistair McCluskey is a serving officer in the British Army. He gained his MA in War Studies from King's College London and is also a graduate of the Advanced Command and Staff Course from the Joint Services Command and Staff College, Shrivenham.

Ross Mahoney is a PhD candidate at the Centre for War Studies, University of Birmingham. He is currently writing a thesis entitled, 'The Forgotten Career of Air Chief Marshal Sir Trafford Leigh-Mallory, 1892–1937: Leadership Development, Succession Planning and Promotion in the Inter-War Royal Air Force'. His most recent publication is, '"The support afforded by the air force was faultless": The Royal Air Force and the Raid on Dieppe, 19 August 1942', *Canadian Military History*, 21 (4) (Autumn 2012), pp. 17–32.

Rob Thompson is a PhD candidate at the Centre for War Studies, University of Birmingham where he is analysing the role of logistics and engineering in the development of the BEF's operational method on the Western Front 1914–18. Previously he taught Military History at the University of Birmingham before becoming an independent military historian. He has published 'Mud, Blood and Wood: BEF Operational and Combat Logistic-Engineering during the Battle of Third Ypres, 1917', in P. Doyle and M. R. Bennett (eds), *Fields of Battle* (Dortrecht, Kluwer Academic, 2002), pp. 237–55. He has presented several papers on the subject of BEF logistics and engineering at various national and international conferences.

Dennis Williams is a PhD candidate at the Centre for War Studies, University of Birmingham where he is currently researching the role of the British Second Army in 1918. He is a former manager in education and children's services, now running a retail business, including second-hand books, specializing in military history. A keen war gamer, he has published a rulebook for nineteenth-century warfare in Europe.

Introduction

Peter Gray, Ross Mahoney and Gary Sheffield

Between 1914 and 1918, the conduct of warfare underwent profound change. Although this change occurred remarkably quickly, the process had its roots in developments that long predated the First World War. The Armistice of 1918 did not mark the end of this process of change, but rather was a point on a continuum. The chapters in this book explore various aspects of the development of warfare in what is from this perspective the most significant year of the First World War, 1918. The focus of the book is the British Empire's land and air forces. The armed forces of other states, notably France and the Germany, also contributed to the remarkable changes in the conduct of war in this period, but this is not their story.

Evolution of artillery

At the heart of the new form of warfighting was a combination of artillery and aircraft. This was in many ways the logical consequence of the remarkable development of military technology over the previous 80 years. The eighteenth and early nineteenth centuries had been a time of technological stasis for armies. Marlborough's and Tallard's armies at Blenheim in 1704 had been equipped with very similar weapons – smoothbore muzzle-loading muskets and cannons, bayonets and swords – as the forces of Wellington and Napoleon at Waterloo 111 years later. The two decades after the end of the Napoleonic Wars had seen, as a by-product of the burgeoning industrial revolution, significant advances in weaponry. At first, these seemed to favour the infantryman. While artillery had been the most lethal weapon on the Napoleonic battlefield, the introduction of the rifled musket (rifle) and the cylindro-conoidal bullet in the mid-nineteenth century gave the foot soldier a weapon of considerable power that had roughly the same range as artillery. The effectiveness of artillery was consequently reduced and small arms filled the gap.[1] In the hundred years prior to ca. 1850, some 50 per cent of casualties on the battlefield were inflicted by artillery, but this had fallen to 5–10 per cent during the Austro-Prussian War of 1866 and the Franco-Prussian War of 1870–1. Even during the Russo-Japanese War of 1904–5, in which there were some developments in artillery (see below), artillery caused a maximum of 15 per cent battle casualties.[2] However, the triumph of the infantryman's rifle was short-lived, for in this period artillery was set on the path of increased accuracy and lethality that led it to be described by Josef Stalin in 1944 as 'the God of War'.[3] Rifled muzzleloaders (such as the Parrot guns used in the American Civil War) superseded smooth bores, bronze guns were replaced by steel, the muzzleloader gave way to breach-loaders such as the British Armstrong weapon of 1859 and solid shot (cannon ball) was supplanted by explosive shells. The latter had been around for a long time: Lieutenant (later Lieutenant-General) Henry Shrapnell had invented the explosive anti-personnel round that bears his name (albeit without the final 'l') in 1784. However improvements to the explosive shell in the 1850s and 1860s produced a much more effective man-killing weapon. So did the development of 'fixed ammunition', that is, a shell incorporated the charge, rather than the projectile with the charge being loaded separately; and smokeless powder, which did something to lift the literal if not metaphorical fog of war from the battlefield.[4]

The introduction of the French 75mm M-1897 'heralded a revolution in the design and capabilities of artillery'.[5] It was a 'Quick-Firing' gun, meaning that as it was fitted with a hydraulic recoil mechanism it did not need to be relaid, that is, laboriously aimed at the target after every shot. This drastically increased the rate of fire to as many as 25 rounds per minute. Relatively light and manoeuvrable, it was able to fire out to 7,500 yards; such was its impact on the French army that it was nicknamed 'God the Father, God the Son and God the Holy Ghost'.[6] Britain, Russia and Germany followed the French lead and produced similar guns.

Most artillery fire remained line of sight: the gunners had to be able to see a target to be able to hit it. Although attempts at indirect fire dated back to the eighteenth century, it was the German and Russian armies in the 1870s and 1880s that took the first steps towards creating an indirect fire capability, based on observers, to correct the fall of shot. Much use was made of indirect fire in the Russo-Japanese War (1904–5), although in Bailey's words 'it was a primitive business'. The British army had tried indirect fire in the South African War. In spite of some scepticism (doubts were expressed about the vulnerability to hostile shelling of the telephone wires that connected the forward observer with the batteries) and neglect, by 1914 the Royal Artillery had taken some tentative steps towards indirect fire.⁷

Evolution of air power

Air power was to be the partner of artillery in transforming warfare during the First World War. As in the case of artillery, the emergence of the use of aircraft in a military role was the outcome of a long process, albeit the inaugural flight of the first practical aeroplane predated the outbreak of the First World War by a mere 11 years. However, the Wright brothers' success in getting their primitive craft airborne at Kitty Hawk, North Carolina in 1903 was not the beginning of air power but rather a step, albeit an important one, in its evolution.⁸ Orville and Wilbur Wright had been preceded by a number of pioneers. A Briton, Sir George Cayley, had designed and flown gliders in the first half of the nineteenth century. Moreover several individuals – including, in the 1890s, a Frenchman, Clement Ader; a German, Otto Lilienthal; and a Briton, Percy Pilcher – had either come close to achieving fixed-wing powered flight or had actually done so, however briefly.

In fact the use, or attempted use, of flight for military purposes had an extremely long pedigree. Medieval Chinese armies had used kites and rockets, but the beginning of modern airpower can be dated to the Montgolfier brothers' experiments with balloons in 1783. Some use was made of balloons for reconnaissance by the French in the Revolutionary Wars that broke out in 1792, although success was limited and the balloon corps was disbanded by Napoleon (who was perhaps surprisingly, technologically conservative in this respect) in 1799.⁹ The first attempt to drop bombs from balloons was made, without a great deal of success, by the Austrians in 1849. Northern forces used balloons for observation during the first part of the American Civil War.¹⁰ In a move that was to prefigure developments during the First World War, on occasions balloons were linked to the ground by telegraph. During the Franco-Prussian War (1870–1) balloons provided a tenuous link between besieged Paris and the outside world; more generally, balloons began to attract significant attention from European soldiers.

An important new era in the evolution of air power arrived in the 1870s, after some 20 years of experiments, with the development of balloons combined with engines – 'airships'. A further stage of development came in the first decade of the twentieth century with the construction of rigid airships (i.e. with the balloon envelope enclosed in a metal frame). At that time such dirigibles offered a real alternative to primitive aeroplanes as a weapon of war. Imperial Germany had a particularly advanced programme of building dirigibles for military and civil use, presided over by Graf (Count) Ferdinand von Zeppelin.

In 1908 the Wright brothers began to demonstrate their aircraft and this quickly caught the attention of the world's military. Coincidentally or not, this was also the year in which H. G. Wells' *The War in the Air* appeared. This was only the most famous work of fiction to predict the use of aircraft in conflict, the earliest appearing in the eighteenth century. By 1914 the major powers had all invested, to a greater or lesser degree, in aircraft. In Britain the response was patchy. The government became aware of the 'strategic implications' of the military use of aircraft in 1908, that is the year before Louis Blériot's pioneering cross-Channel flight, an event that demonstrated the potential vulnerability of Britain's traditional first line of defence, the Royal Navy.[11] In spite of this, it took the efforts of a number of individuals, including Lord Northcliffe, the press baron, and Winston Churchill, First Lord of the Admiralty (1911–15) and an early enthusiast for aircraft (he attempted to learn to fly, to the alarm of his wife) to advance the cause of air power.

The attitude of one particular soldier towards aircraft is of special interest. As commander of First Army in 1915 and then as Commander-in-Chief of the British Expeditionary Force (BEF) from December 1915 until April 1919 Douglas Haig was to play an important role in the development of British airpower. However, he has widely been credited with having, before the war, a dismissive attitude to the military use of aircraft. Haig supposedly said in 1911 that 'flying can never be of any use to the army', and as late as July 1914 is quoted as denying that aircraft could displace cavalry as a means of reconnaissance. Both quotations come from the memoirs of Sir Frederick Sykes. These memoirs are tainted: they were written 30 years after the conversations are purported to have occurred, and Sykes bore a grudge against Haig because of the latter's close relationship with Sykes' rival, Trenchard.[12] In reality, Haig was open to new ideas and new technology. As Chief of Staff, India he was present at a pioneering flight during manoeuvres in India in January 1911 and handed one of the intrepid airmen, Major Sefton Brancker,

> a sealed envelope . . . containing the orders for the following day. Incidentally this was the first occasion on which a British General issued official orders for an aeroplane to fly and bring back information about troops opposed to his . . . We had been out forty-five minutes, covered about twenty-seven miles across

country as the crow flies, and our G.O.C. had a full report of the enemy's position within a hour and a quarter of our start.[13]

This demonstration to Haig of the feasibility of aerial reconnaissance, and other evidence such as his positive references to aviation in private correspondence and his interest in the work of the pioneering airman Samuel Cody, shows that Haig was receptive to the use of aircraft in support of the army long before his arrival on the Western Front.[14] Andrew Whitmarsh's important 2007 article shows that Haig was not alone among senior British army officers in appreciating the potential of aircraft in the years immediately preceding the First World War era. Whitmarsh goes as far as to argue that 'By August 1914, the army saw aircraft . . . as a vital weapons system that in the near future would forever change the conduct of land warfare'.[15] Such evidence suggests that the role of cultural conservatism in the failure to create the artillery/air power revolution may have been overplayed, in the British case at least. A recent comparative study concluded that the Royal Artillery (RA) was 'the most effective artillery force on the Western Front'. The RA was

> rather more effective than the Germans and the French at weaving new technologies into their general planning . . . the British struggled to adapt to large-scale warfare, but once the army demonstrated that it was capable of major operations, it also proved adept at drawing upon skills and technologies that the Germans failed to utilise effectively.[16]

The senior officers who oversaw this transformation were, overwhelmingly, pre-war Regular officers.

A revolution in military affairs?

Over the last two decades much intellectual effort has been expended on the Revolution in Military Affairs (RMA) debate. Spurred by contemporary concerns about US security, the debate was informed by the use of historical examples. The protagonists were usually political scientists, although some historians were involved, and the RMA question has become interweaved with an older, historical debate about 'military revolutions'. The hypothesis that the First World War witnessed a seismic change in warfare has become important both to those concerned with the contemporary 'security' RMA issue, and to military historians seeking to understand the conduct of the Great War.

An immediate problem facing anyone interested in the area is that there is no one universally accepted definition of an RMA. However, the following definition, coined by Andrew W. Marshall of the US Secretary of Defense's Office of Net Assessment, is useful:

> A Revolution in Military Affairs is a major change in the nature of warfare brought about by the innovative application of new technologies which, combined with dramatic changes in military doctrine and operational and organizational concepts fundamentally alters the character and conduct of military operations.[17]

An obvious comment is that RMAs involving technology are different from those that do not, and should be put into a separate category. However, we do not propose to complicate matters further. Whether an RMA that is *not* technologically based is likely to occur in the present age is also beyond the scope of this chapter. And fascinating although the debates about definitions undoubtedly are (what are the precise differences between a Revolution in Military Affairs, a Military Revolution[18] and a Military Technical Revolution?), here these nuances will be set aside, and the term RMA used. Likewise, despite all its faults, Marshall's definition will be used as a benchmark for judging the First World War.

Following Marshall, therefore there are three preconditions for an RMA – technological innovation, doctrinal innovation and organizational adaptation – and the synergy of the three can lead to an RMA. Thus, RMAs are about conceptual developments, not just technology.

A key plank of Marshall's definition of an RMA is that it 'fundamentally alters the character and conduct of military operations'. Tim Benbow's formulation, that an RMA 'refer(s) to a step-change in the basic character of warfare ... [that] fundamentally affect[s] strategy . . . [and] has far greater consequences than routine evolution' makes a similar point.

This points towards the true RMA being a rare phenomenon. The word 'revolution' implies a profound degree of upheaval and disruption on a vast scale.[19] Promiscuous use of the word diminishes the concept. For example, the idea that the German employment of *Blitzkrieg* in 1940 amounted to an RMA is not persuasive. Not only is the very use of term *Blitzkrieg* fraught with problems, but an examination of the character of the German use of all-arms mobile warfare in 1940 reveals two things. First, there was little actually new about it – it is best seen as an evolutionary process that built on previous military developments, not least of 1914–18. As Williamson Murray has argued, it was an 'aftershock' following on from the 'earthquake' of the First World War.[20] Second, *Blitzkrieg* was deeply flawed as an operational method – arguably it only succeeded because of the errors and weaknesses of the opposition.

By contrast, the notion that the artillery- and airpower-based developments of the First World War amounted to an RMA is compelling. They involved technological and doctrinal innovation, and organizational adaptation. Above all, the 'character and conduct of military operations' changed profoundly as a result of these developments. Operations in 1914 looked back to Napoleon. In 1918 they were very different. What had occurred was far more than the incremental advances (allied with a sizeable slice of luck) that produced the so-called German RMA of 1940. Soldiers in 1918 could look back across a deep divide to a vanished past. Subsequent military developments in conventional war have built upon the artillery/airpower RMA of 1914–18, but they have not superseded it.

In the 1990s, Jonathan Bailey, then a senior artillery officer in the British army, put forward the idea of an RMA based on depth fire, beginning around 1915 but peaking in 1917–18. This thesis argued that most of the elements that would eventually come together to create the 'indirect fire revolution' existed before the war, but in Bailey's striking phrase there was a 'failure to meld the components'. In 1914 warfare was linear. As '[t]here were no means of locating targets in depth', and artillery was usually used in direct fire roles, that is, firing at targets that could be seen by the gunners, 'generally at short range, with guns deployed in the open'. 'Adjustment of fire was primitive' and methods of communications between guns and observers were limited and crude. Best use of artillery was hampered by poor mapping, failure to take into account wear and tear on gun barrels (calibration) and not least by the stultifying effect of 'conservative military cultures', manifested in 'lack of imagination and doctrinal laziness'.[21]

Faced with the deadlock of the Western Front, indirect artillery fire emerged as the critical element. Aeroplanes were used to fly over enemy positions and identify targets that would otherwise have been invisible. Equipped with primitive radio, airmen could correct the fall of shot, that is, direct the fire of guns until the shells were landing accurately on the target. This had the effect of greatly extending the danger zone behind the trenches. Troops, headquarters, logistic centres, railway facilities and the like had previously been vulnerable to random shelling as long as they were in the range of artillery; now they could be deliberately and accurately targeted. Counter-battery work – neglected before 1914 – became fundamental. Armies invested in heavy guns, and especially howitzers, and high explosive shells rather than man-killing shrapnel.[22]

The implications of this development were huge. War was now conducted in three rather than two dimensions. Further advances occurred in mapping, aerial photography, survey, calibration and communications. These, plus innovations such as sound ranging and flash spotting, helped produce 'predicted' artillery fire by 1917. Sophisticated developments in command and control harnessed artillery which became a decisive operational-level tool, used effectively by the Germans, British and, to some extent, the Russians.[23] Bailey argues that this was the birth of the 'Modern Style of Warfare'; that the type of conventional warfare conducted ever since has its roots in this artillery- and air power-based revolution that occurred on the Western Front between 1914 and 1918.

Bailey's thesis has commanded wide acceptance; a revised version of his original paper, for instance, appeared in a seminal 2001 collection of essays, *The Dynamics of Military Revolution*.[24] While a number of historians had previously pointed out the significance of the First World War in the development of warfare, it was the work of Jonathan Bailey that, in Colin S. Grey's words, provided the 'conceptualisation of what was effected in 1917–18 [that] was, so it seems, just what the world of historical scholarship was waiting for'.[25]

The chapters

This notion that by the year 1918 a revolution in the conduct of war had occurred on and above the battlefields of the Western Front to such an extent that it was fair to talk of the 'Genesis of Modern Warfare' formed the background for a conference held by the University of Birmingham's War Studies Group in September 2008. The speakers at this conference, held to mark the ninetieth anniversaries of the formation of the Royal Air Force (RAF) and the Hundred Days, were a mixture of established and emerging scholars. The conference featured an eclectic and stimulating collection of papers, largely (and intentionally) British-focussed, that covered air, land and maritime aspects of the military history of 1918. Unfortunately the book-of-the-conference was subject to more than its fair share of mishaps and delays to which such projects are prone, and some of the original speakers proved unable to provide papers for inclusion: hence the absence of any chapters on the maritime dimension of 1918. Fortunately, some other scholars were able to step into the breach, and the editors would like to thank them.

For all the recent work on 1918, there are plenty of areas in need of further scholarly work, and the chapters in this book provide an important series of 'bricks' to help build the 'wall' of our knowledge of 1918.

Jonathan Boff deals with one of the most contentious of Great War topics, the command of the BEF, through the medium of a case study of General Sir Julian Byng's Third Army. 'Bungo's' force was the largest of the five Armies under the overall command of Field Marshal Sir Douglas Haig, and as Dr Boff makes clear, complexity and diversity were the hallmarks of command in this formation. There was some delegation of authority to 'the man on the spot' in accordance with what was regarded, in theory at least, as best practice. However, decentralization was applied patchily, and much depended on the personalities of individual commanders and what Boff refers to as 'a range of non-formal "cultures of command"'. Although much additional work needs to be done on the Third Army's sister formations, it seems highly likely that this pattern was repeated across the BEF. That after four years of war Haig's Armies lacked a uniform approach to command is an interesting comment on the nature and limitations of the BEF's learning process.

Rob Thompson's important chapter deals with a subject which is deeply unfashionable among historians – a few pioneering studies notwithstanding – but of crucial significance to understanding military operations: logistics. By studying the logistics and administration of the Canadian Corps in its preparation for the Battle of Amiens, he shines a light on a topic that too often is simply ignored. The ability of the Fourth Army to achieve surprise on 8 August 1918 was founded on the ability to concentrate troops rapidly and secretly on the Amiens front. This remarkable achievement is testament to the effectiveness and sophistication of the BEF's logistic and staffwork by this stage of the war. Thompson's work is a model of what can be achieved by careful study of logistic records, and neatly complements Peter Dye's chapter on RFC logistics. It is to be hoped that integration of analysis of logistics into wider studies of command and military effectiveness becomes the norm rather than the exception.

Logistics plays a prominent role in Bryn Hammond's study of tanks in the Hundred Days. Much attention has been paid by earlier historians to the BEF's use of tanks, and particularly the question of whether they were mishandled by the high command. Hammond argues persuasively that logistic and other constraints effectively confined the use of armour to set-piece operations, and the tank arm pragmatically accepted and worked within these limitations. This included the use of tanks in 'penny packets', rather than en masse. Although not ideal – the use of 500+ tanks at Amiens was not repeated – the use of armour as part of the BEF's all-arms approach was nonetheless successful. Moreover, up to the very end of the war lessons were being learned and applied within the context of a semi-formal doctrine, and 'a general framework of commonly understood principles and methods'. In view of the theme of this book, Hammond's analysis of cooperation between tanks and aircraft is particularly interesting. In his view, it was 'one of *the* great tactical successes of the last months of the war'.

Niall Barr's discussion of the Battle of the Sambre deals with one of the few actions of the Hundred Days that has any resonance outside a small circle of military historians. This is, as he says, because of the death in this battle of the war poet Wilfred Owen. The death of Owen has often been regarded as 'futile' because he was killed on 4 November 1918, so near the end of the war. But as Barr demonstrates, one the reasons why the war ended when it did was because of the impact of the BEF's victory on the minds of the German High Command: any remaining illusions that anything could be saved from the wreckage was finally swept away. The Battle of the Sambre was the opposite of futile. Niall Barr's careful analysis reveals much about the nature of the fighting in the Hundred Days, and shows that there is plenty of scope for detailed studies of individual actions.

British Second Army was commanded by General Sir Herbert Plumer, arguably Haig's most effective subordinate. It is often forgotten that for much of the Hundred Days Plumer's formation was removed from Haig's command. Second Army was part of the *Groupe d'Armees des Flandres* (Army Group, Flanders – GAF) commanded by the King of Belgians with a French general as his Chief-of-Staff. Dennis Williams examines Plumer's Army in a campaign which, as he argues, has been routinely ignored by most historians. And yet it is a campaign which, as Williams shows, is full of interest. It was a war of liberation, of friendly territory that had been under enemy occupation – a perspective which has vanished from the modern popular perception of the war. Williams argues that Second Army became the principal striking force of the GAF, and coped well with mobile warfare, which presented a number of challenges to troops and commanders alike. No less than logistics, which is one of Williams' concerns, coalition warfare was a vital factor in 1918, and his chapter has some interesting things to say about the realities of fighting in combination with Allies. Although Haig had initially agreed to Second Army's secondment to the GAF, as time passed the arrangement generated some rancorous correspondence as Haig demanded that Foch, the Allied Generalissimo, return Plumer to his command. Plumer too had to tread carefully, on occasion turning a Nelsonian blind eye to orders from GAF. Clearly, Second Army in the Hundred Days would repay further study.

British cavalry in the First World War, for so long the butt of jokes, has recently been subject to scholarly reassessment.[26] The picture that has emerged is very different from the stereotype of an anachronism that had no place in the order of battle of modern armies. It retained, under certain circumstances, a useful role even on the 'hi-tech' battlefield of 1918. Simon Justice's study of Field Marshal Sir Douglas Haig and the Cavalry Corps in October 1918 suggests that cavalry could be highly effective at the operational level. Justice's chapter is another step in the scholarly rehabilitation of cavalry and also, by extension, of Haig. The prevalent idea that Haig's faith in cavalry by itself demonstrated that he was unfit to exercise high command is no longer tenable. Although it may appear counter-intuitive, the evidence overwhelmingly points towards cavalry having a role on the mechanized battlefield of 1918. Imperfect as it was, it remained the BEF's only viable instrument of exploitation.

Turning to the air war, the formation of the RAF was born out of a deliberate process of codifying the lessons and experiences of the changing character of warfare that emerged during the First World War. As the First World War progressed, the roles and functions of air power that are now fundamental were developed. Concepts such as command of the air, reconnaissance, attacking enemy troops and interdicting supply lines, often many miles behind enemy lines, were all developed, applied and, most importantly, proved successful. The chapters presented here examine several key themes related to the formation of the RAF, the world's first independent air force. First, Peter Gray and Chris Luck's chapters examine the process behind the RAF's formation and the senior leadership challenges that the newly formed service and Air Ministry faced during the course of 1917 and 1918. Second, the chapters by David Jordan, Simon Coningham and Alistair McCluskey examine some of the challenges and developments that faced the Royal Flying Corps (RFC)/RAF during the year 1918 and how problems of employing air power were overcome. Finally, Peter Dye's chapter examines a hitherto ignored yet significant area concerning the employment of air power, namely the impact of air logistics on the course and conduct of air operations.

As Peter Dye records in his chapter on the impact of logistics on the utilization of air power during the First World War, the RFC grew from a tiny force of keen and enthusiastic aviators flying fragile, underpowered and barely armed machines into a complex and highly functional weapon of war. More importantly, the RFC and the Royal Naval Air Service (RNAS) contributed to what is now generally accepted as being a true RMA. As each of these papers accepts, by the time of the Armistice air power was being utilized in roles that it continues to handle into the twenty-first century. It is important to note that several extremely significant changes to the character of warfare came about during the First World War. These included the willingness to innovate with major technological change and the formulation, in an active and deliberate manner – and not by happenstance – of a core of air power doctrine. These changes in the character of warfare, however, did not happen merely by accident or some form of osmosis. Some arose from hard-learned lessons from the battlefields of France and Belgium. Others, such as the attempted use of air power at Gallipoli foundered through poor logistics. One of the key factors to come from this increasing dependence on air power was that for it to work, the processes from the acquisition of aircraft, engines, weapons and trained personnel to their employment in what by 1918 had become high-tempo warfare could not be left to accident. More importantly, the vital nature of its contribution to successful operations meant that air power and its support chain could not be left as a second-rate foster child for the erstwhile parents to squabble over. A unified system of procurement and supply had to be developed with its own Board and accountable management structure.

It is somewhat ironic that the world's first independent air force grew from such disagreements in smoke-filled rooms in Whitehall and its nether regions, but in his chapter on the birth of the air ministry and thence the RAF from the RFC and RNAS, Peter Gray has presented the development of the Air Ministry in its bureaucratic context and argues that its formation was essential to deal with the complex problems of strategy, administration and supply. If Britain were to have to the world's first independent air force then it would require an autonomous bureaucratic organ to manage it much as the army was linked to the war office and the navy to the admiralty. As Gray illustrates the origins of the Air Ministry lay in the decision to form a Joint Air War Committee in March 1916 that was designed to improve efficiency between the competing priorities of the RFC and RNAS. This committee eventually evolved into the Air Board and then into the Air Ministry. However, the early history of the Air Ministry was plagued by disputes between the first Chief of the Air Staff, Major-General Hugh Trenchard, and the President of the Air Council, Lord Rothermere. However, the eventual outcome of the formation of the Air Ministry was the search for an air policy analogous with its independent status. This would lead to the formation of the Independent Force (IF), and commanded by Trenchard. It was hoped that this formation, supported by policy decisions at the Air Ministry, would allow the RAF to contribute to victory through independent means. That this did not happen was largely down to the capability of the IF and operational realities. However, the desire to chalk out an independent role signified a portent of future debates surrounding the future of the RAF and the development of a coherent mission for itself.

Chris Luck's chapter on the impact of the Smuts Reports that played a key role in the decision to form the RAF examines several of the key drivers that underpinned the findings of these reports. Formed on 11 July 1917, the Committee on Air Organisation and Home Defence Against Air Raids, sought to examine the arrangements for the home defence of the United Kingdom and the organization needed to support such an endeavour. The key drivers at play that led to the formation of the above committee consisted of political, military and social factors. This complex integration of factors highlights the political and military context of 1917 that created the conditions in which discussions about the formation of an independent air service could take place. Luck charts the process that saw Smuts report's converted into a cohesive policy with the formation of the Air Ministry and the passing of the Air Force (Constitution) Act that was introduced as a bill on 8 November 1917 and passed as law on 29 November. He also notes the importance of Smut's own view on the possibilities inherent in air power and how these played a vital role in findings of the committees convened. Smuts held a futuristic belief in the efficacy of air power and one that would not be realized during the course of the First World War. Nonetheless, the importance of Smuts' thinking was that it founded a holistic and coherent view of air power strategy that was grounded in the belief in the advantages of an organized independent air ministry that could manage the requirements of a key form of modern warfare.

Peter Dye's contribution, as noted, focuses on the importance of logistics and argues that rather than being a product of the changing character of modern warfare it was actually a precipitant with the development of an effective logistics network being its precondition. Central to Dye's view is the idea that it was the emergence of air power that allowed the delivery of overwhelming firepower that was a defining aspect of the character of combat during the First World War. The integration of an effective logistics framework was central to enabling the delivery of that firepower as well as its organic offensive capability. The need for quality, capability and persistence in the delivery of key air power roles was supported by the development of an effective logistics system that allowed the RFC/RAF to achieve an advantage over the enemy. In order to provide an effective logistical support a complex system emerged. Operations in the field were of such a high tempo in 1918 that this system became highly adaptive and laid the foundation for the RAF's mobile logistics system of the Second World War with elements remaining familiar to this day. As Gray notes, central to supporting this complex system was an important function of the Air Ministry that set the strategic priorities for the RAF from which procurement and logistical support flowed into the system in the field.

Three of the chapters presented here detail in various aspects the importance of the Battle of Amiens as the apogee of air power development concerning its support of the land battle in the First World War and one that mapped out its use for the final Hundred Days campaign. As the chapters presented here illustrate the lessons learned were not always implemented. Indeed, for the RAF, Amiens presented an imperfect victory.

In examining the development of the RAF role in the emerging all-arms battle, David Jordan takes a broader view of the context of operations up to 1918. In charting the development of the RFC/RAF up to, and past, its formation, Jordan illustrates the degree to which air power was a defining characteristic of the RMA that was indicative of the 'learning curve' present in all the armies of the First World War. Jordan firmly places the conduct of air operations in 1918 into their appropriate context, the support of ground operations. While aerial combat had emerged in 1915, it is clear that this came about from a desire to defend valuable reconnaissance assets that were being used to provide intelligence and support artillery operations. From this, there further emerged the panoply of air operations that are recognizable today. Indeed, 1916 was an important year for the RFC as Trenchard enunciated the idea of the 'incessant offensive'. The idea of offensive air power has become characteristic of doctrine in numerous air services since this time. This importance of offensive air operations also transferred into an area that has been ignored by historians, the RFC's preparation for the German Spring Offensive of March 1918. The conduct of air operations during the Spring Offensives and its offensive utilization illustrate the degree to which the RFC had become integrated into the structure of the all-arms battle concept that was steadily emerging within the BEF. One parallel with the conduct of air operations in the Second World War that is drawn out by Jordan, and illustrates confusion over the perceptions of roles for air power, comes in the view of its effectiveness in support of infantry. In 1917, as in 1940, the infantry viewed air power as being effective when they could see it in direct support operations. However, from 1917 onward the RFC/RAF increasingly conducted interdiction operations beyond the view of the front line. This led to criticisms that forced Trenchard and Salmond to hold back a portion of their strength for morale purposes. Increasing integrations within the all-arms battle became the key concern for the RAF in the latter stages if the First World War from the Battle of Amiens onward. As both Coningham and McCluskey make clear, this process was not as smooth as might be assumed.

The development of the system of air-ground co-operation that was used at Amiens to achieve victory is detailed in Simon Coningham's chapter. Methods included reconnaissance, artillery spotting, contact patrols, ground support, direct and indirect battlefield support and air superiority. However, as Coningham correctly notes it was only really on the first day that the high level of close co-operation was effective. The key challenge faced by the RAF at Amiens was that there existed a clear lack of planning for what would happen after the first day of the battle. This led to an ad hoc solution to the problem confronting the RAF as it became increasingly difficult to support operation with close support due to issues related to command and control. After the first day it became difficult to maximize the flexibility of the air power, because of problems of target acquisition, concentration and the failure to isolate the battlefield. This influenced RAF thinking during the interwar period, including John Slessor's *Air Power and Armies*, a treatise on the best method of employing air power in support of land forces that chose Amiens as a case study of what air power could achieve if properly employed in an effective manner by an independent air service.[27]

That lessons hard learned would be forgotten, neglected and, in some cases, deliberately ignored was inevitable. In his chapter on the development of air-land co-operation, Alistair McCluskey maps out the problems inherent in this interface between the Battle of Amiens through to 1945. McCluskey challenges the view of David Ian Hall that the problems inherent in the development of a coherent air-land co-operation doctrine lay with the War Office. McCluskey contends that the RAF was equally to blame for the problems that confronted the services in this sphere. He details the contribution that the RAF made to Amiens to great success but is critical of the interwar RAF's overestimation concerning the cost of close co-operation and argues that this was of vital importance. McCluskey contends that during the interwar period the RAF, and Slessor in particular, were guilty of a great deal of subjective analysis of air operations in 1918 that led to key lessons being forgotten. McCluskey maps out the course of tactical air operations during the Second World War and highlights the degree of similarity between them and the Battle of Amiens thus illustrating the fact that Amiens was the forebearer of these successful campaigns. However, a divergence in views exists between McCluskey and Coningham's chapters, with the latter noting that while a degree of institutional amnesia may have existed in the RAF and British Army in the United Kingdom, this was not the case in the imperial conflicts of the interwar period. Lessons were quickly re-learned by officers who had First World War experience and transferred developments from 1918 into the operational context of imperial policing. This process kept alive methods that would be of importance in the Second World War. Nonetheless, as Jordan notes in his chapter it is unfortunate that facets of British military history's lessons are often forgotten; however, as both McCluskey's and Coningham's chapters show, there are still questions over when and how the lessons of air operations in the First World War were re-learned.

There is much work to be still to be done on 1918, not least in integrating studies of land and air operations into wider studies of the evolution of modern warfare, and in particular the notion of a revolution in military affairs. The chapters in this book offer, we believe, useful evidence of the part played during the Hundred Days by the ground and air forces of the British Empire in changing the way war was fought.

Notes

1 Christopher Bellamy, *The Evolution of Modern Land Warfare* (London: Routledge, 1990), p. 42.
2 J. B. A. Bailey, *Field Artillery and Firepower* (Annapolis, MD: Naval Institute Press, 2004), p. 207.
3 Christopher Bellamy, *Red God of War: Soviet Artillery and Rocket Forces* (London: Brassey's, 1986), p. 74.
4 A. Marshall, 'The Invention and Development of the Shrapnel Shell', *Field Artillery Journal* X, 1 (1920), pp. 12, 14–18; Manfred Kühr, 'Artillery', in Franklin F. Margiotta (ed.), *Brassey's Encyclopaedia of Land Forces and Warfare* (Washington, DC: Brassey's, 1996), p. 97; *Encyclopaedia Britannica*, 11th edn (Cambridge: Encylopaedia Britannica, 1910), pp. 865–75.
5 Curt Johnson, *Artillery* (London: Octopus, 1975) quoted in John Terraine, *White Heat: The New Warfare 1914–18* (London: Leo Cooper, 1992 [1982]), p. 52.
6 Terraine, *White Heat*, p. 68.
7 Jonathan B. A. Bailey, 'The First World War and the birth of modern warfare', in MacGregor Knox and Williamson Murray (eds), *The Dynamics of Military Revolution 1300-2050* (Cambridge: Cambridge University Press, 2001), pp. 135–6; Shelford Bidwell and Dominick Graham, *Fire-Power: British Army Weapons and Theories of War 1904–1945* (Boston, MA: Allen and Unwin, 1985 [1982]), pp. 2, 10–12.
8 The following remarks are indebted to John Buckley, *Air Power in the Age of Total War* (Bloomington, IN: Indiana University Press, 1999), pp. 22–41.
9 Gunther E. Rothenberg, *The Art of Warfare in the Age of Napoleon* (Bloomington, IN: Indiana University Press, 1980), pp. 123–4.

10 James L Green, 'Civil War Ballooning during the Seven Days Campaign', www.civilwar.org/education/history/civil-war-ballooning/ballooning-during-the-seven.html
11 Uri Bialer, *The Shadow of the Bomber: The Fear of Air Attack and British Politics 1932–1939* (London: Royal Historial Society, 1980), p. 1. For the context, see Alfred Gollin, *The Impact of Air Power on the British People and their Government, 1909–14* (Stanford, CA: Stanford University Press, 1989).
12 Gary Sheffield, *The Chief: Douglas Haig and the British Army* (London: Aurum, 2011), p. 62. Dr James Pugh has pointed out to Sheffield that the Sykes/Trenchard animosity seems to have intensified with the passing of the years, and Trenchard's comments on Sykes should similarly be treated with caution. See: James Pugh, 'The Conceptual Origins of Control of the Air: British Military and Naval Aviation, 1911–1918' (PhD Thesis, University of Birmingham, 2012).
13 Norman Macmillan, *Sir Sefton Brancker* (London: William Heinemann, 1935), pp. 16–18 (we owe this reference to James Pugh); Basil Collier, *Heavenly Adventurer: Sefton Brancker and the Dawn of British Aviation* (London: Secker and Warburg, 1959), p. 12.
14 Sheffield, *The Chief*, pp. 61–2.
15 Andrew Whitmarsh, 'British Army Manoeuvres and the Development of Military Aviation, 1910–13', *War in History* 14, 3 (2007), pp. 325–46 (quoted from p. 346).
16 Paul Strong and Sanders Marble, *Artillery in the Great War* (Barnsley: Pen and Sword, 2011), pp. 205–6.
17 Quoted in Jeffrey McKittrick, James Blackwell, Fred Littlepage, George Kraus, Richard Blanchfield and Dale Hill. 'The Revolution in Military Affairs', in *Battlefield of the Future: 21st Century Warfare Issues*, edition of *Air and Space Journal* (September 1995), www.airpower.maxwell.af.mil/airchronicles/battle/chp3.htm, accessed 16 January 2013.
18 Bailey, for instance, sees a 'Military Revolution' as opposed to an RMA as 'embod[ying] a more fundamental and enduring transformation brought about by military change'. Jonathan Bailey, *The First World War and the Birth of the Modern Style of Warfare*, Occasional Paper No. 22 (Camberley: Strategic and Combat Studies Institute, 1996), p. 3. For a stimulating discussion of the typology of RMAs, see Tim Benbow, *The Magic Bullet? Understanding the Revolution in Military Affairs* (London: Brassey's, 2004), pp. 13–23.
19 Arguably there have been only three RMAs since 1900 – the artillery/airpower RMA of the First World War, the introduction of nuclear weapons and the as yet incomplete IT-based RMA that, for convenience, can be said to have commenced with the First Gulf War of 1991.
20 Williamson Murray, 'Thinking About Revolutions in Military Affairs', *Joint Force Quarterly* (Summer 1997), p. 73. However, this definition differs from Professor

Murray's in not considering what happened 'on the banks of the Meuse' to have been an RMA in its own right. Williamson Murray, 'May 1940: Contingency and fragility of the German RMA', in Knox and Murray, *Dynamics of Military Revolution*, p. 174.

21 However, see the criticisms of the 'cultural conservatism' argument above. Bailey does not consider the role of financial constraints in limiting the ability of pre-war armies to exploit the possibilities offered by artillery and aircraft.

22 Technically a howitzer is not a gun.

23 For comparative overviews, see Strong and Marble, *Artillery in the Great War*, passim, and Bailey, *Field Artillery*, pp. 240–70. For the British point of view, see Sanders Marble, *'The Infantry cannot Do with a Gun Less': The Place of the Artillery in the BEF, 1914–18* (Columbia University Press, Gutenburg e-book), www.gutenberg-e.org/mas01/index.html; for the German, see David T. Zabecki, *Steel Wind: Colonel Georg Bruchmüller and the Birth of Modern Artillery* (Westport, CT: Praeger, 1994); for the Russian, see Bellamy, *Red God of War*, pp. 36–45.

24 Bailey, 'First World War', pp. 132–53.

25 Colin S. Gray, *Strategy for Chaos: Revolutions in Military Affairs and the Evidence of History* (London: Frank Cass, 2002), p. 173.

26 Stephen Badsey, *Doctrine and Reform in the British Cavalry 1880–1918* (Aldershot: Ashgate, 2008); David Kenyon, *Horsemen in No Man's Land: British Cavalry and Trench Warfare, 1914–1918* (Barnsley: Pen and Sword, 2011).

27 John C. Slessor, *Air Power and Armies* (Oxford: Oxford University Press, 1936).

1

Command Culture and Complexity: Third Army during the Hundred Days, August–November 1918

Jonathan Boff

In the late summer and autumn of 1918, the British army on the Western Front went on the offensive. It had now to fight a war radically different from the trench deadlock to which all sides had become accustomed, as a measure of mobility returned to the battlefield. The Hundred Days campaign of August–November 1918 was no *Blitzkrieg*. For instance, the average daily advance made by General Sir Julian Byng's British Third Army, one of the most active of the attacking formations, was about three-quarters of a mile. The most it moved forward in a single day was just six miles. Nonetheless, the return of relative mobility confronted commanders with a series of new challenges.

One of the most pressing was the exercise of command and control. The increased tempo of operations placed a premium on rapid intelligence and speedy decision-making. However, communications remained a major constraint. The extensive fixed line networks of the trenches were soon left behind, and, although 'the BEF was employing a much more flexible and sophisticated communications system than it had ever done before, tenuous communications were still having a profound impact on its operations', as Brian Hall has shown.[1] New technology offered no quick fix. Wireless, for example, remained in its infancy. Inexperience bred over-long messages which jammed the net. On average wireless messages took 40 minutes to arrive compared with the 55 minutes for those carried by pigeon.[2] So, of the 869 messages passing through the Guards Division signals office on the day it attacked the Hindenburg Line, 27 September, only six went by wireless.[3]

The only way to maintain the pace of operations was to recognize the limitations of the signals system and to work around them. If the chain of command could not be made to work faster, the best way to make decisions more quickly was to reduce the number of links in the chain. One way to do this was for senior officers to go forward and exert more hands-on control, but this was rarely practical. Another was for control to be devolved to more junior commanders, free to use their own initiative. Before the attack at Amiens-Montdidier in early August 1918, General Marie-Eugène Debeney, commanding French First Army, approved all acts of initiative in advance, whatever their outcome.[4] Martin Samuels and Tim Travers have argued that the British army was incapable of this kind of delegation and relied instead on 'restrictive control', whereby commanders received detailed orders which they were to carry out to the letter.[5] Other historians disagree, and suggest that decentralization was a feature of operations in 1918, although they differ about how this was achieved. Robin Prior and Trevor Wilson's seminal work on General Sir Henry Rawlinson, for instance, argues that decentralization was driven from the bottom up. Rawlinson became increasingly marginal to success as the expertise of his subordinates grew and so 'the nature and extent of his job contracted'.[6]

For J. P. Harris and Niall Barr, however, decentralization was contingent on circumstance, rather than on the expertise of subordinates. In their view, during set-piece assaults, 'as a command level Army was crucial'.[7] In less-structured operations, however, responsibility was inevitably devolved, and army and corps HQs sometimes became little more than spectators. Then again, in Andy Simpson's view, devolution of control was the result of deliberate policy choice in line with the pre-war principles of *Field Service Regulations Part I: Operations 1909*, reiterated in the *SS 135* pamphlets issued in 1916–18.[8] This chapter analyses delegation in British Third Army's operations during the Hundred Days. It studies the three kinds of operation that Sir James Edmonds identified as making up the campaign: set-piece assaults on well-prepared positions, improvised attacks on field positions consisting of fortified localities and trenches and pursuit.[9] It argues that historians have underestimated the complexity of British command, that this complexity is rooted in less formal factors and that these need to be studied more closely.

Planning for set-piece attacks was carried out according to a well-established process laid out in *SS 135 The Training and Employment of Divisions*, issued in January 1918. This laid out a seven point top-down planning process, with orders cascading down the organization and each successive lower level of command responsible for filling out details within the objectives set to them.[10] *SS 135* was not designed to be used alone, however, but in conjunction with other, pre-war, manuals such as *Field Service Regulations Part I (Operations)* and *Part II (Organisation and Administration)*, and *Infantry Training 1914*. These stressed the importance of delegation: 'it is essential that superior officers, including battalion commanders, should never trespass on the proper sphere of action of their subordinates.'[11] Orders should state the object, but leave the method of attaining the objective to the subordinate, as the 'man on the spot' likely to have the best knowledge of local conditions. Further, subordinates should be trained to use their 'initiative in dealing with unforeseen developments', and, if necessary, they had not only a right, but a positive duty, to depart from or vary their orders.[12]

Third Army's attack on the Hindenburg Line on 27 September typifies the British approach to set-piece attacks. Informal planning at GHQ and army level got under way on 8 September, with corps and divisions warned for further operations on the seventeenth. Third Army issued formal orders on 20 September, which then trickled down through corps, divisions and brigades, each holding a series of conferences to work out details and co-ordinate where necessary. The battalions slated to lead the assault received their final orders during the course of 25–26 September. The process fits *SS 135* closely: a top-to-bottom cascade of orders, growing increasingly detailed as one moves downstream.

There were, however, significant points of divergence from doctrine. First, the written record makes the process appear considerably more centralized than was the case. In practice, lower level commanders sometimes played an important part in the planning process. On 17 September, for example, VI Corps asked its divisional commanders for their opinions on 11 detailed points concerning the proposed operations. They were asked whether they considered the second objective achievable, and whether that should be conditional on the Canadians taking Bourlon Wood.[13] Divisions were being asked for their input not only on the methods to be used to achieve their objectives but also on the feasibility of those objectives, and on matters of co-ordination between corps.

Secondly, the prescription that commanders 'should never trespass on the proper sphere of action of their subordinates' was inconsistently applied.[14] 2 Guards Brigade, for example, although told to choose their own objectives beyond the first, and instructed to decide the pace of the barrage (in theory, both divisional responsibilities), then found Division 'suggesting' an attack on a single battalion frontage and 'suggesting' lines for assembly, for jumping-off and for the final protective barrage.[15]

Thirdly, *SS 135* allowed for corps to exercise a 'quality assurance' function, approving divisions' plans.[16] Lieutenant General Sir Aylmer Haldane (VI Corps) did indeed vet – and sometimes reject – those of his subordinates.[17] Likewise, Lieutenant General Sir Cameron Shute (V Corps) produced a ten-point critique of one of 21st Division's plans.[18] There is, however, no evidence of other corps commanders doing the same and Haldane's diary suggests that the practice remained controversial: 'It has been, before now, a question whether a copy of orders should be sent to the commander of the next higher formation. In my opinion it is essential.'[19]

How well did the command system cope with improvised attacks in 'semi-open' or 'open' warfare? From 23 August to 3 September Third Army fought a confused and scrappy battle driving east around Bapaume. In place of set-piece attacks, planned and sometimes rehearsed at relative leisure, with nights dedicated largely to relief, resupply and rest, fighting became near continuous. Attacks, ordered at short notice, were often launched with little or no reconnaissance. These were days of near-constant pressure on the Germans, and progress of some kind was made by Third Army almost every day from 23 August, although the New Zealand Division occupied Bapaume, seven miles from the 21 August front, only on 29 August.[20] Many of the 39 brigade attacks undertaken were, in themselves, unsuccessful. The cumulative impact, however, was a factor in the German decision to withdraw to the Hindenburg Line during the night of 2/3 September.

Third Army, on the whole, responded well to the need for faster reaction times, largely by simplifying the command process. As a battalion commander in 99 Brigade (2nd Division), wrote:

> The orders for this attack were given to me personally on the ground by Brigadier General E. Ironside . . . and corroborated in writing on a sheet of paper torn out of his notebook. I mention this as a good example of a commander giving his orders verbally on the ground and the written corroboration being only a few brief paragraphs giving all the necessary information, thus avoiding the mass of written orders which had become so fashionable at this period of the war.[21]

This enabled operations to be mounted quickly. At 09.30 on 24 August, for example, 99 Brigade received orders to attack Mory Copse. By 10.15, Ironside had drawn up a fire plan with the artillery commander. He then rode around to his battalion commanders, the tanks and the brigade on his flank and was ready to attack by 15.30. The attack was successful and casualties totalled only some 50 men, against 100 prisoners taken.[22]

Inevitably, things did not always run so smoothly. At 01.00 hours on 25 August, for example, 187 Brigade, was ordered, having relieved 2nd Division during the night, to attack Mory at 09.00. Since the handover took longer than expected, the brigade commander held a conference at 05.00, at which it was decided to change the start time to 10.30. He informed division that zero hour should be postponed, and was told to set his own start time when ready. Unfortunately, the CO 2nd/4th Battalion York and Lancaster, due to poor telephone communications, had not heard of the conference. When he did, at 08.30, he hurried off to find it, leaving orders for the unit to attack as originally planned. His battalion consequently went forward, largely unsupported, at 09.00. The attack, predictably, failed and the battalion lost eight officers and 214 men.[23]

The role of both army and corps commands was limited in fighting of this nature. Third Army orders, previously specific and detailed, were now perforce general. In the evening of 23 August, for example, Byng ordered merely: 'Advance will be continued tomorrow and no respite is to be given to the enemy'.[24] VI Corps, likewise, issued no full-dress attack orders between 22 August and 1 September. In operations of this sort, corps and army could not keep up with the pace of battle. All higher commanders could, and did, achieve in this kind of warfare, was rotate units in and out of the line, and provide 'ginger' to help maintain momentum.

The outcome was not necessarily consistent delegation. Haldane asked Third Army approval before sending forward 2nd Division on 23 August, although he had no need to do so.[25] Nor was every division happy to have authority devolved to them. On 23 August, IV Corps instructed Major-General Arthur Solly-Flood (42nd Division) to arrange the details of an attack direct with 21st Division (V Corps); Solly-Flood insisted instead on 'a properly co-ordinated attack being arranged between IV and V Corps. He was not in favour of a patch-work arrangement between divisions'.[26]

Another case of delegation from above was field artillery support, a key element in the First World War attack. The highly centralized artillery control which characterized set-piece attacks was clearly inappropriate for more mobile warfare, but it remained a moot point how far command of the guns should be devolved. In 2nd Division, for instance, attaching artillery brigades to infantry brigades proved insufficiently flexible.[27] So, from 26 August, artillery instructions were drawn up, devolving command of artillery batteries even to battalion commanders. This approach became widespread, but by no means universal. In IV Corps, repeated attempts to make divisions responsible for pushing forward batteries, sections or even single guns in close support of the infantry, proved impractical.²⁸ Consequently, on 27 August, Corps decreed that batteries advance attached to specific infantry battalions.²⁹ Although 5th and 42nd divisions complied, the New Zealand Division remained resistant to the idea. As late as 21 September 'there was a devil of a lot of discussion . . . on the forward section and its working' between Division and Corps.³⁰

Sometimes, decentralization was driven by the exercise of initiative from below. For example, in 2nd Division on 29 August, the officer commanding 1st/5th Devons decided to attack along Sugar Factory Road to obtain a good jumping off point for further operations. He arranged infantry and artillery support, and launched a successful assault that he had conceived, arranged and executed without input from above.³¹

Such initiative was not universal, however. One battalion commander complained, for instance, that an opportunity for exploitation was lost on 3 September because he was unable to persuade the regiment on his left to move beyond its first objective without orders: 'the habit had been acquired of limited objectives being laid down and no-one was encouraged to exploit beyond them'.³²

There was controversy whether headquarters should be far forward, to exercise command of their units, or back, to ease control by higher command. XVII Corps ordered that division, brigade and battalion commanders: 'must be right up where they can see the fluctuations of the battle and command. To command by the telephone – basing action on the reports of junior commanders – is a crime'.³³ In IV Corps, however, not only did the GOC (Lieutenant General Sir George Montagu Harper) complain that his division commanders were too often absent when he visited, but 5th Division tried to tie even battalion COs to one spot: 'it is impossible to keep in touch if the battalion commander is moving about all the time'.³⁴ The tension between the certainties of central control and the advantages – and drawbacks – of devolved command is well summarized in a letter from the GSO2, Guards Division who wrote that he returned from a course to the division in late August 1918 and found:

> The whole world mad. . . . Accustomed to the carefully organised and synchronised attacks of 1916 and 1917 I found attacks going off haphazard, with no co-ordination, no preparation and very little artillery support. The Guards Division suffered three thundering good hidings one after the other. . . . But it was wonderful to see . . . company commanders having a chance to command their companies instead of being told what to do by the corps commander.

He contrasts this with his experience on 31 July 1917: he had allowed a battalion to keep two platoons as a battalion reserve, only to be 'told by division that the corps commander insisted on their being given a definite task! There, in a nutshell, is how and why we destroyed ourselves in 1917.'35

The attack of 4 November shattered German resistance and initiated a pursuit which lasted until the Armistice. Pursuit phases earlier in the campaign had tended to be shorter and sometimes more closely resembled a reconnaissance in force, searching for the next line of German resistance, than outright pursuit of a broken enemy.36 It is here, Harris suggests, that we should expect to see the greatest extent of delegation.37 *SS 135* addressed the pursuit operation:

> As the battle develops and the conditions approximate to those of open warfare, there will be less opportunities for working out details of the attack beforehand. To meet these conditions it is necessary that commanders of all grades should be trained to grasp quickly the essential features of a tactical situation, and to issue orders dealing with it. It is equally important that troops should be trained to put these orders into immediate execution.38

Battalions and brigades leapfrogged through to retain forward momentum. Sections of mobile artillery were attached to battalions, and a troop of cavalry to each brigade.39 Progress, however, was slow. Every day at least two miles was made, but never more than three and a half. The enemy was generally not the problem. The weather was poor, the terrain hard going and logistics a serious concern. By 7 November VI Corps had lost contact with all but isolated rearguards of the enemy. In the event, the Armistice rendered this loss of touch militarily insignificant. It does, however, reveal something of the limitations of British command in such fighting.

One, very understandable, explanation for the sticky pursuit was that, at least from 8 November, when German armistice negotiators crossed the Allied lines, senior commanders from Byng on down took their foot off the pedal: 'bearing in mind the general situation, [Byng] did not feel justified in committing troops to offensive operations likely to result in more casualties than was absolutely necessary.'40 It would be not surprising if at least some more junior officers and soldiers were already implicitly following such an approach.

Secondly, the old habits of trench warfare, of advances in continuous lines to a series of limited objectives, were hard to shake off. Although orders were for brigades to push on without waiting for units on their flanks,41 this failed to occur. Haldane complained:

> Divisional generals still, in some cases, will not move forward without an artillery barrage, and continue to order brigades to make certain laid-down bounds and

'leap frog' their troops during an advance. All of these practices cause delay and
. . . the taking away of responsibility from brigadiers, which is properly theirs,
and the resultant destruction of initiative.[42]

The advance of 186 Brigade (62nd Division) on 7 November is a good example. The brigade attacked on a three-battalion front, with companies leap-frogging through to take three successive objective lines. The attackers set off at 06.00 hours and encountered no resistance, reaching the third objective by 10.00. On reporting this success, they were instructed not to lose contact with the enemy and to advance to a line from Vieux Mesnil to the east edge of Bois Delhaye. Moving off at 12.00, they took this objective by 16.00. Division ordered them forward again to occupy the west edge of Bois Hoyaux. 5th Duke of Wellington's set off, only to find 1st/5th Devons on their left not moving: one platoon of the former's C Company made it to the objective, again unopposed, but pulled back when it realized that the rest of the brigade had failed to advance. The brigade advanced little more than two miles all day – less than they had managed against the Hindenburg Line on 27 September. The caution of the advance, and the need for continual 'push' from above to get it moving again, suggest the brigade had become 'sticky' and lacking in initiative.[43] There are, of course, counter-examples. 1 Guards Brigade, for example, on its own initiative, actually gained the first objective it had been set for 4 November during the previous night, using 'peaceful penetration'.[44] There are many instances of initiative at sub-unit level, such as the company led onto its objective by a sergeant after all the officers had been hit.[45]

In general during the pursuit, however, army and corps orders set distant objectives, left considerable latitude to subordinates and delegated control of key assets, such as artillery, appropriately. Some divisions and brigades, however, were simply unwilling or unable at this stage of the war to exercise the initiative required by the situation. A General Staff 'Note on Recent Fighting', issued on 6 November, which criticized infantry for advancing too slowly and pausing on intermediate objectives for too long, suggests the problem was perceived to be widespread.[46]

Overall, command within VI Corps and Third Army presents a complex picture. In set-piece attacks, higher formations drove the planning process, although the views and expertise of subordinates were often incorporated. Army and corps commanders made important decisions where necessary but also left considerable latitude to the 'man on the spot'. There is little evidence of widespread 'restrictive control'. Where decentralization occurred it was a function of a combination of circumstance, subordinates' skill and published doctrine. The principle of delegation, inherent in army doctrine, was flexibly applied in varying degrees according to circumstances. As the campaign wore on and operations became more fluid, however, Third Army seems to have become progressively less comfortable with its command arrangements and the exercise of initiative grew rarer. The more open the warfare, the less delegation seems to have contributed to the maintenance of tempo. Overall, delegation was not always either consistently attempted or achieved. Where decentralization did occur, there is no coherent pattern of its having been driven from either top or bottom.

To understand the complexity of this picture, we need to look beyond the written record and consider less tangible aspects of command, rooted in what Albert Palazzo has called the 'ethos' of the British army.[47] The command culture of an organization, which determines who makes what decisions, is the product of three factors. First, formal procedures, laid down in doctrine, establish principles of performance designed to promote mutual predictability, and so, crucially, trust, between members of the command team. No *fiat*, however, can create trust within a team as effectively as the second variable, the experience of working (ideally, successfully) together. This shared experience interacts with a third factor, personality, to forge a set of norms, sometimes even unspoken, much less codified, which regulate the exercise of command.

The senior leadership of Third Army was long-established by August 1918. Byng had been in command since 9 June 1917, and inherited his MGGS, L. R. Vaughan, from his predecessor. Three of the four corps commanders had fought under Byng since June 1917, and the fourth since December.[48] Below that, the average level of shared experience and cohesion within the command groups of Third Army was high, but not uniformly so, and there was a considerable level of internal variation. The command group of a formation is here defined as the commander, his chief of staff and artillery commander (where appropriate), and the unit commanders beneath him. The average member of a corps command group had been in place for 541 days.[49] However, there was a wide range, and the chiefs of staff of V and XVII Corps had both been in post less than 40 days. Over half the divisions of Third Army – nine – were fighting their first major battles under their corps. The other seven had been under command since the fighting of March-April that year. The average division command team member had been in place for 358 days, although again experience varied considerably both within and between divisions. The average VI Corps brigadier, for example, had served for 274 days, but seven of the 12 had been on the job only since March.

The average battalion commander in the Guards Division had commanded for 249 days, although again the range was broad, from 76 to 404 days. By comparison, in another 'elite' division, the New Zealand, all the brigadiers dated only from April, and only three of the battalion commanders had been there since December 1917.

Casualties, promotions and sackings inevitably generated turnover during the campaign. Different divisions suffered to different extents. 62nd Division had the same three brigadiers at the Armistice as in August, while the Guards went through seven. 3 Guards Brigade alone had no less than five different commanders.

Judging trust by length of shared service in this way risks understating the extent to which the transaction of business was eased by less formal relationships. Even at this stage of the war, commands at brigade level and above were almost exclusively held by pre-war regulars, with all the regimental and personal loyalties, and antipathies, that implies.[50] Two-thirds of battalion COs, likewise, had seen service before 1914.[51] Older ties existed, too. Of 137 senior officers (brigadiers and above) in Third Army, 35 had attended the Staff College, and 23 Eton. At all levels, many officers, regular, Territorial or Special Reserve, knew each other and had worked together in some capacity, even if not as commander and subordinate. For example, MGRA Third Army, A. E. Wardrop, had spent 18 months as CRA Guards Division. G. E. Rasch, CO 2nd Grenadier Guards (1 Guards Brigade) had previously served as GSO3 on the Division staff and as Brigade Major to 2 Guards Brigade.

It is not possible statistically to derive any correlation between length of teamwork and success in the campaign. The common-sense conclusion that teamwork and efficiency went together is, however, reinforced by the evidence of one brigade major regarding his brigadier: 'I knew his mind and methods: a few words would suffice to enable me to write the orders: with still fewer I should know whether they were approved before issue'.[52]

Personality was another source of variation. Some commanders, like Ironside (GOC 99 Brigade), were renowned for their dynamism.[53] 63rd Division provides an interesting case study of the limits allowed to initiative, and, perhaps, of the impact personal relationships could have on the exercise of command. At 16.00 hours on 24 August the GOC, Major-General C. E. Lawrie, gave verbal orders for an attack at 19.30, objectives La Barque and Thilloy. 188 Brigade was to lead, co-operating with New Zealand Division on its left, with 189 Brigade in echelon to its right in support. 188th Brigade was in position by 18.45, but 189 Brigade was running late. By 19.15 it was clear to the commander of the latter, H. D. De Pree, that his units could not be in position in time. He therefore took the initiative to cancel the attack.[54] The New Zealand brigade filed an official complaint, with which Lawrie agreed.[55] He fired De Pree that night, and ordered a fresh attack early next morning.

Had Lawrie over-reacted to a legitimate exercise of initiative by a subordinate? The 188 Brigade commander later argued that 'a glorious chance of taking Thilloy' and cutting off Bapaume had been passed up, that the Germans had therefore been able to reinforce it, and that the result was several days of bloody, fruitless attacks.[56] Thilloy fell only on 29 August. The case was evidently controversial, and a variety of explanations for De Pree's action have been proposed. According to the New Zealand report, De Pree said he had no maps.[57] This hint that inadequate staff work may have been a problem is reinforced by the evidence of a battalion commander in 188 Brigade, and by the fact that the GSO1 was inexperienced, and was actually hospitalized next afternoon with 'over-fatigue'.[58]

A more deep-seated problem may have been that 'relations between HQ 63rd Division and IV Corps were strained, in fact a miniature Gunner *v* Sapper war was going on'.[59] Certainly, Lawrie was dismissed, and 63rd Division transferred to XVII Corps, on 30 August. A range of other plausible explanations for Lawrie's sacking exists. His frontal attacks on Thilloy (25–7 August) were costly and profitless: the division lost nearly 3,500 officers and men in the last week of August.[60] Or perhaps Lawrie was thought wrong to have dismissed a brigadier who exercised appropriate initiative. Within a fortnight, De Pree had another brigade. Then again, perhaps Lawrie just fell foul of politics. De Pree was Haig's cousin and later served as executor to his will.[61] One way or another, it seems clear that personality played at least some role.

One avenue by which commanders sought to set the tone and mould the culture of their commands was by drawing out 'lessons learnt' from operations. Almost all units did this in some fashion.[62] Major-General Torquil Matheson, who took over Guards Division on 11 September, however, seems to have been exceptionally rigorous. In addition to regular after-action reviews, he issued a series of extremely detailed queries, sometimes right down to company level.[63] It is possible to see these as a new divisional commander's attempt to impose his own will and methods on a division which had not lived up to its reputation at the end of August. To subordinates, however, such *post-mortems* must sometimes have seemed less like proper 'quality control' and more like 'second-guessing' by superiors blessed with 20–20 hindsight. Were they always conducive to the promotion of initiative in subordinates?

Haldane's diary provides good, albeit partial, evidence of the culture of command and level of mutual trust in VI Corps. In personal terms, Haldane's attitude towards Byng was generally positive:

> I would do a good deal for Byng as he is always ready to hear what one has to say about the difficulties which have to be surmounted and does not shut one up or slur over them as did Allenby when I had the misfortune to serve under him. Moreover he does not force his own views on one and insist on an attack being carried out in accordance with his ideas, and then when it goes wrong put the blame on one's shoulders instead of taking it himself.[64]

Looking down the chain of command, however, we find that Haldane was wary of some of his subordinates, and they knew it. He had the GOC Guards Division, Major-General Geoffrey Feilding, promoted home. Feilding's replacement, Matheson, was considered sound at least until 6–8 November when Haldane lectured him and Major-General Robert Whigham (62nd Division) on the need to get away from the trench mentality.[65] Of the other divisional commanders in VI Corps, Major-General Cyril Deverell (3rd Division) is not mentioned in the diary in this period, although in April Haldane had ranked him one of the best three commanders to serve under him.[66] Major-General Cecil Pereira (2nd Division) clearly did not inspire confidence, and there are complaints about him from the campaign's beginning. Haldane's frustration grew as Pereira proved 'sticky'.[67] On 23 October, matters came to a head and Haldane decided to sack him unless a good explanation was forthcoming. After a frank interview on 27 October, Pereira kept his job, although the division was not used for offensive operations again.[68]

A useful contrast is provided in the case of V Corps by the diary of the 33rd Division commander, Major-General Reginald Pinney. He resented what he saw as his corps commander's interference. According to Pinney, Major-General David Campbell (GOC, 21st Division) shared his frustration: 'the fortnight's Bosh (*sic*) hunting to which he had looked forward all his service had been absolutely miserable owing to Shute's fussing'.[69] Within a month of coming under Shute's command Pinney sought to resign.

Regardless of the rights and wrongs of this particular relationship, it was clearly dysfunctional. Pinney has also, however, left us evidence of how he dealt with his subordinates. Sometimes, underperformers were carpeted, as was D. C. Owen, CO of 1st Middlesex, for being 'sticky' (*sic*) with one of the brigadiers.[70] Brigadier General A. W. F. Baird, commanding 100 Brigade, when slow to move on 24 October, received a ticking off and a fresh set of written orders, even though Pinney had felt misgivings about the state of his nerves over a month earlier.[71] Brigadier General J. D. Heriot-Maitland (GOC 98 Brigade), however, was told he was 'getting worn and therefore not up to the mark' and replaced.[72] Other subordinates were treated more summarily. When G. K. Olliver (CO, 1st Queen's) neglected to take appropriate action to help casualties around his dug out after a gas attack, he was unceremoniously fired.[73] Most vividly, when Pinney found the CRE, G. F. Evans, miles back from where he should have been on 6 November, he 'BIT HIM' and sent him home.[74] Different personalities, and professional disagreements, taken together, were another source of variation in the 'culture of command'.

This chapter has shown that the exercise of command was more complex in Third Army during the Hundred Days than historians have so far estimated. Delegation played a role in achieving higher tempo, although, paradoxically, the more fluid the situation, the less impact it had. Decentralization was not consistently achieved. It is not possible to establish a coherent pattern of either top-down devolution, or bottom-up assumption, of responsibility. A variety of factors, including a range of non-formal 'cultures of command' partly driven by personality, underlie the complexity of this picture. The human factor remained important even in a war dominated by machines.

Notes

1 Brian N. Hall, 'The British Expeditionary Force and Communications on the Western Front, 1914–1918' (PhD, University of Salford, 2009), p. 309.
2 After-action report (AAR), 21–5 August, 1st Tank Brigade HQ War Diary, TNA WO 95/99. All dates are 1918 unless otherwise specified.
3 GD No. 60/102/G, 3 October, Guards Division General Staff War Diary, TNA WO 95/1195.
4 *'J'approuve d'avance tous les actes d'initiative, quel qu'en soit le resultat'*: First Army General Order No. 562, 3013/3, 6 August, Annexe 517 in Armée, Service Historique, *Les Armées Françaises dans la Grande Guerre*, vol. VII, Annexe vol. I (Paris: Imprimerie, 1922), p. 566.
5 Martin Samuels, *Command or Control? Command, Training and Tactics in the British and German Armies, 1888–1918* (London: Frank Cass, 1995); Tim Travers, *The Killing Ground: The British Army, the Western Front and the Emergence of Modern Warfare 1900–1918* (London: Allen and Unwin, 1987) and *How the War Was Won: Command and Technology in the British Army on the Western Front 1917–1918* (London: Routledge, 1992).

6 Robin Prior and Trevor Wilson, *Command on the Western Front: The Military Career of Sir Henry Rawlinson 1914–1918* (Oxford: Blackwell, 1992), pp. 300, 305, 396–7.
7 J. P. Harris with Niall Barr, *Amiens to the Armistice: The BEF in the Hundred Days Campaign, 8 August–11 November 1918* (London: Brassey's, 1998), p. 27.
8 Three versions of *SS 135* were issued during the war: *Instructions for the Training of Divisions for Offensive Action* (December 1916), *The Training and Employment of Divisions, 1918* (January 1918) and *The Division in Attack* (November 1918). See Andy Simpson, *Directing Operations: British Corps Command on the Western Front 1914–18* (Stroud: Spellmount, 2006), pp. 160–1.
9 J. E. Edmonds and R. Maxwell-Hyslop, *Military Operations, France and Belgium, 1918* vol. V: *26 September–11 November: the Advance to Victory* (London: HMSO, 1947), p. 573.
10 *SS 135* (January 1918), pp. 12–14.
11 *Infantry Training 1914*, p. 121.
12 *FSR I*, p. 23.
13 VI Corps GS 60, 17 September, 2nd Division General Staff War Diary, TNA WO 95/1301.
14 *Infantry Training 1914*, p. 121.
15 GD No. 1/558/G, 15 September, Guards Division General Staff War Diary, TNA WO 95/1195.
16 I am grateful to Dr William Philpott for suggesting this metaphor.
17 Haldane Diary, 26 September, NLS.
18 GS 490/18, 20 August, V Corps General Staff War Diary, TNA WO 95/750.
19 Haldane Diary, 26 September, NLS.
20 See Glyn Harper, *Dark Journey: Three Key New Zealand Battles of the Western Front* (Auckland, NZ: HarperCollins, 2007), pp. 323–490 for a detailed examination of the New Zealand Division in this battle.
21 Letter, Charles Howard, 23 June 1938, Official History Correspondence: Third Army, TNA CAB 45/185.
22 AAR, 24 August, 99th Infantry Brigade, 2nd Division General Staff War Diary, TNA WO 95/1301.
23 AAR, 23 August–3 September, 187th Infantry Brigade War Diary, TNA WO 95/3089.
24 Telegram G. B. 777, Third Army to corps, 17.30 hours, 23 August, Third Army Operations, TNA WO 158/227.
25 Haldane Diary, 23 August, NLS.
26 42nd Division General Staff War Diary, TNA WO 95/2646.
27 Telegram from 2nd Division, 01.30 hours, 24 August, 6th Infantry Brigade War Diary, TNA WO 95/1357.

28 Addendum No. 2 to IV Corps Artillery Instructions No. 257, 20 August; Artillery Instructions No. 259, 23 August; Artillery Instructions No. 261, 24 August; IV Corps CRA War Diary, TNA WO 95/730.
29 Artillery Instructions No. 262, 27 August, IV Corps CRA War Diary, TNA WO 95/730.
30 Diary, Brigadier-General G. N. Johnston (BGRA, NZ Division), IWM 01/12/1.
31 Report to Brigade Major, 5 September, 185th Infantry Brigade War Diary, TNA WO 95/3080.
32 Letter, Charles Howard, 23 June 1938, Official History Correspondence: Third Army, TNA CAB 45/185.
33 Lessons Learnt, 21 August–7 September, XVII Corps General Staff War Diary, TNA WO 95/936.
34 G. 852, 29 September, IV Corps General Staff War Diary, TNA WO 95/718; Lessons from Operations, 21 August–4 September, 5th Division General Staff War Diary, TNA WO 95/1516.
35 Letter, Henry Aubrey-Fletcher, 15 July 1938, Official History Correspondence: Third Army, TNA CAB 45/185.
36 The relevant periods are 3–7 September and 3–5, 9–10, and 24–5 October.
37 Harris, *Amiens*, p. 149.
38 *SS 135*, January 1918, p. 14.
39 AAR, 4–11 November, 186th Infantry Brigade War Diary, TNA WO 95/3085; AAR, 3–10 November, 187th Infantry Brigade War Diary, TNA WO 95/3089.
40 AAR, 27 October–11 November, VI Corps General Staff War Diary, TNA WO 95/775.
41 Guards Division Instructions No. 1 G.D. 1/1082/G, 3 November, Guards Division General Staff War Diary, TNA WO 95/1196.
42 Haldane Diary, 8 November, NLS.
43 AAR, 4–11 November, 186th Infantry Brigade War Diary, TNA WO 95/3085; 5th Battalion Duke of Wellington's Regiment War Diary, TNA WO 95/3086.
44 1st Guards Brigade War Diary, TNA WO 95/1214.
45 2nd Battalion Grenadier Guards War Diary, TNA WO 95/1215.
46 General Staff, Notes on Recent Fighting No. 24, 6 November, LHCMA Montgomery-Massingberd 7/37.
47 Albert Palazzo *Seeking Victory on the Western Front: The British Army and Chemical Warfare in World War I* (Lincoln, NE: University of Nebraska Press, 2000), pp. 8–17.
48 XVII Corps was briefly transferred to First Army in April and rejoined only on 23 August. It had otherwise been in Third Army since early 1916, however, and is here considered to have been part of Third Army on 21 August. Similarly, 63rd Division is considered a part of XVII Corps although it served in IV Corps for a few days in

August, and 33rd Division is included although it joined V Corps only in mid-September.
49 Where the month, but not the exact date, of appointment is known, the 15th of the month is assumed.
50 The only exception in Third Army was Brigadier-General G. H. Gater, GOC 62nd Brigade, 21st Division.
51 At least 22, and possibly 24, of the 36 battalion commanders in VI Corps were regular peacetime officers. (Two had names so common they could not be traced): *Army List*, July 1914 and December 1918.
52 Oliver Lyttelton [Viscount Chandos], *From Peace to War: a Study in Contrast 1857–1918* (London: Bodley Head, 1968), p. 193.
53 Ironside organized the attack on Mory mentioned above. See G. D. Sheffield and G. I. S. Inglis (eds), *From Vimy Ridge to the Rhine: The Great War Letters of Christopher Stone DSO MC* (Marlborough: Crowood Press, 1989), pp. 120–1.
54 63rd Division General Staff War Diary, TNA WO 95/3097.
55 Stopping of the Attack on Thilloy, 1st New Zealand Infantry Brigade War Diary, TNA WO 95/3686.
56 Letter, General Sir John Coleridge, 12 March 1938, Official History Correspondence: Third Army, TNA CAB 45/184.
57 Stopping of the Attack on Thilloy, 1st New Zealand Infantry Brigade War Diary, TNA WO 95/3686; the divisional historian agreed: Jerrold (1923), pp. 305–7.
58 Letter, Lieutenant-Colonel M. C. C. Harrison (CO 2/RIR) undated (but 1938), Official History Correspondence: Third Army, CAB 45/185; Letter, General Sir John Coleridge, 12 March 1938, Official History Correspondence: Third Army, TNA CAB 45/184; 63rd Division General Staff War Diary, TNA WO 95/3097.
59 Letter, General Sir John Coleridge, 12 March 1938, Official History Correspondence: Third Army, TNA CAB 45/184.
60 63rd Division A & Q Branch War Diary, TNA WO 95/3099.
61 Simon Robbins, *British Generalship on the Western Front1914–1918: Defeat into Victory* (London: Frank Cass, 2005), p. 38; 'Biography of Lord Haig', letter to *The Times*, 3 May 1933, p. 15.
62 See, for example, Remarks on Operations, 23 August–15 September 1918, which provided an analytic supplement to detailed AARs for each battle, 186th Infantry Brigade War Diary, TNA WO 95/3085; GS 948/17/1 23, Notes on 2nd Division Conference held 12 October 1918, 2nd Division General Staff War Diary TNA WO 95/1303; 42nd Division Staff ride at Riencourt, 7 September 1918, 126th Infantry Brigade War Diary, TNA WO 95/2656.
63 GD No. 1/738/G and GD No. 1/732/G, both 1 October; GD No. 1/813/G and GD No. 1/803/G, both 10 October; GD No. 1/902/G, 17 October, Guards Division General Staff War Diary, TNA WO 95/1195.

64 Haldane Diary, 22 September and 9 September, NLS.
65 Haldane Diary, 6, 7, 8 November, NLS.
66 Haldane Diary, 10 April, NLS.
67 Haldane Diary, 2, 26 September, NLS.
68 Haldane Diary, 24, 27 October, NLS.
69 Pinney Diary, 15 September, IWM 66/257/1.
70 Pinney Diary, 14 October, IWM 66/257/1.
71 Pinney Diary, 24 October and 21 September, IWM 66/257/1.
72 Pinney Diary, 27 October, IWM 66/257/1.
73 Pinney Diary, 3 October, IWM 66/257/1.
74 Pinney Diary, 6 and 8 November, IWM 66/257/1. Emphasis in original.

2

'Delivering the Goods'. Operation *Landovery Castle*:[1] A Logistical and Administrative Analysis of Canadian Corps Preparations for the Battle of Amiens 8–11 August, 1918

Rob Thompson

On the morning of 8 August 1918 the British Expeditionary Force (BEF)'s Fourth Army and French First Army launched an assault against German forces in the vicinity of Amiens with the objective of freeing the Amiens-Paris railway. By the end of the day an advance of over seven miles was achieved initiating the 'Final Advance to Victory' that ended 96 days later with the signing of the Armistice. The Battle of Amiens differed from previous BEF operations. Comprising the Australian and Canadian Corps, supported by III Corps, it achieved remarkable depth and the territory gained was held and consolidated. Unlike the previous battles of the Somme, Arras, Third Ypres and Cambrai it was an unambiguous and resounding success based upon the lessons and experience of the preceding four years.

Despite the extent of the victory, until recently historians have largely ignored both this battle and 1918 generally preferring to focus on the static warfare of 1915–17. Recent Great War operational scholarship has broadened its remit with an increasing number of texts and monographs examining BEF operations in 1918,[2] including those by Ekins, Harris and Barr, Brown, McWilliams and Steel, Hart, Terraine, Schreiber, Prior and Wilson, Travers, and Wise.[3] The Battle of Amiens occupies a central role in these mainly positive analyses, especially given the dominant participation of the Australian and Canadian Corps in both the battle and the historiography of 1918.

These are welcome contributions to the canon but they are significantly incomplete in their scope. Scholars have been mainly concerned with weapons technology, combat arms tactics, applied operational methodology, command and control [C2], officer leadership and the multifaceted experience of war. In short we know much more about the nature of combat on the Western Front but we know very little about how combat was organized and sustained. This is the realm of logistics and administration, defined by Thorpe in 1917 as all material and human means required for the conduct of war.[4] This dominated mass-industrialized war and defined the nature and parameters of combat.

It is surprising how little attention has been paid to logistics and administration. Thorpe ventured 'the military themselves know next to nothing about logistics'.[5] Van Creveld writing 50 years later noted 'This lack of regard is in spite – or perhaps because – of the fact that logistics make up as much as nine tenths the business of war'.[6] The reason for this disregard is prosaic: combat, despite its horrors is exciting and glamorous whereas logistics and administration is tedious and unexciting. Thorpe likened it to an audience's disregard of stagecraft in favour of the thrill of the performance.[7] Latterly the focus on 1991 Operation *Desert Storm* commanders Colin Powell and Norman 'Stormin' Schwarzkopf, the rapid mobility of the campaign and the technology used, has been subject to significant academic study obscuring the contribution of William 'Gus' Pagonis, Schwarzkopf's logistics expert and the real architect of victory.[8] Heinz Guderian, one of the primary architects of mobile armoured warfare, summed up the dismissive attitude of many commanders when he famously declared that 'Logistics is the ball and chain of armoured warfare'.[9] In contrast Dwight D. Eisenhower, Supreme Allied Commander in North-West Europe 1944–5, noted that 'it was in his [i.e. the German Army] logistic inability to maintain his armies in the field that the enemy's fatal weakness lay'.[10]

Having established the primacy of logistics and administration, we must turn to the body of literature. The comprehensive British Official History covers some of the issues passim in its 14 volumes and there is an additional volume by a sapper, Colonel A. M. Henniker, addressing transportation, albeit at the theatre level rather than operational logistics and administration.[11] The Canadian and Australian Official Histories are similarly scant.[12] Nicholson's memoir *Behind the Lines* does give some idea of division and corps level staff-work.[13] There are also a number of post-war corps histories. The two most important are the relevant volumes of the *History of the Corps of Royal Engineers* and *The Royal Army Service*

Corps.¹⁴ These are technical volumes aimed at specialists and are not widely read. The relevant Canadian and Australian histories tend to be narrative rather than analytical, and are limited to the works by Lindsay, MacNicoll, Kerry and McDill, Murray, and the *Official History of the New Zealand Engineers during the Great War, 1914–1919*.¹⁵

In terms of modern analytical studies there is Brown's *British Logistics on the Western Front 1914–1919*, which like Henniker concerns itself mostly with logistics and administration at the strategic and theatre level rather than the operational or tactical. It argues convincingly that the logistic effort of the BEF was an astonishing and effective achievement up to the operational zone. At the operational level there is Thompson's chapter in *Fields of Battle* analysing operational logistics and engineering at Third Ypres, 1917.¹⁶ Thompson argues that despite general improvement of the BEF operational method it did not extend as far as logistics and engineering. These facets were poorly organized, woefully under-resourced, lacked the proper level of C2 and were inappropriate to the operational methodology. This had a significant impact upon the conduct and outcome of the campaign and had been a persistent problem affecting all previous operations.

There are also a number of texts that concern themselves with the history of military logistics more generally such as the works of John A Lynne, Martin van Creveld and Julian Thompson. These texts by and large avoid the Great War except in passing or confine themselves to naval logistics or the opening moves of 1914.¹⁷ Thus, in spite of the torrent of texts on other Great War subjects there is a gaping hole in our knowledge of the critical area of logistics and administration. Similarly, there is next to nothing in the way of operational analyses of this field. Given the importance of the subject to the wider understanding of the war this lack of material and discussion needs to be addressed.

The vast and complex nature of logistics and administration means this chapter can never hope to redress the balance given the restricted number of words available. What it can do is attempt to highlight some of the issues and their effect on operations that faced the BEF during the second half of 1918 through an analysis of the principal logistic and administrative factors involved in the Canadian Corps' preparations for Amiens.

The overweening focus on 'combat' and ignorance of the logistics and administrative factors involved at Amiens leads to a distorted understanding of the importance of the battle. The significance of Amiens does not lie primarily in the issues of 'all-arms' co-operation, the national 'qualities' of the Dominion troops that undertook the bulk of the assault, the use of tanks; absence of artillery registration, the relative balance of forces or the substitution of firepower for manpower. The Amiens sector was manned by 'second-rate' German troops lacking artillery, meaningful and coherent defensive systems and suffering from poor morale. In contrast Fourth Army morale was high, held a significant firepower advantage and a three-to-one infantry advantage.[18] Given the relative strengths of the forces involved it was clear that this assault would be victorious even if its extent was not.

The most important element of the battle occurred before the battle began: the movement and secret concentration at very short notice of 100,000 men of the Canadian Corps from Arras to Amiens with all their associated materiél. This solved previous intractable operational problems and created a new operational dimension.

During the Third Ypres campaign from late September 1917 onwards, Second Army Commander General Sir Herbert Plumer developed and applied the concept of sequential, limited-depth operations. Prior to this, in the initial operations carried out by General Sir Hubert Gough's Fifth Army, infantry attacked objectives beyond the range of their protective artillery and were vulnerable to German counter-attacks. These counter-attacks would almost invariably push the overextended infantry out of their unconsolidated positions leading to little gain at much cost. By limiting the depth of assault the artillery protected the infantry which could then consolidate and beat off counter-attacks. Applied in rapid sequence the operational effect was cumulative leaving the enemy unable to mount a coherent and effective defence. During the autumn battles it appeared Plumer had found a successful 'system' to defeat the enemy. The success of this 'system' was illusory as the cumulative effect of BEF firepower on the axis of advance annihilated the ground and means of communication to such an extent that the engineers could not cope, artillery fell behind, assaults bogged down and operations were doomed to eventual failure.[19] The achievement of logistical *longitudinal* mobility in 1918 allowed the BEF to launch sequential offensives at different points on the line eliminating the problem of 'self-inflicted' annihilation of the axis of advance while still retaining the benefit of overwhelmingly superior firepower.

Achieving surprise was another major operational problem. The nature of the Western Front, the sheer scale of the forces involved, the need for artillery pre-registration and long bombardments revealed the location and intention of BEF operations. The pre-warned Germans were able to respond to the threat. Throughout 1917 the BEF improved their ability to deceive the enemy, but genuine surprise was not achieved until the Battle of Cambrai in November

1917. This was due principally to improvements in signals security and gunnery techniques. Although Cambrai contains many of the elements found at Amiens it differed in one important respect: it was a 'one off' and relatively small operation undertaken for the most part by troops already occupying the area. The Battle of Amiens, and subsequent operations in 1918, relied on the ability of the BEF to move forces and concentrate them at different parts of the line. If their presence was discovered the enemy could react appropriately. 'Discovery' was largely a function of the time taken to assemble those forces and the faster the assembly the greater the chance of maintaining secrecy. In the context of the allied concentric operations of 1918 secrecy and surprise became largely dependent upon factors of logistics and administration.[20]

Between 1914 and early 1918 the Germans had a significant advantage denied to the Allies. As a single force on a single front they could conceive and operate at the 'grand' operational level. The British and French operated as two distinct national forces on two distinct fronts. They could *co-ordinate* forces and assaults but the absence of a single unified allied command meant they could not fully *integrate* operations as a single force on a single front. The unification of Allied command under Foch in conjunction with significantly improved longitudinal mobility meant the allies could now conceive and function at the 'grand' operational level themselves. This eliminated the German advantage and was an essential component of Foch's 'concentric' operational concept. One practical expression of the concept was the fact that the BEF's largest single formation, the Canadian Corps, participated in two major operations, the Battle of Amiens (8–11 August) and the Battle of the Scarpe (26–30 August), at two different points on the front 40 miles distant from each other in the space of just four weeks.

How was this done? The secondary literature sheds very little light upon this event but fortunately there is a rich seam of little-consulted primary material. All four Canadian divisions produced detailed reports on the Amiens operation and the stable and administratively integrated nature of the Canadian Corps means these reports illuminate far more than just divisional concerns. The most detailed of these primary documents is a report issued by 1st Canadian Division on operations, at Amiens.[21] What is particularly interesting about this 73 page report is its focus on logistics and administration; it has 60 pages devoted to these issues. These include a separate and very detailed 49 page 'Report on Administrative Arrangements' by the divisional Assistant Adjutant and Quartermaster General [AA & QMG], Lt.-Col. J. S. Brown. Together with material from other corps units it is possible to construct a detailed representation of the move of the corps as a whole.

Rawlinson's Fourth Army went to extraordinary lengths to maintain secrecy and proposed moving the Canadian Corps into the line only one day before the assault. The movement of a corps of four divisions under these circumstances was a very difficult objective to achieve. In the case of the Canadian Corps it would verge on the impossible as the Canadian Corps was a much bigger beast than the BEF average. Understanding the sheer size of the corps gives an insight into the nature of the undertaking. Unlike Australian and Imperial formations it had not reduced the number of infantry battalions from 12 to nine in each division. Moreover, it was capable of maintaining those battalions at full strength, that is over 50,000 line infantry.[22] Each division fielded over 20,000 men.[23] All told the Canadian Corps totalled about 100,000 men. To this must be added 25,586 animals, motor transport and artillery resources.[24] In contrast the four divisions of the Australian Corps that attacked alongside the Canadians consisted of less than half this number.[25]

The difficulties inherent in moving such a force were compounded by Rawlinson's obsessive secrecy. Although plans to do 'something' in the Amiens area had been discussed at GHQ as early as May 1918 no firm planning was undertaken until 17 July. Currie, the Canadian Corps commander, learned of the impending operation at a Fourth Army conference at Flixecourt on 21 July where he was forbidden from discussing the plans with anyone except his immediate subordinates. With the objective of maintaining absolute secrecy while at least preparing the Corps to some degree a campaign of misinformation began within the Canadian Corps. The object of this campaign was to prepare the Corps for movement; deceive it as to its final destination and convince the Germans that the Corps was concentrating around Ypres. On 23 July a conference was held where Currie proposed the capture of Orange Hill, overlooking the Canadian positions east of Arras. 1st Canadian Division immediately began reconnaissance and planning activities.[26] A few days later a warning order was received that the corps would be relieved by XVII Corps and preparations for a move north should commence. Entirely unaware of the ruse 2nd Canadian Division, which was already in reserve, complied, with its commander and GSO 1 making several visits to the Ypres sector and discussing plans for an attack south of Kemmel.[27] On 28 July battalions of the 2nd and 3rd Canadian Divisions were designated Corps lead battalions and ordered to move north by strategic train.[28] The rest of the Corps continued its preparations to follow them. To further deceive both the Canadians and Germans all Corps divisional wireless sets were sent north, railheads were organized to receive reinforcements in Second Army area and Casualty Clearing Stations were set up. When corps headquarters moved on 28

July it was 'quietly given out that Corps H.Q. had moved to CASSEL (Second Army Area.)'.[29] Deliberately lax signals security meant the Germans were quickly aware of the 'presence' of the Canadian Corps in the Ypres sector.[30]

The deception programme achieved its triple aims. By 28 July the Corps was prepared to begin its strategic rail move at 12 hours' notice even if it firmly believed its destination to be Ypres. As these battalions moved north and began taking up their positions separate orders were issued on the same day for a move south. Even at this late stage the orders were shrouded in secrecy and formulated on a 'need-to-know' basis. Divisional commanders were interviewed separately by Currie about the proposed Amiens operations and instructed that '*The details were to be transmitted to **NO** others*'.[31] The orders stated that the Corps would be relieved by XVII Corps on the night of 31 July/1 August whereupon they were to be placed in GHQ Reserve (First Army Area) ready to move at 12 hours' notice to Second Army. It was not until 2 August that the 1st Canadian Division AA & QMG was able to issue definite administrative orders for entrainment to Fourth Army and even then troops were not informed of their destination until the train was moving.[32]

The movement of troops from their line positions in one Army to a new Army was not as simple as marching them out and putting them on a train to their new destination. It was a move of such complex detail as to make the actual plans for the assault seem relatively simple. In broad terms the outgoing troops needed to be relieved simultaneously by incoming troops and staged through various rear areas prior to their concentration in designated areas behind the line. They then needed to move from the concentration areas to allocated railheads where they could be entrained to the new Army area. Once they arrived at the receiving railheads they then needed to be detrained and moved to their rear concentration areas. From here they were then moved through stages to their forward concentration positions and subsequently the assault jumping off positions. The BEF lacked the capacity to move all of the Canadian Corps by rail alone and many units, especially artillery and Motor Transport (MT), had to move by road. Suitable concentration areas, billeting and hot food were required. Railheads for equipment and reinforcements required organization while road space had to be managed and trains organized. In this case the extra problems of secrecy and the need to move silently and only at night multiplied what was already an administrative nightmare. Any delay for any reason would have had cumulative effects and could have dislocated the entire operation. During their move to Amiens the Canadian Corps would utilize every form of transport available to the BEF. This included marching, tramways, light railways, broad-gauge trains, horsed transport, MT and even double-decker buses. Secrecy required all moves to be undertaken at night and the long days of August left only eight hours of darkness per day for completion. Finally all of this had to be co-ordinated with the myriad numbers of other BEF supplies, units and formations that were constantly on the move at any given time. Given the paucity of time, the variety and number of units and limited road, track and railway line space available it is a wonder they ever moved at all. To make matters worse a 'three-cornered relief' was in progress at short notice and the Canadians were moving into ill-prepared positions.[33]

The move of the 1st Canadian Division was indicative of the high state of efficiency, flexibility and co-operation of tactical transportation in the BEF. Equally it also demonstrated what could go wrong and what was done to remedy the problems that emerged.

The division began moving from its positions around Neuville Vitasse on the night of 31 July/1 August, the entire relief to be completed by daylight, 2 August. Despite the numbers involved the move of troops out of the line to their initial staging area went remarkably smoothly. This was due to a combination of the extensive light railway [LR] system used in Third Army, the use of MT and the ability of formations to co-operate. Light railways alone moved over 8,500 infantry, machine-gunners and engineers. A shortage of LR trucks meant 1 Canadian Brigade was moved to their concentration area by buses and lorries supplied by First Army at short notice.[34] The use of MT to make up for deficiencies in available rail-based transport was to become one of the hallmarks of this operation, as it would be for the BEF's moves throughout the course of 1918.

Once out of the trenches, problems were encountered due principally to sloppy use of otherwise precise administrative terms. The division was ordered to concentrate in the Liencourt area. This area was a 'sub-area' capable of accommodating only one infantry brigade. Once discovered the congested brigades were directed to Le Cauroy area, an administrative area capable of dealing with the entire division. Although only a minor mistake the consequence was dislocation, congestion, extra marches, missed meals, no billets and no sleep for the troops involved. The transport-heavy artillery were dealt with separately and concentrated in an area four miles north of the infantry. Concurrently the AA & QMG was integrating the move of the attached 6 Brigade, Army Field Artillery [AFA] entraining 30 miles to the south so that all artillery arrived simultaneously.[35] Some idea of the size and complexity of this first-stage move can be grasped when one considers that the division required a 120 square-mile 'corridor' to complete it.

By 2 August the 1st Canadian Division was concentrated and ready to begin the entraining for Amiens. For this the division required 13 artillery trains, 25 infantry trains and three separate stations.[36] Troops marched from Le Cauroy to their stations with the exception of 3 Canadian Infantry Brigade, 3rd Field Ambulance and a battalion of engineers which was some distance away from the station. Lorries were arranged for these units through First Army. Each brigade appointed an Entraining Officer with a permanent staff of 35 troops who worked closely with the Railway Transport Officer [RTO] responsible for each station. Each train also had an 'Officer Commanding Train' [OC Train]. The authority of this man was absolute: rank had no bearing on the matter.[37] The entrainment was carried out near-perfectly and when asked suggestions for improvement the RTOs 'expressed themselves as being perfectly satisfied'.[38]

Not all divisions moved exclusively by rail. 3rd Canadian Division, leaving two days earlier, moved by a mix of tactical trains, buses and staged route march. There were not enough trains to accommodate infantry transport and these moved by road instead. Without transport the division relied on Fourth Army MT to feed the troops after arrival in Amiens until the transport caught up on 3 August. As a contemporary report noted, this was 'A rather expensive and not altogether satisfactory method'.[39] As the troops moved by rail an advanced Divisional Headquarters detachment moved ahead of them by car in order to arrange detraining and billets for the arriving troops. The remainder of the HQ moved to Amiens between 3 and 5 August.

On paper the idea of a secret attack at Amiens had major advantages. The scene of fierce fighting in March 1918, between April and July the Germans concentrated their offensives elsewhere leaving the front quiet. The BEF took advantage of this lull and 'instituted a massive program of railway construction' to ease congestion.[40] By August 1918 much of this work was complete, creating the strategic rail infrastructure required to move large numbers of men to the area. The Amiens area was also full of woods that provided the 'camouflage' necessary for a concealed assembly while allied air superiority assisted by denying German air observation. Attempting to translate these 'paper' advantages into practice stretched the BEF's logistics and administration operational ability to breaking point. At some points the system broke down and as late as 7 August it seemed likely that the operation would have to be called off. The ultimate success of the operation was entirely dependent upon what the logistic system got right and how it responded to what went wrong.

While the strategic logistic infrastructure was good the same could not be said of the operational infrastructure, the most important element of which was roads. The pre-war road needs of rural France had been minimal. The road network consisted mostly of unsealed chalk 'roads' designed for light farm traffic. When subjected to the incessant pounding of thousands of lorries, horses and men these very quickly collapsed. This was the main stimulus for the adoption of a LR policy during static warfare in 1916 and 1917.[41] In Fourth Army area the LR system was virtually non-existent and while cross-country tracks could be made for horsed transport the whole operation was unusually reliant upon roads of which there were few.[42] The main problem however was not so much the paucity and quality of roads but the sheer volume of traffic caused by the concentration of so many troops so quickly. The overriding need for secrecy meant that traffic moved only at night thereby compounding the magnitude of the problem and requiring 'rigid traffic control'.[43]

When the 1st Canadian Division arrived its detraining points were 35 miles from the Amiens front lines, its troops arrived six hours late and faced a 10 mile march to their billets around Hornoy.[44] The approach march of the division to the Bois de Boves was made on the nights of 5/6 and 6/7 August requiring outstanding administration, organization and flexibility. The division created three infantry brigade groups. The first groups to move were the 1st and 3rd and they were moved by omnibus columns. Each bus was capable of moving 25 men up to a total of 4,900 men in a single 196 bus column in the case of the 3rd brigade group.[45] Over the course of two nights 594 buses were required to move 14,850 men.[46] The move of the 1st brigade group did not go well. This was due to poor administration by the Omnibus Company and Fourth Army Roads officers who had allocated a narrow local road instead of a main traffic circuit. Trying to embuss over 3,000 men under these circumstances led to considerable delays. The strain placed upon the bus drivers was also beginning to show as 'The narrowness of the road and the darkness of the night combined with the fact that the bus drivers were very tired resulted in many of the busses running off the road and blocking the column'.[47] Arrangements were much better in the case of the other brigade groups though last minute changes to debussing points required the impromptu use of motorcycle despatch riders to round up the guides waiting at the original points. Although these appear to be minor issues the consequences were not. Other traffic was dislocated and the cumulative delays meant that one of the columns arrived during daylight hours thereby seriously compromising the essential element of secrecy.[48]

Once concentrated in its forward areas the Canadian Corps had other problems to deal with. The forward move of the 3rd Canadian Division to the Boves concentration area went smoothly but they had a particularly difficult task as virtually the entire Canadian Corps and attached artillery were to pass through this area for which they were administratively responsible. To make matters worse there was only one good bridge across the River Avre at this point. This meant that they were not only responsible for the entire Canadian Corps but also 'an enormous amount of ammunition and stores, etc. of all descriptions and a large number of tanks had to be got across'.[49] This 'enormous amount' included 2,000 lorry-loads of heavy ammunition alone. The measures taken to ensure success demonstrate both the high state of BEF administrative efficiency and mirror some elements of the wider BEF 'learning curve'. After discussion at corps and army level it was decided to appoint a specific Area Commandant, Captain A. Robinson of the 49th Canadian Infantry Battalion. Although only a junior officer Robinson was given enormous power and as the Standing Orders make clear 'all orders issued by him must be carried out'.[50] This is a small but illuminating example of the general trend, seen throughout the BEF, towards placing command in the hands of those most capable of carrying out the task. It is also a 'reversion' to the principle of 'Johnny on the spot', a concept central to pre-war Field Service Regulations.

Strict regulations were enforced in Boves Wood: troop were not allowed to leave or enter without permission; fires were forbidden; in the presence of enemy aircraft troops were instructed to 'freeze' and were forbidden to fire back; trees and undergrowth were not to be cut.[51] With so many men and horses in the wood sanitation was a major problem. All human refuse was buried and all horse manure was removed for burial elsewhere at dusk. The whole was policed by the Assistant Provost Marshal [APM]'s troops and mounted orderlies drawn from the cavalry.

The two biggest problems faced by the corps were water and trench munitions supply.[52] The former, along with other factors, seriously compromised secrecy and the latter the operation itself.

The fissured chalk nature of the Somme area means that water quickly drains deep underground and away from the main rivers water is difficult to obtain. This was to become an increasing problem as the advance continued but during the concentration it also presented interrelated problems. The Boves area lacked water and all water needs had to be drawn from the River Avre. Since all available water transport was hidden in the wood this meant a considerable journey for the transport.[53] In addition there were 8,000 horses in the wood, all of which were watered at the River Avre.[54] The result was congestion so serious that the Canadian Corps had no choice but to move and water horses during daylight hours.

This was a serious threat to the secrecy underpinning the operation. The Canadian Corps General Officer Commanding Artillery [GOCRA] noted the 'weather fortunately was overcast otherwise this movement might easily have been picked up by enemy aircraft'.[55] Others also noted a general lack of camouflage security in the forward areas with troops of all types moving freely in daylight and 'it can only have been thanks to our superiority in the air combined with poor visibility and a good deal of luck, that the concentration of troops was not discovered by the enemy'.[56] The 2nd Canadian Division report noted the free movement by daylight of both heavy artillery and ammunition lorries, and added 'it is almost certain that some of this movement was observed by the enemy'.[57] Clearly there was a cumulative and collective failure to properly police movement and it appears that secrecy was at least partially maintained only due to luck and the lack of alertness on the part of the enemy. Many of the problems can be traced to the quality of APMs used for traffic control. All APMs were drawn from 'B' physical category men and were simply unable to stand the rigours: 'The need for physically active men on traffic control duty was never more felt than during the recent operations'.[58] 'A' category personnel were recommended for future operations.

On 3 August the 1st Canadian Division began arranging trench munition supplies and stockpiling for the forward dumps that would be necessary as the battle progressed. The Canadian Corps 'Q' (Quartermaster) informed them that artillery ammunition had priority but that sufficient trench munitions would be dumped in time. By 4 August no supplies were received and the division made urgent demands for grenades, rifle grenades, mortar bombs, flares and 'as much S.A.A. as possible'.[59] By 5 August the division had still not received anything. The situation was becoming critical and corps 'Q' was informed that '. . . munitions *must* be dumped by 5.00 p.m. 6th August', the absolute limit for receipt.[60] By the early afternoon of 6 August there was still no delivery 'and the fact pointed out that the whole operation was liable to be "off" unless something was done immediately'.[61] It was only by 9 p.m. on 7 August, less than eight hours before zero that supplies were finally delivered though numbers of rifle grenades (now one of the primary weapons of the all-arms infantry platoon) were insufficient and there were no trench mortar bombs. This problem was repeated throughout the corps to varying degrees and came very close to halting the operation.

This serious situation arose as a consequence of several interrelated factors. Since the German retirement from the Somme area in early 1917 the BEF realized that it needed to improve its mobility and that the key to this was the use of MT. Throughout the course of 1917 it reorganized MT and by April 1918 it was complete. The reorganization was based upon the concept of 'pooling' at the most effective C2 level. This led to the creation of GHQ Omnibus Companies and the formation of Corps and Army level standardized Mechanical Transport Companies and columns. Instead of each unit possessing its own MT, corps and armies withdrew MT from divisions and allocated MT according to operational need, a more effective use of assets. A similar process had been applied to artillery and machine guns earlier in the war.

On the whole this was a successful change as evidenced by the centrally-coordinated use of bus columns for the mass movement of troops. The Amiens operational method, however, with its emphasis on rapid concentration, highlighted its deficiencies. The lack of LR in the area created a much greater reliance on MT than normal. There was an absolute shortage of lorries; priority was given to the movement of artillery ammunition; divisions were at the 'mercy' of corps and army whose priorities were not necessarily the same; there was no horsed transport available to help clear ammunition railheads leading to delays in artillery ammunition supply and a serious shortage of petrol due to the sudden concentration of MT, tanks and aircraft in Fourth Army area.[62] Horrendous congestion due to poor traffic control added to the problem.

Once corps and Army became aware of the situation the inherent flexibility, professionalism and pragmatism of the BEF administrative and logistical services saved the situation. At all levels a desperate search for lorries and fuel began. Thanks to the 'pooling' system supply lorries were rapidly switched to supplement ammunition lorries and working mileage increased by removing the second driver from each lorry.[63] Emergency supplies of petrol were brought in from as far away as Abbeville and on the evening of 6 August officers were sent out by the corps Senior Mechanical Transport Officer [SMTO] 'to trace up Lorries already on the road, and get as many more working as could be supplied with Petrol'.[64] The situation was saved though it was clear that despite close formation co-operation and the professional, skilled and rapid response on the part of administrative personnel the situation was hardly ideal. The 1st Canadian Division administrative report noted pointedly that in future 'the responsible authorities will ensure that there is an adequate supply, not only of Munitions, but also the means of transporting them'.[65]

The Battle of Amiens was a triumph of all-arms co-operation and the application of the hard-learned operational lessons of the preceding years. From this point onwards the Germans were consistently defeated and pushed back. The BEFs ability to secretly concentrate forces at any point on the line was an essential component in Foch's 'concentric offensive' concept. The ability to mount successive attacks at different parts of the line solved the seemingly intractable problem of diminishing returns and eventual failure that was the hallmark of previous operations. The successful small-scale action by 4th Australian Division at Le Hamel on 4 July 1918 provided the first 'dress rehearsal' for the full-scale operation and despite the weakness of the enemy at Amiens a month later it was clear that this was a significant victory with long-term consequences. Had the Germans been aware of the BEF concentration, or at least acted upon that awareness, they could have brought up reserves and the outcome of the battle may have been very different.

The key element at Amiens was surprise but this was not necessarily a function of improved artillery techniques that did away with the need for pre-registration of fire. Surprise depended entirely on secrecy and that was dependent upon successful logistics and administration. The concentration was far from perfect but how the logistics and administration services dealt with problems is indicative of the high level of skill, flexibility and pragmatism that was obtained in the BEF. By 1918 the BEF had recognized that mobility had two dimensions: the ability to move *to* the battlefield as well as *across* it and Amiens clearly demonstrates the ability of this organization to learn. The audacious and successful attempt to concentrate the Canadian Corps on Fourth Army's front was the triumphant result of this logistical and administrative 'learning curve'. Clearly Amiens was not just a 'Dominion' success but a BEF one and to achieve this had required the effort of the whole of the BEF, from the ports to the front line. When Australian Corps commander Lieutenant-General Sir John Monash declared that the Canadian Corps would 'deliver the goods' he was speaking metaphorically but it was the skilled logisticians and administrative staff of the BEF that turned that metaphor into a reality.[66]

Notes

1 'Landovery Castle' was Canadian Corps' operational codename.
2 For a concise overview of the historiography of 1918 see Ian M. Brown, 'Feeding Victory: The Logistic Imperative Behind the Hundred Days' in Peter Dennis and Jeffrey Grey (eds), *1918: Defining Victory* (Canberra: Army History Unit, 1999), pp. 1–2.
3 Ashley Ekins (ed.), *1918 Year of Victory: The End of the Great War and the Shaping of History* (Auckland, NZ: Exisle Publishing, 2010); J. P. Harris with Niall Barr, *Amiens to the Armistice: The BEF in the Hundred Days Campaign 8 August–11*

November 1918 (London: Brassey's, 1998); Ian M. Brown, *British Logistics on the Western Front 1914–1919* (Westport, CT: Greenwood Press, 1998); James McWilliams and R. James Steel, *Amiens: Dawn of Victory* (Toronto: Dundurn, 2001); Peter Hart, *1918: A Very British Victory* (London: Weidenfeld and Nicholson, 2008); John Terraine, *To Win a War. 1918, The Year of Victory* (London: Sidgewick Jackson, 1978); Shame B. Schreiber, *Shock Army of the British Empire: The Canadian Corps in the Last 100 Days of the Great War* (Greenwood, CT: Praeger, 1997); Robin Prior and Trevor Wilson, *Command on the Western Front: The Military Career of Sir Henry Rawlinson 1914–1918* (Oxford: Blackwell, 1992); Tim Travers, *How the War Was Won: Command and Technology in the British Army on the Western Front 1917–1918* (London: Routledge, 1992); S. F. Wise, 'The Black Day of the German Army: Australians and Canadians at Amiens, August 1918' in Dennis and Grey (eds), *Defining Victory*, pp. 1–32.

4   George Cyrus Thorpe, *Pure Logistics: The Science of War Preparation* (Kansas City, MO: Franklin Hudson, 1917), pp. 4–9.

5   Ibid., p. 4.

6   Martin van Creveld, *Supplying War: Logistics from Wallenstein to Patton* (Cambridge: Cambridge University Press, 1977), p. 231.

7   Thorpe, *Pure Logistics*, p. 4.

8   Damon Schechter, *Delivering the Goods. The Art of Managing Your Supply Chain* (New York, NY: John Wiley, 2002), p. 1.

9   Harold Coyle, *Sword Point* (New York, NY: Pocket Books, 1988), p. 141.

10 Eisenhower quoted in *British Army Doctrine Publication*, Volume 3: *Logistics* (Andover: Director General Doctrine & Development, 1996), pp. 1–2.

11 J. E. Edmonds (ed.) *Military Operations, France and Belgium 1914–1919*, 14 vols (London: Macmillan, 1922–48); A. M. Henniker, *Transportation on the Western Front 1914–1918* (London: HMSO, 1937).

12 C. E. W. Bean (ed.), *The Official History of Australia in the War of 1914–1918*, 12 vols (Sydney: Angus & Robertson, 1920–42) [Bean was the author of six of the volumes]; G. W. L. Nicholson, *Official History of the Canadian Army in the First World War: Canadian Expeditionary Force, 1914–1919* (Ottawa: Queen's Printer and Controller of Stationery, 1962).

13 W. N. Nicholson, *Behind the Lines. An Account of Administrative Staffwork in the British Army 1914–1918* (London: Cape, 1939).

14 H. L. Pritchard (ed.), *History of the Corps of Royal Engineers*, vol. V. *The Home Front, France, Flanders and Italy in the First World War* (Chatham: The Royal Engineers Institute, 1952); R. H. Beadon, *The Royal Army Service Corps: A History of Transport and Supply in the British Army*, vol. II (Cambridge: The University Press, 1932).

15 Neville Lindsay, *Equal to the Task, Volume I. The Royal Australian Army Service Corps* (Kenmore, QLD: Historia, 1992); R. R. MacNicoll, *The Royal Australian*

Engineers, 1902 to 1919 (Netley, SA: Royal Australian Engineers Corps Committee, 1979); A. J. Kerry and W. A. McDill, *The History of the Corps of Royal Canadian Engineers*, vol. I: 1749-1939 (Ottawa: Military Engineers Association of Canada, 1962); J. D. Murray, *The Last Waggon. The Final Story of the Royal Canadian Army Service Corps* (Toronto: Williams and Crue, 2001); N. Annabell (ed.), *Official History of the New Zealand Engineers during the Great War, 1914-1919* (Wanganui, NZ: Bobb & Sharpe, 1927).

16 Rob Thompson, 'Mud, Blood and Wood: BEF operational and Combat Logistico-Engineering during the Battle of Third Ypres, 1917', in Peter Doyle and Matthew R. Bennett (eds), *Fields of Battle: Terrain in Military History* (Dordrecht: Kluwer Academic, 2002), pp. 237-55.

17 Jon Tetsuro Sumida, 'Forging the Trident: British Naval Industrial Logistics, 1914-1918', in John A. Lynne (ed.), *Feeding Mars: Logistics in Western Warfare from the Middle Ages to the Present* (Boulder, CO: Westview Press, 1993), pp. 217-49; van Creveld, *Supplying War*, pp. 109-38; Julian Thompson, *Lifeblood of War: Logistics in Armed Conflict* (London: Brassey's, 1991).

18 Wise, 'Black Day', p. 13.

19 Thompson, 'Mud, Blood and Wood', p. 243.

20 National Archives of Canada [NAC], RG9, 5069 – Fourth Army, General Staff – 'Extracts from Letters and Conferences Concerning the Preparations for the Operations on August 8th, 1918', p. 2.

21 NAC, RG9, 5059, File: 968 – '1st Canadian Division Report on Amiens Operations, August 8th-20th'.

22 NAC, RG9, 5047, File: 911 – General Headquarters 3rd Echelon, Canadian Section, August 1918.

23 Wise, 'Black Day', p. 13.

24 NAC, RG9, 5069 – Fourth Army, Administrative Branches of the Staff, August, 1918 – 'Extra Supplies Issued to the Canadian Corps', horses and mules on strength week ending August 1918.

25 Prior and Wilson, *Command*, pp. 310-16.

26 NAC, RG9, 5059, File: 968 – '1st Canadian Division Report on Amiens Operations, August 8th-20th', p. 1.

27 NAC, RG9, 5059, File: 968 – '2nd Canadian Division Narrative of Operations from March 13th to November 11th, 1918', p. 5.

28 NAC, RG9, 5059, File: 968 – '1st Canadian Division Report on Amiens Operations, August 8th-20th', p. 1.

29 Ibid., p. 2.

30 J. Ferris, *The British Army and Signals Intelligence During the First World War* (Stroud: Sutton Publishing for the Army Records Society, 1992), pp. 19-21.

31 NAC, RG9, 5059, File: 968 – '1st Canadian Division Report on Amiens Operations, August 8th-20th', p. 2. Emphasis in original.

32 Ibid., Appendix 'B', p. 2; NAC, RG9, 4858, File: 153 – 3rd Canadian Division, AA & QMG, August 1918, 'Appendix 'A', 'Move to Fourth Army (July 31st to August 3rd)'.
33 NAC, 4957, File: 504 – General Officer Commanding, Royal Artillery, Canadian Corps – 'Artillery Notes on Attack by Canadian Corps, August 8th 1918', p. 2.
34 NAC, RG9, 5059, File: 968 – '1st Canadian Division Report on Amiens Operations, August 8th–20th' – 'Administrative Arrangements', p. 2.
35 Ibid., p. 2.
36 Ibid., p. 3.
37 Ibid., Appendix 'B', p. 2.
38 Ibid., p. 4.
39 NAC, RG9, 4858, File: 153–3rd Canadian Division, AA & QMG, August 1918, Appendix 'A', p. 1.
40 Brown, *British Logistics*, p. 5.
41 TNA, WO 158/852 – Director General of Transport: 'History of Light Railways 1916–1918', p. 7.
42 NAC, RG9, 5059, File: 968 – '2nd Canadian Division Narrative of Operations from March 13th to November 11th, 1918', p. 6.
43 NAC, RG9, 5059, File: 968 – '1st Canadian Division Report on Amiens Operations, August 8th–20th', p. 6.
44 AA & QMG requests were unsuccessful. See ibid., 'Administrative Arrangements', p. 5.
45 Ibid., Appendix 'E', p. 1.
46 Ibid., p. 8. This does not include any divisional transport which moved separately by road.
47 NAC, RG9, 5059, File: 968 – '1st Canadian Division Report on Amiens Operations, August 8th–20th' – 'Administrative Arrangements', p. 7.
48 Ibid., p. 8.
49 NAC, RG9, 4858, File: 153–3rd Canadian Division, AA & QMG, August 1918, Appendix 'A', p. 1.
50 Ibid., 'Standing Orders for Bois de Boves', 3 August 1918.
51 Ibid.
52 Trench Munitions included Small Arms Ammunition [SAA], grenades and flares.
53 NAC, RG9, 5059, File: 968 – '1st Canadian Division Report on Amiens Operations, August 8th–20th' – 'Administrative Arrangements', p. 32.
54 NAC, RG9, 4858, File: 153–3rd Canadian Division, AA & QMG, August 1918, p. 1.
55 NAC, RG9, 4957, File: 504 – General Officer Commanding, Royal Artillery, Canadian Corps, August 1918, Appendix 'E', p. 1.
56 NAC, RG9, 5059, File: 968 – '1st Canadian Division Report on Amiens Operations, August 8th–20th', Appendix 'D', p. 3.
57 NAC, RG9, 5059, File: 968 – '2nd Canadian Division Narrative of Operations from March 13th to November 11th, 1918', p. 6.

58 NAC, RG9, 4861, File: 164 – 4th Canadian Division, General Staff, '4th Canadian Division Narrative of Operations, Battle of Amiens, August 8th to August 13th, 1918', Appendix '1', p. 6. For APMs in the First World War see G. D. Sheffield, *The Redcaps: A History of the Royal Military Police and Its Antecedents from the Middle Ages to the Gulf War* (London: Brassey's, 1994), pp. 50–1, 69, 74–5, 78–9.
59 NAC, RG9, 5059, File: 968 – '1st Canadian Division Report on Amiens Operations, August 8th–20th' – 'Administrative Arrangements', p. 10.
60 Ibid., p. 11. Emphasis in original.
61 Ibid., p. 11.
62 Ibid., p. 11. NAC, RG9, 5021, File: 788 – Canadian Corps Mechanical Transport Column, 5 August 1918.
63 Ibid., 7 August 1918.
64 NAC, RG9, 5059, File: 968 – '1st Canadian Division Report on Amiens Operations, August 8th–20th' – 'Administrative Arrangements', p. 11.
65 Ibid., p. 11.
66 John Monash, *The Australian Victories in France* (London: Hutchinson, 1920), p. 75.

3

'After Amiens': Technology and Tactics in the British Expeditionary Force during the Advance to Victory, August–November 1918

Bryn Hammond

Introduction

On 8 August 1918, the British Expeditionary Force (BEF), together with their French allies, launched a major offensive which finally accomplished an overwhelming physical and psychological victory over the German forces on the Western Front. In this, the Battle of Amiens, the BEF successfully combined infantry, artillery, aircraft and armour in an orchestrated operation, applying to good effect the lessons of four years' fighting. The BEF's attack broke its opponent's defences and penetrated to a depth of up to eight miles, inflicting heavy casualties and causing significant loss of *matériel* that the Germans could ill-afford.

Experience had taught the high command that if casualties in any offensive were to be minimized, it was essential for attacks to be made on a wide front by infantry with good artillery support and close co-operation by tanks. By the end of the fourth day of the battle, these conditions no longer prevailed at Amiens, and the attack was rightly closed down.

In switching their attention to other parts of the front, the British commanders then faced the necessity of maintaining operational tempo while ensuring that the lessons of Amiens were disseminated and applied in subsequent operations. This was especially true in connection with the tactical employment of armour. During the following months and until the end of the war, and against an increasingly popular perception among all ranks that tanks offered a means to reduce casualties in the offensive, and consequent demands to use them in operations, senior commanders endeavoured to manage the available assets as effectively as possible. Their responses combined innovation and pragmatism but were frequently conditioned by the realities of logistical and operational considerations as well as environmental factors such as terrain and the weather.

This chapter examines how the BEF's assimilation of tanks into the so-called all-arms battle held up under the pressure of events during the last months of the war. In doing so, it stresses certain key factors that defined the environment in which this task was undertaken and reviews the Tank Corps' own analyses of its performance after Amiens.

Operational tempo: A two-edged sword

The generals' desire for maintenance of operational tempo was significant in its effect on tank use on the Western Front in the latter half of 1918. While striving to keep the Germans on the back foot after Amiens, the high command created an environment that was counter-productive to the reduction of tank-infantry co-operation to an effective drill honed by practice before battle. The almost continuous nature of operations worked to preclude extended periods of training. After the Cambrai Battle in late 1917 which had 'defined the standard of training and planning required for truly successful co-operation between tanks and other arms',[1] any opportunity for infantry and armour to rehearse together was recognized as a significant factor in successful tank-infantry co-operation. The publication of *S.S.204 Infantry and Tank Co-Operation and Training*[2] in March 1918 had represented a concomitant attempt by General Headquarters (GHQ) to offer practical direction on how this training might be carried out. However, in reality, few such opportunities arose after Amiens.

Nevertheless, the high command continued to recommend the value of training in its doctrinal publications. Yet *S.S. 214 Tanks and their Employment in Co-operation with Other Arms*, published in August 1918, could offer little more than suggestions for army and corps school instructors to be attached to tank units to train junior officers and NCOs in the hope of gradually disseminating knowledge and ideas. This was surprising in what was, in other respects, a valuable document full of practical and sound advice based on combat experience.[3]

The significance of this lack of training opportunities and the value placed by tank unit commanders on training in co-operation is illustrated by the remarks of Lieutenant-Colonel Harry Johnson of 1st Tank Battalion in reviewing operations with 30th American Division at Bellicourt on 29 September 1918: 'All the old lessons have been again learned [sic] . . . One suggestion only will cover all the points I desire to make; greater facilities for training in the attack are essential to secure greater efficiency.'[4]

Operations involving armour in late 1918 were also constrained by the actual numbers of tanks available to the BEF for use in the fighting which, in turn, were complicated by the closely-linked issues of tank supply and salvage. These matters have been given more detailed consideration elsewhere[5] but, essentially, because tank wastage in mid- to late 1918 was many times greater than was anticipated, stocks of spares were severely depleted and supplies of replacements were inadequate. As a consequence, men usually engaged on repairs were instead salvaging parts from abandoned tanks.[6] Meanwhile, tanks that might otherwise have returned to action after suffering battle damage were cannibalized to compensate for the spares shortage. In addition, the desire for a rapid tempo in operations involved frequent switching of attacks from one sector of the front to another. This presented insurmountable logistical problems (given the available transport and technologies) when assembling tanks for use en masse in each of these widely-separated attacks.[7]

The approach adopted by GHQ and the Tank Corps to the deployment of available armour was entirely sensible, given the logistical and operational circumstances. They allotted a tank brigade (consisting of two or more battalions) to each of the three armies undertaking the major offensive operations in France, that is, First, Third and Fourth. This meant that the somewhat rigidly established logistical support arrangements needed to maintain the tanks of each unit in the field could be built on and expanded as necessary and not severely disrupted as they would surely otherwise have been.

Logistics were especially important in defining the circumstances for tank use in the final advance. It was only in early 1918 that a sophisticated and relatively robust infrastructure for the equipment, supply and reinforcement of the Tank Corps in France and Belgium was fully established. There was now a vast array of workshops, supply and equipment dumps and training bases along the Ternoise valley north-west of Arras. In addition, the introduction in February of the first roll-on, roll-off cross-Channel train ferry service capable of carrying numbers of tanks loaded on rail flat cars, gave significant advantages to tank units at the front.[8] Yet, despite these important developments, the very nature of the fighting in late 1918 with an advance continuously away from the established bases and supply dumps presented a host of logistical challenges that undoubtedly influenced the numbers of available tanks in some operations.

This point should, however, be treated with a degree of caution. There was a significant period between 4 and 18 September 1918 in which there was an absence of tank operations. Although this period offered benefits in the planning and execution of attacks involving armour, it did not witness a significant rise in available tank numbers for the next phase of operations. Indeed, Brigadier-General Anthony Courage commanding 5 Tank Brigade was especially vocal in criticizing a relatively small number of tanks from one battalion being spread too thinly for action on 18 September.[9] Clearly, other factors were at work in connection with the tanks available for action from mid- to late September.

Tanks were usually deployed in larger set piece battles because of their relative mechanical fragility (especially in terms of durability of their tracks) and their heavy logistical requirements which basically demanded the use of railways for their transportation and supply. Moreover, limiting the distance tanks were required to travel under their own power and on their own tracks before being committed in action increased the likelihood of both them and their crews arriving at the point required in good enough physical condition to be of use in combat.

It is also important to recognize that in the operations in the last months of the war the set piece battles for which tanks were most suited by logistical considerations took place over a greatly reduced time period between initial planning and execution. As Andy Simpson points out, 'Even though the set piece operations, such as the attacks on the Hindenburg Line, look ponderous, they were launched at a far greater speed than their equivalents in 1917.' In one example, mentioned by Simpson, the planning and execution of an attack by units of IV Corps on 23 August took a total time of 19 hours from the start of the initial conference involving divisional and corps commanders to zero.[10]

While this reduced cycle was an indication of how efficient the staff work of the BEF had become by 1918 and how strong was its logistical base,[11] it gave rise to unexpected problems for the tank arm. Since the planning and execution of operations was now considerably devolved, with corps and divisions making arrangements with tank brigades, this should, in theory, have produced a closer mutual understanding between the various arms undertaking an attack. However, when combined with the desire demonstrated by all corps commanders to have some tanks (even in small numbers) allotted to them for any assault they were about to make, the end product instead was a return to the much-derided 'penny-packeting' of tanks in sections or companies among each of the attacking corps.

In 1916, given the paucity of tanks available and a desire to make use of what there was, there had been little option for army and corps commanders other than to commit tanks in 'penny-packets'. Indeed, there had been a number of successful occasions of their use in this manner in the latter part of the Somme battle in that year.[12] However, by 1918, a more robust Tank Corps defence was mounted against this approach, which disrupted command and control arrangements.[13] The response from GHQ, in the person of Lieutenant-General the Hon. Sir Herbert Lawrence, was to warn of the consequences of penny-packeting but, once more, to be pragmatic in accepting the need if operational circumstances demanded. In a memorandum of 1 September, intended to address 'the unfamiliarity of many Divisional and Brigade Commanders with the functions and limitations of Tanks' which had produced disproportionate tank losses to the results attained, Lawrence wrote:

> The units and formations of the Tank Corps have been so organized in order to facilitate their handling both tactically and administratively. This organization has been frequently departed from in order to meet local conditions. Although at times this may be unavoidable it should be borne in mind that such a departure from the normal organization must result in a loss of fighting efficiency.[14]

This pragmatic approach was in keeping with Lawrence's intention not to manage the detail of tank operations but more appropriately to ensure a defined general framework for the conduct of such operations.

Inevitably, given the continuing requests for tanks to be made available for operations, the splitting up of tank battalions and companies continued and, equally inevitably, produced its own problems. A complaint from one tank battalion commander after operations on 18 September that 'The time for preparation was insufficient for proper co-operation with three corps'[15] did not prevent this distribution of tanks from one unit among several corps being repeated on 8 October 1918 when those from two battalions were split across four corps and eight divisions.[16]

The demand for tanks in the fighting of late 1918 in combination with the logistical constraints on their availability and further compounded by tank casualties from action, necessitated another pragmatic response from both the tank arm and the higher echelons of the BEF. While both continued to expound the tactical principles associated with each type in use, the realities of the fighting prompted occasions when *any* tanks of whatever type were what were demanded and used – especially on the second and subsequent days of a major offensive. This was particularly the case with the Medium A 'Whippets'. Notionally 'intended to exploit success when the enemy's line has been broken',[17] they were sometimes used in direct contact with the infantry.[18]

Notwithstanding these issues, significant tactical successes were achieved in a variety of circumstances. In common with the units of all arms, the Tank Corps was industrious in post-battle analysis and used the results of this analysis to inform tactics and technology for future operations. From these after-action reports it is instructive to see how the tank arm regarded its own performance in the fighting from late August 1918 to the war's end.

The Royal Air Force and the Tank Corps

One undoubted area of significant progress and success (and perceived as such by both the Tank Corps and Royal Air Force) was in the use of RAF aircraft to assist tanks in offensive operations. In January 1918, Brigadier-General Hugh Elles, commander of the Tank Corps in France, had asked Major-General Sir Hugh Trenchard for Royal Flying Corps assistance for tanks in offensive operations. Elles' principal point was that when the tanks got ahead of the infantry and beyond, or at the extreme range of, the British artillery fire, they were likely to encounter German anti-tank guns at point blank range as happened at Flesquières during the Cambrai Battle. His request was for aircraft to give warning of such anti-tank guns and, if possible, to keep down their fire.[19] The two general principles of Elles' request encapsulated the areas in which tactics and technology were developed for aircraft to co-operate with tanks during the rest of the war and which, in the Final Advance, were being refined and conducted with considerable success.

The principal step forward in air co-operation after Amiens was the allocation of a second RAF squadron to the role of counter anti-tank work. No. 73 Squadron, which flew Sopwith Camels, was specifically assigned to the task of ground attacks on German field guns that might operate in an anti-tank role and first saw action in this capacity on 23 August.[20] Between that date and 11 November, according to the squadron history, 'continuous low-flying was carried out, and a total of 153,600 rounds were fired at, and 1,176 25-lb bombs were dropped on, ground targets. The record for one day being 25,000 rounds fired and 160 25-lb bombs dropped'.[21] This ground-attack work complemented that of the existing tank co-operation squadron, No. 8, which flew Armstrong-Whitworth FK8 two-seater general purpose aircraft.

Once again, this decision to employ a second squadron arose from the actions of Elles who, on 16 August, had written to Major-General John Salmond, now commanding the RAF in France, regarding 'the importance of having definite aircraft units detailed to engage anti-tank guns'. In suggesting that, 'for the protection of the Tanks from the fire of hostile guns, a complete unit of fighting machines should be detailed to carry out this work and have no other mission', Elles acknowledged that he might be perceived to 'be making too great a demand on the RAF but I put it forward as I consider it to be of such importance if the Tanks are to be able to fulfil their tasks to the full'.[22]

Typically, the role of the two squadrons in operations where they both participated was as follows. At least one machine from No. 8 Squadron was to be up during the attack to keep the co-operating tank brigade or battalion headquarters informed as to the advance of the tanks and any points where they were held up. Other aircraft from this squadron were to bomb and machine gun any German artillery which they witnessed firing at tanks, and keep under periodical machine gun fire all places where German guns were likely to be.[23] Meanwhile, No. 73 Squadron machines actively roamed the attack front looking for likely locations for anti-tank guns to be sited. Major Trafford Leigh-Mallory, who had overall responsibility for the two RAF tank co-operation squadrons, had swiftly concluded that using such aircraft to send down Zone Calls for British artillery to open fire on the hostile batteries was out of the question since the anti-tank guns did not generally start to fire till the tanks were between 1,500 and 1,000 yards away.[24] Consequently,

> the only sound principle was obviously immediate action on the part of the aeroplane with bombs and machine guns, with a view to driving the German gunners from their guns until the Tanks had overrun the position.[25]

This scheme to which the two squadrons worked derived first from a thorough post-action reconnaissance of the Amiens battlefield conducted by Leigh-Mallory and Brigadier-General Henry Karslake, the Tank Corps' senior staff officer. The two examined the positions of German anti-tank guns during the various phases of the fighting.[26] The principle then established was for the RAF squadrons and Tank Corps officers to discuss the location of anti-tank guns and draw up a map showing the places where the tanks would be most exposed, and the most likely places from which they could be fired at by anti-tank guns. It was soon found that the tanks did not require as much assistance at the commencement of a battle, when they were advancing under a barrage as they did later, when the artillery protection thinned and gradually diminished.[27]

As the fighting went on, the airmen's knowledge of the anti-tank guns increased and was greatly enhanced after 2 September with the capture of a document detailing the German methodology for allotting guns for anti-tank work and the kinds of positions they were to take up. According to Leigh-Mallory:

> This gave us a great deal of valuable information, and greatly increased the use we could make of the existing Counter Battery Maps, which of course only lasted while we were fighting to break down the Trench System. The scheme worked in the following way: The pilot and observer copied the likely anti-tank positions on to their own maps, in the area over which they were going to fly, each machine only having about 2,000 yards of front to watch. They were to machine gun and bomb periodically all the likely places in their area, whether they were seen as active or not, and then when they actually did see a gun firing, to attack it with everything they had got. In this way, by looking at the right sort of places, a great number of anti-tank guns were spotted as soon as they opened fire. As time went on we could reckon on at least 50% of the places so marked actually being active.[28]

RAF co-operation with the Tank Corps was only one strand of the very important ground-attack work the air arm undertook in 1918. But it was, without doubt, one of *the* great tactical successes of the last months of the war.

Getting things right?

A review of combat analyses produced by units of the Tank Corps after Amiens and in the immediate post-war period suggests the Corps believed that its tactical principles and methods in the last months of the war were, largely, appropriate to the circumstances.[29] 'Tactical Experiences of all past Tank Corps Operations Collected and Issued by the 3rd Tank Group' stated that:

> The co-operation as laid down in S.S. 214 and 'The Infantry and Tanks Training Leaflet, No. 12' issued by I[nspectorate].G[eneral]. of Training, are both considered to contain the essential point of co-operation which have been brought out in the recent operations; the co-operation as laid down in these pamphlets is universally approved by tank commanders.[30]

S.S. 214 has been mentioned above. Its publication had been intended to provide the BEF with tactical guidance for tank use in late 1918. Analysis of tank operations in the latter part of 1918 show it was widely used, supporting the remarks in the 3rd Tank Group document.³¹ But given the fact that, unlike most previous doctrinal publications, the Tank Corps had had a significant amount of involvement in the creation of both documents, it is hardly surprising that the tank arm felt they were appropriate to their needs and that a particular section or paragraph of *S.S. 214* dealt with most or all of the situations that had been encountered. This was also the case with the Inspectorate-General of Training's *Training Note No. 12 Infantry and Tanks* published in September 1918, which was 'really excellent and fill[ed] a long felt want' according to one Tank Corps staff officer in January 1919.³²

While this could be regarded as complacency, a more positive interpretation (and one supported by clear evidence) is that these publications were closely based on an analysis of the 'lessons of the fighting' detailed in the after-action reports produced by tank and infantry units. To take one example, *S.S. 214* carried stern warnings that:

> When, in any operation, continuity of attack is necessary, tank echelons must be organized in sufficient depth to enable the first echelon to reorganize by the time the last echelon goes into action. This means that from the beginning of the battle a strong reserve of tanks must be kept in hand. The hasty improvisation of reserves while the battle is in progress leads not only to a general disorganization of tank units, but also to the destruction of telegraphic and railway communication owing to the lateral movements of tanks. Unless all arrangements are made beforehand, infantry attacks are also liable to be delayed owing to the tanks arriving late at the assembly points.³³

This was clearly a reference to the experiences of Cambrai where a strong reserve of tanks had not been kept in hand and where the minor tank units (sections) operated to some extent in echelons, but where no echelons were employed by the Tank Corps as a whole. Furthermore, again and again, on 21 November 1917 and subsequent days, Cambrai had featured badly-coordinated and poorly-executed attacks in which tank co-operation was frequently unreliable and inadequate and liaison with the infantry ineffectual and fitful.³⁴

Yet the same combat analyses make clear that the need to adhere to this tried and trusted guidance was as strong as ever in the war's final months. As one tank battalion commander advised after his unit's operations on 23 and 24 October:

> I would suggest that, in view of the character of the present operations, in future the greater weight of Tanks be held in reserve to be thrown into the battle as it develops and the strong points and positions which the enemy

intends holding become apparent. If all tanks are committed to a fixed plan of action before the battle commences there will probably be none available to assist the infantry in any specific operation, which is to be undertaken on the spur of the moment.[35]

In the same way, the IGT's *Training Note* also drew on actual combat experiences. It suggested training exercises that might illustrate: the initial advance, dealing with machine gun opposition, dealing with enemy who had not been 'mopped up', how a tank might assist neighbouring infantry, infantry assistance to tanks, what to do when the tanks were out of action and action after the capture of the final objective. All these were likely or, in some cases, frequent occurrences during the fighting.[36]

Training Leaflet No. 12's simple 'bullet points' concerning an exercise covering action after the capture of the final objective neatly encapsulated all the crucial elements of learning in connection with this phase of operations and in particular that after the final objective was reached and the infantry had pushed out patrols and started consolidation, tanks should withdraw to the nearest cover. Only when the tank unit commander had ascertained from the infantry commander that the situation was OK, should the tanks withdraw to a rallying point flying red, white and blue flags.[37]

The necessity for tanks to withdraw under cover and not to stay out in front of the infantry had been recognized before Amiens[38] but success on 8 August seemingly prompted a loss of caution concerning this aspect of the assault. Operations between 21 and 24 August were reminders of the dangers inherent in undertaking this role, prompting one tank brigade commander to state frankly that it was 'asking for trouble if Tanks hang about or patrol in front of an objective'.[39] Yet in spite of the losses suffered, the doctrinal guidance issued on the subject and the warnings of many (including Lawrence in his 1 September memorandum),[40] demands for tanks to cover consolidation continued although, in the latter part of the fighting, operation orders became more definite in instructions to counter this.[41]

The risks to their tanks and themselves during consolidation were clear to the crew members as illustrated by the remarks of one concerning orders for his company's attack on 3 September:

> Imagine our poor tanks crawling along the brow of a slope for an indefinite period, in full daylight, in full view of the enemy's gunners! It seemed to us as if we were to be deliberately offered up as a sacrifice to appease the anger of certain infantry commanders.[42]

An interesting justification was given on this occasion for consolidation work:

> There had been complaints in previous actions that tanks, after reaching their final objectives, had gone home and left the infantry to meet unaided any counter attacks that might have come. So in this particular show it seemed to us that we were not to have the slightest chance offered us of going home![43]

Here was a good demonstration that different arms in late 1918 drew entirely contrary lessons from after action analysis.

Thus, lessons might be learned inconsistently. To continue on the subject of consolidation, 3rd Tank Group's Tactical Experiences report also remained concerned regarding tank support for infantry consolidation:

> In the past tank commanders have on many occasions, been much too keen to move their tanks elsewhere and to leave an objective, before the Infantry have actually arrived to take it over. This must be carefully guarded against by Tank Commanders and should never happen if they are carefully watching the advance of the Infantry.[44]

The tank arm also acknowledged therefore the fine balance between success in giving the right amount of assistance and failure in 'abandoning' the infantry.

Yet, despite the potential for inconsistency in how the tank arm considered the lessons arising from the fighting at Amiens and afterwards, this was in fact largely avoided. In many cases, learning was consistent and appears to have been widely disseminated both within and beyond the Tank Corps.[45] Innovation in responses to battlefield problems was also evident and especially so in the technological responses. Two examples were the 'crib' and smoke.

The fascine was a medieval siege device reintroduced to the modern battlefield in late 1917 to counter a particular problem the tanks encountered there, that is, a means to cross the wide trenches the Germans were increasingly employing in their defensive systems. It was an enormous bundle of brushwood about 5 feet in diameter that weighed over 1½ tons. One was carried on the top of each tank and secured there by chains. It proved valuable at Cambrai but the need for an improved version was identified and lead to the production of the 'crib' – 'an immense hexagonal [open] crate of timber and steel, carried as before on top of the cab'.[46] This comparatively lightweight device was available for use in operations in late September 1918.[47]

The necessity for greater use of smoke to mask the movements of tanks had been a lesson from the 1917 Ypres fighting[48] and at Amiens in 1918 both artillery barrages mixed with smoke[49] and co-operation from the Royal Engineers No. 2

Special Company using Livens Projectors to screen tanks and infantry on 3rd Canadian Division's front were employed.[50] In addition, at least one tank battalion had provided its tank crews with rifles and rifle grenades. These were to 'be fired out of the top of the tank should it be desired by Tank Commander to temporarily cover themselves with a smoke screen.'[51]

After Amiens, the Tank Corps concluded that the 'necessity of smoke protection for Tanks operating in daylight was again conclusively proved' but it is interesting that the idea of tanks providing their own local smoke protection had been firmly grasped and was being immediately pushed forward. The first edition of *Weekly Tank Notes* issued on 10 August 1918 noted a decision that 'all fighting types of Tanks will be equipped with Commander Brock's exhaust smoke device'.[52] This decision was already being enacted by the time orders were being issued for the operations with Third Army which commenced on 21 August[53] and the devices proved especially useful in the capture of Bourlon village on 27 September.[54] However, it is clear that the ambition to equip all tanks with such devices was not met in reality and most tanks were still using smoke grenades for local smoke protection.[55] Nevertheless, although the technology fell short in this case, the pragmatic use of smoke rifle grenades was typical of the Tank Corps' clear and consistent response to the lessons of previous fighting.

Conclusion

British armoured operations in late 1918 may be said to have been characterized by a degree of pragmatism and practicality within a general framework of commonly understood principles and methods.

This would suggest that such operations were conducted along the lines suggested by Albert Palazzo, that is, the use of an effective 'ethos' compensating for a formal series of doctrinal principles.[56] However, there is clear evidence that in the tactical employment of tanks, as in all other areas of its conduct of operations, the BEF did evolve and apply a 'doctrine', albeit a semi-informal one based on the pre-war *Field Service Regulations* (FSR).[57] The report on 'Tactical Experiences' issued by 3rd Tank Group contained several references to the applicability of principles defined in *S.S. 214* and *Training Note No. 12*, and the latter made specific reference to FSR when stating that the actions of infantry and tanks in the firing line should be governed by the principles of mutual support.[58] Since *S.S. 214* was based on combat experience, the link between doctrinal theory and operational practice was a strong one.

What is of particular interest concerning the BEF's use of tanks in late 1918 is the dichotomy between, on the one hand, the tactical flexibility and technological innovation the BEF continued to demonstrate during this period and, on the other, the rigid logistical and practical constraints under which it was necessary to carry out operations. Most especially, the logistical arrangements necessary to support the tanks in the field were the chains that bound them to use in particular circumstances, that is, set piece operations.

These limitations were understood and accepted by the tank arm. Indeed, in some cases, tank brigade and battalion commanders had to remind corps and divisional commanders of these practical constraints when they had been requested to co-operate in a planned attack at short notice. With the same corps and divisional commanders pressing for more tanks for use in operations and with the numbers of available tanks under pressure from mechanical wear and tear and a shortage of the right spares, it is remarkable that the Tank Corps managed to deliver on its tasks on so many occasions in the war's last months.

Throughout the period, the processes for after action reporting continued. Frequently the suggestions drawn from the lessons of operations were minor enhancements or changes to existing tactical principles or technologies. Generally, the tank units believed that the principles they were guided by were the correct ones. What remained keenly felt was the absence of training opportunities. Two days before the war's end (a fact of which he was, of course, unaware), one experienced senior tank officer was still stressing the need for as much training as possible to be undertaken during the winter months.[59] Nevertheless, even without extensive training opportunities in the war's final months, armoured operations had been highly successful and the tank, while not the 'war-winning weapon' had made a significant contribution to the BEF's overall success.

Notes

1 Christopher Brynley Hammond, 'The Theory and Practice of Tank Co-operation with Other Arms on the Western Front during the First World War' (PhD, University of Birmingham, 2005), p. 178.
2 S.S.204 Infantry and Tank Co-operation and Training (March 1918).
3 S.S.214 Tanks and their Employment in Co-operation with Other Arms (August 1918).
4 The National Archives [TNA] WO 95/109 [Lieutenant-Colonel H. H. Johnson] 'Report on BELLICOURT Operations, 29th September 1918' [n.d.].

5   In particular, see David J. Childs, *A Peripheral Weapon?: The Production and Employment of British Tanks in the First World War* (Westport, CT: Greenwood Press, 1999) and Tim Travers, 'Could the Tanks of 1918 Have Been War-winners for the British Expeditionary Force?' *Journal of Contemporary History* 27 (1992), pp. 389–406. For criticism of Travers' overly-simplistic analysis of British tank deployment on the Western Front, see Bryn Hammond, *Practical Considerations in British Tank Operations on the Western Front, 1916–1918* (University of Salford Centre for European Security Working Papers in Military and International History No. 2) (Salford: University of Salford, 2011).
6   Ministry of Munitions, *History of the Ministry of Munitions. Volume XII: The Supply of Munitions*, Part III (London: HMSO, 1922), p. 69 and Tank Museum [TM]: [Major S. G. Brockbank], *History of the Central Workshops*, Chapter 2, p. 2.
7   This point is well made in Childs, *A Peripheral Weapon?* p. 182.
8   The roll-on, roll-off ferry service between Richborough and Calais commenced on 10 February 1918. Colonel A. M. Henniker (compiler), *History of the Great War Based on Official Documents by Direction of the Historical Section of the Committee of Imperial Defence: Transportation on the Western Front, 1914–1918* (Nashville, TN, 1992 [1937]), pp. 240–1. See also F. O. Stanford, 'The War Department Cross-Channel Train Ferry', *Minutes of the Proceedings of the Institution of Civil Engineers* 210, 1920 (1920), pp. 208–38.
9   Courage criticized the employment of 21 tanks from 2nd Tank Battalion in support of attacks by three corps on a 14-mile front; not least because it affected command and control arrangements. TNA: WO 95/112 [Brigadier-General A. Courage] '5th TANK BRIGADE. REPORT on Operations of 18th September 1918 by 2nd Tank Battalion with IIIrd, Australian and IXth Corps', 18 October 1918.
10 Andrew Simpson, 'The Operational Role of British Corps Command on the Western Front, 1914–1918' (PhD Thesis, University College London, 2001), pp. 191–4.
11 Ibid., p. 191.
12 See Trevor Pidgeon, *Tanks on the Somme: From Morval to Beaumont Hamel* (Barnsley: Pen and Sword, 2010) for more detail on these operations.
13 Especially those of tank battalions and companies.
14 Australian War Memorial [AWM]: AWM 25 925/4 Lieutenant-General Sir H. A. Lawrence to Armies, GHQ O.A.109, 1 September 1918.
15 TNA: WO 95/113 [Lieutenant-Colonel H.R. Pape], '2nd TANK BATTALION REPORT ON OPERATIONS of 18th September 1918', 2 October 1918.
16 TM: RH: 5 1TB (BOX 1) '1st TANK BRIGADE. REPORT ON OPERATIONS ON 8th AND 10th OCTOBER 1918', 26 October 1918.
17 See, for example, AWM: AWM 25 925/4 'TACTICAL EMPLOYMENT OF TANKS IN BATTLE', 22 August 1918 and Imperial War Museum (IWM) : Weekly Tank Notes, No. 3, 24 August 1918.

18 TNA: WO 95/106 '3rd (LIGHT) TANK BATTALION. REPORT ON OPERATIONS BY "A" COMPANY ON 3RD OCTOBER 1918', 10 October 1918 offers one example. Here, 'Owing to the absence of Heavy Tanks, the Infantry Commander on the spot requested A.235 ("CRIEFF") and A.223 ("COMME-CI") to deal with an enemy strong point in B.2u.c.7.8., which was then holding up the advance.'
19 TNA: AIR 1/1074 Major-General H. M. Trenchard to Brigadier-General J. F. A. Higgins, 18 January 1918.
20 H. A. Jones, *The War in the Air: Being the Story of the part played in the Great War by the Royal Air Force*, vol. VI (Oxford: Clarendon Press, 1937), p. 469.
21 TNA: AIR 1/176/15/185/1 'History of 73 Squadron RAF', November 1918.
22 TNA: AIR 1/1074 Elles to Advanced HQ, RAF; GHQ; HQ, RAF, G.24/13, 16 August 1918.
23 See, for example, TNA: WO 95/99 '1st Tank Brigade ADDENDUM to ORDER No. 37 TANK and R.A.F. CO-OPERATION', 19 August 1918, which was concerned with planning for operations commencing on 21 August 1918.
24 TNA: AIR 1/1671/204/109/26 [Major T. L. Leigh-Mallory] 'HISTORY OF TANK AND AEROPLANE CO-OPERATION', 31 January 1919.
25 TNA: AIR 1/1671/204/109/26 'HISTORY OF TANK AND AEROPLANE CO-OPERATION'.
26 TNA: PRO AIR 1/2388/11/80 [Trafford Leigh-Mallory] 'War Experiences of Trafford Leigh-Mallory', 28 September 1925.
27 TNA: AIR 1/1671/204/109/26 'HISTORY OF TANK AND AEROPLANE CO-OPERATION'.
28 TNA: AIR 1/1671/204/109/26 'HISTORY OF TANK AND AEROPLANE CO-OPERATION'.
29 At the war's end, each Tank Corps brigade and battalion, as well as various ancillary units such as the supply, workshop and gun carrier companies, produced war histories detailing the unit's involvement in operations. In many cases, these suggested lessons from the fighting and tactical and technological improvements based on these learnings. In addition, from August 1918, the Tank Corps produced 'Weekly Tank Notes', which highlighted aspects of tank operations and was a means to broaden tactical knowledge and experience. Three newly-created Tank Groups also circulated information on the tactical experiences of units under their command. One such document, 'Tactical Experiences of all past Tank Corps Operations Collected and Issued by the 3rd Tank Group', together with the various unit 'war experiences' and the 'Weekly Tank Notes' provides much of the material for this section.
30 TM: RH: 5 2TB/4TB 896–7, 'Tactical Experiences of all past Tank Corps Operations Collected and Issued by the 3rd Tank Group', November 1918.

31 Hammond, 'Theory and Practice', p. 371.
32 IWM Department of Documents (DOCS): Maxse Papers, 69/52/12, File 59, Boyd Rochfort to Maxse, 22 January 1919. 'Training Leaflet No. 12 Infantry and Tanks' is in the same file. Lieutenant-Colonel Harold Boyd-Rochfort was GSO2 at Tank Corps HQ at the time.
33 *S.S.214 Tanks and their Employment in Co-operation with Other Arms* (August 1918), p. 7.
34 See Bryn Hammond, *Cambrai 1917: The Myth of the First Great Tank Battle* (London: Weidenfeld and Nicholson, 2008), passim. Throughout this narrative of Cambrai, I have sought to stress that the Tank Corps was as conditioned by the years of trench warfare and, consequently, as ill-prepared for 'open warfare' as all other arms of the BEF when the nature of the fighting changed on 21 November 1917.
35 TNA: WO 95/103 [Lieutenant-Colonel John Micklem], '10TH TANK BATTALION REPORT ON OPERATIONS. 23rd & 24th OCTOBER 1918', 27 October 1918.
36 IWM DOCS: Maxse Papers, 69/52/12, File 59, 'Training Leaflet No. 12 Infantry and Tanks'.
37 IWM DOCS: 69/52/12, File 59, 'Training Leaflet No. 12 Infantry and Tanks'. The flags were to indicate these were British tanks withdrawing and not captured tanks being used by the Germans.
38 See, for example, TM: RH 2 4A: 1789 '5th TANK BRIGADE REPORT ON TANK OPERATIONS 4/7/1918', 23 July 1918.
39 TNA: PRO WO 9/108 [Brigadier-General E. B. Hankey], '4th Tank Brigade Report on Operations August 22nd to 24th, 1918', 28 August 1918.
40 AWM: AWM 25 925/4 Lawrence to Armies, O.A.109, 1 September 1918.
41 See, for example, TNA: PRO WO 95/3122 'INSTRUCTION NO.4 Issued under [66th] Div[isona]l. Order No.97 TANKS', 6 October 1918.
42 Liddle Collection, Brotherton Library, Leeds University, GS 0270 [Second Lieutenant Norman] Carmichael interview.
43 Liddle Collection, GS 0270, Carmichael interview.
44 TM: RH: 5 2TB/4TB 896-7, 'Tactical Experiences', November 1918.
45 This is a point of difference with Jonathan Boff's admirable recent analysis of combined arms tactics in the Hundred Days, which argues that certain factors prevented the coherent dissemination and application of a single tactical doctrine within the BEF. See Jonathan Boff, 'Combined Arms during the Hundred Days Campaign, August-November 1918', *War in History* 17, 4 (2010), pp. 459–78.
46 Captain D. G. Browne, *The Tank in Action* (Edinburgh: William Blackwood and Sons, 1920), p. 441.
47 There is good photographic evidence of tanks fitted with cribs on 29 September 1918 in the Imperial War Museum Photograph Archive. See, for example, Q 9370.

48 Liddell Hart Centre for Military Archives [LHCMA]: Fuller Papers I/TCOII, [Colonel A. Courage], '2nd BRIGADE TANK CORPS. REPORT ON Tank Operations, 31st July 1917', 21 August 1917. Courage suggested that 'Tanks should not be employed until the ground has been captured which overlooks them; or as an alternative, a much more extensive use of smoke for barrage purposes than has hitherto been the case.'
49 See, for example, TNA: PRO WO 95/113 [Lieutenant-Colonel E. D. Bryce] '2nd TANK BATTALION OPERATION ORDER No. 1', 6 August 1918.
50 TNA: PRO WO 95/108 '4th Tank Brigade Order No.19 INSTRUCTION No. 9 Smoke', 5 August 1918.
51 TM: RH 86: TC 14 Bn 415 [Lieutenant-Colonel G. A. McL. Sceales] '14th Battalion, Tank Corps Order No. 1 Instruction No. 6 Administration', 6 August 1918. Each tank company of the battalion was issued with 14 rifles, 14 cups and 161 grenades and could expend two of these for practice purposes if they wished.
52 IWM: Weekly Tank Notes, No. 1, 10th August 1918.
53 TM: RH5 1TB (Box 1), '1st TANK BRIGADE ORDER No. 37', 19 August 1918. These orders indicate the process was not complete. Whilst some tanks from 10th Tank Battalion were so equipped, others were still issued with No. 37 Smoke Rifle Grenades.
54 TM: RH: 86 TC 7 Bn, VII TANK BATTALION REPORT on OPERATIONS 27th September 1918, [n.d.].
55 Thus, 10th Tank Battalion's commander was still suggesting that 'each Tank be provided with an apparatus for emitting smoke from the exhaust', after operations on 23-4 October. TNA: WO 95/103 '10TH TANK BATTALION REPORT ON OPERATIONS. 23rd & 24th OCTOBER 1918', 27 October 1918.
56 Albert Palazzo, *Seeking Victory on the Western Front: The British Army and Chemical Warfare in World War I* (Lincoln, NE: University of Nebraska Press, 2000).
57 See Gary Sheffield's review of Palazzo's work in the online *Journal of the Australian War Memorial*, www.awm.gov.au/journal/j35/palazzoreview.asp, accessed May 2011.
58 IWM DOCS: 69/52/12, File 59, 'Training Leaflet No. 12 Infantry and Tanks' which referenced *FSR* Part I, para 103-4.
59 TNA: WO 95/102 [Brig.-Gen. H. K. Woods] '2nd TANK BRIGADE REPORT ON OPERATIONS: 23rd & 24th October 1918', 9 November 1918.

4

The Last Battle of the BEF: The Crossing of the Sambre-Oise Canal, 4 November 1918

Niall Barr

Almost every British school pupil has heard of Wilfred Owen, perhaps the most famous of the Great War poets, and of his tragic death one week before the Armistice. But far fewer have heard of the Sambre-Oise Canal or the events which took place there on 4 November 1918. Yet this engagement may well rank as one of the few battles of the Great War to have not only military implications but direct political consequences concerning the Armistice negotiations.

The Battle of the Sambre has been often overlooked, perhaps because of the 'rush' to reach the armistice which seems to afflict most studies of the Great War. It is a strange fact that while military historians have tended to ignore this action, much literary effort has been expended in recounting Wilfred Owen's last days by biographers.[1] Pat Barker's *The Ghost Road*, the final novel of her 'Regeneration' Trilogy ends poignantly at the banks of the Sambre with Wilfred Owen's death.[2] Yet, however evocative and powerful these novels are, *The Ghost Road* does not necessarily give a reliable or accurate account of the battle – nor should military historians leave such significant events entirely to their literary colleagues. In fact, there are many good reasons why this unremarked battle is worthy of greater attention. As the last major action of the British Expeditionary Force (BEF) in the Great War, it is possible to examine what, if anything, the British Army had learnt during four years of warfare on the Western Front. The assault on the Sambre-Oise canal is also a clear example of 'ordinary' British troops acting as shock troops and accomplishing considerable feats of arms. Finally, the action is also an excellent example of a complicated engineering operation which is an often overlooked aspect of studies concerning the Great War.

By November 1918 it was clear that the tide of war had swung irrevocably against Germany. Through a grinding series of offensives during August, September and October, the Allied Armies had worn down the last strength of the German Army in the West. The German Supreme Command composed of the famous duo of Hindenburg and Ludendorff had many worries but perhaps the most pressing was the obvious fact that Germany's Allies could not endure for much longer. Austria-Hungary, Bulgaria and Turkey were all on the verge of collapse. Albeit reluctantly, and without clearly admitting that Germany was comprehensively defeated, negotiations for an armistice began on 3 October at Ludendorff's insistence. However, by the end of October, there had been no agreement on what form the armistice should take. Meanwhile, Ludendorff's black mood had lifted and he was now more optimistic about Germany's situation. With his advice now fatally compromised, Ludendorff was forced to resign on 27 October.[3]

General Wilhelm Groener, who replaced Ludendorff as First Quartermaster-General, initially viewed the military situation on the Western Front with a limited degree of optimism. On 1 November he fiercely denounced Dr Drews, Minister of the Interior, when he reported the clamour for the abdication of the Kaiser. Hindenburg later wrote: 'By the end of October the collapse was complete at all points. It was only on the Western Front that we still thought we could avert it'.[4] Even this might be considered wishful thinking but Groener did not share the illusions which had clouded Ludendorff's judgement. Groener believed the only way to save the German Army in the West was to order an immediate withdrawal to the line of the Meuse river even though this too was in reality 'nothing more "than a line on the map"'.[5] In giving up the territory which Germany had conquered and occupied for the past four years it was hoped that the German Army could hold out during the winter along this line and possibly reach a compromise peace in the spring of 1919.[6] However, this amounted to a considerable retreat, and the German forces would need to hold the Allied Armies at bay for some time to rest their troops and remove the enormous quantities of supplies and material they had accumulated over three years of static warfare. It was due to this situation that the line of the Mormal Forest and the Sambre-Oise canal began to assume great importance as the last major defence line which might be held by the German rearguard against the BEF and thus enable the German Army to make good its escape.

After the last major fighting around Le Cateau and Bohain on 23 October, the British Fourth Army slowly closed up to the canal and the Mormal Forest. Field Marshal Sir Douglas Haig, Commander-in-Chief of the BEF, was not willing to give the Germans the respite they needed and issued orders on 29 October for the next major blow. He planned that his Third and Fourth Armies, in conjunction with the French First Army, would mount a major attack along the front from Le Quesnoy to Oisy in the south. Fourth Army was to mount an attack across the Sambre-Oise Canal and through the Mormal forest further north – a frontage of 15 miles, but the total frontage of the combined attack was 30 miles.[7] This was designed as a massive blow which would puncture the German's last major defence line and quite possibly bring about the disintegration of the German army which Haig had been trying to achieve for so long.

Third Army's attack would be mounted across reasonably open terrain, while the northern divisions of Fourth Army were confronted by the Forest of Mormal. However, the IX and XIII Corps of Fourth Army faced the greatest obstacle in the form of the Sambre-Oise Canal. The canal ran along roughly half of Fourth Army's front from Landrecies in the north to Oisy in the south. As the canal was 70 feet wide bank to bank, 35 feet wide at water-level and 6–8 feet deep with a muddy bottom, fording had to be ruled out. The Germans had also inundated the low-lying ground around the canal, which combined with the numerous small streams, the ancient Sambre river and drainage ditches also formed minor obstacles.

There were also wide canal reservoirs just south of Lock No. 1 which also made any crossing attempt difficult. However, the lock gates at Catillon, Ors, Landrecies and Lock No. 1 provided a narrower gap of 17 feet and thus were attractive crossing points. There was also the difficulty that although the Germans had been cleared off most of the west bank, they still held important points at Catillon, Le Donjon, a fortified farmhouse south of Ors, and the Happegarbes spur. This spur was key terrain as it dominated the canal as far as Catillon. It was the scene of heavy fighting during 2 and 3 November but fierce German counterattacks meant that it could not be held before the main assault on 4 November.[8]

Quite clearly, the Sambre-Oise Canal was not an easy obstacle to overcome. Indeed the 16th Highland Light Infantry history stated that the Sambre-Oise canal crossing was: 'an even more perilous emprise than the crossing of the St Quentin Canal'.[9] Not surprisingly, the Germans were planning to hold this line 'at all costs'. However, by November 1918, this meant that the position was held only by a rearguard which depended heavily on a machine gun defence supported by scattered batteries and single field guns. As late as 16 October Haig had considered avoiding the canal altogether by asking Rawlinson 'to transfer his main strength to his left which would advance on the north bank of the

Sambre ... towards Valenciennes'.[10] However, the terrain on the east bank of the canal quickly became open, rolling dairy farmland. If the canal could be crossed successfully, the British troops would find perfect ground to push on and exploit the victory.

Clearly, an assault on such a difficult obstacle would require careful planning but since Haig only finally decided on an attack on 29 October, and the divisional orders were distributed on 31 October this left just five days to plan and prepare before the attack. The operation had to be planned very rapidly yet the experienced British staff were able to draft effective plans in the short time available. General Sir Henry Rawlinson (GOC Fourth Army) laid down two main objectives to be secured by IX and XIII Corps. The first objective was the 'Red Line' which rested east of Landrecies, Ors, Catillon and Lock No. 1, in order to carry the advance well beyond the canal, and to allow the construction of heavier transport bridges without interference. The second objective was a line of exploitation two miles on from the canal. This was perhaps overambitious and was not achieved on the day.

Fourth Army, now shorn of the Australian Corps which was in well-deserved rest, was composed of just two corps. XIII Corps was deployed opposite the Forest of Mormal and the town of Landrecies. It was to mount an attack on Landrecies at 06.15 hrs in conjunction with Third Army. While the 18th and 50th Divisions pushed into the forest, 25th Division was to cross the canal at Landrecies.[11] The assault by IX Corps was to be mounted half an hour earlier at 05.45 hrs, by 32nd Division at Ors and, further south, the 1st Division would attack at Catillon and Lock No. 1. However, each division was treated as independent in the detail and execution of its crossing. In 1918 the divisional staffs were trusted to produce a workable plan and indeed, the 32nd Divisional orders and 'Notes on Future Operations' were a model of clarity and foresight. These instructions were issued down to company level which proves that the importance of disseminating orders down to the troops was understood by 1918.[12]

It was recognized that: 'surprise will only be obtained if all our preparations are concealed to the last moment' and everything was done to preserve secrecy before the attack. The BEF had learned the value of surprise by 1918. Artillery was also of prime importance to the attack. Artillery batteries were moved into position gradually, with the majority remaining silent and camouflaged until the attack. There were some silent periods of 30 minutes to assist in the sound ranging necessary for counter-battery work. In total 31 Royal Field Artillery brigades and 19 heavy and 13 siege artillery batteries were assembled (amounting to over 1,000 guns) and a sophisticated barrage plan was worked out which, it was hoped, 'would crush . . . all enemy fire at the crossing points'. Unfortunately, the true importance of one snippet of intelligence was not realized. It was noted that there was considerable activity along hedges and at farms in the forward battery area east of the canal. The 32nd Division orders noted that there was 'a very large concentration of M[achine] g[un]s and infantry close to the canal bank, and a large number of scattered batteries and single guns in the area enclosed by our Red objective line'. This meant that the British barrage plan, which would stand on the canal for 5 minutes, before lifting 300 yards and standing for another 30 minutes, before moving on at 6 yards a minute, would not deal properly with the main German defences ranged along the canal bank.[13]

Other weapons were also tasked to support the attack. A trench mortar company was allotted to each division to fire smoke to cover the crossings, while a machine gun company was similarly deployed to fire a machine gun barrage prior to the attack. While it was realized that the terrain was generally unsuitable for tanks, they were allotted to the attacks on Catillon and Landrecies to assist in clearing the defended houses.

The Royal Air Force also made a major contribution with intensive aerial reconnaissance of the entire area to give as much information about the canal and the German defences as possible. For the attack itself, squadrons were allotted to ground strafing in the German rear areas, while others were to assist the ground troops by dropping smoke bombs to cover the crossings and attacking targets of opportunity. The procedure for air-ground co-operation through a system of red flares and metal discs was emphasized and practised before the attack.

All of these preparations reveal the BEF as a proficient organization which was confident in its abilities and knew its job. The 32nd Division's 'Notes on Future Operations' ended on a positive note:

> The Divisional Commander has full confidence that difficult though their tasks may be in some respects, all ranks will shew the same determination as on previous occasions to add another great victory to the honour of the Division by breaking a line which enemy commanders have stated to be of the utmost importance to them.

The speed and efficiency with which this complex operation was planned and organized shows the BEF at the very height of its powers.[14]

However, perhaps the most important aspect of the preparations lay with the Royal Engineers. The crossing of the canal presented Fourth Army and its attacking divisions with a considerable engineering problem and the Royal

Engineers which supported each division had to work very rapidly to be ready in time. Once the Engineers had gained all possible information about the canal, they then had to find material for bridging – and build the bridges. Recces were begun after the operations of 17–18 October when forcing the canal became a likely task. Information about the canal was obtained from liberated French inhabitants, Corps intelligence staff and aerial photographs. The Royal Engineers found it difficult to spare the personnel necessary for foot patrols as everyone in the Field Companies were already fully occupied. With enemy alarm posts still in position on the western bank, the ground recces were made even more difficult.[15]

The 25th Division had perhaps the most difficult task as the engineering equipment had to be carried across one and half miles of rough country before the canal was reached at Landrecies. The 20-foot wide ancient river was also an obstacle, which meant that conventional bridging pontoons could not be driven up in wagons. Indeed, the supporting brigades of the division doubted that the 75 Brigade's attack was possible. Luckily, 'swimming was ruled out by the GOC as a feasible manner of crossing' and instead it was planned to throw infantry bridges across at three places at and on both sides of Landrecies lock. Two footbridges 22-feet long were made to bridge the lock if the lock gates were destroyed. Lifebelts were issued, and Berthon boats held in reserve. However, the standard Cork rafts, which each weighed 300 lbs, which were usually used for river crossings, were too heavy to carry through the rough country before the canal was reached. The 46th Division had had difficulty with them at the Bellenglise canal crossing and so these were rejected and rafts constructed from petrol tins were used instead.[16]

These rafts consisted of 16 petrol tins attached to a timber framework and were much lighter at 95 lbs each but this was still heavy enough for two Pioneers to carry over one and half miles, while a sapper, armed with a hand-axe cleared the way. The plan was that the rafts would be launched, the sapper would paddle across, a line being paid out by the Pioneers. On reaching the far bank, the sapper would take the second line, which was fixed to the front of the raft, secure it to the bank and then the raft could act as a ferry by being pulled backwards and forwards with an infantryman being taken across each time. After the first wave was across, the rafts would be formed into bridges. Although logical, this was too cumbersome an operation to perform under fire.[17]

There was no time for a rehearsal to test the technique and the best that could be arranged was a demonstration on the Selle river on the afternoon of 2 November in which a platoon of infantry made an attack followed by the sappers.

The Sappers duly paddled across, ferried infantry and built bridges. However, it was noted that:

> The realistic nature of the operation was somewhat marred by the enormous crowd of spectators; who found amusement in the efforts of one or two of the infantry to balance themselves on the rafts. There was a general feeling of doubt I think, as to whether the operation would really be feasible under fire. One CO gave it as his opinion that it would be a 'Sporting Event'.[18]

This hardly boded well, and in previous years of the Great War might well have led to a disaster.

The 1st Division on the other hand, had a real stroke of luck in finding a German Pioneer store at Bohain. It was later recalled that:

> Bohain had been an important German Pioneer Park, and the accumulation of various engineer materials there was almost intoxicating; my stores officers was so delighted with it that I had the greatest difficulty in getting him to come home, even for his meals.[19]

The division's engineers found 700 petrol tins, wooden barrels and German light steel floats designed specifically for assault bridges. It was recalled that 'These light steel floats appeared so certain to be useful that wagons were sent to take them all away before they appealed to the cupidity of any other Division'.[20]

The staff of 1st Division planned to attack at three points. Catillon would be cleared by 3 Brigade, while 1 Brigade crossed the canal 1,000 yards south of Catillon. It was decided that the first waves should carry complete bridges so that no constructional work would be needed at the canal bank. Four assault bridges were constructed with the German floats, although not using German methods. The bridges were taken apart and rebuilt to give greater flexibility, and each bridge had a hinged storming ladder. These produced the lightest and most portable bridges used in the attack, which could be carried easily as a complete bridge by six men, with two men per pier. Another two bridges were built using the standard British equipment of cork floats and separate roadways. It was noted that these were: 'Best for permanent work and under fire, but do not lend themselves to launching as complete bridges and are therefore, not suitable for use at the actual moment of assault'.[21] A further two bridges were built from petrol tin floats which were found to be light and steady and again could be launched as complete bridges.

Further south, 2 Brigade, led by the 2nd Royal Sussex would attempt to cross at Lock No. 1 where the gap to be spanned was 17 feet, which made the engineering task slightly easier. Four single span bridges were constructed with a launching lever and a pair of wheels so that they could be thrown across the lock quickly. These were supplemented with four stouter bridges without the special launching device. These bridges were designed for the infantry assault, but after the attack it was planned to put heavier bridges across the lock to allow transport and artillery to use the crossing.

32nd Division planned its main crossing to be made by 96 Brigade 1,000 yards north of Ors. A subsidiary attack would be made by 14 Brigade at Ors itself. The plan was to span the gap in the old bridge and meanwhile build a bridge out of petrol tin rafts 200 yards south of Ors. The 1st Dorsetshires were given the task of crossing at Ors and instructed that: 'In the event of the battalion being unsuccessful in their crossing, I was to ensure that the enemy opposite me were pinned to their ground and not permitted to interfere with the main crossings on the 96 Bde front'.[22]

Meanwhile, 96 Brigade had to rely on the standard cork rafts which had been rejected by both other divisions. This meant that the bridges built by 218 Field Company were heavy, at 300 lbs per raft, and difficult to carry up to the canal. Once the canal was reached, the bridges would have to be built under fire and it would take time to build once the canal had been reached – which was estimated at half an hour.[23] This was far from ideal, particularly given the fact that the crossing point could be enfiladed by fire from the Happegarbes spur which remained in German hands. It is quite possible that, with both other divisions having secured large quantities of engineer stores that there was no alternative available for 218 Field Company but to use the cork floats. There seems little doubt that the 1st Division's planning, equipment and bridges were superior to either the 25th or 32nd Divisions' but also that this had only been made possible by appropriating all of the material left behind by the Germans at Bohain. Indeed there were serious flaws in both the 25th and 32nd Division's plans and equipment for the crossings. The fact that each division acted independently in the planning for the crossing meant that engineering equipment and stores were jealously guarded and expertise was not distributed according to the difficulty of the crossing point. This lack of communication was to have serious repercussions during the crossing.

By midnight on 3 November all was ready for the coming attack. The night was dark with rain until midnight, and then a thick fog formed which lasted until 09.00 hrs. The attack began at 05.45 hrs when the British barrage crashed down along the entire front. On the 1st Division front, almost everything went according to plan. 3 Brigade, supported by two tanks which rolled down the street, quickly overcame the German resistance at Catillon. 1,000 yards down the towpath, 1 Brigade encountered very little resistance. As soon as the barrage lifted off the east bank of the canal at three minutes after zero, the bridges were carried 300 yards to the canal. A solitary German machine gun post was silenced by Sergeant Cook of 23 Field Company. Meanwhile, the four floating bridges were in position ten minutes after zero. Indeed there was a race between the first two battalions as to who would get across first. In the event, 1st Cameron Highlanders were 30 seconds faster than the Loyal North Lancashires. The German protective barrage was slow in opening and fell west of the canal well behind the leading troops and there was was no heavy shelling subsequently perhaps because it was not an obvious crossing point. The battalions quickly fanned out and reached the bridgehead line by 08.00 hrs. The village of Bois de L'Abbaye was seized after hand to hand fighting by the Camerons.[24] Thus, 1 Brigade's attack south of Catillon, and the clearing of Catillon by 3 Brigade, were all completely successful and achieved without many casualties which was in direct contrast to the much more difficult crossing at Lock No. 1 by 2 Brigade.

As the British barrage opened, the first wave of infantry from the 2nd Royal Sussex and sappers from 409 Field Company advanced, and all closed up to within 100 yards of the barrage. Three minutes after zero, the barrage lifted 100 yards, and the leading waves advanced. But since this was an obvious crossing point, the Germans responded with a very heavy hostile barrage 50 yards west of the canal, and heavy machine gun fire came from the lock houses and Bois de L'Abbaye further north. Some of the leading wave got past the German barrage area before it fell, but heavy casualties were still suffered and this German shellfire nearly caused disaster. Unfortunately, a small stream west of the canal proved a more serious obstacle than originally expected and this caused delay – as the planks brought to bridge it proved too short and roots, debris and barbed wire limited the points where bridges could be laid over the stream. Some men of the leading platoon waded across the stream and scrambled up the lock bank while one man actually crossed the remnants of the lock bridge. But the stream could not be bridged without waiting for the main bridging parties.[25] By this time the following waves of sappers and infantry, carrying the bridges for the lock itself were approaching the stream and shells landed among them causing confusion and delay. The rear waves began to close up so that there was now a considerable crowd of men all held up. Not only was there confusion but: 'So intense was the enemy's fire that even the stoutest troops hesitated, and it seemed impossible for any men to get to the lock and yet live'.[26]

At this point, Major George Findlay of 409 Field Company and Lieutenant-Colonel Johnson of the 2nd Royal Sussex made a critical contribution to the attack. Both of them stood where the fire was hottest and gathered their men for another attempt. Although Findlay was soon wounded, he reorganized his sappers and got volunteers from the infantry to repair the bridges damaged by shell fire. Working under such heavy fire, 409 Field Ccompany suffered 50 per cent casualties during the attack. Meanwhile, Lt-Col Dudley Johnson of 2nd Royal Sussex came forward to see the progress and realized that further delay would only lead to greater casaulties. He also collected men to help the sappers and personally lead them forward, but a further salvo landed right among them, literally blowing them back onto the rear waves.[27]

Johnson and Findlay continued to work with calmness under fire, collected more volunteers and again led their men forward. Once more scratch parties manhandled the bridges and this time placed one of the bridges meant for the lock over the stream. The troops were now able to cross the stream, and then scramble up the steep embankment. Taking cover by the canal bank, the men fired at the Germans in the lock houses while some men stood on the top of the bank firing their Lewis guns from the hip. This silenced the machine gun post in the lock house and under this covering fire, a second bridge was pulled up the bank to the edge of the lock. Wheels and launching lever were fixed and the bridge laid across the lock at 6.10 hrs. As soon as the bridge was laid, Major Findlay dashed across, followed by the infantry who dealt with the Germans in the lock house. Soon there were three bridges across the lock and within a short time the whole of the 2nd Royal Sussex was across the canal and advancing in extended order. The battle cost the Sussex 100 casualties, but they took 200 prisoners, two field guns, seven trench mortars and 50 machine guns. Both Findlay and Johnson won the Victoria Cross for their part in the action and without their inspiration the attempt to cross at Lock No. 1 would almost certainly have failed.[28]

Further north, the 32nd Division also experienced mixed fortunes in its attempts to assault the canal. When the artillery lifted off the canal bank five minutes after zero, the whole of the west bank was occupied – except south of Ors at le Donjon where the Royal Scots were held up by fire.

At Ors itself, the Dorsets managed to force a crossing for 14th Brigade – which was contrary to the expectations of the divisional staff, who had looked to the 96 Brigade for success. However, the Dorsets attempt to cross quickly across the remnants of the bridge at Ors failed. Men rushed forward with sappers who carried bridging materials but were met by heavy machine gun fire – and a German field gun firing straight across the old bridge. The attempt had to be abandoned. A northern crossing by collapsible boat also failed as the boat capsized.

Nonetheless, the battalion managed to cross 200 yards south of Ors 25 minutes after zero. The petrol tin bridge there was constructed without interference as the Germans did not spot this bridge due to the fog and the Dorsets were able to cross without much opposition and capture 150 prisoners. Once across the canal, the Dorsets were able to push on to Rue Vert and here they took another 223 prisoners, 30 machine guns and three howitzers. By 08.15 hrs, the Dorsets and Royal Scots were established along the road running parallel to the canal through Rue Verte and the eastern outskirts of Ors. The Germans in Le Donjon, now encircled, surrendered at 10.45 hrs.[29] The success of this secondary attack by the Dorsets was critical, as it turned out, to avoid failure across the 32nd Division's front.

Matters were very different on the main crossing of 96 Brigade where 16th Lancashire Fusiliers and 2nd Manchesters, supported by 218 Field Company and 16th Highland Light Infantry (Pioneers), were not so lucky in their attempt to cross at the elbow in the canal north of Ors. At 03.30 hrs the two battalions moved to their forming up lines in the fields close to the canal and lay down. When the barrage crashed down at 05.45 hrs, the men got ready and five minutes later the infantry and engineers dashed up to the bank of the canal. As the engineers started to build the bridges from the cork rafts, the infantry gave covering fire to help them. Unfortunately, these two battalions encountered stronger German resistance than anywhere else along the canal that day. The Germans still occupied the Happegarbes spur on the west bank further north, and although this was cleared by the 15th Lancashire Fusiliers by 07.00 hrs, there was still enfilading fire from here during the crossing attempt.[30] The main resistance came from German machine gun nests deployed on the canal bank and on the slope up towards La Motte Farm. There were also German artillery batteries behind this ridge which had not been suppressed by the British artillery preparation. These German guns brought down heavy fire on the troops by the canal and their shellfire constantly broke up the bridges which the engineers were desperately trying to build. At the canal bank, both battalions encountered a storm of fire. At the Fusiliers' crossing point, the sappers completed the bridges in half an hour in the face of great difficulties. Some men rushed across the bridge but it was quickly damaged and German machine gun fire was constantly hitting the bridge. The bridge was repaired again and a handful of men crossed before it was broken. Lieutenant Colonel James Marshall came forward, took charge of the situation and organized the repair parties, but all of the first party were soon killed or wounded. Nonetheless, Marshall's personal example meant that other volunteers soon sprang up. Throughout the repair of the bridge, Marshall stood on the canal bank, helping and encouraging the work under a storm of fire. Once the bridge was repaired again, Marshall tried to rush across at the head of his men but he was shot and instantly killed. With his death, the Fusiliers abandoned their attempt to cross and took cover by the canal bank.[31]

At the 2nd Manchesters' crossing point, the German fire was, if anything, even heavier and it was noted that: 'Thirty yards away from the pioneers were German canalside nests of machine guns which stuttered in metallic bursts as the building went on in the deep gloom. Flares lit the waters in phosphorescent spasms and silhouetted the builders into easy targets.'[32] The men of 218 Field Company suffered very heavy casualties. Two officers were killed and two wounded while the rest of the men were all killed, wounded or gassed. This left only Major Arnold Waters and Sapper Adam Archibald who desperately continued to build the bridge from the heavy cork floats. As they worked, German bullets struck sparks from the wire binding the floats and the wood they were handling was hit repeatedly. It seemed as if they both would be killed – but they worked on.[33]

Meanwhile, 2nd Lt. James Kirk of the 2nd Manchesters took a Lewis gun and four magazines and paddled across the canal on one of the rafts. He fired away at the German machine guns until he ran out of ammunition. More ammunition was paddled across to him and he continued to fire even though wounded in the arm and the face. Eventually he was shot dead and fell over his gun. It was said of him that 'only his supreme contempt of danger and magnificent self-sacrifice' enabled the bridge to be built.[34] Once the bridge was finished, Archibald collapsed from the effects of gas poisoning but his conduct was considered 'beyond all praise' and 'that anyone should have lived through such close and accurate fire is little short of miraculous'.[35] Waters completed the task alone and then led two platoons of the Manchesters across the bridge. It was later considered that this attempt was only successful 'due to his extraordinary bravery and example'.[36] Unfortunately, shell fire soon destroyed the bridge and further attempts to repair it proved fruitless. Wilfred Owen, serving with the 2nd Manchesters, was remembered as acting coolly under fire and encouraging his men. It is not known exactly where he fell but it appears that he may have been killed while on a raft in the canal.[37] After these desperate attempts had failed, the battalion took cover behind the canal bank. Over 200 casualties had been suffered in the two battalions and it was decided that any further attempts to cross would simply result 'in purposeless loss of life'.[38] So many British soldiers had died during the war in ill-conceived attacks which had resulted in 'purposeless loss of life' but this time, given the preparations and the success of the other attacking troops, the soldiers of 96 Brigade had simply been very unlucky: they had attacked the most awkward stretch of canal and met the best organized defence.

At 08.30 hrs, both battalions were ordered to hold their present positions and then to move south and cross over the Dorsets bridge, south of Ors. The troops of 14 Brigade, now across the canal, were ordered to hold until 96 Brigade had crossed on the bridge south of Ors. This rapid alteration of orders, and co-ordination between the two brigades, was made possible by the divisional wireless net. The battalion headquarters were established close together so that they could share one looped wireless set which was linked to the brigade headquarters, which in turn communicated with the divisional headquarters using a heavier trench set. These wireless communications allowed a much more rapid response to a change in situation by the higher headquarters and allowed the brigades to be much more flexible than was possible earlier in the war. Once 96 Brigade had crossed the canal, both battalions worked their way north east to recover their original place in the line – and captured the German artillery batteries which had caused so much havoc earlier in the day. Thus the setback was only temporary in military terms, but casualties had been severe. By the end of the day, 16th Lancashire Fusiliers could only muster 100 men and 96 Brigade had suffered a total of 700 casualties.

Further north, the 25th Division experienced great success in its assault on Landrecies. The division attacked at 06.15 hrs – half an hour after the 1st and 32nd Divisions had begun their assault. At 5.45 hrs, in the darkness before dawn, a racket of firing broke out all along the line, mainly from machine gun batteries grouped along the front. Their noisy fire was deliberately designed to drown out the sounds of two tanks which rolled up from the rear into position for the attack. First light was showing through the mist when at 6.15 hrs, the rattle of MGs was drowned out by the thunder of the British barrage as the British artillery opened fire all along the line, and the attack began.[39] The artillery barrage halted 300 yards east of the canal while machine guns were brought forward to cover the crossings with direct and indirect fire. Smoke shells were fired on the high ground east and south of the canal and aircraft dropped smoke bombs on Landrecies as well. Four tanks accompanied the infantry to the canal and four supply tanks transported the heavier bridging material. This was perhaps the best example of how, when resources were available, the BEF could co-ordinate the activities of all arms to achieve success.

The advance was led by the troops of 75 Brigade. The Warwicks encountered stiff opposition in the chateau of Fauborg Soyers, the western suburb of Landrecies, where they were held up and lost the barrage. Lance-Corporal Amey stormed the building alone and eventually, with the help of a tank, the German resistance collapsed.[40] With the capture of the chateau, the Warwicks were able to reach the canal. The road bridge over the canal was blown up at 10.30 hrs by a German officer who then galloped off on a black horse. However, the left company of the battalion found an intact German bridge 500 yards north of the road bridge and used this to get across the canal.[41] Most of the Gloucesters crossed at the lock gates which had been rushed by a small party of the 182nd Tunnelling Company who overpowered the German demolition party just before they were going to blow them. Meanwhile, the Worcesters found that the thick fog meant that the carrying parties became intermingled with the infantry and some became involved in the fighting. When the ancient river was reached, Sergeant Wood and Sapper Barbour jumped into the water and cut the leads to the demolition charges from a large trestle bridge before it was blown. Sergeant Wood was remembered as: 'That gallant sapper sergeant appeared from nowhere and disappeared as he came, as if he were a ghost of the battle of four years ago'.[42] Two floating bridges were also laid across the ancient river and the advance continued to the canal. Scared by the heavy barrage, the Germans had left one plank bridge over the canal intact and another two floating bridges were built immediately across the canal. German artillery and machine gun fire from the east bank was rapid but unaimed as the bank was smothered in dense clouds of smoke from shells and aircraft bombs. Indeed, the barrage was so heavy that a German battery positioned near the footbridge was silent as the crews had taken cover in shelters nearby. As soon as the barrage moved on, D Company of the Worcesters charged the guns and captured two officers and 50 men before they could man their guns. Meanwhile, C Company of the Worcesters gained the river bank north of Landrecies and brought up their petrol tin rafts. Bullets were hitting all along the bank and splashing in the water, but the rafts were paddled across and a covering party was organized while the ropes and tackle were set up. It was fortunate that, given the effective smoke screen, this was the only place along 25th Division's front where the engineering plan actually had to be used.[43]

By 9.20 hrs all three battalions had crossed the canal: the Worcesters, Gloucesters and Warwicks crossed almost simultaneously along the divisional front, though each unit as well as the Engineers claimed that their men were the first to reach the opposite bank and the town of Landrecies. The houses of Landrecies had been well prepared for defence but with the British attacking from the south, west and north, and with such heavy artillery fire in support: 'the defence was fairly swept away'.[44] Although there was a sharp fight at the crossroads south east of the town, Landrecies was captured quickly. After the fighting was over: 'the inhabitants of the town emerged from their cellars in transports of joy'.[45] There was great enthusiasm from the French inhabitants and a few days later at a ceremonial march they announced that one street would be renamed Boulevard Charles as a compliment to the division and its Commanding General, General Sir Ronald Charles. It is important to remember that the Allied advance in the autumn of 1918 was also a war of liberation for the people of northern France and Belgium. Many prisoners and stores were captured in Landrecies – including a regimental commanding officer and his staff, and a sick parade of German invalids. The British captured 838 prisoners and 27 guns in Landrecies, and such was the German demoralization that some even surrendered to the supply tanks.

It was later noted that:

> The capture of Landrecies was an operation beset with many difficulties, but thanks to good leadership, the bravery of the troops, the skill and devotion of the divisional engineers and pioneers, the 75th Brigade met with the success and good fortune which such a well planned and boldy executed operation deserved.[46]

In fact, 75 Brigade had been fortunate to achieve such a high degree of surprise although the rapidity of the attack was certainly down to good planning and judgement. 75 Brigade also seems to have benefitted from a heavier artillery barrage and air support than the other divisions recieved.

After the patchy resistance experienced during the crossings, the British troops found that the Germans were thoroughly demoralized by the success of the assault and many Germans simply gave up the fight. The 1st Northamptonshires which came up in support in the 1st Division sector found that: 'Once the canal had been crossed, the resistance put up by the enemy was small and beyond rounding up a few machine guns which gave battle here and there, there was no infantry fight worthy of mention, as the enemy infantry seemed only too ready to "Kamerad."'[47] By the end of the day, the main objectives had all been achieved, and Fourth Army, along with the other British Armies, were able to push the Germans back rapidly. To the north, Third Army had taken Le Quesnoy, while the 18th and 50th Divisions had pushed through the Forest of Mormal. With the German rearguard position broken, there was now little to stop the advance of the British armies. Haig noted in his diary that evening that: 'The Enemy seems to have placed all his strength in this front line. Consequently when this was overcome he had no reserves in rear with which to oppose our advance.'[48] The pursuit of a broken enemy which Haig had been working towards for so long, was finally a possibility. Yet as late as 31 October, Haig and his army commanders had been agreed that 'the enemy has not been sufficiently beaten as to cause him to accept an ignominious peace'.[49] It was these views, along with his opinion that the British Army would not fight simply to grind the Germans into the dust, that informed Haig's opinion on the Armistice – that the fighting should be terminated as quickly as possible and that the Germans should not be backed into a corner.

After touring the front on 5 November, it was clear to Groener that the front had ruptured and that the German Army might well be broken up in the field. The simple fact was that the German troops now fleeing from the Allied armies were no longer capable of sustained resistance. Groener's gloomy prognosis was that, to save the Army from destruction, an armistice was needed immediately. On 6 November he told the German chancellor: 'We shall have to cross the lines with a white flag. Even a week is too long to wait. It must be Saturday [9 November] at the latest.'[50] Until the events of 4 November, many of Germany's leaders, including the Kaiser and Groener, had clung to the hope that they might be able to hold the Western Front together for just a little longer. The action of the Fourth Army in crossing the Sambre-Oise canal and pushing through the Forest of Mormal, combined with the advance of the Third Army, had thrown the German rearguards off the last possible defence line before the river Meuse. It was in this context that these relatively minor military successes assumed critical importance in forcing the final crisis in the German Army's High Command by finally forcing them to confront the reality that the war was lost. Events within Germany soon assumed greater importance as the crisis gathered pace but the battle on 4 November 1918 can perhaps be seen as the final catalyst which led to the German collapse.

One of the puzzles of this battle concerns the excellent fighting performance of 'ordinary' British troops in action. At the end of the Second World War, some units became noticeably 'combat shy', for the obvious reason that few people have ever wished to be the last soldier to die in a war which was clearly coming to an end. Yet British troops fought with real determination on 4 November

1918, even though the end of the war was in sight. Perhaps one of the answers to this question comes from the XIII Corps report of the fighting:

> It might have been anticipated . . . that a certain reluctance to take unnecessary risks would have manifested itself among troops, whose years of weary effort were on the point of being crowned with success. The very reverse was the case. Each successive victory steadily accelerated the disintegration which was taking place in the German ranks, and as steadily increased the daring and vigour of our blows.[51]

It would appear, judging by the events of the Battle of the Sambre, that the soldiers of the British Army in November 1918 smelt victory and did not want to be deprived of such a hard earned laurel. Perhaps Haig misjudged the situation in November 1918. It is not clear whether Haig's decisions were also influenced by the very real logistic problems which would have attended any further Allied advance, but it may well be that the BEF would have been prepared to fight on to total victory. Certainly, the Battle of the Sambre proved that the BEF had become a very competent and capable force, and almost unrecognizable from the enthusiastic but untrained army of two years before. There is clear evidence that the BEF had learned and developed from the hard years of trench warfare. Few of the capabilities which made the canal crossing possible in November 1918 were present in July 1916, apart from the undoubted bravery and determination of the troops. Rapid and competent planning which took a realistic view of capabilities and placed an emphasis on speed and suprise, co-ordinated and effective artillery bombardment, air superiority combined with effective air-ground co-operation, tank-infantry co-operation where appropriate, infantry platoon tactics, effective engineering capability and wireless communications all combined to produce a very powerful fighting formation. The BEF, with its increased expertise and weaponry, really could now tackle the most formidable obstacles.

However, although we can acknowledge the fighting power of the BEF as it stood at the end of the war, we must also remember that the Battle of the Sambre was indeed a tragic action. The Army certainly recognized the importance of the Battle of the Sambre with the award of seven Victoria Crosses to men who fought there. Yet today, the events of 4 November 1918 have faded from memory and it is the death of Wilfred Owen which stands out due to his subsequent fame as a war poet. It seems a sad fact that in Ors cemetery where Owen is buried, it is often only his grave that is surrounded by poppy tributes when many other men also paid the ultimate price just one week before the end of the war. Perhaps it is now time, nine decades on, to remember those events in full.

Notes

1. See Dominic Hibberd, *Wilfred Owen: The Truth Untold* (London: Weidenfeld and Nicholson, 2002); Jon Stallworthy, *Wilfred Owen: A Biography* (Oxford: Oxford University Press, 1974); Helen McPhail, *Portrait of Wilfred Owen: Poet and Soldier, 1893–1918* (Petersfield: Gliddon Books in association with The Wilfred Owen Association, 1993).
2. See Pat Barker, *Regeneration* (London: Viking Press, 1991); *The Eye in the Door* (London: Viking Press, 1993); *The Ghost Road* (London: Viking Press, 1995).
3. Roger Parkinson, *Tormented Warrior: Ludendorff and the Supreme Command* (London: Hodder and Stoughton, 1978), pp. 182–3.
4. Charles Messenger (ed.), Field Marshal von Hindenburg, *The Great War* (London: Greenhill, 2006), p. 222.
5. Robert B. Asprey, *The German High Command at War* (New York, NY: W. Morrow, 1991), p. 485.
6. Gordon Brooke-Shepherd, *November 1918: The Last Act of the Great War* (London: Collins, 1981), pp. 337–8.
7. J. E. Edmonds and R. Maxwell-Hyslop, *Military Operations France and Belgium 1918* vol.V *26 September–11 November: the Advance to Victory* (London: HMSO, 1947), p. 463.
8. Archibald Montgomery, *The Story of the Fourth Army in the Battle of the Hundred Days, August 8th to November 11th, 1918* (London: Hodder and Stoughton, 1920), pp. 240–2.
9. Thomas Chalmers, *A Saga of Scotland: History of the 16th Battalion, the Highland Light Infantry, City of Glasgow Regiment* (Glasgow: J McCallum and Co., 1930), p. 124.
10. Gary Sheffield and John Bourne (eds), *Douglas Haig: War Diaries and Letters 1914–1918* (London: Weidenfeld and Nicholson, 2005), p. 483.
11. Montgomery, *Fourth Army*, pp. 243–5.
12. 'Notes on Future Operations', 32nd Division War Diary, October 1918, WO95/2372, TNA.
13. Ibid.
14. Ibid.
15. W. Baker-Brown, *History of the Corps of Royal Engineers*, vol. V (Chatham: The Institution of the Royal Engineers, 1952), p. 394.

16 Report on XIII Corps Engineer Work During Operations 1 October, 1918–11 November, 1918, WO95/827, TNA.
17 Ibid.
18 Ibid.
19 C. E. P. Sankey, 'Assault Bridging', *The Royal Engineers Journal*, August 1922, p. 67.
20 Ibid., p. 69.
21 Ibid., p. 60
22 Regimental History Committee, *History of the Dorsetshire Regiment, 1914–1919, Part 1: The Regular Battalions* (Dorchester: Henry Ling, 1932), p. 139.
23 XIII Corps Engineer Work, WO95/827, TNA.
24 Montgomery, *Fourth Army*, p. 249.
25 Baker-Brown, *Royal Engineers*, p. 397.
26 Montgomery, *Fourth Army*, p. 249.
27 G. D. Martineau, *A History of the Royal Sussex Regiment, 1701–1953* (Chichester: Moore & Tillyer, 1955), p. 159.
28 Ibid., pp. 160–1. See also Montgomery, *Fourth Army*, pp. 286, 289.
29 John Ewing, *The Royal Scots 1914–1919*, vol. II (Edinburgh: Oliver and Boyd for the Association of Lowland Scots, 1925), p. 734.
30 J. C. Latter, *The History of the Lancashire Fusiliers 1914–1918*, vol. I (Aldershot: Gale and Polden, 1949), p. 435.
31 Ibid., p. 434. Marshall was awarded the Victoria Cross posthumously; see Montgomery, *Fourth Army*, p. 293.
32 Chalmers, *Saga*, p. 124.
33 Montgomery, *Fourth Army*, p. 251.
34 Ibid.; Kirk was awarded the Victoria Cross posthumously, see Montgomery, *Fourth Army*, p. 291.
35 Archibald was awarded the Victoria Cross, see Montgomery, *Fourth Army*, p. 281.
36 Ibid.; see also Gerald Napier, *The Sapper VCs: The Story of Valour in the Royal Engineers and its Associated Corps* (London: The Stationary Office, 1997), pp. 231–2; Waters was awarded the Victoria Cross, see Montgomery, *Fourth Army*, p. 298.
37 McPhail, *Portrait*, p. 61.
38 Mongtomery, *Fourth Army*, p. 251.
39 H. T. Clarke and W. K. Peake, *1/8th Battalion, The Worcestershire Regiment, 1914–1918* (London: War Narratives Publishing Company, 1919), p. 479.
40 Amey was awarded the Victoria Cross. See Montgomery, *Fourth Army*, p. 281.
41 Ibid., p. 480.
42 Ibid., p. 481.
43 Ibid.
44 M. Kincaid-Smith, *The 25th Division in France and Flanders* (Uckfield: Naval and Military Press, 2010 [1925]), p. 221.

45 Clarke and Peake, *1/8th Battalion*, p. 481.
46 Montgomery, *Fourth Army*, p. 253.
47 Clarke and Peake, *1/8th Battalion*, p. 482.
48 Sheffield and Bourne, *Douglas Haig*, p. 485.
49 Ibid., p. 483.
50 John W. Wheeler-Bennett, *Hindenburg: The Wooden Titan* (London: Macmillan, 1936), p. 186.
51 Report on XIII Corps Engineer Work During Operations 1 October, 1918–11 November, 1918, WO95/827, TNA.

5

War of Liberation: British Second Army and Coalition Warfare in Flanders in the Hundred Days

Dennis Williams

References to British Second Army in the histories of the Hundred Days are scarce. Seek a reference to the Battle of Courtrai, say, even in books that deal specifically with 1918 and the Western Front, and you will nearly always draw a blank.[1] British Second Army operated under foreign command and independently of other British forces, with the initial role of flank guard to the Belgian Army and supporting French forces. Such circumstances have caused the Army to be forgotten in assessments of the final stage of the war.

The *Groupe d'Armees des Flandres* (Army Group, Flanders – GAF) was composed of Belgian, British and French forces, under the leadership of Albert, King of the Belgians, with a French Chief of Staff. This coalition force, formed at the start of the Hundred Days, with Second Army being the British contribution, would proceed to liberate most of west Belgium by the time of the Armistice.[2]

Flanders is the ancient name for the area of land along the North Sea coast in west Belgium, linking to the French coast along the English Channel. The name means literally 'flooded land' (a description which all British Expeditionary Force (BEF) troops would no doubt have readily endorsed) reflecting the elaborate drainage system which channels most of its heavy rainfall into the river Yser. The area is largely flat and therefore the series of relatively low ridges (no more than 160 feet high), east of the main town of Ypres, provide a commanding view of the entire plain. Thus these ridges and the small villages and key pieces of ground in and around them were of considerable strategic value.[3]

The rivers Lys and Schelde provide natural lines of defence and their south-west/north-east configuration meant that British Second Army, deployed on the right flank of the GAF, was the first of the coalition forces to confront these barriers. It was Second Army's ability to force a crossing of these rivers, and thus turn the flank of the German defenders, which created the momentum for the advance of the Belgian and French armies.

The majority of Belgium had been under German occupation for four years. An attempt to set up an independent Flanders under German influence which would have had an army to fight alongside the German army had failed as most Flemish-speakers remained loyal to Belgium. Some 115,000 Belgians were deported for labour in Germany, resources were seized for German consumption and homelessness and starvation became a fact of life for many, despite humanitarian aid from allied and neutral countries.[4] While the majority of occupied Belgium was under the administration of a Governor General, most of the fighting took place in areas under military administration.

Operations in Flanders were included within the scheme developed by Haig and Foch for a general series of coordinated advances across the Western Front, to capitalize on the success at the Battle of Amiens. Both commanders were anxious to secure a commitment from the Belgian King that his troops would take part in the planned offensive. On 2 September 1918, Marshal Foch requested a plan from the British and Belgian GHQs for an advance in the north. One week later it was agreed that the general offensive would include action on the northern stretch of the Front; the aims included the clearing of ground between the River Lys and the coast, the clearance of the Flanders coast and the establishment of a line through Ghent to the Dutch frontier. To achieve this, a special army group was established and Haig agreed that the British Second Army commanded by General Sir Herbert Plumer would operate as part of the group, under the overall command of King Albert. The GAF would comprise the Belgian army, the British Second Army and three French corps. The French Sixth Army staff under General Degoutte as Chief of Staff, would service the command structure.

The Operations Report for British Second Army in September 1918 states that:

> Opposition stiffened considerably on the 4th [September] and subsequently, and the reluctance of the enemy to suffer the dislocation of his scheme of defence found frequent expression in counter-attacks. A sturdy opposition has been offered by the troops fronting us, and they have shown no signs of yielding

positions of value without fighting. It was with increasing reluctance, from 10th September onwards, that the enemy gave ground, and our rate of progress thenceforward was appreciably lessened.[5]

At this stage of the war, British troops advanced into the unknown. They could face no resistance, suffer harassing fire, become drawn into a firefight with machine-gun posts or artillery or receive a full counter-attack. The psychological pressure thus created, as much as the physical risk of injury and death, placed very heavy demands upon soldiers and their leaders. This unpredictable and staccato pattern of warfare – as the enemy acted to defend ground or not – was to be a distinctive feature of the final days of fighting.

Three other features would define the nature of the conflict in Flanders during the Hundred Days. The first was the notorious Flanders weather. This was able to produce stifling dry heat on one day, yet change to torrential rain within 24 hours. The impact upon the advancing forces would be considerable and is referred to regularly in contemporary writings and in the *Official History*. Next, the variable weather exacerbated the transport problems created by the poor quality of the roads in the area. Sustaining supply lines and in particular the bringing forward of artillery support was a major challenge in order to maintain the momentum of an advance; to convert a *breakthrough* into a *breakout*. Finally, the Flanders terrain was divided by a series of rivers, generally running north to south, and canals, which created a succession of natural defensive lines.

What of Second Army itself? Peter Simkins concludes that Plumer, due to his instincts for promoting teamwork and practical approaches to problems, together with a sound feel for tactics, 'did as much as anyone, and more than most, to encourage and develop the type of all-arms attack that proved the key to victory in 1918'.[6] Such qualities also encouraged the promotion of lower-level command and initiative which was to prove essential during the more open warfare of autumn 1918.[7]

At the time of the Final Advance in Flanders, Second Army retained four corps: II, X, XV and XIX. However the order of battle consisted of just ten divisions in total, nine of which had been with the army during the summer. 29th Division was originally a Regular Army Division. All the rest, 9th (Scottish), 14th (Light), 30th, 31st, 34th, 35th, 36th (Ulster), 40th and 41st, were New Army Divisions. The Army during this period was made up completely of British troops – there were no units from other parts of the Empire. Arguably it was the weakest, on paper at least, of the British Army formations during the Hundred Days. Six of its divisions had faced the Michael offensive in March; of these, a number had also been moved north to recuperate and five divisions thus found themselves instead repeating their experience in response to the Georgette offensive in northern France and Flanders. Battalions and brigades had faced the experience of having survivors pulled together in temporary composite formations, to retain cohesion in command and control.[8]

In May 1918 there were ten divisions in the BEF overall, marked with a red circle on the daily situations reports at GHQ, indicating that they had been reduced to cadre divisions. Five of these, reconstituted, were with Second Army in August 1918. Of the 100 battalions making up the Army, over half were listed as service or pioneer battalions; 40th Division had five former garrison battalions.[9]

New drafts into units were not always of the best quality. The 15th (Service) Battalion Loyal North Lancs, from an initial cadre of about ten officers and 40 Other Ranks (ORs) was boosted by new drafts during June to 43 officers and 937 ORs – but 254 of the new arrivals were then deemed to be medically unfit.[10] The 2nd Battalion Prince of Wales' Volunteers (South Lancs Regiment), which had been part of a composite unit following the Battle of the Aisne, stayed in France and received new drafts to bring it back up to strength.[11] The 15th (Service) Battalion KOYLI, was attached to 40th Division from June 1918. The Battalion, initially designated as a Garrison battalion, was composed of mainly B1 and B2 classified soldiers, many transferred from Labour battalions.[12]

David Bilton's history of the Hull Pals refers to 'the extreme youth of the replacements' and that 'many men of less than perfect health were being sent to the front line'.[13] On 2 August 1918 Major-General C. L. Nicholson, the commander of 34th Division, noted 'all Battalions were down to an average strength of less than 250, short of officers and very tired. . . . though quite willing to advance, I did not think the men were in a condition to go more than about 3 miles.'[14] Unlike other British armies, Second Army was not allocated any tank formations, though there were instances of cooperation with French tanks.

The re-organization and re-equipping of the Belgian Army, following its withdrawal behind the River Yser in 1914, had produced a front line strength of around 170,000 in 1918. The Belgian troops had undertaken no major action in the interim, concentrating on monitoring German activity and policing the flooded areas of no man's land. Their enthusiasm combined with a lack of combat experience was comparable with the newly arrived American forces.[15] Though the French Army had overcome the discord of the previous year it faced serious manpower problems. 'Some front line units were composed almost entirely of men in their forties', as Clayton notes.[16] Many divisions were under-strength and there were ongoing issues regarding supplies, replacements and casualty rates. Morale remained brittle and it was all too clear to the French soldier that he lacked the material support which the British and in particular the Americans enjoyed.[17]

The troops which faced Second Army belonged to the German Fourth Army. The troops were of varied experience and quality; most had enjoyed a period of rest following the fighting earlier in the year. The German positions were well-organized, with maximum use being made of pill-boxes, dug-outs and wire from earlier fighting, in order to provide for effective defence in depth. Machine-gun positions were heavily concealed, and snipers deployed in numbers. The high ground gave clear lines of sight across the battlefield; a shell-torn terrain, pock-marked by craters and former trenches, and littered with the debris of previous conflict, impeding the movement of men, animals and machines.[18]

The fight for control of the air was another factor in the Flanders campaign. The RAF together with its French and Belgian counterparts enjoyed a numerical superiority during the campaign and the success that this led to is illustrated by the high number of enemy aircraft destroyed in this period.[19] This victory gave a significant advantage to coalition troops – when the weather permitted. It allowed effective reconnaissance of German troop activity and positions, a crucial requirement given the fresh terrain over which the troops would be advancing. The allied aircraft carried out regular interdiction of enemy communications, headquarters and transport and troop formations.[20]

General Plumer was experienced in working with allied forces and commanders. As well as commanding colonial and volunteer troops early in his career, he had his more recent time in Italy to draw upon, where he had made a positive impression upon the Italian leadership. During the Spring 1918 fighting he had sustained good relations with both Belgian and French allies.[21]

Inclusion within the GAF, and the flank guard role it was allocated, could be interpreted as a downgrading for Second Army.[22] Yet the setting up of the GAF was a clever political manoeuvre by Foch as Supreme C-in-C; it allowed him to incorporate the Belgian Army in the planned series of offensives, through accommodating the desire of King Albert for the Belgian Army to be seen to lead the liberation of their country. Albert had consistently refused to put his troops under foreign command, arguing this was contrary to the country's constitution. He had always wanted to view his army as independent of the Allied forces, and, while stating his willingness to work cooperatively, was obsessed with maintaining Belgian independence. He was adamant in retaining sole command of the Belgian Army, and the prospects of a coalition force with himself at its head, persuaded him to agree to cooperation with the allies in the final push in 1918.[23]

It was in everyone's interest for the fresh Belgian troops to take part in the forthcoming offensive. Britain, or perhaps more specifically Haig, was concerned to ensure that France did not claim the credit for liberating Belgium, and that French troops did not lead an advance for which British troops had fought to create the conditions. Haig both wanted and needed to keep Plumer in situ because of the latter's proven ability to manage his way successfully through the political complexities of coalition warfare. Haig wanted to ensure that the Belgian Army would actually fight during the forthcoming series of attacks;[24] the presence of a British Army under a commander with a thorough knowledge of the area would be a considerable incentive. Another consideration should have been the condition of Second Army, which was on paper the weakest of Haig's armies. Haig probably feared that the force was not capable of much more than a holding role on the flank of an army group, and the overriding requirement was to give the Belgians the confidence to attack. In addition to Plumer's diplomatic abilities he was an experienced commander who could nurse a weakened British Army through the fighting to come.

The Battle of Ypres: 28 September–3 October 1918

The GAF received its first orders from the King of the Belgians on 19 and 21 September, signed 'au nom du roi' by General Degoutte. Second Army was to provide flanking cover to the Belgian forces to the north, and to establish a bridgehead south of the River Lys.

Plumer had issued his main operations order before receipt of Degoutte's instructions, in line with the GHQ briefing he had received three days previously. The GAF was to attack between Dixmude and St Eloi, to break through the enemy's lines and then use these as the base for further exploitation. The implication in the Official History is that the thoughts and actions of Degoutte did not impress Plumer or the writer of the History.[25] Harris and Barr comment that 'Plumer and his staff . . . regarded Degoutte as officious and inefficient and to have thought that he did little to co-ordinate planning between themselves and the Belgians'.[26] Powell comments 'It now fell to Plumer to remedy faulty staff work in the GAF and to carry out much of the essential co-ordination necessary between his own Army and the Belgians, especially the scope and details of the artillery programme'.[27] Despite this and subsequent events, relations between

Degoutte and Plumer apparently remained good, although Belgian criticism of the performance of the French forces would subsequently emerge.[28]

In accordance with Second Army's reputation for thorough preparation, a large-scale model of the positions to be attacked was constructed at Army HQ. Officers from each attacking division were brought in to be briefed on the overall attack and their position within it.[29] On 24 September a joint conference took place between leaders of the Belgian Army and British Second Army in order to agree upon the practical arrangements for the attack. Discussion concentrated upon the artillery, with the British favouring a surprise attack without a preliminary bombardment. The Belgians were concerned at the ability of their forces to breach defences without an initial bombardment and so it was agreed that they would commence a barrage three hours before Z-hour. The Belgian right wing would receive creeping barrage support from II Corps heavy artillery. During the battle, '200 hostile artillery positions were kept under fire during the operations and very little hostile shelling was reported'.[30] The Belgian forces were also allocated air support from the eight squadrons of the 5th Group RAF.

The ground over which the attacks would be launched was the battlefields of autumn 1917; the physical consequences of the earlier conflict were all too real. British troops would have to advance across a barren landscape scarred by warfare: 'The artillery bombardments of 1917 had destroyed the fragile drainage system and left a wilderness of water-filled shell craters, decaying trenches, rusting wire entanglements and all the debris of a war that had passed by'.[31] The cratered ground would prevent deployment of the GAF cavalry reserve.

Despite the problems created by the terrain for communications, transport and supply, the outcomes of the military action were very different from previous Allied offensives in the area. 28 September 1918 saw a total advance by the attacking corps of between four and six miles. British troops established a new line beyond Ypres ridge and Houthulst Forest. The Belgians reached Passchendaele that day; the British retook Wytschaete.

Further orders from Degoutte were received after Plumer had already determined the next day's actions. Degoutte stated that resistance had been weaker opposite the British Second Army and the Belgian right flank and it was here the attack must be pressed without pause. The Official History records dryly that 'Plumer saw no reason to modify the orders he had already given'.[32]

Significant further advances were made. A notable feature was co-operation on the adjoining flanks between British 9th Division (II Corps) and Belgian forces. This saw a joint offensive which achieved a breakthrough of the prepared German defensive position, *Flanders Line I*, and by late afternoon, units were in place in front of *Flanders Line II*. Plumer confirmed the role of Second Army in acting as flank guard for the Belgians, emphasizing the aim of covering and securing the crossing points of the Lys. Most of the country which had been scarred by previous battles now lay to the rear of the front line forces; the troops would now be able to liberate towns and villages which had been under German occupation since 1914. The enemy would no longer have the benefit of defending amid the detritus of previous battles. However the new terrain would be unfamiliar to the attackers, increasing the need for quality maps and the support of air reconnaissance.

Continuing bad weather, in particular the torrential rainfall on the night of 29–30 September, prevented the badly-needed RAF operations, as well as disrupting supply traffic. With the limited number of decent roads, delivery of ammunition and rations to advancing troops was near-impossible; enemy activity became a 'minor consideration as compared with the problem of communications'.[33] Second Army improvized via 'corduroy' roads and through the extension of existing railway lines. For example, by day three of the battle the German railway system east of Ypres had been linked up to the railway station at Passchendaele.

The limited experience of the Belgian Army meant it had difficulty dealing with the requirements of this new and mobile warfare, and Second Army had to slow its advance in order to maintain cohesion with its ally. On 2 October advance units of Belgian and Allied troops were cut off from supplies and were without food. To avoid these having to pull back, 80 aircraft were deployed to air-drop 15,000 rations to them; an overall load of 13 tons. Small sacks were used, each with five or ten packs, and padded with earth to absorb the shock of hitting the ground after being thrown out of the aeroplane.

With the worsening transport and supply problems, plus German reserves strengthening the defensive lines of the *Flanders Positions*, the battle ceased on 2 October. The British were two miles short of Menin (which had been an objective in the autumn of 1914). Although Degoutte wished for a new general advance to commence on 7/8 October, the date was eventually set by Albert as 14 October. He was worried at the scale of Belgian casualties and demanded increased preparation for the next phase.

The Battle of Ypres saw overall British Second Army casualties of 303 officers and 4,392 other ranks. For the Belgians, 2,000 soldiers had been killed and 10,000 were sick or wounded; their total net loss was 4,500 including 50 per cent of the officers. Second Army had captured 4,672 prisoners and about 100 guns. Overall, the GAF had taken over 10,000 German prisoners, 300 guns, 100 trench mortars and 600 machine guns.[34]

The Battle of Courtrai: 14–19 October 1918

At Zero hour of 05.35 on 14 October 1918, British Second Army launched its opening assault in the Battle of Courtrai. Overall the GAF had 32 divisions (13 Belgian, ten British and nine French), faced by the German Fourth Army of 24 divisions. The Second Army's role was to again protect the right flank of the GAF. This time the French XXXIV and VII Corps were designated as the main strike force with immediate flanking support from Belgian divisions on either side. The aim was to seize Roulers and from there, advance to Thielt and Ghent. The *Official History* states innocently that 'all that was required of the Second Army was a wheel to the right up to the Lys'.[35]

However Plumer was apparently mindful of the potential for his Army to do rather more than its flank guard role. His actions suggest that he felt empowered by the success of his troops to attempt a more audacious role than that originally intended. This reflects Haig's view at this time, that it was the British armies on the Western Front that were fighting most effectively.[36] As well as his new-found belief in the potential of Second Army, Plumer is also likely to have been influenced by his lack of confidence in Degoutte, and the increasing evidence of weakened German resistance and intelligence of enemy preparations for further withdrawal. On 11 October he issued a modification to his earlier orders, changes which implied a switch to the offensive; authorizing advanced guards to establish bridgeheads south of the river Lys.

Initial successes were repeated on 15 October with Plumer's orders urging units to consolidate the gains of the previous day, send forward patrols and to establish bridgeheads across the Lys, if possible to achieve 'without undue loss'. XV Corps, employing the cover of artillery and machine guns, put temporary bridges across the Lys and established a firm bridgehead. This was a crucial move as it allowed enemy defences on the right (southern) bank of the Lys to be outflanked. To the north, II Corps in conjunction with the Belgian right wing made good progress despite encountering considerable resistance in the initial stages of the attack.

The progress made by French forces in the north was considerably slower, an advance of four kilometres in comparison with the ten kilometres achieved by the Belgian Southern *Groupement* and II Corps. Unsurprisingly, Foch was less than happy with this situation and he subsequently arranged for a reorganization of French forces to create the *Armée Francaise de Belgique*, with French Sixth Army under General de Boissoudy.[37]

16 October saw the four divisions on the right of Second Army holding a line across the Lys, while the rest of the army occupied the north bank of the river. The heavy howitzers and long-range guns of II Corps engaged targets south of the Lys, whereby harassing fire and bombardment of targets selected by the infantry was conducted. The artillery of the other Corps moved forward as conditions permitted, crossing the Lys as soon as appropriate bridging was in place. Information from prisoners together with observed evidence, suggested that the enemy was looking to undertake a planned withdrawal to the Schelde. Though advancing British forces encountered strong covering detachments of artillery, machine-guns and small arms, they were able to execute pursuit of the retreating enemy.

That same day, reflecting his own unhappiness with the limited progress of the French forces, King Albert issued orders which altered the flank guard operations of Second Army (not that Plumer had shown himself restricted to that role). XV and X Corps were to push eastwards, south of the Lys; XIX and II Corps were to consolidate their positions and clear the enemy from the vicinity of the Lys and Coutrai. Albert was actually seeking to suspend operations as soon as possible, due to his concern at the level of Belgian casualties. The Official History states that 'General Plumer again ignored the orders of the GAF. . . . [directing] XV and X Corps to advance to the Tournai-Courtrai railway. . . . XIX and II Corps were to make all preparations to cross the Lys when the situation demanded'.[38]

During the following few days, units along the Second Army line crossed the Lys in the face of resistance by the German covering forces. Where daylight crossings were deemed too dangerous an offensive was launched by night. The variations in the depth and breadth of the Lys meant that a variety of bridging arrangements were used including rafts, a barrel bridge and pontoon bridges. Second Army extended its left flank northwards, relieving part of the Belgian line; on 19 October Courtrai was taken. By the first light of 20 October, the whole of Second Army was across the Lys.

As a consequence of continuing German withdrawals to the north and along the coast, the French and Belgians were able to accelerate their advance. On 17 October the Belgians entered Ostend, King Albert entering on a British destroyer flying the Belgian flag. Two days later they were in Zeebrugge and Bruges, with Albert formally entering the latter city on 20 October.

19 October also saw a General Directive from Foch, instructing the GAF to advance in the general direction of Brussels. In response, Albert now issued further orders for the GAF to move speedily to cross the Lys and the Deynze-Ecloo

canal, thus denying the Germans the time to organize resistance. If resistance was encountered then 'the principal part in dislodging him would fall to the British Second Army'.[39] This recognized that the success of the Army in already crossing the Lys allowed it to now move rapidly towards the Schelde, thereby assisting French and Belgian forces to cross the Lys and enter the open ground ahead.

Between the Lys and the Schelde: British Second Army 20 October–11 November 1918

Second Army issued special instructions stating that 'the fighting of the last few days has become more mobile than has hitherto been the case and is now practically open warfare'.[40] The need to keep close up to the enemy as he retreated was constantly emphasized:

> [The Army had the] policy of harassing the Germans without intermission, even though the main advance might be temporarily held up owing to the difficulty of getting supplies forward across the devastated regions in the wake of the pursuers, and the desire to avoid needless casualties. These harassing tactics, in the conditions of open warfare now prevailing, gave ample scope for initiative and skill on the part of company and platoon commanders.[41]

Progress along the line was hampered by the slow advance of the French on the left; the enemy was increasing its resistance in front of Second Army because it was essential to hold these positions until its units opposing the French could themselves pull back. Plumer accordingly set the line of the Schelde as the next objective. Involved in what has been designated as the 'Action of Ooteghem' were X Corps (34th Division), XIX Corps (41st Division) and II Corps (9th and 36th Divisions) with the co-operation of the French 164th Division and a French cavalry brigade. The attack was a partial success, The southern divisions (34th and 41st) achieved their objectives but II Corps was frustrated in its attempt to reach Ooteghem.

The first seven days of action beyond the Lys produced a limited advance by Second Army of a maximum of seven miles; and unlike the British right wing, none of the French or Belgian forces had yet reached the Schelde. The large amount of civilian traffic being generated as areas were liberated created problems for the British artillery. The Germans used a high proportion of gas shells which also caused casualties among civilians.[42] On 31 October three Second Army divisions fought the 'Action of Tieghem', designed to clear a way forward for a full advance onto the Schelde. Two companies of French tanks were deployed to assist, with Major-General Nicholson, commanding 34th Division, noting that these proved to be 'of great value on the right'.[43]

From 14–31 October, Second Army captured 7,422 prisoners, 172 guns plus considerable numbers of machine-guns and trench mortars. During this same period, 76 German aeroplanes and four balloons were destroyed, for the loss of 30 British planes.[44]

From that point on Plumer commenced plans for a forced crossing of the Schelde. Artillery, sufficient to protect the west bank and conduct counter-battery work, was maintained in action; all other guns were to be held in preparation for supporting the crossing. Provisional orders were prepared to take advantage of any identified reduction in the German defences. Bridging material was being brought together and probing patrols were sent forward regularly including two minor bridging operations. The enemy continued to resist in force, employing harassing fire including gas bombardments. Despite this, the British succeeded in establishing a number of advance posts on the eastern bank of the river.

Haig had become exasperated with the delay in returning Second Army to his command. Foch wanted to allow Albert to enter Bruges at the head of an allied force but Haig insisted that Second Army had fulfilled its agreed task. No definitive reason has been established for Haig's determination to bring Second Army out of the GAF coalition; nor for Haig to adopt the most extreme (and for him, most exceptional) position and threaten his resignation if he did not get his way. Speculation covers a number of possible considerations including the fact that the British Army was carrying the weight of the fighting and making most progress; concern that the French forces were not pulling their weight; fears over the casualty rates (acknowledging the pressures from London on this issue). From a distance the degree of feeling in the dispute that arose between Haig and Foch over this question seems quite disproportionate, and some blame has been directed at the GHQ staff, and Haig's Chief of Staff Lieutenant-General Sir Herbert Lawrence. The matter was in due course resolved over 'tea and cakes' initiated by Foch (though Haig pointed out that he never 'took tea'!).[45] On 4 November, British Second Army was removed from the GAF and restored to Haig's command, as part of the BEF.

By 9 November it was clear that German forces were retreating from the Schelde and Second Army sent forward advance units, using pontoon bridges and boats, onto the eastern bank. During the final three days of the war, Second Army advanced 22 miles, reaching the River Dendre.

The Army's final act before the Armistice took place on 11 November when a squadron of 7th Dragoon Guards, attached to X Corps, advanced towards the bridge over the Dendre at Lessines. At around 10.45 the troops charged the village, taking 130 prisoners and a machine gun; more importantly, the bridge, which was wired for demolition, was captured intact. A further 41 prisoners were captured on higher ground overlooking the village; it now being after 11.00, these prisoners were released. During the period 1–11 November, 719 prisoners were captured by Plumer's Army. This was in addition to 18 guns, six trench mortars, 142 machine-guns, two complete trains and 10 locomotives.[46]

Thus the British Second Army concluded its war. Since the initial advance in Flanders began on 18 August, Second Army had fought two major battles, seven major supporting actions and advanced 53 miles across Belgium in 86 days.

Conclusions

From this summary narrative of British Second Army operations, certain themes emerge from the Hundred Days campaign. The GAF pushed the Germans out of most of west Belgium, experiencing the sort of scenes more often associated with the liberation of Western Europe in the Second World War, as the following example illustrates:

> On the 18th [October, 1918] General Woodcock and the headquarters of the 101st Brigade made a triumphant entry into Lauwe, which was the first Belgian Town we had entered which was still inhabited. The inhabitants gave the general a demonstrative and enthusiastic welcome. The enemy was evidently in full retreat, and a crowd of liberated civilians were met on all sides.[47]

It is no mistake to present the Battle for Flanders in the autumn of 1918 as a 'War of Liberation', though this is a description that is at odds with current popular perceptions of the war in Britain.

At the start of the campaign it would perhaps have been difficult to be confident about the offensive potential of British Second Army and its component units and troops. The advantages of the weather and terrain, allied to the available weaponry, offset to a considerable degree any disadvantages that the Germans suffered in terms of the declining quality of their troops and numerical inferiority. British Second Army was itself beset with problems of troop quality and the rate of casualties meant that obtaining replacements was a continual headache. The problems of transport and supply, and the ongoing challenge of attempting to move artillery forward to support infantry attacks further beset the Army. In general this challenge was tackled successfully, as one regimental history makes clear, referring to the 'wonderful work' of the transport services:

> The railhead was far behind, the roads were bad, every bridge had been destroyed, and the distances that had to be covered to reach [the battalion] increased almost daily by about ten miles. Yet on no single occasion did the supply of daily rations fail to arrive.[48]

As well as the demands of logistics, the Army had to adjust to the changed open nature of the warfare, and ensure its soldiers were sufficiently trained and skilled in the all-arms tactics of the BEF. Casualty lists were high but this does not appear in general to result from failures in planning or command. This was a product of the nature of the more open warfare being undertaken, with British troops operating out of the protection of trenches. The success of the Army in overcoming these challenges is demonstrated by the scale of the advance and the recognition by its partners of its performance. It restored the standing of the BEF in the eyes of the French, for whom British troops had suffered unfavourable comparisons with the newly arrived fresh American forces (a case of familiarity breeding contempt perhaps). Anthony Clayton in his history of the French Army concludes that 'Respect for the British suddenly returned following [British Second Army's] success in Flanders'.[49]

Plumer was not able to operate independently, although he took a very positive view of his Army. He was within a coalition and officially subordinate to Belgian (or arguably, French) control. At the strategic level, the Army had to conform to coalition requirements, and to plan and pace its advance in the interests of its allied neighbours. Yet despite being restricted initially to the role of flank guard, the performance of the army was such that it subsequently became designated by King Albert as the advance force for the GAF. The British impressed their allies at both command level and in the field.

It is to Second Army's credit that it found various ways of addressing or coping with the majority of the problems which confronted it during the Hundred Days. During this period Plumer's British Second Army became the main strike force of the GAF due its successful application of battlefield techniques which maximized the resources in men and material available to it, and responded to the challenges of climate, terrain and a determined enemy. There is no doubt that, as Peter Simkins concludes, the circumstances in Flanders in the autumn of 1918 allowed 'a rolling series of limited-objective and all-arms attacks to be conducted on an almost daily basis. As a leading proponent and practitioner of [such tactics], Plumer surely deserves considerable credit for his contribution to the BEF's "learning curve" and his part in the eventual German defeat'.[50]

The Flanders campaign was a success achieved by the common British 'Tommy'. In the advances of the Hundred Days, the soldiers of Second Army fought a series of battles in support of coalition forces to liberate western Belgium; a success which should feature in any list of major achievements by the British Army.

Notes

1. Even a book as recent as Peter Hart, *1918: A Very British Victory* (London: Weidenfeld and Nicholson, 2008) contains no reference to Second Army in Flanders.
2. Unless noted otherwise, the campaign narrative in this chapter is based upon J. E. Edmonds, *Military Operations, France and Belgium, 1918* vol. IV: *8th August–26th September: The Franco-British Offensive* (London: HMSO, 1947); J. E. Edmonds and R. Maxwell-Hyslop, *Military Operations, France and Belgium, 1918* vol. V: *26 September–11 November: the Advance to Victory* (London: HMSO, 1947), p. 573; J. P. Harris with Niall Barr, *Amiens to the Armistice: The BEF in the Hundred Days Campaign 8 August–11 November 1918* (London: Brassey's, 1998); The National Archives (TNA), WO 158/218, Operations on the Second Army Front.
3. For a brief pen picture see Winston Groom, *A Storm in Flanders: The Ypres Salient 1914-1918 – Tragedy and Triumph on the Western Front* (London: Cassell, 2003), chapter 3.
4. A. Garcia, 'Soup and Stoicism – Feeding occupied Belgium during the Great War', *Stand To! The Journal of the Western Front Association* 82 (April/May 2008), pp. 57–60.
5. WO 158/218.
6. Peter Simkins, 'Herbert Plumer', in Ian F. W. Beckett and Steven J. Corvi (eds), *Haig's Generals* (Barnsley: Pen and Sword, 2006), p. 154.
7. Ibid., p. 159.
8. See A. F. Becke, *Order of Battle Part 4: The Army Council, GHQs, Armies and Corps 1914-18* (London: HMSO, 1945), and *The Long, Long Trail*, www.1914–1918.net.
9. See Becke, *Order of Battle Part 4* and *The Long, Long Trail*.
10. H. C. Wylly, *The Loyal North Lancashire Regiment*, vol. II *1914–1919* (London: Royal United Service Institution, 1933), p. 359; TNA, WO 95/1890, War Diary of 15th L.N.L. June 1918.

11 H. Whalley-Kelly, *'Ich Dien': The Prince Of Wales's Volunteers (South Lancashire) 1914–1934* (Aldershot: Gale and Polden, 1935), p. 62; WO 95/2336, War Diary of 2nd S. Lancs, July 1918.
12 R. C. Bond, *The History of the King's Own Yorkshire Light Infantry in the Great War 1914–1918* (London: Lund Humphries, 1929), p. 986; TNA, WO 95/2612, War Diary of 15th KOYLI, June 1918.
13 David Bilton, *Hull Pals: 10th, 11th, 12th & 13th (Service) Battalions of the East Yorkshire Regiment – A History of 92 Infantry Brigade, 31st Division* (Barnsley: Pen and Sword, 1999), p. 156.
14 Imperial War Museum (IWM), 01/14/1, Major-General C.L. Nicholson diary, 2 August 1918.
15 R. Pawly and P. Lierneux, *The Belgian Army in World War 1* (Oxford: Osprey Publishing, 2009); Philip J. Haythornthwaite, *The World War One Source Book* (London: Arms and Armour Press, 1993), pp. 148–53.
16 Anthony Clayton, *Paths of Glory: The French Army 1914–18* (London: Cassell, 2005 [2003]), p. 181.
17 Ibid., pp. 177–96.
18 Edmonds, *Military Operations 1918* vol. IV; Edmonds and Maxwell-Hyslop, *Military Operations 1918* vol. V; Martin Marix Evans, *1918: The Year of Victories* (London: Arcturus, 2002); Groom, *Storm*.
19 Analysis of TNA, WO 158/218 records 192 enemy aircraft destroyed for the loss of 90 RAF machines.
20 Ibid.
21 Charles Harrington, *Plumer of Messines* (London: John Murray, 1935), Geoffrey Powell, *Plumer: The Soldiers' General: A Biography of Field-Marshal Viscount Plumer of Messines* (London: Leo Cooper, 1990).
22 Simkins, 'Herbert Plumer', p. 148.
23 Elizabeth Greenhalgh, *Victory through Coalition: Britain and France during the First World War* (Cambridge: Cambridge University Press, 2005), pp. 253–60; William Philpott, *Anglo-French Relations and Strategy on the Western Front 1914–18* (Basingstoke: Palgrave Macmillan, 1996), p. 159.
24 Haig diary, 5 September 1918, in Gary Sheffield and John Bourne (eds) *Douglas Haig: War Diaries and Letters 1914–1918* (London: Weidenfeld and Nicholson, 2005), p. 457.
25 Edmonds and Maxwell-Hyslop, *Military Operations 1918* vol. V states 'going dead against the expressed opinion of General Plumer, it was laid down that "it is not necessary in the first instance to attack the Wytschaete-Messines area..."' (p. 58) and 'General Degoutte made no attempt to co-ordinate action at the junction of the Belgian and British Second Armies, and it was discovered by General Plumer that several points of difference required adjustment' (p. 60).

26 Harris and Barr, *Amiens to the Armistice*, p. 300.
27 Powell, *Plumer*, p. 273.
28 Greenhalgh, *Victory*, p. 255.
29 Harris and Barr, *Amiens to the Armistice*, p. 300.
30 WO 158/218.
31 J. H. Johnson, *1918: The Unexpected Victory* (London: Arms and Armour Press, 1997), p. 141.
32 Edmonds and Maxwell-Hyslop, *Military Operations 1918* vol. V, p. 76.
33 TNA, WO 158/218.
34 Edmonds and Maxwell-Hyslop, *Military Operations 1918* vol. V, p. 91.
35 Ibid., p. 271.
36 See Haig's Diary, 10, 17, 19 October 1918, in Sheffield and Bourne, *Douglas Haig*, pp. 472, 474, 476; Harris and Barr, *Amiens to the Armistice*, p. 291.
37 Greenhalgh, *Victory*, p. 255.
38 Edmonds and Maxwell-Hyslop, *Military Operations 1918* vol. V, p. 287; see also Greenhalgh, *Victory*, pp. 255–6.
39 Edmonds and Maxwell-Hyslop, *Military Operations 1918* vol. V, p. 292.
40 IWM 01/14/1 – GSI No. 15 23rd October 1918, extract from *Field Service Regulations Part 1*.
41 Whalley-Kelly, '*Ich Dien*', p. 66.
42 TNA, WO 158/218.
43 IWM, 01/14/1 Nicholson diary, 31 October 1918.
44 TNA, WO 158/218.
45 Greenhalgh, *Victory*, pp. 255–61.
46 TNA, WO 158/218.
47 Wylly, *Loyal North Lancashire* II, p. 151.
48 L. Nicholson with H. McMullen, *History Of The East Lancashire Regiment 1914–1918* (Liverpool: Littlebury, 1936), p. 559.
49 Clayton, *Paths of Glory*, p. 192.
50 Simkins, 'Herbert Plumer', p. 159.

6

Behind the Lines: Sir Douglas Haig and the Cavalry Corps, September–October 1918[1]

Simon M. Justice

The principles underlying the nature of Field Marshal Sir Douglas Haig's command of the British Expeditionary Force (BEF), and the relationship between Haig and General Sir Henry Rawlinson (GOC Fourth Army) in particular, have proved of interest to scholars.[2] Peter Simkins argues for a balanced view of the Field Marshal's command style, noting that by mid-1918 there was a well-established culture of personal meetings and conferences with his direct subordinates, and that the time given to his Army commanders was increased as Haig felt necessary. This was especially true in the case of Rawlinson. Haig and the Fourth Army commander held at least 14 one-to-one meetings during the Hundred Days campaign. No other Army commander could boast of as many meetings with the Commander-in-Chief (C-in-C).[3] This evidence tends to support the growth of a more consultative and collaborative effort that allowed Haig, by the late summer of 1918, to relinquish day-to-day command of the Armies on the Western Front and act as more of a 'hands-off' C-in-C in line with pre-war doctrine. Haig felt able to adopt this role not least because he was more confident in the abilities of his subordinates. As he wrote to the Chief of the Imperial General Staff, General Sir Henry Wilson, in October 1918, 'we have a surprisingly large number of very *capable* generals'.[4]

Under the new system Rawlinson, and his fellow Army commanders (General Sir Henry Horne, First Army; General Sir Herbert Plumer, Second Army; General Sir Julian Byng, Third Army; General Sir William Birdwood, Fifth Army),[5] were then allowed to conduct operations free of the C-in-C's direct control; a development in command policy in direct contrast to Haig's previous interventions, arguably associated with most (if not all) of the 'failures' of the previous campaigns. There is, however, compelling evidence that Haig was as willing to intervene directly during the Hundred Days as he ever was during his tenure as C-in-C, if he saw the need. This is particularly apparent during his planning for operations beyond the Hindenburg Line.

Edmonds, Haig and the Cavalry Corps

Offensive operations between the Hindenburg Positions and the River Selle, 8–25 October 1918, encompassed the range of tactical situations typical of siege and mobile warfare. Of these, the engagement of the Cavalry Corps in the 'Pursuit to the Selle'[6] signifies a transitional point in the return to a war of movement. This period marks a critical phase in the Cavalry Corps' campaign, and a true test of its ability to affect the outcome of the war.

The British Official Historian, Brigadier General Sir James Edmonds, dismissed the contribution of the Cavalry Corps to actions before the Selle in October 1918 as largely irrelevant. While it is true that the nature of the Cavalry Corps represented a unique problem and opportunity cost in logistic terms, his assertion that 'the cavalry had done nothing that the infantry, with artillery support and cyclists, could not have done for itself at less cost' lacks credibility.[7] A closer examination of the evidence contained in Edmonds' own narrative and supporting sketches suggests an alternative view, namely that on this occasion the Cavalry Corps, far from being extraneous, proved to be a formation uniquely well-equipped to spearhead and facilitate the considerable gains of the 'Pursuit to the Selle'. Indeed, it came close to pulling off the war-shortening coup that Sir Douglas Haig desired, albeit not in the way that he envisaged.

A review of Haig's contemporary interactions with government, his peers and his subordinates, reveals two important possibilities. First, that Haig's foresight enabled timely and pertinent planning for the return to mobile warfare. Second, that Haig's personal contribution in the direction of the Cavalry Corps during September and October 1918 gave it a chance to fulfil its raison d'être as a strategic/operational instrument of exploitation. The ability of the Corps to fulfil its potential and, thereby, the extent to which Haig's intervention influenced results in the field, is the focus of this essay. However, before turning to the Selle operations and the Cavalry Corps' preparations, it is necessary briefly to consider the context.

In the spring of 1917 a state of semi-open warfare existed while the German armies opposing the BEF retired to the Hindenburg Line. The orderliness of the withdrawal precluded significant cavalry operations.[8] Indeed, during that period, Haig made it clear to his commanders that the precious Cavalry Corps was not to be used in operations against the retreating enemy, directing instead that:

> It is essential that the Cavalry Corps should be in a condition to deliver an effective blow against the enemy after battle. This moment has not yet arrived. In the existing conditions the fullest use should be made of the [Army] Corps Cavalry [i.e. squadrons of cavalry attached to infantry corps] and lightly equipped advanced guards. . . .[9]

Haig had already turned his mind to the ground beyond the Hindenburg Line and the long-awaited decisive use of his arm of exploitation. He recognized that reversion from siege to open warfare required the acquisition, or recollection, of different skills and mind set. He set to work to ensure the Cavalry Corps was ready, even reduced as it was from its previous maximum establishment of five cavalry divisions to a mere two.[10]

Sharpening the sword: The Cavalry Corps training exercise – 17 September 1918

Final preparation of the Cavalry Corps for its special purpose began when control of the formation was technically passed from GHQ to Sir Henry Rawlinson at the end of July 1918.[11] By now Haig was concerned with relinquishing direct control of operations and the creation and maintenance of an environment within which his army commanders could attain independent success. Rawlinson in June 1917 recorded Haig telling him that 'last year he had only one Army Com[mande]r. (me) now he had five who knew their business'. Haig had built up their confidence and belief that they did indeed 'know their business'.[12] Nonetheless, a little over a month after Rawlinson took 'ownership', Haig demonstrated that in reality he had not completely relinquished personal direction of the Corps. Following a conference with Lieutenant-General Charles Kavanagh (GOC Cavalry Corps) and Lieutenant-General Sir Ivor Maxse (now Inspector General of Training) Haig issued his training plan, which explicitly revealed his vision for unleashing the Cavalry Corps, and its objectives.[13]

In this document, Haig gave warning that he would be holding a field inspection 'In about 10 days time... when I will set... a problem connected with "the pursuit".[14] In the first of three preceding points, he noted the deterioration of enemy discipline under intense Allied pressure. In the second, he stressed that he would not allow the use of the Cavalry Corps, which included infantry and machine gun units, until conditions were aligned with those contained in the pre-war doctrinal document of which he had a major part in devising, namely *Field Service Regulations* (FSR). Part I, paragraph 112 of FSR dealt with 'The Pursuit',[15] namely open warfare against an enemy in retreat. Haig was careful to stipulate the likely use of sacrificial enemy rearguards composed of 'his freshest troops' to cover the coming retirement. Crucially, in his third point, Haig modelled the specific nature of the opposition and real future battlefield by detailing the points of resistance, and objectives to be set by Kavanagh for the field inspection 'in order to prepare it [the Cavalry Corps] for action in about a fortnight'.[16] Machine guns were to be the main obstacle, covering an enemy withdrawing in columns, and the similarly important goal of 'some important railway centre or other vital point in the enemy's comm[unicatio]ns....' Elaborate instructions for Haig's 17 September exercise were issued down to brigade level on the day before the event.[17]

The 'fictitious' circumstances of the exercise stated that the British Armies had inflicted a series of defeats on the enemy and were engaged in the pursuit of a demoralized, disorganized and retreating opponent to a last line of prepared defences. Aerial reconnaissance had provided evidence of 'no continuous system of defences' behind this line.[18] The scheme would unfold on the premise that the British forces had, on that day, broken through the enemy defence lines and that the C-in-C had 'decided to launch the Corps in pursuit [of the *defeated* enemy] and to support it with his general reserve'.[19] The exercise was to begin with 1st Cavalry Division, three motor machine gun batteries and six armoured cars in readiness, and detachments moving forward to keep in touch with the advancing infantry. 3rd Cavalry Division, with two motor machine gun batteries and six armoured cars, was prepared to pass through the former. 34 Infantry Brigade and Household Machine Gun Brigade were to act in support of 1st Cavalry Division.[20] Air and other support came from No. 6 Squadron RAF[21] and the Corps Cyclist Battalion. Opposition on the day was provided by 198 Infantry Brigade of 66th (2nd East Lancashire) Division.[22]

All being prepared, the exercise went ahead as planned, observed by Haig, under the watchful eyes of more than 70 umpires.[23] The Chief Umpire was Major-General H. C. C. Uniacke, Deputy Inspector General of Training,[24] and the overall Director, Maxse. The Canadian Cavalry Brigade was not involved.

A lengthy post-mortem

Performance in the scheme was discussed in three appraisals: a debriefing document that included a lengthy narrative, a Cavalry Corps conference held on 19 September and Haig's own comments delivered on 22 September. The debrief, though not dated or signed, is likely a form of minute from a conference convened immediately following the conclusion of the exercise, and attended by Haig, Maxse, Uniacke, all umpires, directing staff and commanders of the units involved.[25] The discussion of the preconceived 'General' and 'Special' ideas in the narrative is worthy of examination in some detail. The published objectives further confirm the focus of Haig, and now Kavanagh, on Le Cateau, the Selle and the ground before these features: 'forcing the passage of a river . . . dealing with hostile machine gun nests . . . attacking villages and woods . . . destroying a railway centre.' It should be noted that these four items were the key objectives and that the umpires had instructions to 'pay special attention to the tactical methods adopted . . . as regards [them]'.[26]

The instructions were explicit, noting that success against these objectives could be obtained by employing 'the chief essential . . . fire and movement'.[27] The process was further defined to include 'The combination of dismounted fire action and shock action. Covering fire from machine guns and artillery. Rapidity of turning movements. Skilful use of ground.'[28] The narrative's illustration of the defence allowed, importantly, for the effects of a continuous advance following a morning rupture of the lines. It featured a demoralized and tired enemy, with hastily prepared defences at river crossings which were not organized or continuous. The scenario also showed the surviving units of the retreating 'Whites' '*defeated in the early morning*, and driven from [their] fortified positions . . . offering a weak and scattered resistance.'[29]

Each of the three appraisals mentioned above illustrated success and failure during the scheme. First, in the narrative, which consisted of six pages of foolscap typescript, the performance of each part of the composite force was analysed. That of the cavalry and artillery is discussed here.[30] With regard to the main mounted bodies and close support, the tactical use of dismounted troops to pass over a river and take a defended crossing in rear to force the passage was commended. There was criticism of repeated attempts, by squadron and then troop, to take machine gun and rifle posts before the same river at the gallop which 'failed, with what would have proved in action severe loss'. The ordering forward of the Household Machine Gun Brigade and 34 Infantry Brigade when they 'were 12 and 13 miles respectively from the most advanced line of troops' was noted, as was the failure to enter a village under fire. Praise was given to the outflanking of an enemy-held ridge by a detachment which passed it on either side across clear ground while a supporting regiment mopped it up, to the identification by patrols of a post which was subsequently put out of action by the Royal Horse Artillery (RHA) and to the fixing from the front of another position which was then taken by being 'galloped from a flank'. In general, over-reliance on 'shock action' to overcome machine guns and posts was seen as a prevailing fault. Additionally, the delays (of hours) in moving forward after the capture of objectives, even over 'sparsely defended ground', was criticized. Complete gaps in defences were missed and in some cases the artillery was left out of touch by poor manoeuvres. Ominously, not all possible river crossings were explored, so that undefended bridges were not reported and the opportunity to bypass or take defended villages from the rear was missed. Credit was generously given to the demonstration of 'sound tactical ability, quickly applied' when a crucial post at a crossroads was eliminated, widening a gap between two defended villages to permit the passage of supports unscathed by the defence. In reviewing artillery performance the narrative was direct and simple – it needed more practice: 'Artillery support for attacks on infantry posts was the exception rather than the rule.' By the time some gun sections, supposedly working with the leading regiments, were coming to action, they were firing at ranges approaching two miles. Out of touch, some sections never caught up with the pursuit, a fault attributed mostly to the 'officer in charge of the guns' and battery commanders. The document stated that the RHA must move faster to limber up and take opportunities to get forward. The guns should be in sight of the objective and assaulting troops, and reserves should not be used solely when the advance was held up. Lastly, forward sections must 'move in close support of the advance for the engagement of machine guns, etc., at short range'. In short, more daring was required: 'the pursuit demands and allows risks not admissible in other circumstances.'[31]

The second further debate on performance took place during a conference held at Cavalry Corps HQ on Thursday 19 September.[32] It had a similar but narrower tactical focus. Identified were a number of important areas to be addressed concerning the pursuit. These included getting commanders as far forward as possible, passing information to rear units faster by adding more motor cyclists to each regiment and brigade, and giving and acting on orders more swiftly. Also recognized was the need to take more risks in using reserves earlier and, in essence, simply getting faster at preparing to move. Three major edicts were thought necessary. First, troops (i.e. combined forces, not small cavalry units) were to be allocated specific tactical objectives without stipulating their attack by frontal assault. Second, neighbouring formations should not be constrained by map boundaries if crossing them facilitated the advance to their objective. Third, armoured cars should advance by bounds, have definite objectives and not advance long distances unsupported. In general, it was felt that the 'closest co-operation between Armoured Cars and Cavalry is necessary'. Training would focus on 'dealing with M.Gs. by fire and movement' and patrols operating not invariably at full speed but rather advancing by bounds for economy of effort and 'horse flesh'. It is the concept, design and direction of these training schemes, and their analysis by the officers in command, against which the actions of the Cavalry Corps before the Selle (and Haig's grasp of the situation which faced him), must be considered. His distilled thoughts are evident in the plan for operations beyond the Hindenburg Positions.

On 21 September, Saturday, Haig told the Secretary of State for War, Lord Milner, that '*every available man should be put into battle at once*' for a chance to obtain a decision in 1918.[33] On the same day, he held one of the frequent conferences with his army commanders to discuss the imminent assault on the Hindenburg Line. Here it was agreed that 'the objective of the main British effort will be the line Valenciennes – Le Cateau – Wassigny'.[34] (This was known to the Germans as the Hermann Position.) It was not until 22 September, Sunday, the day that he issued the general orders for the assault on the main Hindenburg system,[35] that Haig gave his considered opinion on the cavalry training scheme of 17 September.[36]

To the green fields beyond[37]

The C-in-C did not add greatly to previous tactical debates on the manoeuvres but stressed the need for fire and movement, for the use of all-arms, for speed, for complete reconnaissance, for close or at least closer support and for decisive command. It is not absolutely certain to which audience his comments were addressed. It is clear, however, that he was speaking only to Kavanagh and Rawlinson when he stated the need 'to act boldly, quickly and to accept risks, but the result of risks thus accepted should promise to have a direct influence on the decision of the battle and, perhaps, of the campaign'. In this statement, Haig emphasized that responsibility for the decision to release the cavalry would lie with his subordinates, reminding all concerned that the overriding objective was to get to grips with the bulk of a retreating enemy. He was in no doubt that the Cavalry Corps would prove the decisive force on the battlefield, saying 'The problem before us is not one of screening an advance, but that of a *vigorous offensive against certain definite objectives*'.[38]

Specific aims for the Cavalry Corps were given one week later: to pass 'through the Fourth Army as soon as the enemy's defences on the line MONTBREHAIN – BEAUREVOIR have been captured', by which was meant the Beaurevoir or Hindenburg Reserve Line.[39] Rawlinson's temporary control of the Cavalry Corps would then cease and it was to 'operate independently under the orders of GHQ'; that is, under the control of Haig himself.[40] The orders conclude with three main objectives: to move towards Le Cateau and Busigny capturing the respective rail junctions, to co-operate with Third and Fourth Armies and attack the enemy flank and rear and to cut enemy communications about Valenciennes.

These orders were explained personally to Kavanagh and his Chief of Staff, Brigadier-General Archibald 'Sally' Home, over lunch at GHQ on 29 September. It was predicted that the Corps would come into action the next day.[41] An expectant and confident Kavanagh was here informed that the decision to launch the Corps would be his, not Rawlinson's.[42] The opportunity would not present itself until the second week in October.

The pursuit: 9 October

In the last week of September, and the first week of October 1918, the Germans were finally, and completely, evicted from their Hindenburg Line defences.

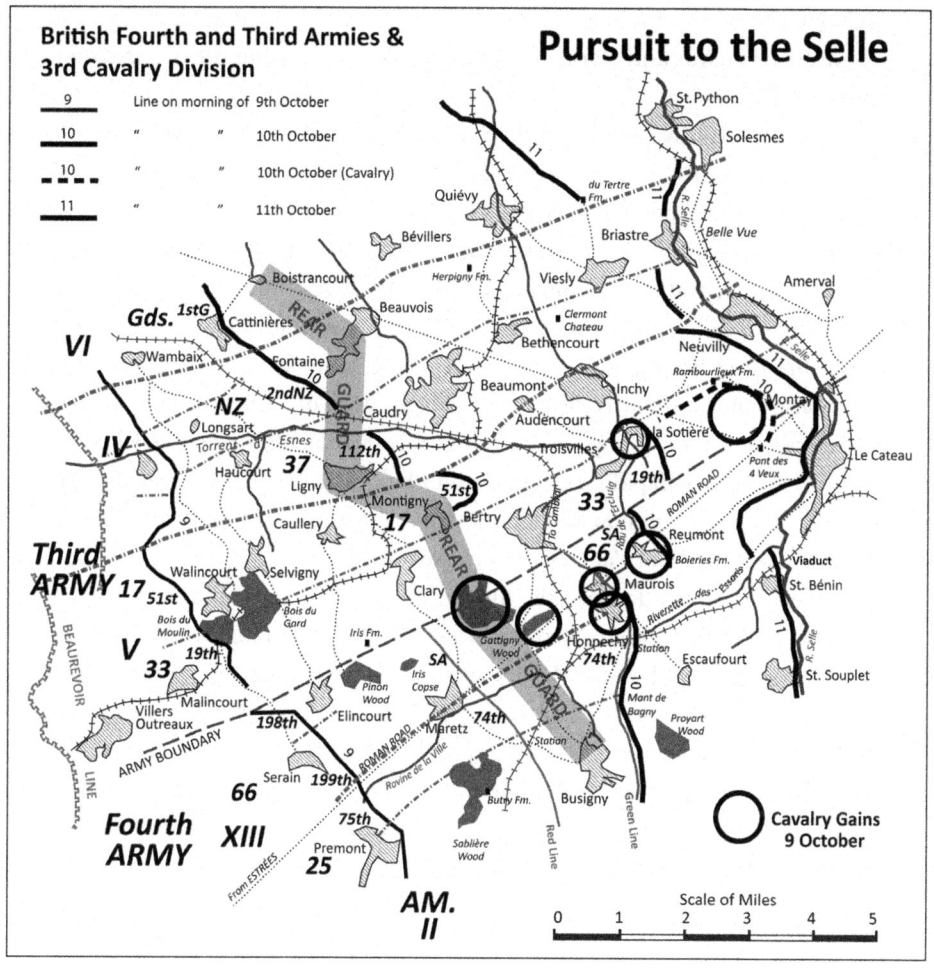

During the early hours of 9 October the enemy opposite Fourth Army began a covert, orderly retirement to the Hermann Position, leaving rearguards in a wide band of 'centres of resistance' about three miles from the BEF start lines which, as it happened, formed a 'rearguard zone' about a half-mile beyond the Fourth Army's initial objectives for that day.[43] No surprise, then, that the 66th (2nd East Lancashire) Division, on that Army's left flank, encountered little opposition in covering the two and a half miles to its first objectives.[44] 3rd Cavalry Division was in close touch. Its 6 Cavalry Brigade advanced south, and the Canadian Cavalry Brigade north of the Roman Road,[45] while flanking formations also moved forward. Immediately to their left 33rd Division, operating on the far right (south) of Third Army – and without a barrage – got on quickly. By 11.00, its advanced guards and a brigade of field artillery assisted in the occupation of most of Clary.

Both infantry divisions were then pinned down by artillery and machine-gun fire from Gattigny Wood. The Canadian Cavalry Brigade, deploying their own machine guns and horse artillery, and with two armoured cars, launched a mounted attack on the wood from north and south. The capture of the feature was completed, and 230 prisoners, a 5.9-inch howitzer and 40 machine guns taken, by 11.45.[46] Mobile once more, 66th Division advanced and, coming under fire from Bertry, which was in the Third Army area, ignored formation boundaries and summarily cleared the village ahead of 33rd Division (who did not move until relief troops arrived at 14.00). Kavanagh now received orders to 'push forward as rapidly as possible on LE CATEAU and after reaching that place . . . carry out mission already allotted . . . by the C-in-C',[47] namely cutting communications about Valenciennes to the north-east.

Kavanagh decided to seize the high ground at Honnechy – Maurois and at 14.00 6 Cavalry Brigade attacked Honnechy, alongside a simultaneous Canadian cavalry assault on Maurois. As 6 Cavalry Brigade, advancing to the assault, passed through 74 Infantry Brigade, which had been held up near Maretz since 11.00, the latter rose and followed on. Both attacks were completed sometime around 14.40 by which time 66th Division had reached its final objective and the Germans were retiring in numbers. 6 and Canadian Cavalry brigades were then ordered to capture Reumont and two spurs: east towards St. Bénin and north towards la Sotière, both objectives being held in force. With la Sotière under attack to the north-east, a rush against Troisvilles by 33rd Division (having been able to go straight through Bertry unhindered – see above), inflicted heavy casualties on the enemy and enabled direct observation of the Inchy – Le Cateau road. 4.5-inch howitzers were quickly brought to bear on the packed columns of retreating troops travelling along it.

By 16.30 the Canadian Cavalry had completed the capture of Reumont and la Sotière, having captured 30 prisoners and used *arme blanche* weapons – that is, the sword – to kill numerous enemy.[48] 6 Cavalry Brigade were held up at the line of St. Souplet, Reumont, and withdrew to support when their ground was occupied by 66th Division. 7 Cavalry Brigade came up, pushing a patrol forward to overlook Le Cateau, and two armoured cars entered the town, reporting it still in German hands. It was getting dark when the Canadian Cavalry Brigade pushed on another mile to take the high ground before Montay. The Canadians stayed in the front line overnight while 7 Cavalry Brigade was relieved by the Corps Cyclists who arrived at 18.15.[49]

Since the morning of 8 October the Cavalry Corps had suffered 605 casualties in men, of which seven officers and 77 other ranks were fatalities. Horse casualties were approximately 1,300 which represented about 8 per cent of the combined horseflesh of the two cavalry divisions. The operations of 9 October were mainly undertaken by 3rd Cavalry Division whose losses were 338 men wounded, and four officers and 53 other ranks killed. More than 500 prisoners had been taken together with over 60 machine guns and ten 'guns'.[50]

Postscript: 10–17 October

On 10 October the morning mist rendered air observation impossible. At 06.00 7 Cavalry Brigade relieved the Canadian Cavalry Brigade, having received orders the night before that their previous objective, Valenciennes, stood.[51] Patrols scouting north-eastwards drew severe fire and the brigade suffered significant losses when it crested the ridge before the Selle.

After retiring to Troisvilles, additional patrols were sent further north along the Selle river, but found the course between Neuvilly and Briastre, and the village of Viesly (west of Briastre), strongly defended. At 13.50 Kavanagh was granted permission to retire. Further south, at dusk, 5 Cavalry Brigade withdrew their final advanced troops from Vaux Andigny to Bohain. They had been unable to make any further gains. The pursuit was over and the Cavalry Corps' actions were at an end.

Between 10 and 16 October the British formations flanking Le Cateau wheeled into position along the line of the Selle, a manoeuvre which, for the most part, was complete by 12 October. It was not until 17 October, however, that supplies, materials, ammunition, artillery and tanks, were brought up in sufficient quantities to enable a prepared assault across the Selle to take place. Not only had munitions, etc. to be brought over ten miles, it was across rolling countryside, which although generally unspoiled, was crossed by thoroughly broken communications. Whereas they had been surprised by the attack on 8 October, the orderly withdrawal of the following night and day had enabled the Germans to destroy the intervening road and rail network most effectively. This hampered the pursuit and ensured that supplies had to be moved by horse, mule and on foot. The engineers spent the pause in operations split between efforts to repair road and rail links, dismantling delay-action mines and preparing many bridges to be thrown across the river.[52]

Conclusion

Just three weeks previously, 3rd Cavalry Division had been practicing, semi-successfully, against machine guns represented by chalk arrows and football rattles.[53] Now they had repeated the exercise for real. The Canadian Cavalry Brigade in particular had demonstrated the skilful use of fire, movement and tactical awareness which Haig demanded. The Canadians' seizure of the high ground between Rambourlieux Farm and Pont des Quatre Veux, their successive deployment of machine guns and horse artillery in the attacks on Gattigny Wood, Maurois, Reumont and la Sotière, their employment of dismounted troops and the shock of mounted assaults at the gallop, had carried the day. Likewise the all-arms attack on Honnechy, including 6 Cavalry Brigade[54] at the gallop, under a prepared barrage and supported in force by 74 Infantry Brigade and armoured cars,[55] was completed quickly even under heavy shell and machine-gun fire. In all of the day's cavalry actions speed had been required and achieved. It is impossible to imagine that cyclists could have done as well, even if supporting field artillery had been able to get forward along cratered roads further obstructed by downed bridges.[56]

The Canadian Cavalry Brigade had been excused 'remedial' battle practice in Haig's September training scheme. It did not need it. In the capture of Moreuil Wood on 30 March 1918 it demonstrated a high level of competence in the utilization of motor machine-gun units and horse artillery, and in both mounted and dismounted action.[57] This contrasted with other units in 1st and 3rd Cavalry Divisions during the spring crisis.[58] Haig's pursuit plan was conceived and critiqued in part on the basis that the Canadians had got it right in March. Who better, therefore, to deploy the Canadians against Gattigny Wood, where they again 'killed many Germans with the sword'[59] than Major-General A. E. W. Harman? As acting commander of 3rd Cavalry Division (he had replaced Major-General John Vaughan on 5 May 1918)[60] Harman proved to be an adept commander of combined cavalry and infantry units on at least two occasions. On 23 March, during the (mainly dismounted) actions of the cavalry in the first German spring offensive, Harman was placed in command of a joint force of 700 cavalrymen and 600 infantry from various units, together with some machine-gunners, in what became known as 'Harman's Detachment'.[61] This unit remained detached throughout the month, fighting variously with British and French forces around Ham and Roye.[62] The next month Harman was given leave to use 'Pompey' Elliott's 15 Australian Brigade as he saw fit in the defence of Villers-Bretonneux on 4–5 April, a move which no doubt impressed the fiery Australian.[63]

Edmonds' narrative of events of the pursuit,[64] and the sketches showing the disposition of First, Third and Fourth Armies overnight on 9/10 October 1918,[65] reveal that the advance of all three Armies had stalled in or before the rearguard zone,[66] with one exception. The 3rd Cavalry Division had *pulled* the infantry of 66th and 33rd Divisions five miles through and beyond the rearguard zone. At the end of the day, however, the Cavalry Corps made an error of strategic importance. Since 29 September Kavanagh's focus had been the attainment of Le Cateau and the disruption of enemy communications about Valenciennes, to the north-east.[67] All patrols in the afternoon and evening of 9 October, and even on the morning of 10 October, probed north-east into, demonstrably, the most heavily defended localities and highest troop concentrations (a result of German formations being bottled up by the severing of the main road into Le Cateau). No scouts had gone south or south-east. Edmonds, an accomplished military engineer, specifically directed attention to this part of the Hermann Position in his note regarding 9 October.[68]

This potentially open two-and-a-half mile stretch of the River Selle may have revealed a crossing point. More importantly, in the middle of the 'gap' was St. Bénin and its viaduct, probably not demolished until midday on 10 October at the earliest.[69] While the destruction of the viaduct caused significant problems for the infantry assault on 17 October,[70] it may be left to another engineer to explain the consequences of missing an opportunity to save this critical rail crossing.

> In the last week before the Armistice [the Fourth] Army advanced another twenty-five miles, but the destroyed viaduct at St. Bénin held up any advance of rails. At the date of the Armistice the only reliable railheads for the Fourth Army were fifty miles behind the armistice line and, owing to the state of the roads, *horse transport* was being used to carry the loads forward.[71]

This had been no Megiddo; the German armies were not routed and fleeing into death-trap defiles. There was to be no decisive war-shortening last effort by the Cavalry Corps. But Kavanagh's men had come very close. The Cavalry Corps' achievement was to prove that modern cavalrymen had been up to the challenge of taking on the rearguards in centres of resistance. They and their commanders in the field had taken the initiative and exploited success, pulling the infantry advance after them. In open warfare the Cavalry Corps had demonstrated that the bold application of speed, shock and stealth could win.

Sir Douglas Haig had the foresight to understand the realities of mobile warfare in late 1918, and it was Haig who prepared the only arm of exploitation he had to make the most of it.[72] As has so often been levelled as an accusation he was, after all, a *Cavalryman*.

Appendix

Pursuit to the Selle: Cavalry corps order of battle – 9 October 1918[73]

GOC   Lieut.-Gen. Sir C. T. McM. Kavanagh

    BGGS   ..   ..   Brig.-Gen. A. F. Home
    DA and QMQ   ..   ..   Brig.-Gen. J. C. G. Longmore
    GOCRA   ..   ..   Brig.-Gen. H. S. Seligman
    CRE   ..   ..   Lieut.-Col. W. H. Evans

Corps Cyclists
    XVIII Corps Cyclist Bn.

6 Squadron, RAF (RE8)

17th (Armoured Car) Tank Bn.

Corps Signal Troops
    Cavalry Corps Signal Sqn.
    Cavalry Corps Wireless Sqn.
    AD and 'GG' Cable Sections

Cavalry Corps Bridging Park, RE
Cavalry Corps Troops MT Co.

              4th Guards Brigade
              (Brig.-Gen. Hon. L. J. P. Butler)
              4th Bn., Grenadier Guards
              3rd Bn., Coldstream Guards
              1/1st Bn., Honourable Artillery Co.

              4th Guards Light Trench Mortar Battery
              A/58 Battery, RFA

              Household Machine Gun Brigade
    No.1 (1st Life Guards) Bn., Guards Machine Gun Regt.
    No.3 (Royal Horse Guards) Bn., Guards Machine Gun Regt.

Pursuit to the Selle: Cavalry corps order of battle – 9 October 1918

1st Cavalry Division   **Maj.-Gen R. L. Mullins**
    GSO1   ..   ..   Lieut.-Col. R. E. Cecil
    AA and QMG   ..   ..   Lieut.-Col. J. Blakiston-Houston

    1st Cavalry Brigade
    (Brig.-Gen. H. S. Sewell)
    2nd Dragoon Guards
    5th Dragoon Guards
    11th Hussars

    'I' Battery, RHA
    (6 × 13 pdr. Guns)
    1st Cavalry Machine Gun Sqn.

    1st Signal Troop

    2nd Cavalry Brigade
    (Brig.-Gen. A. Lawson)
    4th Dragoon Guards
    9th Lancers
    18th Hussars

    'H' Battery, RHA
    (6 × 13 pdr. Guns)
    2nd Cavalry Machine Gun Sqn.

    2nd Signal Troop

    9th Cavalry Brigade
    (Brig.-Gen. D'A. Legard)
    8th Hussars
    15th Hussars
    19th Hussars

    'Y' Battery, RHA
    (6 × 13 pdr. Guns)
    9th Cavalry Machine Gun Sqn.

    9th Signal Troop

  7th Brigade, RHA and Ammunition Column
  1st Field Squadron, RE
  1st Signal Squadron
  HQ 1st Cavalry Divisional RASC
  1st Cavalry Divisional MT Co.
  1st Cavalry Divisional Aux. (Horse) Co.
  1st, 3rd and 9th Cavalry Field Ambulances
  1st, 10th and 39th Mobile Veterinary Sections

Pursuit to the Selle: Cavalry corps order of battle – 9 October 1918

3rd Cavalry Division   Maj.-Gen. A. E. W. Harman
    GSO1 . . . . Lieut.-Col. G. P. L. Cosens
    AA and QMG . . . . Lieut.-Col. T. W. Pragnell

    6th Cavalry Brigade
    (Brig.-Gen. E. Paterson)
    3rd Dragoon Guards
    1st Royal Dragoons
    10th Hussars

    ―――――

    'C' Battery, RHA
    (6 × 13 pdr. Guns)
    6th Cavalry Machine Gun Sqn.

    6th Signal Troop

    7th Cavalry Brigade
    (Brig.-Gen. A. Burt)
    7th Dragoon Guards
    6th (Inniskilling) Dragoons
    17th Lancers

    ―――――

    'K' Battery, RHA
    (6 × 13 pdr. Guns)
    7th Cavalry Machine Gun Sqn.

    7th Signal Troop

    Canadian Cavalry Brigade
    (Brig.-Gen. R. W. Paterson)
    Royal Canadian Dragoons
    Lord Strathcona's Horse
    Fort Garry Horse

    ―――――

    Royal Canadian HA Brigade
    (two batteries of 4 × 13 pdr. guns)
    Canadian Cavalry Machine Gun Sqn.

    Canadian Signal Troop

    4th Brigade, RHA and Ammunition Column
    3rd Field Squadron, RE
    3rd Signal Squadron
    HQ 3rd Cavalry Divisional RASC
    3rd Cavalry Divisional MT Co.
    3rd Cavalry Divisional Aux. (Horse) Co.
    6th, 7th and Canadian Cavalry Field Ambulances
    13th, 14th and 'A' Canadian Mobile Veterinary Sections

Notes

1. An earlier version of this essay was published in a private members journal as Justice, S.M. 'Behind the Lines: Sir Douglas Haig and the Cavalry Corps, September-October 1918', *Records: The Journal of the Douglas Haig Fellowship*, (14) (November 2010), pp. 36–55.
2. See, for example, Peter Simkins, 'Haig and the Army Commanders', in Brian Bond and Nigel Cave (eds), *Haig: A Reappraisal 70 Years On* (Barnsley: Pen and Sword, 1999), pp. 78–97; Robin Prior and Trevor Wilson, *Command on the Western Front: The Military Career of Sir Henry Rawlinson 1914–1918* (Barnsley: Pen and Sword, 2004 [1992]).
3. Simkins, 'Haig and the Army Commanders', p. 96.
4. Quoted in Gary Sheffield, *The Chief: Douglas Haig and the British Army* (London: Aurum, 2011), p. 319.
5. For these commanders see for example Simon Robbins, *British Generalship in the Great War: The Career of Sir Henry Horne (1861–1929)* (Farnham: Ashgate, 2010); Peter Simkins, 'Herbert Plumer', in Ian F. W. Beckett and Steven J. Corvi (eds), *Haig's Generals* (Barnsley: Pen and Sword, 2006), pp. 141–63; Jonathan Boff, *Winning and Losing on the Western Front: The British Third Army and the Defeat of Germany in 1918* (Cambridge: Cambridge University Press, 2012); Prior and Wilson, *Command*; and John Lee, 'William Birdwood', in Beckett and Corvi (eds), *Haig's Generals*, pp. 33–53.
6. See Appendix, 'Pursuit to the Selle: Cavalry Corps Order of Battle – 9 October 1918'.
7. J. E. Edmonds and R. Maxwell-Hyslop, *Military Operations, France and Belgium, 1918* vol. V: *26 September–11 November: the Advance to Victory* (London: HMSO, 1947) [hereafter *Military Operations 1918* vol. V.], p. 235.
8. V. John, 'The British Cavalry on the Western Front in 1918' (MA, University of Birmingham, 2007), p. 11 gives the sole example of recognizable cavalry action from this period in 1917 as that of two squadrons of 8th Hussars, supported by armoured cars and horse artillery; David Kenyon is more expansive in acknowledging a more significant, if sparse, contribution by the Corps in D. Kenyon, *Horsemen in No Man's Land: British Cavalry and Trench Warfare 1914–1918* (Barnsley: Pen and Sword, 2011), pp. 86–132.
9. The National Archives (TNA), WO 95/575 Cavalry Corps Papers: General Staff, 'OAD 347, Directive to Fourth Army, Fifth Army, Cavalry Corps (20 March 1917)'.
10. Sheffield, *The Chief*, p. 322 argues that Haig 'was asking too much of the ... [Cavalry Corps] in its current shrunken state'.
11. TNA, WO 95/575, 'OAD 900/4, Directive to Lieut-Gen Sir C.T. McM. Kavanagh, Commanding Cavalry Corps (29 July 1918)'.
12. Quoted in Simkins, 'Haig and the Army Commanders', p. 97.

13 TNA, WO 95/575, 'Memorandum: Instructions to Kavanagh and Maxse (6 September 1918)'.
14 A 'Field Inspection' entailed the observation of an elaborate training exercise with detailed goals and objectives.
15 *Field Service Regulations 1909 (Amended Edition), Part I (Operations)* (1914). Chapter VII, Section 112.
16 In the original version, handwritten by Haig for typing by Maj-Gen G. P. Dawnay (BGGS Staff Duties GHQ), and also present in TNA WO 95/575, Haig amended this to 'a fortnight' from 'the 20th Sept'. The assault on the main Hindenburg System (Siegfried I Stellung), that part of the Siegfried Position(s) in front of Fourth Army and the Cavalry Corps, took place on 29 September 1918. The Hindenburg Support and Reserve (Beaurevoir Line) Systems were not finally overcome until 5 October. For a description see J. P. Harris and Niall Barr, *Amiens to the Armistice: the BEF in the Hundred Days' Campaign, 8 August–11, November 1918* (London: Brassey's, 1998), pp. 232–5.
17 TNA, WO 95/575, 'Cavalry Manoeuvres (16 September 1918)' is a collection of documents gathered in nine discrete appendices.
18 Ibid. 'Appendix "A", General Idea'. This is clearly a reference to the Hindenburg positions (Siegfried Stellungen) and the sketchy defences of the Hermann Position from ten miles or so beyond the third, Hindenburg Reserve or Beaurevoir Line. See also Edmonds and Maxwell-Hyslop, *Military Operations 1918* vol. V, Note *II*. pp. 228–9.
19 Ibid. Appendix 'A' *Special Idea.* Author's italics.
20 34 Infantry Brigade was a unit of 11th Division, First Army, in the van of that army's advances south of the Sensée Canal on 9 October 1918. The Household Machine Gun Brigade consisted of 2nd (Life Guards), 3rd (Royal Horse Guards), 102nd (Lincolnshire and E. Riding Yeomanry) and 103rd (City and County of London Yeomanry) Battalions, Machine Gun Corps. The Motor Machine Gun Batteries were provided by No. 1 Motor Machine Gun Brigade and the armoured cars by 17th Tank (Armoured Car) Battalion.
21 Flying RE8 reconnaissance/bombers.
22 The instructions for units involved are contained in TNA, WO 95/575, 'Cavalry Manoeuvres 16/9/1918 Appendix "D" Cavalry Corps Special Instructions'. The composition of the Cavalry Corps (and opposing force) for the event is detailed in TNA, WO 95/575, 'Cavalry Manoeuvres 16/9/1918 Appendix "F" List of Units Taking Part in Operations'.
23 Kenyon, *Horsemen*, p. 217 argues that the time Haig as C-in-C devoted to 'this kind of micro-management is questionable'.
24 Library of the Royal Artillery Institution, Firepower!, Woolwich, London, Uniacke Papers, U/I/1, 'Nominal Roll of Officers served on, or attached to, Staff of the

Inspector General of Training in France 1918/19 (1919)'. Uniacke had been appointed DIT on 9 July 1918; he was formerly GOCRA Fifth Army.

25 TNA, WO 95/575, 'Cavalry Corps: General Staff War Diary January 1918 – March 1919 (17 September 1918 4:00 pm)'.
26 TNA, WO 95/575, 'Cavalry Manoeuvres 16/9/1918 Appendix "G", Instructions for Umpires (September 1918)'.
27 Ibid.
28 Ibid. This approach was not a departure from recommended tactics. For tactical debates within the British cavalry see S. Badsey, *Doctrine and Reform in the British Cavalry 1880–1918* (Aldershot: Ashgate, 2008) and Kenyon, *Horsemen in No Man's Land*.
29 Author's italics.
30 TNA, WO 95/575, 'Narrative and Criticism of Cavalry Corps Exercise, September 17th, 1918' (n.d.). All quotations and examples in this paragraph are taken from this document unless otherwise noted.
31 The corresponding wording in *FSR* is 'All pursuing troops should act with the greatest boldness, and be prepared to accept risks which would not be justifiable at other times' *FSR* part I, chapter VII, para. 112, point 4.
32 TNA, WO 95/575, 'Conference held at Headquarters Cavalry Corps, 19th September 1918'. All quotations and examples in this paragraph are taken from this document unless otherwise noted.
33 Haig's Diary, 21 September 1918 in Gary Sheffield and John Bourne (eds), *Douglas Haig: War Diaries and Letters, 1914–1918* (London: Weidenfeld and Nicholson, 2006), p. 463; emphasis in original. Haig had previously flagged up this point, and the urgent requirement for mobile troops, to Milner on 10 September. Haig's Diary 10 September 1918, in ibid., p. 458.
34 Haig's Diary, 21 September 1918, in ibid., p. 463.
35 OAD 932 (22 September 1918). Reproduced in Edmonds and Maxwell-Hyslop, *Military Operations 1918* vol. V, pp. 14–16.
36 TNA, WO 95/575, 'Remarks by the Commander-in-Chief on the Cavalry Exercise held on 17th of September, 1918 (22 September 1918)'.
37 Taken from a book chapter title, 'To the Green Fields Beyond', in A. J. Smithers, *A New Excalibur: The Development of the Tank 1909–1939* (London: Leo Cooper, 1986), pp. 189–99.
38 Haig's emphasis.
39 TNA, WO 95/575, OAD 928, 'Directive to GOCs First, Second, Third, Fourth, Fifth Armies, Cavalry Corps (29 September 1918)'. These orders remained in force throughout the coming actions before the Selle.
40 Ibid.
41 Haig's Diary 29 September 1918 in Sheffield and Bourne, *Douglas Haig*, p. 467.

42 Ibid.
43 Narrative fact in this passage is taken from Edmonds and Maxwell-Hyslop, *Military Operations 1918* vol. V, pp. 212–35 and associated sketches, unless otherwise noted. The retirement was also taking place opposite the French to the south, Third Army, and the right wing of First Army to the north. Edmonds does not supply a sketch of the Corps actions, which took place chiefly along the juncture between Fourth and Third Armies (3rd Cavalry Division). For clarity the author has re-arranged events in chronological, rather than formation order.
44 66th (2nd East Lancashire) Division did not arrive until about 11:00. Fog is given as one reason for delay but they also carried out the initial advance under cover of a creeping barrage.
45 The straight Roman Road from Estrées to Montay (Le Cateau) ran just south of the juncture between Fourth and Third Armies.
46 As an example this is more than the entire Motor Machine Gun Brigade in support of 3 Cavalry Division (36 machine guns).
47 TNA, WO 95/439, 'Urgent Operation Order G. 319 (9 October 1918, 11:45)'.
48 Library and Archives Canada, Volume 4956, Reel T-10772-10773, File: 496, 'Fort Garry Horse War Diary, October 1918: Appendix "A" – Narrative 9th October 1918'.
49 See Edmonds and Maxwell-Hyslop, *Military Operations 1918* vol. V, p. 235.
50 All statistics from TNA, WO 95/575, '*Narrative of Operations – 8th to 10th October 1918* (20 October 1918).
51 TNA, WO 95/439, 'Urgent Operation Order G. 322 (9 October 1918, 19:30)'. This order also confirmed the standing objectives for IX, XIII and AEF II Corps. For the Americans this remained the line, south to north, Molain – St. Souplet – St. Bénin.
52 H. A. Baker, 'History of the 7th Field Company, R.E., during the War, 1914–18', *The Royal Engineers Journal*, XLVI (December 1932), pp. 615–32; R. U. H. Buckland, 'Experiences at Fourth Army Headquarters: Organization and Work of the R.E.', *The Royal Engineers Journal* (September 1927), pp. 385–413; M. R. Caldwell, 'History of the 12th Company Royal Engineers (concluded)', *The Royal Engineers Journal*, XXXIX, 2 (June 1925), pp. 272–87.
53 TNA, 'WO 95/575, Cavalry Manoeuvres 16/9/1918 Appendix "G", Instructions for Umpires (September 1918)'.
54 It should be noted that this (cavalry) brigade was attacked from the air and massed machine guns from Escaufort with some success, having been forced to concentrate to go under a railway bridge while approaching the village: Edmonds and Maxwell-Hyslop, *Military Operations 1918* vol. V, pp. 217–18. Detail for the narrative in this section is drawn from this volume unless otherwise noted.
55 The armoured cars of the 17th Armoured Car Battalion, Tank Corps contributed significantly in most, if not all, of the Cavalry actions of 9 October.

56 As has been already noted, it was already dark before the supporting Corps cyclists caught up with the pursuit. In fact, none of the Corps supporting infantry units got forward enough to become engaged on 9 October. The Royal Engineers Squadron(s) repaired a large number of cratered roads and defused a number of roadside mines. See TNA, WO 95/575, Cavalry Corps Narrative of Operations 8–10 Oct 1918'.

57 See Andrew Iarocci, 'Engines of War: Horsepower in the Canadian Expeditionary Force, 1914–18', *Journal of the Society for Army Historical Research*, 87, 349 (2009), pp. 59–83. Moreuil Wood is covered in pp. 77–9 where 'many of the Germans were killed with the sword' (p. 77); See also John, 'The British Cavalry on the Western Front in 1918'.

58 For the most part the British cavalry forces, by brigade, had been forced to fight as 'Dismounted' units in March and April 1918.

59 Edmonds and Maxwell-Hyslop, *Military Operations 1918* vol. V, p. 218.

60 A. F. Becke, *Pt.1 – The Regular British Divisions* (London: HMSO, 1935), p. 17. For Vaughan, see his *Cavalry and Sporting Memories* (London: The Bala Press, 1954). He had served with Haig in the 7th Hussars.

61 J. E. Edmonds, *Military Operations, France and Belgium, 1918* vol. I: *The German March Offensive and its Preliminaries* (London: Macmillan, 1935), p. 334.

62 Ibid., pp. 498–9.

63 J. E. Edmonds, *Military Operations, France and Belgium, 1918 Vol II: March–April: Continuation of the German Offensive* (London: Macmillan, 1937), p. 127. Another perspective of this engagement is given in P. Simkins, '"The Absolute Limit": British Divisions at Villers Bretonneux, 1918' (unpublished paper, 1997). See in particular pp. 11–12.

64 Edmonds and Maxwell-Hyslop, *Military Operations 1918* vol. V, pp. 212–29.

65 See Edmonds and Maxwell-Hyslop, *Military Operations 1918* vol V. Sketch 16, *Third Army 8th–19th October 1918*. Sketch 17, *Fourth Army 9th–11th October 1918*. Sketch 18, *First Army Right Wing 8th–19th Oct. 1918*.

66 The Fourth Army was perched on the 'Green Line' or line of exploitation set for them prior to 9 October. The Third Army was largely stopped on or before their final pre-set objectives.

67 1st Cavalry Division is not mentioned in Edmonds' narrative. They were reported opposite Busigny (secondary objective) during the day. Busigny had been pulverized by the 12-inch and 14-inch guns until five hours after Zero.

68 That is, his note that aerial reconnaissance had shown there was no prepared position between Le Cateau and St. Souplet as late as 14 October. Edmonds and Maxwell-Hyslop, *Military Operations 1918* vol. V, pp. 212–29; note II, p. 229.

69 St. Bénin was in the American II Corps area. It was not captured (by XIII Corps) until the afternoon of 10 October. It was handed over to the American II Corps that night.

70 XIII Corps were to assault across the Selle at this point. The inundation forced the 50th (Northumbrian) Division south into the American zone and a narrow 600-yard frontage just to the north of St. Souplet from which to attempt the crossing. See also Joint Services Command and Staff College Archive, Shrivenham, UK, Montgomery-Massingberd Papers, 'Narrative of Operations, October 16th to 18th 1918' (n.d.).
71 H. L. Pritchard, *History of the Corps of Royal Engineers,* vol. 5: *The Home Front, France, Flanders and Italy in the First World War* (Chatham: Institution of Royal Engineers, 1952), p. 660; italics in original.
72 For an alternative view, see Kenyon, *Horsemen*, pp. 236–7.
73 Headquarters, Corps troops and 1st and 3rd Cavalry Divisions. 5th Cavalry Brigade (2nd Cavalry Division) under Brigadier-General N. W. Haig was attached to IX Corps, Fourth Army. The other 2nd Cavalry Division units were distributed between First, Second and Third Armies.

7

The Air Ministry and the Formation of the Royal Air Force

Peter Gray

The standard depiction of the formation of the Royal Air Force (RAF), and its subsequent fight for survival, rarely covers the bureaucratic context with its quest for a governmental entity capable of ordering *materiel*. It is relatively easy to conjure images of Zeppelins and Fokkers wreaking havoc, but the reality was underpinned by a more prosaic problem centred on administration and supply issues. This chapter aims to examine the formation of the RAF in this wider context.

From its inception in 1912, it was inevitable that there would be competition between the component parts of the 'Flying Corps' (consisting of a 'Naval Wing, a Military Wing, and a Central Flying School for the training of pilots') for resources and over operational policy issues.[1] This 'marital bliss of 1912 was, however, short-lived' when the Naval Wing became the Royal Naval Air Service (RNAS) and its Military counterpart, the Royal Flying Corps (RFC).[2] Further major change towards a unified air entity would require the impact of Jackson and Bramall's harbingers of change: defeat, cost and public opinion.[3] For military aviation, these came to a head at the end of 1915 and into 1916 at the height of the so-called Fokker scourge.[4] This represented a sufficiently serious defeat to have been able to convince people that 'something was seriously wrong with our air administration and that nothing short of radical change would set it right'.[5] The effects of the 'Fokker scourge' were exacerbated by the apparent impunity with which the German Zeppelins were able to drop their bomb loads on British targets.[6] These raids caused two, quite specific, reactions from the public that would have far-reaching consequences for the organization of air power in the interwar years. The first of these was the outcry that the raids should be stopped by interception prior to the planes reaching London (in particular); and the second was the demand that Germany should suffer similar treatment.[7] The debate, in Parliament in particular, was inflamed by the use of high rhetoric with, for example, accusations that RFC pilots were being 'murdered by the government' in having been sent to fly in substandard machines.[8] Inevitably, the furore was taken up by Lord Northcliffe and his *Daily Mail*.[9]

Although technological developments were in the 'pipe-line' to defeat the 'Fokker scourge', the momentum for change was too great and the government set in place an enquiry under the chairmanship of Mr Justice Baihache KC to investigate the perceived 'maladministration'.[10] In practice, this enquiry made little headway with the Admiralty refusing to give evidence and a collective lack of support for its aims.[11] In parallel with this enquiry, the Joint Air War Committee was set up in March 1916 under the chairmanship of the Earl of Derby (who was not in the Cabinet at the time, but 'would have the closest possible contact with it');[12] its main objective was to tackle the competition between the Army and the Royal Navy for aircraft which Hankey (as Secretary to the CID) described as a 'matter of utmost difficulty' and over the limited output of engines as 'almost a scandal'.[13] Internal disagreements prevented this entity ever functioning.[14] The crucial factor, however, was the Committee had no executive powers with which to force one side or the other to concede hard won ground.[15] It was therefore replaced by an Air Board under the chairmanship of Lord Curzon (Leader of the House of Lords). The unsatisfactory state of affairs continued with both Services ordering their own material without consultation, and frequently without even informing the Air Board.[16] The acrimony was described by Lloyd George as follows:

> When Lord Curzon put forward his plan along these lines [for the formation of a department with the sole and complete control over production of machinery for aerial warfare], he was in turn challenged by Mr. Balfour [First Lord of the Admiralty] in a very caustic and amusing memorandum. To this Lord Curzon replied in suitable terms. It was clear that if the controversy did not conduce to the provision of aeroplanes it at least provided excellent entertainment for those who were privileged to read these documents and to hear the discussions.[17]

Furthermore, it is evident that the Prime Minister (Asquith) was unwilling to bring the matter to a head.[18] It has nevertheless been suggested that by dogged determination, and continuing to exist, Curzon's Air Board set a blueprint for future co-ordinated aircraft supply which could be taken forward by its successor.[19] For future generations, the legacy of Curzon's 'bludgeon' (against Balfour's rapier) was the gradual attrition of the Admiralty's grip on air policy.[20] In effect, Curzon took on Trenchard's line that the RNAS should concentrate on work with the Fleet while the RFC did everything over the land (including strategic bombing and the possible reprisals demanded by public opinion).[21]

The lack of formal standing of Curzon's Air Board was remedied in the New Ministries and Secretaries Bill, which became law on 22 December 1916, and provided that the President of the Board 'shall be deemed to be a Minister appointed under this Act' and hence the Air Board became a Ministry.[22] But as Spaight went on to point out, this Act did more than give statutory existence to the old board; it became a real Ministry, albeit one with limited powers.[23] Furthermore, Curzon was at pains to suggest that this new Ministry would be permanent, and not just for the duration of hostilities. The membership of the new Board was set out in an Order in Council of 6 February 1917 with Lord Cowdray (an industrialist who had been a Liberal MP and was made Viscount Cowdray in order to take this post) at its head; the powers ascribed to the Board have been described as 'elastic'.[24] To some extent this, along with the transfer of responsibility for production to the Ministry of Munitions reduced the chaos, and friction, over the supply of aircraft and engines.[25] Indeed, the Air Board, and its growing staff in the Hotel Cecil (on the Strand, but now demolished), became something of a supply ministry with added responsibility for personnel and general administration.[26] But there was a critical gap in the field of policy, in particular in the balance between air defence and offence.[27]

The major accusations against the efficiency, or relevance, of the Cowdray Board stemmed from its apparent inability to prosecute raids against Germany or, as events were about to show, to defend London against German attacks.[28] The attack by German Gotha bombers on 7 July 1917 on London, 'without any effective challenge', inevitably caused considerable concern.[29] The ensuing debate in both Houses of Parliament covered the now traditional issues of retribution and improved home defence.[30] Accordingly, Lloyd George decided that, although the House had broadly accepted his explanation that the Army in France came first, he considered that 'we must go far more thoroughly into the matter, with a view to ensuring the best possible use of the air weapon alike and for defence'.[31] Lloyd George had also developed a marked distrust of his military advisers and used the opportunity to 'break the strategic stranglehold of the military command'.[32] He therefore set up a formal committee consisting of himself and Lieutenant-General Jan Smuts who was to confer with representatives from the Admiralty, the General Staff, Commander-in-Chief Home Forces and 'such other experts as we might desire'.[33] Smuts produced two reports for the War Cabinet and the literature deals with his progress in considerable detail.[34] Smuts' Second Report (Committee on Air Organisation and Home Defence Against Air Raids (2nd Report) dated 17 August 1917) denounced the Air Board as being 'merely a Conference'.[35] Smuts emphasized that although the Board had 'nominal authority to discuss questions of policy, it had no real power to do so'.[36]

Smuts' report then went on to contrast (as opposed to the normal practice of drawing parallels in the functions of) the Air Service with the use of artillery; in this he emphasized that the air arm could 'conduct extensive operations far from, and independently of, both Army and Navy'.[37] This ability, and arguably desirability, of independent operations was to become a cornerstone of Trenchard and his Air Ministry's rhetoric for the period up to the formation of Bomber Command. Smuts acknowledged that the 'subjection' of the Air Board and service could be justified in its infancy, but saw every reason why it should now be raised to the status of an 'independent Ministry in control of its own war service'.[38] The report also considered that the 'maintenance of three Air Services is out of the question'.[39] Of the eight specific recommendations in the report, number two is important for the context of the organization that was subsequently to evolve. It recommended that:

> under the Air Ministry an Air Staff be instituted on the lines of the Imperial General Staff responsible for the working out of war plans, the direction of operations, the collection of intelligence, and the training of the air personnel; that this Staff be equipped with the best brains and practical experience available in our present Air Services, and that by periodical appointment to the Staff of officers with great practical experience from the front, due provision be made for the development of the Staff in response to the rapid advance of this new service.[40]

The War Cabinet discussed the report a week later and accepted the recommendations of the report, despite a lengthy discussion initiated by the First Lord of the Admiralty (Geddes) who was prepared to accept the new Ministry, but wanted to keep the RNAS intact within the Admiralty.[41] This viewpoint was one that would return, with considerable vigour, in the interwar years with direct connotations for the future of the new service and its component commands.

In addition to accepting the recommendations, the War Cabinet appointed a further Committee, under Smuts' chairmanship, to bring the new service into being and prepare the necessary legislation 'for submission to Parliament at the earliest possible date'.[42] The new Committee proceeded with its work reporting to the War Cabinet on a regular basis and finally recommended that the legislation was ready at the meeting on 6 November 1917.[43] The Air Force (Constitution) Bill became law on 29 November 1917 and had two 'remarkable characteristics'.[44] The first was that the 'Air Force Act' under which the discipline of the new service would be based, and its commanding officers empowered, was merely a schedule to the 'Constitution Act'; this made it the only Act on the Statute Book with no date and the only one to have entered law by this unorthodox means.[45] The second issue would have more significance as the new organization took shape in that it was largely an 'enabling measure' providing a structure around which the real detail would be added by Orders in Council.[46] In the House of Lords, Lord Curzon acknowledged that it was 'a skeleton upon which the flesh and blood will have to be reared as time goes on'.[47] As Spaight has emphasized, the debates in Parliament showed clear intent that the new Air Council was to be a permanent fixture and not there merely for the duration of the War.[48] The Lord Privy Seal (the Earl of Crawford) stated in his opening address that:

> Aircraft can no longer be regarded as a sub-department of the Admiralty or of the War Office. The air is one. It is a unity, far more than the sea is and a hundred times more than the land is.[49]

Although the intent of Parliament was clear, especially to a lawyer like Spaight, it would not prevent the Admiralty from returning to the fray. The Air Council was based on the Army model, not least because it was 'thoroughly well understood by the vast majority of the officers concerned'.[50] Furthermore, Major Baird, the Under-Secretary of State for Air, detailed the role and responsibilities of the Chief of the Air Staff (CAS) as being:

> The Chief of the Air Staff is charged with advising His Majesty's Government as to the conduct of air operations in all questions of air policy affecting the security of the Empire, including Home defence. He is further charged with liaison with the Allies, with the Admiralty, and with the Army Council as regards policy, operations, and intelligence.[51]

The first part of this requirement was self-explanatory, but the second element stressed the key role of senior leaders in managing the interfaces between their organization and those others with which they must make common endeavour.[52]

One of the other key facets of leadership at the highest levels is the requirement that an organization must be fit for purpose. In this context, the building blocks were theoretically in place. Nevertheless, even the most perfect organization (if such a thing exists) can only function as well as the personalities (and egos) allow it so to do, especially when the system is under stress. In the case of the embryo RAF, Lloyd George singularly failed to recruit a workable 'top team' and the inevitable strife ensued.[53] Notwithstanding the turbulence over Secretaries of State and the resignation of Trenchard from his post as CAS, the Air Ministry sought, not only to find suitable accommodation, but also to build an Air Staff along the lines of that in the War Office.[54] Given that one of the reasons for the establishment of the new Ministry was to allow air policy to be formed outside the traditional bastions of the Admiralty and the War Office where it had been subservient to the demands of the parent services, it is not surprising to see moves towards this end. Sir William Weir replaced Lord Rothermere as Secretary of State on 25 April 1918 and was to 'prove to be a dedicated proponent of the doctrine of strategic air power'.[55] Trenchard had been replaced by Major-General Sykes as CAS and one of Weir's first acts was to force Trenchard into accepting command of the Independent Force in France.[56]

The Independent Force[57]

Although Weir and his new CAS were keen advocates of the strategic potential of air power, their thinking was based more on intuition than on established, or detailed theoretical work.[58] Sykes came into post acknowledging that the 'final blow against a great land power must be the Army', but victory 'could be won with the assistance of an overwhelming strategical [sic] bombing force'.[59] The detailed strategy was to follow and was to be embellished as time went on, not least to justify the continued existence of the RAF and its potential for independent offensive air operations. The reality at the time was that the government had long been under remit from public opinion to take the air war to the German people as retaliation. Sykes saw the role of the new entity as being 'to strike far, wide and hard at the enemy's manufacturing centres, submarine bases and communications' and pressed on with his 'cherished project'.[60]

It should not, however, be imagined that work on this scheme only commenced when Weir and Sykes took office. In October 1917, when the War Cabinet discussed the 'forthcoming offensive', reference was made to the great and growing demand on the part of the British public for retaliation. The War Cabinet:

> Approved the arrangements outlined above in regard to machines and objectives, and the Prime Minister impressed on General Trenchard the importance of

making a success of the forthcoming air offensive, having regard to the effect that such a success would have on the *moral* [sic] of the people at home.[61]

The scheme was based on the deployment of two squadrons (one for day and the other for night operations) to Ochey (near Nancy) under the command of Colonel Newall (later to become CAS). Targets were to include the 'Lorraine iron-works, and, when conditions were favourable, Mannheim and Stuttgart'.[62] Notwithstanding the Prime Minister's direction to Trenchard, the withdrawal of the aircraft from Haig's offensive (Third Ypres – 'Passchendaele') sparked immediate protest from the Chief of the Imperial General Staff (CIGS) and further debate in the War Cabinet.[63] The reality within Newall's 8th Brigade was that the demands from the Army were such that priority was given to communications targets behind German lines (in France) and aerodromes near the lines.[64]

Matters improved little when Trenchard took command of the Force on 6 June 1918, not least because German defences continued to exact a heavy toll on the bombers necessitating diversion of resources into attacking the defenders' airfields.[65] In his final despatch (dated 1 January 1919), Trenchard had seen his two real alternatives as being:

1. A sustained and continuous attack on one large centre after another until each centre was destroyed, and the industrial population largely dispersed to other towns; or
2. To attack as many of the large industrial centres as it was possible to reach with the machines at my disposal.[66]

Trenchard chose the latter option largely because of the small numbers of aircraft and their limitations 'imposed on long-range bombing by the weather'.[67] Trenchard further justified his choice:

> By attacking as many centres as could be reached, the moral effect [sic] was first of all very much greater, as no town felt safe, and it necessitated continued and thorough defensive measures on the part of the enemy to protect the many different localities over which my force was operating. At present the moral effect of bombing stands undoubtedly to the material effect in a proportion of 20 to 1, and therefore it was necessary to create the greatest moral effect possible.[68]

It is an interesting postscript to this despatch to note that Weir, whose term as Secretary of State was limited to the duration of the war at his own request, had advised Trenchard to keep the 'final operational despatch educational for the benefit of the armchair critics'; Weir also shared his own views of the success of the Force.[69] The clear implication was that Weir saw Trenchard returning to high office and was keen that he should not burn his boats.

It is a difficult task to analyse the effectiveness of any bomber offensive, even one as limited in scale as that carried out by the Independent Force. In the first instance, the desired effect has to be plainly stated. If the rationale for the Force was merely retaliatory then the very fact that it was formed and operated may be said to have implied success. Measuring the effect on enemy morale was (and is) all the more difficult. It is instructive to note the views of those directly involved in this limited offensive action. Trenchard was unequivocal and trenchant in his private views:

> Thus the Independent Force comes to an end. A more gigantic waste of effort and personnel there has never been in any war.[70]

Although these words from Trenchard's (private) diary written on 11 November 1918 have been widely quoted, it could be argued that they reflect his personal frustration at finishing the War in what he perceived to be an operational backwater, rather than directing the main force in support of Haig's army. Furthermore, his attitude belies the fact that much of the Force's activities were in support of the army either against communications targets or enemy airfields. While there may have been some efficiencies had the force operated within Salmond's organization (what had been the RFC in France under Trenchard for much of the War), these could hardly be described as 'gigantic'. According to his biographer, Salmond's view was that the war would have been won and lost on the north-western front and that the army needed the support of every aircraft that could be used.[71] In his defence of his strategy, Sykes was at pains to point out that he was working to Cabinet direction and that it was not his role to demur from this.[72] He went on to say that the 'sudden emergencies' would have been catered for by the switch of resources.[73] Sykes was also keen to elaborate on the strategy. His autobiography was published in 1942 in which he defended his actions from criticism in Slessor's work *Air Power and Armies*.[74] Sykes effectively said that even if the 'sole object of war is the destruction of the enemy's army', then destruction of armaments factories, fuel supplies and communications were perfectly valid aims.[75] Given the animosity between Trenchard and Sykes, there is a risk that the former's language had more to do with their clash than the reality of the situation; by the same token, Sykes had clear views on 'Trenchard's predilection for the tactical offensive'.[76] The implication in this is that Sykes saw himself as the more clear-sighted, especially with hindsight.

In terms of the wider literature in assessing the operational effectiveness of the Independent Force, the Official History was predictably upbeat about its performance and defended Trenchard in particular for his prioritization of airfield targets in that his organic assets were all that were available for the task.[77] The *War in the Air* also confirmed that the results justified Trenchard's policy.[78] The debate among scholars is interesting because it reflected (and continues to reflect) debates which were to recur over the effectiveness of the strategic air offensive against Germany in the Second World War. Although C. G. Grey only dealt with the Force in passing, he implied that it had value purely because its operations were independent of the War Office and the Admiralty.[79] Furthermore, because they were directed from the Air Ministry, these operations were, in theory, independent of Haig; but in practice, Trenchard could be relied upon to work very clearly within his erstwhile master's intent. As a keen advocate of the potential of strategic bombing, Jones lamented the lack of opportunity for the Force to prove itself and, by implication, was critical of the commanders for being insufficiently far-sighted in applying the necessary resources and thus not exploiting the possible advantages, instead choosing to fight an air war which favoured the Germans.[80] Cooper was altogether more pragmatic emphasizing the practical and technological limitations of the aircraft, their ordnance and the ability of the crews to bomb accurately by day and especially by night.[81] He highlighted the delays that occurred in production, but is sceptical about the impact on morale.[82] Webster and Frankland have stressed in the introduction to their four-volume contribution to the Official History of the Second World War, *The Strategic Air Offensive against Germany 1939–1945*, that the Independent Force was 'no more than aspiration. Its significance was in the future, not in the struggle of 1918'.[83]

This review of the Independent Force not only provided the precedents for many of the historiographical debates that were to follow the strategic air offensive in the Second World War, but it also set the tone for the often heated discussions that were to follow in Whitehall in the aftermath of the First World War and through into interwar years. The immediate months saw Churchill, as Secretary of State for War and Air, unceremoniously bundle Sykes off to be Controller of Civil Aviation 'and console him with a GBE'.[84] Trenchard was then in post as CAS from 1919 to 1930 and oversaw, first the survival of the new Service, and then its development towards the organization that would police the Empire, win the Battle of Britain and wage the strategic air offensive against Germany. Other air arms would follow the example of the RAF in attempting to gain independence from other services. It is not surprising that rivalry between navies and armies could have hugely damaging consequences in operational terms if the quarrels were not stamped upon. It is, however, somewhat ironic that the deep issues behind the formation of the first independent air arm stemmed from bureaucratic wrangling that the government of the day failed to control.

Notes

1. Walter Raleigh and H. A. Jones, *The War in the Air: Being the Story of the part played in the Great War by the Royal Air Force*, vol. I (Oxford: Clarendon Press, 1922), p. 198. See also H. A. Jones, 'The Birth of the Royal Air Force', *Journal of the Royal United Services Institution [JRUSI]* 83 (1938), p. 1 who cited the original wording from the Haldane Report of February 1912. From a historiographical viewpoint, Raleigh's opening volume of the Official History of the Royal Air Force has not been much praised and it is interesting that his co-author should publish this piece in the *JRUSI*. See Malcolm Cooper, *The Birth of Independent Air Power: British Air Policy in the First World War* (London: Allen and Unwin, 1986), p. xvii.
2. F. F. G. 'The Royal Air Force- Administration, Organization and Direction' *JRUSI* 82 (1937), p. 89.
3. General Sir William Jackson and Field Marshal Lord Bramall, *The Chiefs: The Story of the United Kingdom Chiefs of Staff* (London: Brassey's, 1992), p. 7.
4. See C. G. Grey, *A History of the Air Ministry* (London: George Allen and Unwin, 1940), pp. 51-4. Grey was an interesting character; he was editor of the *Aeroplane* magazine and often expressed views that were extremely critical of the government on air issues. For a more pragmatic source, and one which is effectively an 'inside voice' as a member of the Air Ministry see J. M. Spaight, *The Beginnings of Organised Air Power* (London: Longmans, 1927), p. 32.
5. Spaight, *The Beginnings of Organised Air Power*.
6. See Cooper, *The Birth of Independent Air Power*, p. 42.
7. See Tami Davis Biddle, *Rhetoric and Reality in Air Warfare: The evolution of British and American Ideas about Strategic Bombing, 1914 - 1945* (Princeton: Princeton University Press, 2002), pp. 22-4, Cooper, *The Birth of Independent Air Power*, p. 43. For an example of contemporary reporting, see 'Air Debate', *The Times*, 17 Feb 1916 in which the First Lord of the Admiralty (Balfour, on behalf of the Prime Minister) confessed to Parliament just how far behind the United Kingdom is in the aerial prowess.
8. See Grey, *A History of the Air Ministry*, pp. 55-6 for the exploits of Mr. Noel Pemberton Billing MP who was the Member for East Hertfordshire. Billing had an early interest in aviation and founded the Supermarine Workshops in 1911; he was allowed to resign from the RNAS in 1916 (as a Squadron Commander) to enter politics to lobby on behalf of the flying services – which he did with 'vehemence and plain speaking'.

9   Ibid. See J. Lee Thompson, *Northcliffe: Press Baron in Politics 1865-1922* (London: John Murray, 2000).
10 Ibid., p. 57.
11 Cooper, *The Birth of Independent Air Power*, p. 44.
12 Spaight, *The Beginnings of Organised Air Power*, p. 70.
13 Lord Hankey, *The Supreme Command; 1914-1918* (London: George Allen and Unwin, 1961), p. 549.
14 Ibid.
15 Cooper, *The Birth of Independent Air Power*, p. 47. For a political view see D. Lloyd George, *War Memoirs of David Lloyd George*, vol. IV (London: Nicholson and Watson, 1937), p. 1,849.
16 Hankey, *The Supreme Command*, p. 550.
17 Lloyd George, *Memoirs*, vol. II, p. 977. For much of the correspondence, see CAB 42/25/10.
18 Ibid., p. 978.
19 Cooper, *The Birth of Independent Air Power*, p. 57.
20 Hankey, *The Supreme Command*, p. 551.
21 Cooper, *The Birth of Independent Air Power*, p. 58.
22 Spaight, *The Beginnings of Organised Air Power*, p. 93.
23 Ibid., p. 94.
24 Ibid., p. 100.
25 Ibid., p. 104.
26 Ibid., p. 116.
27 Ibid.
28 Ibid., p. 121. See also Lloyd George, *Memoirs*, pp. 1859-64.
29 Quotation from 'The Story of the Raid: The Enemy's Escape Unscathed', *The Times*, 9 July 1917.
30 See 'The Raid: Demand for Machines', *The Times*, 9 July 1917 for the Lords and 'Commons and Air Raid: Secret Sitting', *The Times*, 10 July 1917.
31 Lloyd George, *Memoirs*, pp. 1862-3. For his statement to the House see 'Commons and Air Raid: Secret Sitting', *The Times*, 10 July 1917.
32 Cooper, *The Birth of Independent Air Power*, p. 98.
33 Lloyd George, *Memoirs*. War Cabinet Meeting 11 July 1917, CAB 24/22 copied in AIR 8/2, E5. Also produced at Appendix II to Jones, *War in the Air: Appendices*.
34 See Cooper, *The Birth of Independent Air Power*, ch. 8, and John Sweetman, 'The Smuts Report of 1917: Merely Political Window-Dressing?' *Journal of Strategic Studies* 4, 2 (1981), pp. 152-74.
35 The National Archives (TNA), CAB 24/22 (GT. 1658) 'War Cabinet: Committee on Air Organisation and Home Defence against Air Raids (2nd Report)', 17 August 1917, para. 4.
36 Ibid.

37 Ibid., para. 5.
38 Ibid.
39 Ibid., para. 8.
40 Ibid., para. 10 (2).
41 TNA, CAB 23/3, War Cabinet 223, Minutes, 24 August 1917, para. 12.
42 Ibid.
43 TNA, CAB 23/4, War Cabinet 266, Minutes, 6 November 1917, para. 10.
44 Spaight, *The Beginnings of Organised Air Power*, p. 141.
45 Ibid.
46 Ibid.
47 HL Deb, 21 November 1917, vol. 26, c. 1122.
48 Spaight, *The Beginnings of Organised Air Power*, p. 144.
49 HL Deb, 21 November 1917, vol. 26, c. 1106.
50 Major Baird, Under-Secretary of State for Air to the House of Commons as part of his presentation of the 1918 Air Estimates: HC Deb, 21 February 1918, vol. 103, c .959.
51 Ibid., cc 959–60.
52 Stephen J. Zaccaro, *The Nature of Executive Leadership: A Conceptual and Empirical Analysis of Success* (Washington, DC: American Psychological Association, 2001), p. 13.
53 Of the many accounts of Trenchard's appointment and resignation, followed by that of his Secretary of State (Lord Rothermere) see Malcolm Cooper, 'A House Divided: Policy, Rivalry and Administration in Britain's Military Air Command 1914-1918', *Journal of Strategic Studies* 3, 2 (1980), pp. 178–201.
54 The staff of the British Museum, for example, were less than enamoured at the prospect of the Air Staff taking over the Museum – see TNA, CAB 24/35, Letter from British Museum Staff dated 12 December 1917.
55 Cooper, *The Birth of Independent Air Power*, p. 128.
56 Ibid., p. 129. For the most comprehensive account of Sykes, see Eric Ash, *Sykes and the Air Revolution 1912–1918* (London: Frank Cass, 1999), and for Weir, see W. J. Reader, *Architect of Air Power. The Life of the First Viscount Weir of Eastwood* (London: Collins, 1968).
57 As Sykes pointed out, the terms, 'Independent Air Force (sometimes of the RAF)', 'Independent Bombing Force' and 'Independent Striking Force' were all used interchangeably in 1918: Sir Frederick Sykes, *From Many Angles; An Autobiography* (London: Harrap, 1942), p. 219.
58 See Sykes, *From Many Angles*, pp. 220–7, Ash, *Sykes and the Air Revolution*, p. 159 and Cooper, *Birth of Independent Air Power*, pp. 130–1.
59 Sykes, *From Many Angles*, pp. 226–7.
60 Ibid., p. 224.
61 TNA, CAB 23/4, War Cabinet Meeting 244, 2 October 1917, para. 2.

62 Ibid.
63 TNA, CAB 24/28 for Robertson's Memorandum to the War Cabinet of 6 October 1917 (GT2234) and CAB 23/4 War Cabinet Meeting 247, 9 October 1917, para. 9 for the debate that ensued. See also Haig's diary, 4 October 1917, in Gary Sheffield and John Bourne (eds), *Douglas Haig: War Diaries and Letters 1914–1918* (London: Weidenfeld and Nicholson, 2005), p. 333 for Haig's record of Trenchard's report that 'All members of the War Cabinet seem to have lost their heads over the German bombing'.
64 Cooper, *Birth of Independent Air Power*, p. 132.
65 Ibid., p. 135. See also Jones, *War in the Air*, vol. VI, p. 119 for a description of German defences. See also p. 135 for the actual dates of Trenchard's arrival in the area; the date quoted is that on which the force formally came into being.
66 The Despatch is available in full in AIR 6/19 (Air Council Memoranda) and quoted extensively in Jones, *War in the Air*, vol. 6, p. 136.
67 Ibid.
68 Ibid.
69 Andrew Boyle, *Trenchard: Man of Vision* (London: Collins, 1962), p. 314.
70 Royal Air Force Museum, Personal Papers of Marshal of the Royal Air Force Viscount Trenchard, MFC 76/1/32, dated 11 November 1918.
71 John Laffin, *Swifter than Eagles: A Biography of Marshal of the RAF Sir John Salmond* (Edinburgh: Blackwood, 1964), p. 130.
72 Sykes, *From Many Angles*, pp. 236–7.
73 Ibid., p. 237.
74 John C. Slessor, *Air Power and Armies* (Oxford: Oxford University Press, 1936).
75 Sykes, *From Many Angles*, p. 237.
76 Ibid., p. 226.
77 Jones, *War in the Air*, p. 163. See also the Appendices Volume at Appendix XIII for the statistical breakdown of the raids; the Remarks column gives an interesting reflection on the realities of the operations.
78 Ibid., p. 137.
79 Grey, *A History of the Air Ministry*, p. 85.
80 Neville Jones, *The Origins of Strategic Bombing: A Study of the Development of British Air Strategic Thought and Practice up to 1918* (London: Kimber, 1973), p. 212.
81 Cooper, *Birth of Independent Air Power*, p. 135.
82 Ibid.
83 Sir Charles Webster and Noble Frankland, *The Strategic Air Offensive against Germany, 1939–1945* (London: Her Majesty's Stationary Office, 1960), p. 41.
84 Boyle, *Trenchard*, p. 329.

8

The Smuts Report: Interpreting and Misinterpreting the Promise of Air Power

Christopher Luck

John Sweetman's assertion that 'No consideration of the origins of the Royal Air Force would be complete without mention of Lieutenant-General J. C. Smuts, and in particular, the second of his two reports on air power' is entirely correct in its premise.[1] Smuts' vision, as mentioned in Chapter 7, of air power independence, perhaps even dominance, formed the logic of his call for an independent British air force. But while his call for organizational independence was clearly justified for reasons of efficiency and effectiveness, his unqualified assertions concerning air power's strategic potential, or more correctly defined independent action, conferred an expectation that air power would always be dominant and could perhaps achieve victory single-handedly. One of the unfortunate consequences of Smuts' prognostication, despite its temporal and contextual anchor, is that air power continues to be accused of failing to perform when its independent use does not, in and of itself, deliver victory. Despite air power's clear value, this accusation of 'failure' was most recently trumpeted in the harsh critique of air power's contribution during the July 2006 Israeli-Hezbollah conflict. *Washington Post* columnist Phillip H. Gordon decried the 'strategic bombing fallacy' and 'wishful thinking' of the Israeli air strategy.[2] The history of independent strategic air power, he claimed, was one of perennial over optimism', as reflected by such claims as Smuts', and later Winston Churchill's in a speech in Boston, Massachusetts, in 1949, that 'For good or ill, air mastery today is the supreme expression of military power, and fleets and armies, however necessary, must accept a subordinate rank.'[3] Tami Biddle argues that the 'heady promises' of the Smuts Report were divorced from the 'reality of Britain's Independent Force'. She also claims that British airmen failed to scrutinize 'objectively their experience in World War I', leading to a failure of perception about the efficacy of independent strategic bombing.[4]

The roots of these critiques can be traced to Smuts' *Second Report of the Prime Minister's Committee on Air Organisation and Air Defence Against Air Raids*, arguably the 'most important single document in the history of air power'.[5] The German bombing of London (May–July 1917) although ineffective to the modern eye, 'exerted a strong moral effect simply because of their relative novelty'.[6] The bombing and Smuts' report led to 'a massive reorganization of Britain's armed forces which would affect her strategic doctrines for the next fifty years and more'.[7]

Subsequent air power thought and development concentrated on Smuts' future vision of air power's potential and hindered thinking on how air power can and should be used to achieve strategic, that is, politically desired, objectives, obscuring its indispensable instrumentality to the joint fight and to the detriment of 'auxiliary' aviation. This vision continues to bedevil policymakers and public opinion about what to expect from the air instrument. The following evaluation of the historical roots of air power, as imbedded in the second Smuts report, and its strategic application, may help to correct faulty perceptions of air power's utility and answer whether it has caused 'major, and quite gratuitous, political damage' to air power thinking.[8]

The Western Front devoured armies and engendered a tremendous sense of waste, with participants on both sides hating the slaughter, yet finding themselves unable to disengage from it.[9] The manoeuvres of the first weeks of the Great War followed the German Schlieffen Plan and the French Plan XVII. These plans intended to produce battles of encounter and movement leading to a short, sharp war of decision. British optimism that the commitment of the British Expeditionary Force (BEF) would quickly tip the balance for victory in France's favour was also sadly mistaken.[10] After the Allied defensive stand on the Marne and the 'Race to the Sea', movement ceased. The opposing armies dug in, shattering the preconceptions of all the belligerents. The stasis continued, despite bloody attempts to break the deadlock, leading both sides to adopt a strategy of attrition. By 1917, the general situation appeared bleak for the Allies, with pessimism rising that they would soon have to pursue a disadvantageous peace.

When Britain declared war on Germany on 4 August 1914, the Royal Flying Corps (RFC) mobilized and took to the field under the command of Brigadier-General Sir David Henderson. The first aircraft arrived in France the following day and the 63 deployed aircraft included BE2s, BE8s, Bleriots and Farmans.[11] Reconnaissance was air power's key function during this early stage of the war.[12] Although reconnaissance remained king, by year's end aircraft had conducted both bombing and aerial combat, though the primitive aircraft then in use 'offered no prospect of breaking the stalemate'.[13] Airmen soon realized that this was not to be a short war, and that 'the key to victory had just changed from winning the mobilization battle to winning the production-training-technology battle'.[14] According to the official history, the 'war, if it was to be won, could only be won in the workshop and the training school'.[15]

In 1915 organized bombing and the struggle for air superiority began.[16] On 31 May, the first attack on London occurred and by October the War Office began experimenting with coordinated defence efforts around London.[17] Most raids were little more 'than symbolic' because of the 'tiny bomb loads'. Yet the propaganda value was enormous because they made the British government appear powerless.[18] Colonel Hugh Trenchard took command of the RFC in France on 19 August, while Henderson returned to the War Office to deal with the requirements of rapid expansion.[19] During the autumn the RFC made extensive efforts to cut communications by bombing railways, rolling stock and depots.[20] As the number of aircraft armed with machine guns grew it became increasingly difficult to conduct missions without first contesting the air.[21] At this time Trenchard came to the conclusion that the best protection was the 'strategic offensive', or 'by fighting and subduing the enemy airmen far away from the aeroplanes flying in direct co-operation with the Army'.[22]

In 1916, both sides developed their tactics and adjusted their organizations to meet evolving challenges.[23] British bombing tactics switched from small detachments bombing many targets, to the 'mass bombing of single targets'.[24] The Zeppelins flew four times as many raids as they had in 1915 but caused only two-thirds the damage of previous attacks. At the same time, losses of airships were rising prohibitively compared to their successes.[25] The Royal Naval Air Service (RNAS) had little success in directly defeating the threat posed and under intense public scrutiny, handed responsibility for air defence back to the RFC in February.

In 1917, as air services grew, the air war 'evolved into a mass struggle of attrition', similar to the war below in the trenches. The air war stretched from the 'ground to 20,000 feet into the heavens'.[26] Meanwhile, Gotha bombers began their raids on England in the spring.

In the early stages of the war government interest in, and awareness of, aviation, remained minimal.[27] A hands-off approach to production proved to be problematic as the demands of total war impinged on Britain's ability to cope with two of the air war's greatest difficulties: organization and supply, and more specifically, engine supply and manpower. The reality was that the aircraft and engine production infrastructure was geared to a small force and a quick war. With a British aircraft industry unable to adequately supply both services, each competed with the other for scarce resources.[28] To make matters worse, orders were haphazardly placed and the uncoordinated effort caused confusion. The British services and the government had yet to understand or adjust to the demands of the war, leaving the 'battle of the air' to be won or lost at home.[29] With no common policy to adjudicate and allocate scarce resources, British aviation was deeply mired in a crisis of expansion.[30] Services 'contracted for their planes, motors, etc. at varying prices so that each branch tended to bid up costs ...'.[31] The shortfall in aircraft and engines caused Haig to complain bitterly that until he had the aircraft numbers he required for the Army's requirements in the field, strategic bombing had to be regarded as a 'luxury'.[32]

Air policy on the Western Front was shaped by Trenchard's policy of 'supporting the army' in a 'relentless offensive' and was surrounded by controversy since its inception. By 1917, especially following 'Bloody April', political considerations 'began increasingly to influence the development of air power'.[33] But Trenchard's demand for a constant air offensive mirrored the approach approved of by the Chief of the Imperial General Staff (CIGS), General Sir William Robertson, who informed Haig in April 1917 that the 'best plan' for victory was that of 'breaking down the enemy's army'.[34] Trenchard's singlemindedness has been critiqued as bordering on stubbornness, being expensive in aircraft and airmen and, while gaining control of the air, had 'little value in a war as static as that on the Western Front'. He was, according to this line of thought, a 'soldier of the old tradition', who preferred to command more by instinct than by 'science and analysis'.[35] His policy was also criticized as being bereft of strategic utility.[36] The Official Historian opined that the offensive patrols 'were too much a matter of routine, that their direction and co-ordination were not always sufficiently characterized by an alert imagination'.[37] Thus, Trenchard's offensive mindset created an additional burden to what was an already inadequate training system.[38] The training system continued to produce 'poorly trained pilots who did not survive aerial combat', which only exacerbated the problem.[39]

Trenchard believed that any shift in effort away from supporting the field army would seriously undermine the war strategy, and he was sceptical of promises of surplus aircraft.[40] Although the offensive policy was a 'very blunt instrument', it was a microcosm of the larger war and reflected the mentality of the military leaders of a focus on the Western Front and Army support.[41] Such a policy, with its tacit acceptance of the doctrine of attrition, when combined with the lack of aircrew replacements and aircraft, left Trenchard with little scope for other activities in 1917.[42]

Thus air strategy on the Western Front reflected overall strategies. Through mid-1917, however, air power had been unable to deliver decisive military blows, although it was perceived that 'under certain conditions air power could exert considerable psychological pressure'.[43] Arguably, the greatest psychological impact was from bombing by the Germans against civilian population centres.[44] This did cause some loss of production, fear and an increased consumption of resources in an attempt to secure the populace.[45] The actual cost of the damage and the low numbers killed were at odds with the subsequent vision of bombing's potential.[46]

Limitations in navigation, aircraft endurance, bombing accuracy, as well as improved enemy defenses prevented bombing from being decisive.[47] Compounding all these limitations was the absence of an overall air strategy that blended and harmonized the functions of air power with national goals. By the spring of 1917 competition for resources, accusations of inefficiency and lack of policy convinced a growing body of concerned leaders of the need for an independent Air Ministry. At the same time, the German raids created a public demand for retaliation. These cries became increasingly loud and reached a climax in the summer of 1917, following the daylight raids on London. The response of the Prime Minister, David Lloyd George, was to appoint Smuts to investigate the whole issue of aerial operations.[48]

Smuts had the rare ability to think clearly in both the political and military spheres. Thus, in mid-1917, when Britain was on the edge of a strategic crisis, his skill in visualizing the political implications of military decisions, while simultaneously seeing the military ramifications of political decisions, was timely and fortuitous. He saw 'fragments leading to wholes which are superior to the mere sum of their constituent parts'.[49] This early expression of complexity was germane to his success in grasping a 'picture of the future'.[50]

With a reputation as a soldier, statesman and intellectual and a bent for grand strategy, Smuts arrived in Britain in March 1917 to a shower of honours.[51] Already appointed to the Imperial War Cabinet, he was also appointed to the British War Cabinet, as Lloyd George felt that he 'could be safely trusted to examine into the intricacies of any of our multifarious problems and unravel and smooth them out'.[52] His not being wedded to the Western Front, with a mind 'free of prior commitment to the grand-strategic landscape', made him one of the very few senior military men who had 'not got trenches dug deep into his mind'.[53] It was to this soldier-statesman, with a 'fresh and able mind free from departmental prejudices' that Lloyd George entrusted the chairmanship of the war priorities committee, which was chartered to match industrial production to the demands of war and additionally to find a solution to the German air attacks on England.[54]

On 25 May 1917, Gothas bombed the Kent towns of Shorncliffe and Folkstone.[55] On 13 June, they bombed London, killing 162 and injuring 432, with all the bombers escaping.[56] The impotence and shortcomings of existing defensive measures were again evident on 7 July when a further 54 people were killed and 190 injured in London.[57] Smuts witnessed this raid and did not fail to note the significant psychological impact on the British population.[58] These attacks were 'dramatised in the press and exploited in politics', and forced the Prime Minister to call a secret session of Parliament on 10 July to discuss air defence.[59] Newspaper editorials deplored the psychological shock of the attacks as a 'national shame', declaring that Britain had been 'humiliated and disgraced'.[60] Parliament and the public clamoured for defence, retaliation and 'victory through air power', with George Bernard Shaw declaring that 'this war will be won in the sky, not in the trenches'.[61]

Public opinion turned sharply against the government for its failure to prevent the raids and against anyone who tried to rationalize the German attacks.[62] Public pressure for retaliation demanded action despite the fact that the cost in lives from aerial bombardment for the whole war was less than a 'single "quiet" day at the Front', and total property damage cost 'less than half what the Great War cost the British each day'.[63] Lloyd George visited the bombed-out citizens of the West End of London to placate them, but even 'his Welsh rhetoric could not forestall the night-time smashing and looting of Hackney shops bearing German names' and other such 'mob savagery'.[64]

Powerful social forces have often compelled politicians to change policy, and with it military organization.[65] This time would provide no exception. Lloyd George already objected to the way 'Haig and Robertson squandered men on the Western Front', and the losses of the Somme confirmed in his mind that the 'soldiers had been given too free a hand'.[66] He felt that Herbert Asquith had 'surrendered to the Allied military strategy which had decreed a war of attrition'.[67] In 1917 he had his hands full with labour troubles that threatened to inhibit the government's ability to prosecute the war.[68] Pressured by the German raids and becoming increasingly sceptical of victory on the Western Front, Lloyd George looked to Smuts to examine aviation's organization and use.[69] Lloyd George was 'no air strategist', but the declaration of his intent to 'bomb Germany with compound interest' represented astute politics in difficult times.[70]

It was inevitable that the army general staff and Lloyd George would clash, as they held totally opposed views on strategy.[71] The 'generals maintained that the politicians, by their muddling, were responsible for the various defeats in the field' and the politicians blamed the generals for the horrifying military losses and misfortunes.[72] Public and political reluctance to feed the slaughter mill led to government and press speculation that Haig and the general headquarters were out of control.[73] Lloyd George was particularly critical of Haig's ability and felt that his lack of 'intelligible and coherent expression' was a sign of a lack of 'mental precision'.[74] By mid-1917, Lloyd George had determined to break the 'strategic stranglehold' of the military commanders.[75] This determination influenced his decision towards aviation policy.[76] The Prime Minister laboured to impose his own 'notions of a more practicable strategy' that envisioned defensive operations in the west and the weakening of the enemy by a peripheral strategy.[77] One observer of these disagreements believed the military officers failed to see the war 'as one vast politico-military problem', thinking that 'it would be fatal to mix up politics with strategy'.[78]

Thus, by 1917, British war policy was gripped by an abiding pessimism, with Britain seemingly 'under the shadow' of defeat.[79] The fact that Germany had not been defeated by the combined might of the Entente brought many policymakers to the brink of despair.[80] Russia fell to revolution in 1917, and its withdrawal cost the Entente half its manpower at a time when war demanded ever greater numbers. After the disastrous Nivelle offensive, the French Army was incapable of large-scale attacks.[81] The Italians suffered significant reverses at the hands of a German-Austrian offensive and were reduced to a 'beaten and unarmed horde of refugees'. Unrestricted submarine warfare sent British merchant tonnage to the seabed at an alarming rate and the Allies seemed in danger of losing the war, through starvation.[82] Lloyd George believed the growing food shortage would decide the war as actual defeat would transpire from the social discontent generated.[83] Although fears of revolution were exaggerated, they coloured the atmosphere in which policy was formulated.[84] The cabinet could only conclude that unless solutions were found to the host of seemingly intractable problems, Britain would be driven out of the war.[85]

As suspicion grew that victory might not be possible, thoughts turned to a compromise with Germany, a 'peace without victory'.[86] The strategic situation, however, had deteriorated to such an extent that hopes of a favourable peace, that is, one that curbed Germany's growing power, seemed well out of reach.[87]

Lloyd George believed that Britain would lose the war 'unless the civilians asserted themselves over the military', while Smuts, confident that Germany could be brought to terms by shattering its morale on the home front, supported refraining from unsatisfactory negotiations.[88] Smuts thought that although the German line could not be broken, 'remorselessly hammering away' at it might 'break his heart'.[89] Aircraft could help win the war by vaulting the static front and attacking the enemy's industrial capability and morale.[90]

Thus, in 1917 the Allied Powers appeared to be on the brink of military defeat, with the generals unable to think outside their Western school of strategy and the logic of attritional warfare.[91] Lloyd George struggled to influence the military to achieve 'strategic goals by practicable means'.[92] Although CIGS was impatient about 'the attention being given to the feelings of the population of London', Smuts had seen enough to realize that 'the population had been shaken', and the psychological factor had to be taken into account.[93] For Lloyd George, the use of air power appeared as a solution to the 'arid strategists'. This potential intuitively matched his developing belief that an 'absolute priority should be given to avoiding wastage of manpower by means of . . . changes in tactics'.[94] Lloyd George was determined that the use of the air weapon be investigated by 'a fresh and able mind, free from departmental prejudices', and saw in Smuts the answer.[95]

Thus the politico-strategic context, the overlapping of the functions of the two air services, their competition for resources, all came together to produce a drastic rethinking of the way in which military aviation should be organized. The frightening novelty of the summer air attacks only added to Lloyd George's conviction to stop the enemy from the 'bad business' of air raids and to respond in kind.[96]

On 11 July, Smuts was appointed to the Committee on Air Organisation and Home Defence Against Air Raids. Lloyd George was the only other member but took no active part.[97] Smuts' mandate was to examine (i) the 'defence arrangements for Home Defence against air raids and (ii) the air organization generally and the direction of aerial operations', and to do so quickly.[98] He was aided by the erudite and perceptive Henderson, now the Director-General of Military Aeronautics. Smuts was far from satisfied with the overall organization of the British air effort.[99] He produced two reports that were issued on 19 July and 17 August 1917. The first was on defence against air raids.[100] This report, which was accepted in full by the war cabinet, recommended centralized control of air defence under a single senior officer; reorganization of anti-aircraft guns, observers and balloon-barrages; training for formation flying in combat and the provision of sufficient air defence units to protect London, the nerve-centre of the Empire.[101]

His second report of 17 August 1917 has been described as having 'revolutionary implications' and as being the 'most important paper in the history of the creation of the Royal Air Force'.[102] Its central message was the importance of air power and the need to separate it from the restraints of the older services in order to end 'competition, friction, and waste'.[103] Smuts argued that the subordination of the Air Board and Air Service to the two services was no longer justifiable because the Air Service 'can be used as an independent means of war operations', with 'absolutely no limit to the scale of its future independent war use'.[104] He then concluded that the Air Board should become an independent ministry in charge of an independent service. This bureaucratic independence was based on what Smuts saw as being air power's potential to attack and devastate an enemy to the extent that the 'older forms of military and naval operations become secondary and subordinate'.[105]

Having been assured that sufficient aircraft would be available in 1918, Smuts called for an Air Staff to plan and direct the 'great surplus' of aircraft being made available by the programme of aircraft production, for 'independent air operations'.[106] Smuts' clarion call for a separate staff was based on the belief that 'careful staff work in advance' was even more essential in air operations than in military and naval operations that rested on centuries-old routines and experience.[107] He further argued that the future air policy for the whole war had to be settled by 'competent' staffers, so appropriate airframes and engines were built, rather than ones that were 'useless for independent strategical operations'.[108] A new Ministry and Air Service were required to handle the 'new instrument of offence' properly, without losing 'the great advantages which the new form of warfare promises', as neither the Army, Navy or Air Board 'could possibly cope with the vast developments involved', without collapsing onto 'chaos and confusion'.[109]

Smuts argued that given the stalemated Western Front, air attacks on industrial and communication targets deep behind the enemy's lines were likely to be an 'important factor in bringing about peace'. To avoid 'hopeless confusion', Smuts recommended absorbing 'both the existing services under arrangements that fully safeguard the efficiency and secure the closest intimacy between the Army and the Navy and the portions of the Air Service allotted or seconded to them'.[110] This was intended to prevent the Army and Navy from delaying or circumventing the report.[111] On 24 August the War Cabinet accepted in principle that a separate air service be formed.[112]

While the air organization committee was dealing with the work of amalgamating the RFC and RNAS, the general headquarters in France expressed misgivings about the whole policy.[113] Neither Trenchard nor Haig was enthusiastic about Smuts' report, and both were committed to the primacy of the Western Front and RFC support of the army.[114] The War Office forwarded a copy of Smuts' report to Haig for comment. Haig reacted forcefully against the formation of an Air Ministry, and argued that the notion that the war could be won in the air, rather than on the ground, was 'a mere assertion unsupported by facts'.[115] He remained committed to the policy that 'all available aircraft were needed in close support of the land forces' and that the creation of an independent Air Ministry 'was a dangerous diversion of much needed resources'.[116] Trenchard so vehemently disagreed with Smuts that he called the establishment of a separate air force 'the successful culmination of a German plot aimed at dislocating the RFC in the field'.[117] He also raised the concern that an Air Ministry under civilian leadership, without dominant army and navy input, would lose 'its sense of proportion' when reacting to 'popular and fictional comment'. He further argued that the inevitable response would be a pandering to 'the spectacular, such as bombing reprisals and home defence', rather than concentrating limited 'essential means' on army and navy cooperation.[118]

Haig's response of 15 September, which owed much to the pen of Trenchard, pointed out the lack of credible evidence justifying the report's predictions for strategic bombing. He presciently wrote that 'the science of defence against aircraft attack may develop considerably in the future'.[119] Haig was also sceptical about production of a surplus of aircraft for independent bombing, especially considering the 'repeated' failure of past promises to provide aircraft in adequate numbers, or even to match attrition.[120] The scorn that Haig and Trenchard piled upon Smuts' report, added to a returned governmental complacency, meant that it 'was about to be shelved'; only Smuts kept pressing for action.[121]

Haig's response arrived just as renewed attacks in September, known as the Moonlight Raids, had caused the government to revisit the air issue.[122] Smuts was requested to investigate the latest attacks. His conclusion was still that existing preparations for any action were 'backwards', and the fact that a separate air organization was pending was all that was preventing an 'outburst of popular indignation' which might bring the Government down.[123]

On 18 September, Smuts submitted a further memorandum, which both Weir and Henderson supported, arguing that the solution to the problem required a holistic examination of air strategy within an overall war policy, which would then lead to an 'aerial plan of campaign'. Smuts added that if manufacturing output was to be synchronized with the spring 1918 campaign plan, time was short. A comprehensive approach meant that a plethora of other factors also had to be addressed: producing training aircraft, building additional airfields and supporting infrastructure and training pilots and mechanics. In essence, Smuts argued, the 'whole question of air expansion was really one of fundamental war policy'.[124]

In October, no fewer than four committees, under the chairmanship of the 'seemingly omniscient' Smuts, were dealing with air matters: the Air Raids Committee, the Air Reorganization Committee, the War Priorities Committee and the Air Policy Committee.[125] Smuts reported on the whole situation, recommended priorities and outlined the impact these priorities might have on the army and navy. He recommended a committee that was empowered to address all munitions priority for the war effort. Smuts' proposal was accepted on 8 October, and the War Priorities Committee was formed with powers to settle all questions of priority for munitions production.[126] This was a revolutionary step that, for all intents and purposes, made Smuts the de facto minister of defence. British strategy had taken a noticeable step forward.

However, for a moment 'it seemed that the Cabinet's decision of principle' would be put into limbo, to the 'despair' of those who 'realised the importance of a unified air service'.[127] War Cabinet discussions on 15 October reveal some disquiet about the disruptive effects of forming an Air Ministry.[128] The Cabinet seemed to develop a consensus for the air services to be coordinated, but for the formation of an Air Ministry to be left to the future. In the interim, an air policy committee, once again under the chairmanship of Smuts, substituted for the Air Ministry.[129] Lord Milner circulated a memorandum on 26 October questioning the wisdom of depending on Smuts' air policy committee to deal with all the complexities and issues involved in implementation of a comprehensive air strategy. Notwithstanding these concerns, Smuts' committee had, by the end of October, sketched out the plan for the new organization, made the arrangements for its establishment and drafted the required legislation, which became known as the Air Force Bill.[130]

The appointment of the RAF senior leadership proved contentious. Lord Rothermere was appointed the first Secretary for the Air Force. Rothermere's brother, Lord Northcliffe, had already publicly turned down an offer of the post from Lloyd George, preferring to critique the government's air policy through his paper, *The Times*.[131] Trenchard was appointed as the first Chief of the Air Staff (CAS) on 18 January. His appointment caused Haig significant consternation, as he felt that 'the proper place for Trenchard was 'in actual command of the Flying Corps in the field in France'.[132] Disagreements between the political and military heads of the new service soon cast 'a shadow of legitimacy' over the newly formed service.[133]

It was not long before Rothermere and Trenchard disagreed over responsibilities.[134] Haig recorded in his diary on 16 December 1917 that Trenchard believed that the Air Board was 'off their heads as to the future possibility of aeronautics for ending the war'.[135] Thus, Trenchard arrived at the Air Council with 'no sympathy for the setting up of an Air Ministry'. This drove Lord Beaverbrook to state that Trenchard 'was a father who tried to strangle the infant at birth though he got the credit for the grown man'.[136] Trenchard resented Rothermere's penchant for seeking aviation advice from others, and Rothermere thought Trenchard an intolerant know-it-all 'of dull, unimaginative mind'.[137] Rothermere 'rosily imagined great reprisal raids against German cities', while Trenchard felt that matters of air policy were his to decide and 'hewed to the operational reality' of limited-range bombers and poor weather.[138] At loggerheads with his civilian superior, Trenchard resigned on 18 March.

To minimize the political repercussions of Trenchard's departure, and in light of the German Michael offensive, the resignation was not accepted until 13 April.[139] Smuts was asked to comment on the business with Trenchard. He supported the release of Trenchard and wrote Lloyd George, 'My deepest sympathy is with you. . . . Now is the time for quietness and strength. . . . I have no doubt we shall pull through this crisis both in a military and political sense'.[140] Major-General Frederick H. Sykes, a known advocate of strategic bombing, was appointed to succeed Trenchard.[141] Rothermere resigned on 25 April after Trenchard's supporters attacked his competence in the House of Commons, and was succeeded by Sir William Weir, another 'true believer' in strategic bombing and the architect of the 'surplus fleet'.[142]

Although Weir considered Trenchard's resignation as CAS to be 'unjustifiable', he recognized his importance to the RAF and felt that he was the only airman with sufficient experience and authority to command the new Independent Force of the RAF.[143] He persuaded Trenchard to assume command by allowing him to report directly to him, thus bypassing Sykes.[144] Yet Trenchard was a reluctant commander, still sceptical of strategic bombing's potential.[145] He had never wanted the air force split from the army and wrote of the Independent Force that 'a more gigantic waste of effort and personnel there has never been in any war'.[146] He therefore continued throughout his tenure to support the army in the field.[147]

Lloyd George anticipated destructive attacks on enemy cities.[148] This reasoning was based substantively on negative, or defensive, experience from the Gotha raids.[149] However, the greatest percentage of effort continued to be expended on targets that directly supported the army at the front. This prompted the Director of Flying Operations, Percy Groves, to write 'that this policy is a violation of the policy of the Independent Force'.[150] With the promised numbers of aircraft not materializing and the events on the battlefield diverting Trenchard from his official mandate, the meagre and ill-trained force was barely capable of conducting the mission for which it was formed and was not tested as its advocates had hoped.[151]

The consequences of defeat in the Great War were potentially devastating and arguably irreversible. With the fate of empires hanging in the balance, strategy had to wring every possible advantage from dwindling resources. Air power was one such resource, and although it was not yet an instrument 'capable of achieving decision . . .', it had become an 'important weapon'.[152] The formation of the Air Ministry was the first step in coordinating the overall air effort for the war and, specifically, in developing the air policy for the independent mission and ensuring continuing air support to the army and navy 'under the command of air force officers'.[153]

Smuts' vision for air power was based on the assumption of surplus and suitably capable aircraft being available through 1918, but he had significantly overestimated what aircraft were capable of at that time.[154] The inadequate performance of the Independent Force's aircraft meant low load-carrying ability, limited range, slow speeds and low altitudes, which made them vulnerable to interception.[155] Inadequate aircrew training produced pilots who lacked the flying skills to operate effectively in the inclement weather and at night.[156] When suitable targets were found, pilots had a low chance of hitting them because of crude bomb-sights and low-yield bombs caused little damage even when targets were hit.[157] The lack of technically efficient means of delivery seriously reduced any chance of the Independent Force achieving its mission.[158] Organizationally, the lack of a coherent, systematic campaign plan led to ineffective operations. The absence of meaningful trials and experimentation further hindered performance.[159]

Thus, the potential of air power to achieve independent success was more hoped for than empirical. Smuts lacked evidence from practical experience of strategic bombing to sustain the forecasts he made for its emerging potential. He placed his faith in an exaggerated belief in the destructive and psychological impact of the air weapon.[160] While civil populations were alarmed by the bombing, their morale did not collapse. Once the initial panic subsided, life went on.[161] Improved defences further reduced the potential effectiveness of strategic bombing through 1918.[162] In the event, the little bombing conducted by the Independent Force was plagued by significant losses to enemy fighters and flak.[163] The unescorted bombers proved easy pickings for strong German defences and foreshadowed similar losses in the future.[164] Smuts failed to perceive, or allow for, a simple fact: at the time he wrote an effective strategic force was at best remotely possible and at worst technologically infeasible.[165]

Smuts' analysis of the situation in 1917 was heavily shaped by the unfavourable grand-strategic situation. He was poignantly aware of the growing distrust between the politicians and the generals as he searched for a path leading to victory.[166] The fact that an independent Air Ministry would be run by a civilian and not a general bode well for strategies other than attrition. From the vantage point of his position in the war cabinet, Smuts saw that pressure was exerted by the general public, the press and parliament. The decision to form an Air Ministry and an independent air service appeared neither illogical nor irrational, but absolutely necessary. An Air Ministry would ensure that the anticipated surplus aircraft would not be diverted to the army and navy, and would end the manifold inefficiencies of the separate air services. Perversely, the fact that the surplus failed to materialize emphasized the importance of Smuts' independent Air Ministry in imposing discipline on the air instrument.

There were long-term negative effects of the Smuts Report. His clarion call for air dominance led to unwarranted extrapolation, speculation and zealous advocacy for strategic bombing.[167] Before the end of the war, Sykes, Groves and Colonel William 'Billy' Mitchell of the American Expeditionary Forces, carried the theory of strategic bombing to the logical extreme of expecting the next war to be won entirely by a pre-emptive air strike. This led the RAF to develop a strategic bomber deterrent that manifestly failed to stem the tide of Nazism. The almost mystical belief in strategic bombing's efficacy short-circuited efforts to deal with the problems of range, protection, bomb weights, targeting, poor weather and night flying and navigation.[168] Meanwhile, the hard-won skills gained in tactical ground-attack operations were discarded.[169]

History suggests that the realities of time, space, equipment, logistics, higher direction and national character must be taken into account in the application of air power. The Great War was no exception. The ability to grasp the complex whole of war and to ground it in its strategic context is difficult and requires a 'radical intellect in a traditional temperament'.[170] Smuts possessed just such a radical intellect, but he lacked the moderating influence of a traditional temperament. His visions of air's dominance and perhaps solitary ability to effect strategic goals were flawed, and they continue today to impale airmen on an overly high measure of effectiveness. But his genius was in seeing that air power had the *potential* to produce strategic effect both on the battlefield *and* far removed from it, and needed centralized control under airmen released from the mental climate of the soldier and the sailor.

Smuts' holistic approach to air power fostered development of a coordinated policy, doctrine and economy of force – the necessary ingredients of an effective air strategy. By looking to the future, Smuts established the organization to think and act elementally. His call for an independent air ministry to coordinate, manage and develop the air weapon anticipated air power's coming of age as an equal military instrument of power, and gave impetus to the search for Clausewitz's *'shorter route to the goal'*.

The Great War was a crucial, formative period for air power, but the war did a great deal more for aviation than aviation did for the outcome of the war.[171] How one evaluates Smuts' interpretation and misinterpretation of air power thus depends very much on how long a historical perspective one takes. For today's air power strategists, Smuts' enduring 'lessons' are that air power occupies a unique geography, requiring independent elemental expertise to meld it into a truly holistic approach to war strategy, and that the strategic, and therefore political utility of the instrument, is always contextual and contingent.[172] This, properly imbibed, should prevent further 'gratuitous, political damage' to air power thinking.

Notes

1 John Sweetman, 'The Smuts Report of 1917: Merely Political Window-Dressing?' *Journal of Strategic Studies* 4, 2 (June 1981), pp. 152–74; esp. p. 152.
2 Phillip H. Gordon, 'Air Power Won't Do It', *Washington Post*, 25 July 2006, p. 15.
3 Asher Lee, 'Trends in Aerial Defense', *World Politics* 7, 2 (January 1955), pp. 233–54; esp. p. 233.
4 Tami Davis Biddle, *Rhetoric and Reality in Air Warfare: The Evolution of British and American Ideas about Strategic Bombing, 1914–1945* (Princeton: Princeton University Press, 2002), pp. 289, 291, 301.
5 Tony Mason, *Air Power: A Centennial Appraisal* (London: Brassey's, 2001), p. 26.
6 Malcolm Cooper, 'Blueprint for Confusion: The Administration Background to the Formation of the Royal Air Force, 1912–19', *Journal of Contemporary History* 22, 3 (July 1987), pp. 437–53; esp. p. 445.

7 H. R. Allen, *The Legacy of Lord Trenchard* (London: Cassell, 1972), p. 17.
8 Colin S. Gray, *Modern Strategy* (Oxford: Oxford University Press, 1999), p. 231.
9 David Stevenson, *1914–1918: The History of The First World War* (London: Penguin, 2004), p. xix.
10 Ibid., p. 36.
11 H. A. Jones, *The War in the Air*, Appendices (Oxford: Clarendon Press, 1937), p. 154.
12 Walter Raleigh, *The War in the Air*, vol. I (Oxford: Clarendon Press, 1922), pp. 298, 329.
13 John H. Morrow, Jr., *The Great War: An Imperial History* (London: Routledge, 2004), p. 46.
14 Eric Ash, *Sir Frederick Sykes and the Air Revolution 1912–1918* (London: Frank Cass, 1999), p. 59.
15 Raleigh, *The War in the Air*, vol. I, p. 407.
16 Air Historical Branch, *The Royal Air Force in the Great War* (Nashville, TN and London: Battery Press, 1996), p. 51. nb: Originally released in 1936 as Air Publication 125 under the title *A Short History of the Royal Air Force*.
17 H. A. Jones, *The War in the Air*, vol. III (Oxford: Clarendon Press, 1931), pp. 90–135.
18 Lee Kennett, *The First Air War 1914–1918* (New York, NY: Simon and Schuster, 1991), p. 55.
19 H. A. Jones, *The War in the Air*, vol. II (Oxford: Clarendon Press, 1928), p. 124.
20 Ibid., pp. 127–34.
21 Ibid., pp. 135–44.
22 Ibid., p. 165.
23 Ibid., pp. 147–9.
24 Ibid., p. 181.
25 Jones, *The War in the Air*, vol. III, p. 243.
26 Morrow, *The Great War*, p. 193.
27 Cooper, 'Blueprint for Confusion', p. 439.
28 Allen, *Lord Trenchard*, pp. 13–15.
29 Malcolm Cooper, *The Birth of Independent Air Power: British Air Policy in the First World War* (London: Allen and Unwin, 1986), p. 35.
30 Ibid., p. 53.
31 Barry D. Powers, *Strategy Without Slide-Rule: British Air Strategy 1914–1939* (London: Croom Helm, 1976), p. 43.
32 Hilary St. George Saunders, *Per Ardua – The Rise of British Air Power 1911–1939* (Oxford: Oxford University Press, 1945), p. 218.
33 Michael Paris, *Winged Warfare: The Literature and Theory of Aerial Warfare in Britain 1859–1917* (Manchester: Manchester University Press, 1992) pp. 238–9.
34 RFC HQ Memorandum, Offence and Defence, 22 September 1916, The National Archives (TNA), AIR 1/522/16/12/5; Hew Strachan, *The First World War* (London: Viking, 2004), p. 251.

35 Philip S. Meilinger, 'Trenchard and "Morale Bombing": The Evolution of Royal Air Force Doctrine Before World War II', *Journal of Military History* 60, 2 (April 1996), pp. 243–70; esp. p. 248; Paris, *Winged Warfare*, p. 190; Biddle, *Rhetoric and Reality*, pp. 27–8; Vincent Orange, *Slessor: Bomber Champion – The Life of Marshal of the Royal Air Force Sir John Slessor, GCB, DSO, MC* (London: Grub Street, 2006), p. 22.
36 Biddle, *Rhetoric and Reality*, p. 28; Edward H. Sims, *Fighter Tactics and Strategy 1914–1970* (New York, NY: Harper Row, 1972), p. 43.
37 Orange, *Slessor*, p. 22.
38 Biddle, *Rhetoric and Reality*, p. 28.
39 Ash, *The Air Revolution*, p. 104; Biddle, *Rhetoric and Reality*, p. 28; Paris, *Winged Warfare*, p. 217.
40 Alan Morris, *First of Many: The Story of the Independent Force, RAF* (London: Jarrolds, 1968), pp. 12–20.
41 Biddle, *Rhetoric and Reality*, p. 27.
42 Cooper, *Independent Air Power*, pp. 74–81.
43 Robin Higham, *100 Years of Air Power and Aviation* (College Station, TX: Texas A&M University Press, 2003), p. 33.
44 Ibid.
45 Ibid., p. 53.
46 Ibid., p. 31.
47 John Buckley, *Air Power in the Age of Total War* (Bloomington, IN: University of Indiana Press, 1999), p. 59.
48 Paris, *Winged Warfare*, p. 239.
49 Jackie L. Joiner, 'General Jan Christiaan Smuts' (MA, Air University, 1965), p. 13.
50 Joiner, 'Smuts', p. 14.
51 W. K. Hancock, *Smuts: The Sanguine Years 1870–1919* (Cambridge: Cambridge University Press, 1962), p. 107; David R. Woodward, 'The Imperial Strategist: Jan Christiaan Smuts and British Military Policy, 1917–1918', *The South African Military History Society Military History Journal* V, 4, at http://rapidttp.com/milhist/vol054dw.html, accessed 21/07/08, p. 1.
52 Anon, 'Gen. Smuts At The War Cabinet' *The Times*, Issue 41512, 23 June 1917, p. 5; Joiner, 'Smuts', p. 23.
53 *Oxford Dictionary of National Biography* [ODNB], s.v. 'Smuts, Jan Christiaan'; Hancock, *Smuts*, p. 435; Woodward, 'Imperial Strategist', p. 2.
54 H. A. Jones, *The War in the Air*, vol. V (Oxford: Clarendon Press, 1936), p. 11; Hancock, *Smuts*, p. 107; ODNB, s.v. 'Smuts, Jan Christiaan'; Sweetman, 'The Smuts Report', p. 155.
55 Anon, 'Lessons of the Air Attack', *The Times*, Issue 41489, 28 May 1917, p. 7; Anon, 'No Warning Of Air Raid', *The Times*, Issue 41491, 30 May 1917, p. 3.
56 Neville Jones, *The Origins of Strategic Bombing: A Study of the Development of British Air Strategic Thought and Practice up to 1918* (London: Kimber, 1973),

p. 131; Air Historical Branch, *The Royal Air Force in the Great War*, p. 237; Biddle, *Rhetoric and Reality*, pp. 29–30.

57 Air Historical Branch, *The Royal Air Force in the Great War*, p. 237; Scot Robertson, *The Development of RAF Strategic Bombing Doctrine, 1919-1939* (Westport, CT: Praeger, 1995), p. 16.

58 Jones, *The War in the Air*, vol. V, p. 10; Jones, *The Origins of Strategic Bombing*, pp. 135–6.

59 See: Anon, 'Attack On London', *The Times*, Issue 41525, 9 July 1917, p. 8; Anon, 'Air Raid on London', *The Times*, Issue 41525, 9 July 1917, p. 9; Anon, 'Commons and Air Raid', *The Times*, Issue 41526, 10 July 1917, p. 7; Tony Mason, *Air Power*, p. 23.

60 Raymond H. Fredette, *The Sky on Fire: The First Battle of Britain 1917-1918 and the Birth of the Royal Air Force* (London: Cassell, 1991), p. 79; George K. Williams, *Biplanes and Bombsights: British Bombing in World War I* (Maxwell, AL: Air University Press, 1999), p. 36; Morris, *First of Many*, p. 12.

61 John H. Morrow Jr., *The Great War in the Air: Military Aviation from 1909 to 1921* (Washington, DC: Smithsonian Institution Press, 1993), p. 246.

62 Jones, *The Origins of Strategic Bombing*, pp. 132–3.

63 Biddle, *Rhetoric and Reality*, pp. 30–1; Stephen Budiansky, *Air Power: The Men, Machines, and Ideas that Revolutionized War, from Kitty Hawk to Gulf War II* (New York, NY: Viking, 2004), p. 97.

64 Morris, *First of Many*, p. 12.

65 Allan R. Millet, Williamson Murray and Kenneth Waltman, 'The Effectiveness of Military Organizations' in Allan R. Millett and Williamson Murray (eds), *Military Effectiveness: Volume I – The First World War* (London: Unwin Hyman, 1988), p. 3; Michael Howard, 'The Forgotten Dimensions of Strategy' in *The Causes of War*, 2nd edn (London: Unwin, 1983), pp. 105–6.

66 Morrow, *The Great War*, p. 158; C. R. M. F. Cruttwell, *A History of the Great War 1914-1918* (Oxford: Clarendon Press, 1934), p. 392.

67 David Lloyd George, *War Memoirs of David Lloyd George*, vol. III (Boston: Little Brown, 1934), p. 49.

68 Biddle, *Rhetoric and Reality*, p. 32.

69 David Kaiser, *Politics & War: European Conflict from Philip II to Hitler* (Cambridge, MA: Harvard University Press, 1990), p. 328; Jones, *The Origins of Strategic Bombing*, p. 135; Robertson, *RAF Strategic Bombing Doctrine*, p. 16.

70 Fredette, *The Sky on Fire*, pp. 151–2; Budiansky, *Air Power*, p. 97; Robertson, RAF *Strategic Bombing Doctrine*, p. 16.

71 For a detailed analysis of Lloyd George's struggles with his generals see David R. Woodward, *Lloyd George and the Generals* (Newark, DE: Delaware University Press, 1983); V. H. Rothwell, *British War Aims and Peace Diplomacy 1914-1918* (Oxford: Calrendon Press, 1971), p. 7.

72　Lord Beaverbrook, *Men and Power 1917-1918* (New York: Duell, Sloan and Pearse, 1956), pp. xxxix–xli.
73　Ash, *The Air Revolution*, p. 97.
74　David Lloyd George, *War Memoirs* VI (Boston: Little Brown, 1937), p. 357.
75　Beaverbrook, *Men and Power*, p. 186.
76　John Gooch, 'The Maurice Debate', *Journal of Contemporary History* 3, 4 (October 1968), pp. 211–28, esp. p. 212; Cooper, *Independent Air Power*, pp. 98–9.
77　George L. Cook, 'Sir Robert Borden, Lloyd George and British Military Policy, 1917–1918', *The Historical Journal* 14, 2 (June 1971), pp. 371–95; esp. pp. 371–2.
78　Rothwell, *War Aims and Peace Diplomacy*, p. 114.
79　Jones, *The War in the Air*, vol. VI, p. 1; F. S. Northedge, '1917–1919: The Implications for Britain', *Journal of Contemporary History* 3, 4 (October, 1968), pp. 191–209; esp. p. 191; Brock Millman, 'A Counsel of Despair: British Strategy and War Aims, 1917–18', *The Journal of Contemporary History* 36, 2 (April 2001), pp. 241–70; esp. p. 244.
80　Millman, 'A Counsel of Despair', p. 246.
81　B. H. Liddell Hart, *The Real War 1914-1918* (Boston: Little Brown, 1964 [1930]), pp. 300–1.
82　Paul M. Kennedy, 'The First World War and the International Power System', *International Security*, 9, 1 (Summer, 1984), pp. 7–40, 21, 34.
83　George, *War Memoirs*, vol. III, p. 199.
84　H. A. Jones, *The War in the Air*, vol. VI (Oxford: Clarendon Press, 1937), p. 1; Millman, 'A Counsel of Despair', p. 251.
85　Ibid., pp. 248–9; Kaiser, *Politics & War*, p. 326.
86　Kaiser, *Politics & War*, p. 327; Fredette, *The Sky on Fire*, p. 71; Hancock, *Smuts*, p. 464.
87　W. B. Fest, 'British War Aims and German Peace Feelers during the First World War (December 1916–November 1918)', *The Historical Journal* 15, 2 (June 1972), pp. 285–308; esp. p. 300.
88　Woodward, *Lloyd George*, p. 117; Fest, 'British War Aims', pp. 294–6.
89　George, *War Memoirs*, vol. III, pp. 441–2.
90　Jones, 'The Origins of Strategic Bombing', pp. 136–7.
91　Rothwell, *War Aims and Peace Diplomacy*, p. 7; Biddle, *Rhetoric and Reality*, p. 27.
92　Paul Kennedy, 'Britain in the First World War' in Millett and Williamson (eds), *Military Effectiveness*, vol. I: *The First World War*, p. 41.
93　Jones, *The War in the Air*, vol. VI, pp. 10–11.
94　Rothwell, *War Aims and Peace Diplomacy*, p. 144.
95　Lloyd George, *War Memoirs*, vol. IV (Boston: Little Brown, 1934), p. 118.
96　Ibid., p. 115; Jones, *The War in the Air*, vol. VI, pp. 4–6.
97　Ibid., p. 7.
98　Ibid.

99 Robertson, *Strategic Bombing Doctrine*, p. 17.
100 'Report of Lieutenant-General J. C. Smuts's Committee, July 1917', in Jones, *The War in the Air*, vol. V, pp. 487–91.
101 Hancock, *Smuts*, p. 439; Robertson, *RAF Strategic Bombing Doctrine*, p. 17.
102 'Second Report of the Prime Minister's Committee on Air Organisation and Home Defence against Raids', dated 17 August 1917, in H. A. Jones, *The War in the Air* Appendices, p. 8; Robertson, *RAF Strategic Bombing Doctrine*, p. 17; Jones, *The War in the Air*, vol. VI, p. 11; Powers, *Strategy Without Slide-Rule*, p. 90.
103 Morrow, *The Great War in the Air*, p. 247.
104 'Second Report', in Jones, *The War in the Air* Appendices, p. 10.
105 Ibid.
106 Biddle, *Rhetoric and Reality*, p. 33; 'Second Report', in Jones, *The War in the Air* Appendices, pp. 10–11; Sweetman, 'The Smuts Report', pp. 162–4.
107 'Second Report', in Jones, *The War in the Air* Appendices, p. 11.
108 Ibid., pp. 10–11; Sweetman, 'The Smuts Report', p. 165.
109 'Second Report', in Jones, *The War in the Air* Appendices, pp. 11–12; Powers, *Strategy Without Slide-Rule*, p. 90.
110 'Second Report', in Jones, *The War in the Air* Appendices, p. 12.
111 Biddle, *Rhetoric and Reality*, p. 33.
112 Jones, *The War in the Air*, vol. VI, p. 13.
113 Ibid.
114 Biddle, *Rhetoric and Reality*, p. 33; Smith, *British Air Strategy*, p. 19.
115 Jones, *The War in the Air*, vol. VI, p. 14 and Biddle, *Rhetoric and Reality*, p. 33.
116 Smith, *British Air Strategy*, p. 19.
117 Ash, *The Air Revolution*, p. 190.
118 Jones, *The War in the Air*, vol. VI, p. 14.
119 Biddle, *Rhetoric and Reality*, p. 34.
120 Jones, *The War in the Air*, vol. VI, p. 14.
121 Fredette, *The Sky on Fire*, p. 197.
122 Anon, 'Air Raid On London', *The Times*, Issue 41575, 5 September 1917, p. 6; Anon, 'The Moonlight Air Raid', *The Times*, Issue 41576, 6 September 1917, p. 7.
123 J. M. Spaight, *The Beginnings of Organised Air Power: A Historical Study* (London: Longmans, 1927), p. 138.
124 Jones, *The War in the Air*, vol. VI, p. 16.
125 Cooper, *Independent Air Power*, pp. 115–17.
126 Jones, *The War in the Air*, vol. VI, p. 17.
127 Saunders, *Per Ardua*, p. 222.
128 Spaight, *Organised Air Power*, p. 132.
129 Cooper, *Independent Air Power*, p. 116.
130 Spaight, *Organised Air Power*, p. 138.

131 Lord Northcliffe made public his refusal of the position in an open letter to the Prime Minister, see: Lord Northcliffe, 'The Air Ministry – Letter to the Editor', *The Times*, Issue 41637, 16 November 1917, p. 7.
132 Jones, *The War in the Air*, vol. VI, p. 23; Cooper, *Independent Air Power*, p. 120.
133 Ibid., p. 128.
134 Ibid., p. 122; Powers, *Strategy Without Slide-Rule*, pp. 101–2.
135 Beaverbrook, *Men and Power*, p. 220.
136 Ibid.
137 Morrow, *The Great War in the Air*, p. 319.
138 Biddle, *Rhetoric and Reality*, p. 36; Cooper, *Independent Air Power*, p. 122; Smith, *British Air Strategy*, pp. 20–1.
139 Cooper, *Independent Air Power*, p. 123; Biddle, *Rhetoric and Reality*, p. 36; Fredette, *The Sky on Fire*, p. 207.
140 Beaverbrook, *Men and Power*, pp. 223–4.
141 Ibid., p. 226; Biddle, *Rhetoric and Reality*, p. 36; Cooper, *Independent Air Power*, pp. 129–30; Paris, *Winged Warfare*, pp. 241–2.
142 Jones, *The War in the Air*, vol. VI, pp. 24–7; Cooper, *Independent Air Power*, pp. 124, 128; Powers, *Strategy Without Slide-Rule*, p. 94; Morrow, *The Great War in the Air*, p. 320.
143 Morrow, *The Great War in the Air*, p. 324.
144 Ibid., p. 320.
145 Biddle, *Rhetoric and Reality*, pp. 37, 41–2; Saunders, *Per Ardua*, p. 221.
146 Morrow, *The Great War in the Air*, p. 320.
147 Biddle, *Rhetoric and Reality*, p. 40; Cooper, *Independent Air Power*, p. 132; Powers, *Strategy Without Slide-Rule*, pp. 105–6; Robertson, *RAF Strategic Bombing*, pp. 22–3; Morrow, *The Great War in the Air*, pp. 320–3.
148 Lloyd George, *War Memoirs*, vol. IV (Boston: Little Brown, 1934), p. 103.
149 Robertson, *RAF Strategic Bombing*, p. 19.
150 Biddle, *Rhetoric and Reality*, pp. 42–3; Cooper, *Independent Air Power*, p. 134.
151 During 1918, the Independent Force received only 427 of the 1,817 bombing aircraft sent to the Front. At the armistice, only 10 of 99 squadrons and 140 of 1,799 aircraft of the RAF on the Western Front were under Trenchard's command; Cooper, *Independent Air Power*, p. 136; Powers, *Strategy Without Slide-Rule*, p. 106; Morrow, *The Great War in the Air*, p. 324.
152 James S. Corum, *The Luftwaffe: Creating the Operational Air War, 1918–1940* (Lawrence, KS: University Press of Kansas, 1997), p. 15.
153 Robertson, *RAF Strategic Bombing*, p. 21.
154 Buckley, *Total War*, p. 67.
155 Paris, *Winged Warfare*, pp. 232–4.
156 Cooper, *Independent Air Power*, p. 143.

157 Biddle, *Rhetoric and Reality*, pp. 41–2.
158 Buckley, *Total War*, p. 61.
159 Biddle, *Rhetoric and Reality*, p. 47.
160 Paris, *Winged Warfare*, p. 239.
161 Biddle, *Rhetoric and Reality*, pp. 57–66.
162 Buckley, *Total War*, pp. 61–2.
163 Biddle, *Rhetoric and Reality*, p. 44.
164 Cooper, *Independent Air Power*, p. 151.
165 Ibid., p. 154.
166 David Stevenson, *Cataclysm: The First World War as Political Tragedy* (New York, NY: Basic Books, 2004), pp. 272–3.
167 Biddle, *Rhetoric and Reality*, p. 67.
168 Buckley, *Total War*, p. 62.
169 Ibid., p. 68; Paris, *Winged Warfare*, p. 243.
170 Harold R. Winton, To *Change an Army: General Sir John Burnett-Stuart and British Armored Doctrine, 1927–1938* (Lawrence, KS: University Press of Kansas, 1988), p. 240.
171 Buckley, *Total War*, p. 69.
172 Colin S. Gray, *Explorations in Strategy* (Westport, CT: Greenwood Press, 1996), chapters 1 and 4.

9

The Genesis of Modern Warfare: The Contribution of Aviation Logistics

Peter Dye

The German Army in the Hundred Days campaign was in a state of shock created by the momentum of successive Allied attacks and the debilitating effect of constant retreat in the face of an apparently untiring enemy. The British Army's success was built on innovative tactics and hard-earned operational competence. Significant as these attributes were, they only became decisive because of persistent logistic excellence. This was not simply a matter of quantitative superiority (which undoubtedly existed by 1918) but the result of a comprehensive and highly sophisticated logistic system that met the ebbs and flows of operational demand while retaining flexibility and responsiveness. In this context, the ability to sustain mobile warfare during the Hundred Days campaign was as remarkable as the ability to meet the Western Front's unprecedented materiel demands in the previous four years.

The development of air power during the First World War illustrates the central role of logistics in enabling battlefield success. This chapter addresses how logistics enabled an immature technology to be transformed into an effective weapon – in the form of the Royal Flying Corps (RFC), and from April 1918 its successor the Royal Air Force (RAF) – that was both the precondition and precipitant for modern warfare. It was air power that allowed the British Expeditionary Force (BEF) to deliver overwhelming kinetic effect through predicted artillery fire. Finally, the chapter will discuss how the aviation logistic principles and practices developed on the Western Front provided the foundation for RAF post-war planning and presaged operational success in the Battle of Britain.

The First World War and its aftermath largely shaped the twentieth century. In scale and intensity it was quite different from any other war previously fought. It was also a conflict in which technology dominated events to a degree unparalleled in human conflict. This was never more evident than in the rapid expansion of the flying services and the increasing impact of air power on the battlefield. The large numbers of high-performance aircraft operating on the Western Front in 1918 bore little resemblance to the few, underpowered, unreliable and generally ineffective machines of 1914. It also witnessed the birth of the world's first independent air service, the RAF.

The idea that the four years of bitter fighting on the Western Front represented something more than just the first total war in history only emerged in the 1990s. The end of the Cold War led some to argue that a fundamental change was occurring in how wars would be fought in the future. The world (or more precisely the American military) stood at the threshold of a Revolution in Military Affairs (RMA). This concept had emerged from the ideas first outlined by Michael Roberts in 1956 about a 'military revolution' in early modern military history.[1] Roberts focussed on the 100 years from 1560 in which changes in military technology had led to large political and social consequences. His ideas were subsequently developed by others, notably Geoffrey Parker, to explain the rise of the West to global dominance over the period 1500–1800.[2] Since then, other 'military revolutions' have been identified (by one account there have been at least 23 since the fourteenth century),[3] although this may be more to do with a natural desire to find patterns in events than rigorous analysis.

Colin Gray has written on the arguments for and against RMAs.[4] He has been particularly critical about the claims for historical antecedents, pointing out that profound change need not be revolutionary and where military revolutions have occurred they have often ridden on the back of revolutionary social, economic and political changes. Even so, he has supported the view that the First World War did produce an RMA, endorsing the proposition first expressed by Jonathan Bailey that:

> Between 1917 and 1918, a RMA took place which, it is contended, was more than merely that; rather it amounted to a Military Revolution which was the most significant development in the history of war to date, and remains so. It amounted to the birth of what will be called the Modern Style of Warfare with the advent of 'three dimensional', artillery indirect fire as the foundation of planning at the tactical, operational and strategic levels of war. This was indeed so revolutionary that the burgeoning of armour, airpower and the arrival of

the Information Age since then amount to no more than complements to it – incremental technical improvements to the efficiency of the conceptual model of the Modern Style of Warfare – and they are themselves rather its products than its peers.[5]

At this point, I am conscious of Christopher Duffy's warnings – in the context of the Battle of the Somme – about the desire of writers to fit technical and tactical advances into a learning curve.[6] To his mind, the notion of a military revolution has not only distorted the study of early modern history but also led some historians to date the birth of twentieth-century mechanized warfare to the last years of the war, rather than 1916 when the British Army first successfully co-ordinated the action of artillery, aircraft and infantry. Given the generous timescales in which both Michael Roberts and Geoffrey Parker placed their military revolutions, it may seem strange to argue about the exact year in which the 'modern' style of warfare first emerged. What is not in debate, however, is that warfare was transformed during the First World War. My concern is that the role of air power in this process has not been properly understood and the essential contribution of logistics largely overlooked.[7]

The Modern Style of Warfare, as described by Jonathan Bailey, has the following characteristics:

- It takes place over an extended area and is three-dimensional;
- Time (tempo) is critical;
- Intelligence is the key to targeting;
- High value targets can be hit accurately;
- Firepower is applied to achieve specific effect;
- Command, control and communications [C^3] systems are available to fuse these characteristics.

Each of these elements depends on air power. To take the first point, without the ability to operate in the third dimension there can be no three-dimensional warfare. This was achieved on the Western Front because the RFC was able to establish and maintain air superiority. But this had to be fought for and could only be sustained through continuing effort (as much against the weather as the enemy) and at considerable cost. Trenchard's doctrine of the offensive – sometimes characterized as a visceral attempt to demonstrate the warrior ethos of the RFC – was aimed at securing and maintaining the ability to operate at will across the battlefield while denying the German Air Service the same advantage. From the French experience at Verdun, the RFC had concluded that air power was achieved through offensive action – not defensive patrols that drained resources and handed the initiative to the enemy.

The RFC, with its ability to achieve effect at distance, day and night and through air reconnaissance to anticipate and counter the enemy's actions, enabled commanders to achieve significantly greater operational tempo. Coupled with airborne communications, in the form of wireless telegraphy and, towards the end of the war, wireless telephony, the RFC was able to provide a more comprehensive, detailed and timely picture of the battlefield than had ever been achieved before.

The vital importance of intelligence has already been highlighted. As significant as flash spotting and sound ranging were in identifying enemy batteries and vital points, these techniques were limited (particularly in the mobile battle) and depended on large-scale accurate mapping which itself relied on aerial photography and air reconnaissance. Arguably, it took the RFC until 1917 to develop the necessary equipment and consistently provide the map makers with the quality they needed. The 1/20,000 and 1/10,000 maps covering the entire Western Front, produced by the Royal Engineer (RE) Survey Sections, together with daily air photography, provided the accuracy needed by the garrison and field artillery to neutralize enemy batteries in the short, intensive preliminary bombardment that was the foundation for British success in 1918.[8]

It was not just the artillery war where air power played such a central role. The RFC was able to deliver firepower to specific effect as the operational situation demanded. The fighter squadrons that machine-gunned and bombed German columns in March 1918 were the same that had previously protected the corps squadrons in their artillery co-operation duties and the same that a few months later flew close air support against German anti-tank guns during the Battle of Amiens.

In terms of C^3, the RFC was essential to the effective co-ordination and synchronization of firepower. As Bidwell and Graham have observed, 'The starting point and pivot for the new artillery techniques was the RFC pilot'.[9] In reality, this had been evident from the very earliest days of the war. Many of the techniques and systems that were employed so successfully at the Somme were in fact introduced more than a year earlier. Squared maps and the clock code to allow aircraft to control artillery fire were invented in the autumn of 1914 by two RE officers belonging to No. 9 (Wireless) Squadron. The same unit undertook much of the experimental work to make wireless telegraphy a viable technique, such that RFC aircraft were able to direct artillery fire with considerable effect as early as May 1915, during the Battle of Festubert. By 1916, individual batteries were provided with dedicated RFC wireless operators, while each corps squadron had one or more artillery liaison officers with landlines to the divisional artillery staffs. Nearly all (90%) counter-battery observation was done by airmen using wireless and, as a result, 'the success of the artillery battle had come to depend on the weather being suitable for flying'.[10]

None of this may seem particularly novel or contentious. It has been well described by John Terraine, Shelford Bidwell and Dominick Graham among others:

> The most momentous contribution – greater than the tank – was from the maturing air force, the RFC/RAF, on its own initiative developing tactical air support and later strategic support, feeding reliable information to the intelligence staff and also enhancing the scope and accuracy of artillery fire. Improvements in radio telegraphy and the invention of the thermionic valve benefitted the air arm, leading to the first steps towards revolution in what we now call C^3I [Command, control, communications and information].[11]

Everything hinged, however, on the ability to operate in the third dimension. By 1916, the technology, techniques and systems were all in place to make intimate co-operation between the RFC and the artillery the norm, but to make it fully effective required that the RFC achieve air superiority.[12]

Winning the air battle depended on:

- Quality (relative to the enemy);
- Capability (the deployment of effective tactics and systems);
- Persistence (sufficient aircraft in the right place at the right time).

The RFC's logistic organization played a vital role in meeting each of these requirements, but by enabling continued operations in the face of combat attrition and high wastage, it also endowed the RFC with a critical advantage. The relative technical efficiency between the RFC and the German Air Service waxed and waned throughout the war. In general, no side ever enjoyed an overwhelming advantage such that they could operate with impunity. The innovative tactics and systems introduced by the RFC were important but, ultimately, counted for nothing unless they could be deployed where and when required. The ability to consistently field more aircraft than the enemy, irrespective of wastage, allowed the RFC to win the air battle on the Western Front.

By the Armistice, the total strength of the RAF on the Western Front (including the Independent Force) comprised some 1,800 front line aircraft and 51,000 personnel – a considerable increase on the 66 aircraft and 1,000 personnel deployed by the RFC to France in August 1914.[13] Perhaps, though, we should ask ourselves, why so few and why so many? The 1,800 front line aircraft represented only 12 per cent of those that had actually been delivered to the RFC in France during the course of the war (some 15,000 machines).[14] On the other hand, only 8 per cent of the 51,000 personnel were classed as combatants[15] – the equivalent figure for the BEF was 65 per cent.[16]

The logistic system supporting air operations on the Western Front was clearly rather different from anything seen previously. John Terraine has observed that 'the Great War was from the beginning the greatest war of technical innovation ever fought', adding that modern wars had become, as a war of masses with modern weapons sustained by modern mass production, 'a matter of organization and specialist skills in all the complex areas of logistics'.[17]

Of these complex areas, it was aviation that demanded the most comprehensive and sophisticated support arrangements. In fact, to sustain the RFC in the field it proved necessary to bring mass production to the front line. Operating aircraft on the Western Front required significant numbers of skilled and semi-skilled tradesmen. Low reliability, particularly of engines, frequent accidents and the effects of weather – even if overnight hangarage was available – made maintenance and repair a continuous activity. There were limits however to what could be achieved at squadron level, so a large network of depots, Army Air Parks (AAP) and repair and salvage sections were also created. The depots and parks rapidly expanded to store aircraft and spares as well as to undertake salvage, repair, modification and maintenance.

It was the unexpected scale and complexity of these tasks that provided the greatest challenge. The tempo of air operations and the key logistic drivers were quite different from all that had gone before. Attrition was extremely high – as a result of accidents and low reliability as much as from enemy action – demanding a constant supply of new aircraft and aircrew. For example, between March and October 1918 over 6,500 aircraft were struck off the strength of the front line squadrons, of which 4 per cent was attributed to poor airfields, 29 per cent to forced-landings, 36 per cent to enemy action, 6 per cent to time expiry and 25 per cent to pilot error (Figure 9.1).[18]

Engine wastage posed a particular problem. Although damaged engines could often be repaired, and generally survived a crash better than the airframe, a larger pool of engines was needed to cope with low reliability and the need for regular overhauls. In the early part of the war, engines could not be run for more than 20 hours without overhaul. This had risen to an average of 35 hours by 1917 and, for some types, to 100 hours by the end of the war. Even so, the increase in operational flying meant that total arisings (lost, damaged or unserviceable engines) continued to outstrip aircraft losses. The difficulties of transportation, the need to reduce pipeline times and a desire to avoid impeding new production in the United Kingdom, encouraged the creation of a dedicated engine factory at Rouen. By the Armistice the Engine Repair Shops comprised over 5,000 RAF personnel and was producing over 400 repaired and overhauled engines each month.

The disparity between new production and supply, particularly in engines, meant that salvage and repair could make a significant contribution to operations (Figure 9.2).[19]

Obsolescence, design and manufacturing shortcomings and shortage of critical equipment also required a high level of modification and rework – all to be undertaken in the field. A wide range of special equipment, tools and a

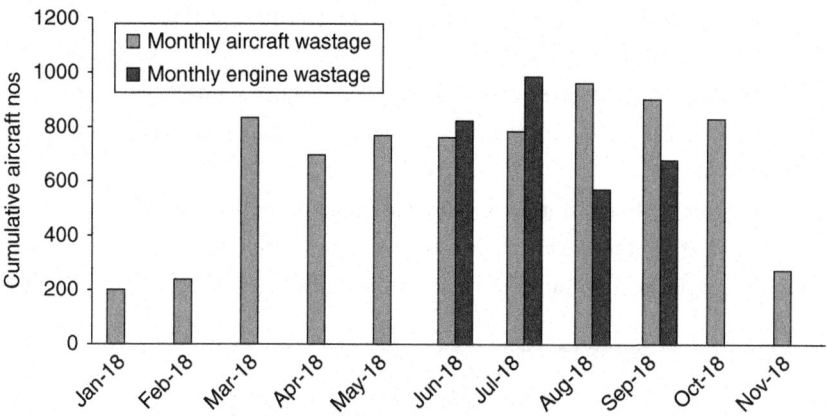

Figure 9.1 Aircraft and engine wastage – 1918
Source: TNA AIR 1/926/204/5/915, AIR 1/998/204/5/1242 & 1243

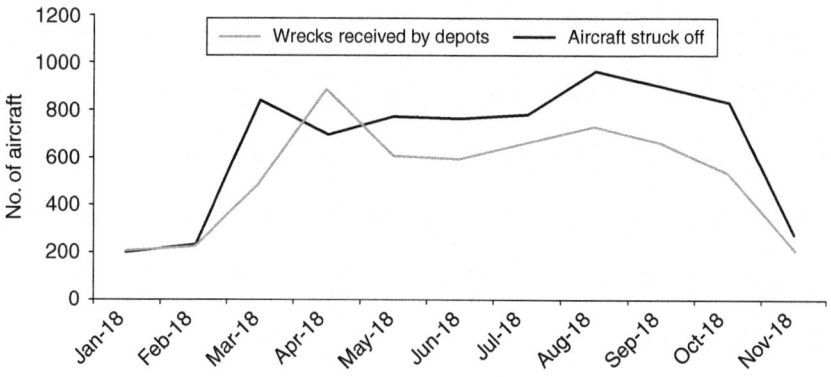

Figure 9.2 Aircraft Salvage – 1918
Source: TNA AIR 1/1111/204/5/1895

myriad of individual parts and components had to be readily available to support these activities as well as to carry out routine maintenance. This necessitated the creation of an extensive ground organization, employing large numbers of skilled and semi-skilled personnel, underpinned by a supply chain that stretched from the front line, via the repair depots and AAP, to the factories at home (Figure 9.3).

Aircraft and their component parts largely populated this pipeline, together with a constant flow of technical information, spares, equipment and personnel. However, unlike previous logistic systems, it was not one dominated by consumables but by scarce, high-value items that flowed to and from the front line.[20] Finally, the entire system – including the depots – had to be mobile to allow air power to be concentrated at specific parts of the front. As a result, and unlike any previous arm, non-combatants hugely outnumbered combatants. This was no subtle shift in the balance of roles but a step change in the 'teeth-to-tail' ratio. A characteristic of the 'modern' style of warfare that has become more pronounced over the succeeding decades across all arms and all environments – air, land and sea.

The logistic system embracing these varied activities had few if any parallels. By the Armistice, the RAF's technical inventory comprised more than 50,000 separate line items. No single organization had ever had to manage a stock

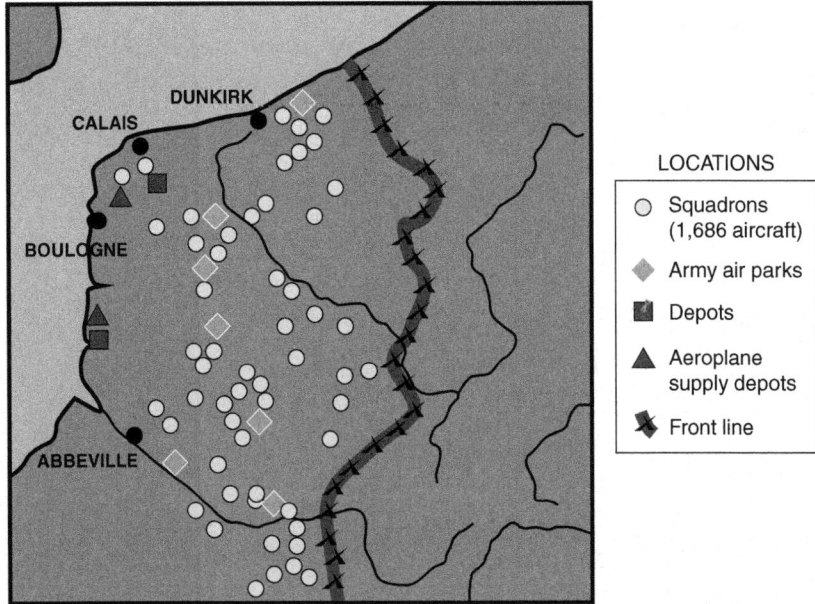

Figure 9.3 RAF logistic organization – August 1918

holding of this size or complexity; a challenge made all the more difficult by the delicate nature of much of the equipment involved, rapid obsolescence and high modification rates. The effective and timely support of operations on the Western Front and in more distant theatres, not only made heavy demands on the supply chain but also forced a high degree of self-reliance among the deployed units.

The foundation for logistic excellence was a plentiful supply of motor vehicles. From its foundation in 1912, the RFC's squadrons and support units were provided with a wide range of lorries, cars and motor cycles to provide mobility in the field and to transport personnel, stores and equipment. The RFC was, in effect, the first fully-mechanized corps in the British Army. By October 1917 just over 2,700 vehicles were employed on the Western Front in support of air operations.[21] The largest single group (2,533) comprised heavy and light tenders – including specialist repair vehicles – approximately 10 per cent of all lorries employed by the BEF, even though the RFC represented just 1.1 per cent of the BEF's total manpower.[22] Specialist RFC transport units included Air Ammunition Columns, responsible for the supply of ordnance to each brigade and Tent Detachments responsible for dismantling, moving and erecting airfield and depot tentage. The latter capability proved particularly important during periods of rapid movement as it freed squadron personnel to concentrate exclusively on engineering and maintenance duties. A further innovation in September 1917 was the creation of Reserve Lorry Parks (RLP). Each brigade was provided with a dedicated RLP holding a pool of some 30 lorries, achieved by reducing the vehicle establishment of the individual squadrons and AAPs. This strategic reserve was employed to meet short-notice or urgent requirements at the direction of HQ RFC.[23]

The success of the RFC and RAF logistic system in meeting the front line's needs was exceptional. The average monthly aircraft wastage rate was equivalent to 37 per cent in 1917 and closer to 52 per cent in 1918. In the last ten months of the war, combat losses alone amounted to a little over 2,800 aircraft. When accidents and other causes are included, the total number of aircraft written off came to more than 7,300 – or 400 per cent of front line strength. Yet aircraft availability grew through the year as did the flying effort (Figure 9.4).[24]

By July 1918, the RFC was flying nearly twice the operational hours (60,000) as a year previously during the Third Battle of Ypres (32,750).[25]

The wastage in aircrew reached similarly high levels. In the nine months to October 1918, the RAF lost more than 3,600 pilots. Although a significant proportion were killed or wounded in combat, many died in accidents. The single largest cause of wastage, however, was the requirement to rest aircrew

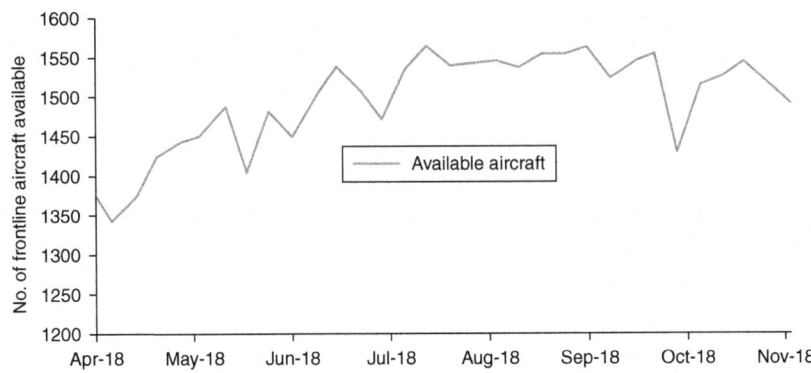

Figure 9.4 Available RAF aircraft – 1918
Source: TNA AIR 1/1073/204/5/1655

before their efficiency was impaired and the need to feed experienced instructors into the flying training system. For planning purposes, the RFC assessed the productive life of a pilot on the Western Front as about three months (depending on role). Many pilots flew for much longer than this and did several tours but, on average, some 550 new pilots were required each month just to maintain the front line squadrons at full strength.

Serviceability rates – a good indication of engineering effort and supply efficiency – remained consistently high. Throughout the Somme and Third Ypres the number of serviceable aircraft never fell below 88 per cent. Even during the difficult Bloody April period it remained above 86 per cent. Notwithstanding the high wastage of 1918 and the significantly increased flying effort, serviceability rates continued to be maintained at around 90 per cent (Figure 9.5).[26]

This achievement reflects both the skills and hard work of front line squadron personnel and the ability of the supply system to provide spares and replacement equipment where and when needed.

The March 1918 German Offensive, although anticipated, severely tested the RFC's logistic system. The impact is best illustrated by examining the Brigade serviceability rates. Although the data is not complete – the daily reporting regime briefly faltered in the face of the rapid German advance – the increased flying effort allied to the disruption caused by having to move airfields at short notice saw serviceability fall (at least in the short term). Up to 21 March (the opening day of the German offensive) the daily percentage of aircraft serviceable across I, II, III and V Brigades varied between 100 per cent and 80 per cent (Figure 9.6).[27]

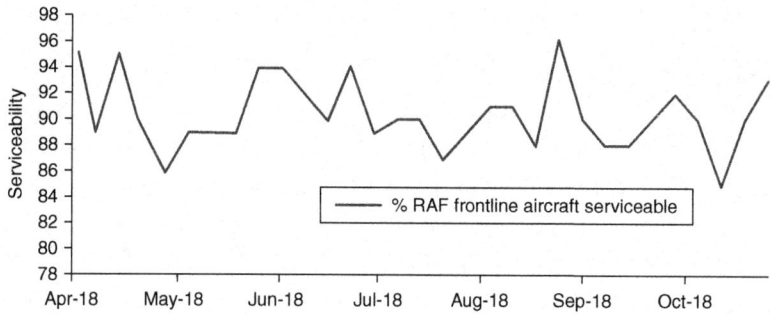

Figure 9.5 Weekly front line serviceability – April–November 1918
Source: TNA AIR 1/1073/204/5/1655

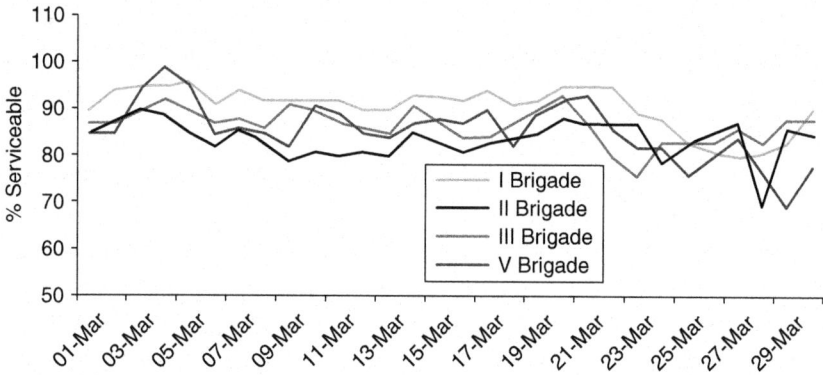

Figure 9.6 RFC brigade serviceability rates – March 1918
Source: TNA AIR 1/838/204/5/285 & AIR 1/838/204/5/287

Thereafter, it ranged from 90 per cent to as low as 70 per cent The impact was particularly marked on units immediately in the path of the attack (III and V Brigades) and less so on those further north (such as I and II Brigades), although within a week the impact across all brigades was notable. Even so, the supply of aircraft and spares did not falter, as Salmond made clear in a personal letter to Trenchard, 'Thanks for the supplies of machines which have kept us going very well'.[28]

The selfless efforts of the ground crew in keeping the squadrons operating during these difficult days are recorded in numerous accounts. Guy Knocker, a pilot with No. 65 Squadron equipped with Sopwith Camels, wrote to his parents on 1 April 1918 that:

The mechanics are working frightfully hard at present as there are beaucoup crashes and buses to repair and very little time to do it in. No workshop or anything and all work has to be done in the open or in a sort of extempore hangar.[29]

The ready availability of transport meant that the movement of units and the delivery of spares and supplies continued in the face of a German attack that threatened to break through to the Channel Ports. Major-General John Salmond commented that 'The transport has stuck it all right so far, but I visualize a large number of moves in the future and shall be obliged for the extra vehicles of the extra Lorry Park'.[30] The RFC's inherent mobility was reflected in the relatively modest materiel losses (other than aircraft) suffered by the front line squadrons. Units were largely able to pack up and move complete with their equipment despite the rapid German advance. By 25 March 4,300 hydrogen tubes, 1,500 bombs, 40 light aircraft tents, one car, two lorries and two light tenders had been abandoned or destroyed.[31] Among the major moves prompted by the German advance was the complete relocation of the main aeroplane depots at St-Omer and Candas, both organizations relocating to sites closer to the Channel coast within a matter of days and without any interruption in the supply of new or repaired aircraft.

Although the German Spring Offensive and the Hundred Days Campaign demanded unprecedented mobility on the part of the flying squadrons, as well as a significant number of logistic units, there was no significant or enduring impact on the supply of spares or replacement aircraft. Even with the rapid changes in airfields from August onwards, aircraft availability continued to grow while serviceability rates were maintained. Indeed, the forcible uprooting of so many units ensured that they were much better placed for the mobile warfare that emerged from August onwards. In one sense, therefore, the German March Offensive better prepared the RAF's logistic organization for the challenge of supporting the flying squadrons through the Hundred Days campaign.

For the 15 RE8 equipped corps squadrons employed on the Western Front (forming the heart of the RAF's artillery co-operation effort) aircraft serviceability stayed above 90 per cent until the end of September, although there was a steady decline over the summer (Figure 9.7).[32]

Just as importantly, however, front line numbers were maintained at over 300 machines throughout the Hundred Days campaign – reflecting the ability to replenish losses notwithstanding the wastage suffered during some of the heaviest air fighting of the war (Figure 9.8).[33]

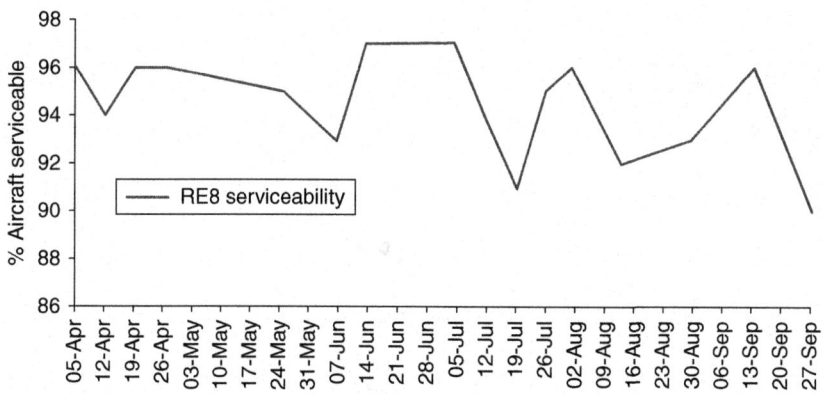

Figure 9.7 Art co-op (RE8) serviceability – 1918
Source: TNA AIR 1/1019/204/5/1379 & 1383, AIR 1/951/204/5/1020

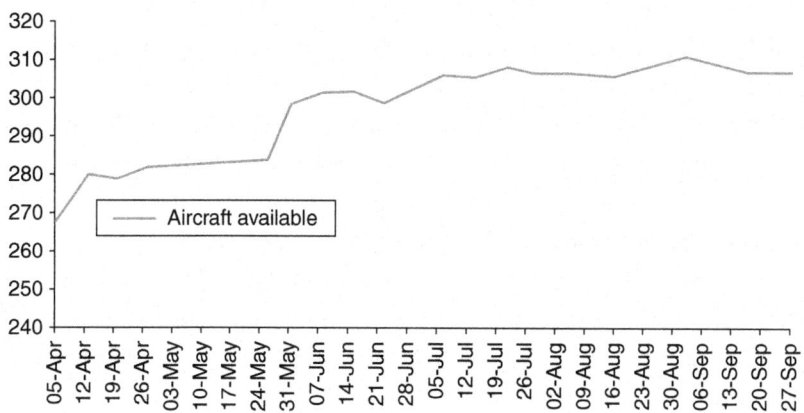

Figure 9.8 Available art co-op aircraft (RE8) – 1918
Source: TNA AIR 1/1019/204/5/1379 & 1383, AIR 1/951/204/5/1020

Significantly, the combat losses suffered by the corps squadrons fell from 30 per cent in 1917 to 17 per cent in 1918 – the brunt of the air fighting being borne, as intended, by the single-seat fighter squadrons.

The degree of mobility required by the RAF during 1918 can be judged from the frequency of airfield moves compared to the previous year. For the group of corps squadrons equipped with the RE8, changes in airfields occurred on average three times a month during 1917. The German March Offensive saw this rise to 20 moves in a single month before it fell back in June and July to the 1917 average. However, with the Allied advance it rose rapidly from August onwards reaching a peak of 25 airfield moves in October alone (Figure 9.9).[34]

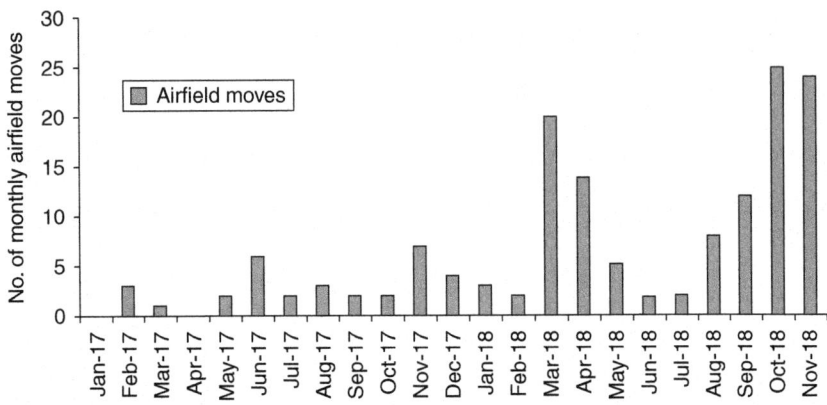

Figure 9.9 Art co-op sqn (RE8) – Airfield moves 1917/1918
Source: Jefford, RAF Squadrons

All of this came at a price. Logistic excellence was not cheap. By the Armistice, the total cost of the RAF to the nation, in materiel and human terms, amounted to £200M per year – or 4 per cent of Gross Domestic Product. Daily expenditure had reached over £0.5M, or 7 per cent of Britain's total daily war expenditure. This was set to rise still further with some £165M of outstanding aviation orders, more than half the production commitments of the Ministry of Munitions. In fact, it was the sheer cost of the air services and the evident inefficiency and squabbling about the allocation of scarce resources that led directly to the formation of the Air Council in 1916 and, ultimately, the establishment of a separate Air Ministry and subsequently, an independent air force.

The result of this huge investment was the production each month of more than 4,300 aircraft and 5,300 engines (including those repaired or rebuilt) and a trained output of 1,200 pilots and 3,000 other ranks. Without this effort, average monthly losses of 2,200 aircraft and 3,000 engines (written off and damaged) and some 800–900 pilot casualties would have rapidly curtailed operations (Figure 9.10).

By the Armistice, the RAF held 22,171 aircraft on charge but just 6,740 were assigned to operational duties (comprising the Western Front, Italy, the Middle East, Macedonia, home defence and anti-submarine operations) and of these, only 2,896 could be regarded as effective – the remainder being in store, in transit or under repair. As some 10–15 per cent of front line aircraft were unserviceable at any one time; this left just 2,500 available to be employed on active operations. When the civilian labour involved in aircraft and aero-engine production and associated spares, together with those engaged in repair activities are added

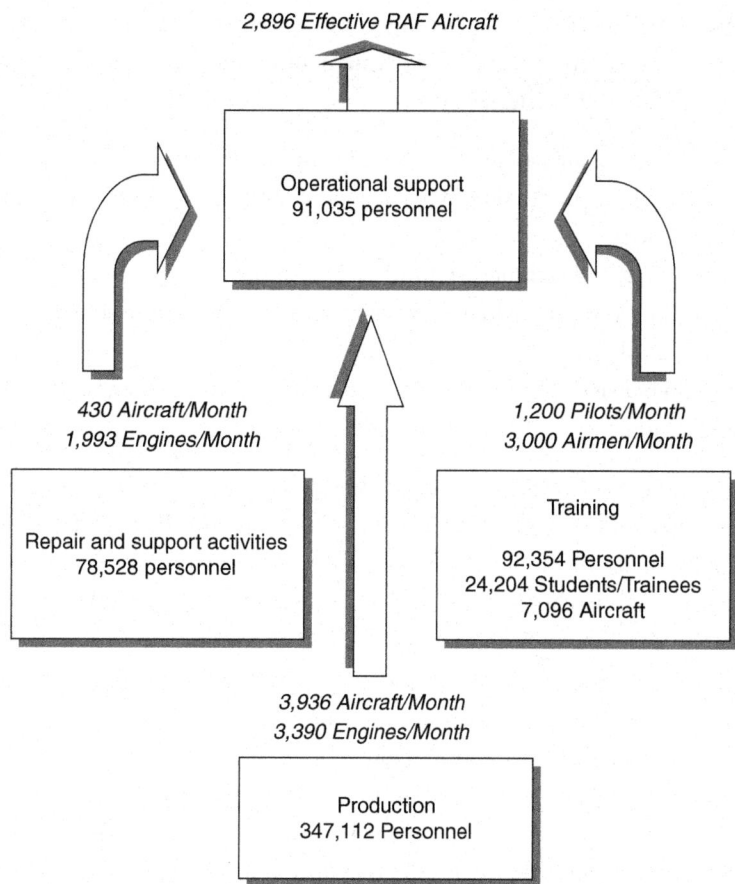

Figure 9.10 Supply of RAF aeronautical material – October 1918

together, the total number of personnel involved in supporting the RAF rises to around 630,000 (including trainees, instructors and support staffs).[35] In other words, a single serviceable front line aircraft required over 240 personnel (uniformed and civilian) to support, maintain and operate it.[36]

When one reflects on the capacity, resources, ingenuity and sheer relentless effort spent to build and sustain the RFC it is little wonder that Martin van Creveld has argued that 'modern war' only emerged with the logistic revolution that occurred between 1914 and 1916. In his view, logistics prevailed over operations and strategy and only when this challenge was addressed was victory possible.[37]

The RAF's experience on the Western Front profoundly affected the Service's thinking during the interwar period. The view that air warfare was an attritional as well as a technological struggle was firmly embedded at both the organizational and individual level. Not surprisingly, the planning that underpinned the expansion of the RAF during the re-armament period[38] envisaged a future air war that would be characterized by:

- High wastage in aircraft and crews requiring significant reserves;
- Substantial new production to make good combat losses and to counter obsolescence;
- A large flying and technical training organization;
- An agile and responsive logistic system capable of reacting to rapid technological change;
- A comprehensive system of aircraft and aero-engine recovery, repair and modification.

The RAF invested heavily in creating substantial reserves and a large, widely dispersed network of depots and storage units to support the high attrition that war would bring. The ability to recover and rapidly repair aircraft and engines was central to this scheme – although it was subsequently found necessary to expand the system to include a large UK-based civilian repair organization. The RAF's success in the Battle of Britain, where fighter and pilot wastage approached the levels seen on the Western Front, was due as much to its logistic superiority as any other factor. As a result, Fighter Command grew steadily stronger throughout the fighting while the Luftwaffe steadily weakened.[39]

These characteristics continue to define air power to this day. The heavy demand for resources, the high tempo of technological change and the need for an agile and flexible engineering organization were as relevant in Iraq and Afghanistan as they were in 1918 and 1940. There is no doubt that the First World War defined an enduring relationship between logistics and air power that shows little sign of weakening a ninety or more years on from the formation of the RAF.

Finally, it is necessary to return to Jonathan Bailey's definition of Modern Warfare. While there are no issues with the first part of his statement, it is highly debatable whether air power was simply the *product* of the modern style of warfare. An alternative proposition is that taken by the German official historians of the Somme who concluded that the RFC had deployed large numbers of compact formations of fighters that were technically superior, and developed a novel way of conducting aerial warfare aimed at:

- an aggressive battle to win air superiority which extended well behind the enemy rear;

- the systematic beating-down of German batteries in concert with artillery;
- combat reconnaissance for the infantry, combined with lending support in the attack, assuring communication between the fighting troops and the command.⁴⁰

There is little doubt, therefore, that air power was not the *product* of the modern style of warfare but the *precipitant*, while logistic excellence was the *precondition*.

Notes

1. Jeremy Black has summarized the background to this concept and the current state of the debate in 'Was There a Military Revolution in Early Modern Europe?' *History Today* 57, 8 (July 2008), pp. 34–41.
2. Geoffrey Parker, *The Military Revolution: Military Innovation and the Rise of the West, 1500–1800* (Cambridge: Cambridge University Press, 1988). It is difficult to avoid the conclusion that the end of the Cold War engendered a narrow, western-centric and triumphalist interpretation of history. For example, see Victor Davis Hanson, *The Western Way of War: Infantry Battle in Classical Greece* (Oxford: Oxford University Press, 1989).
3. Williamson Murray and MacGregor Knox, 'Thinking about Revolutions in Warfare' in Williamson Murray and MacGregor Knox (eds), *The Dynamics of Military Revolution, 1300–2050* (Cambridge, Cambridge University Press, 2001), p. 13.
4. Colin Gray, *Strategy for Chaos: Revolutions in Military Affairs and the Evidence of History* (London: Frank Cass, 2002), pp. 140–1.
5. Jonathan Bailey, *The First World War and the Birth of the Modern Style of Warfare*, Strategic and Combat Studies Institute Occasional Paper No 22 (Camberley: Strategic and Combat Studies Institute,1996). A version of this paper with some changes appeared as 'The First World War and the Birth of Modern Warfare', in Murray and Knox (eds), *The Dynamics of Military Revolution*, pp. 132–53.
6. Christopher Duffy, *Through German Eyes – The British and The Somme 1916* (London: Pheonix, 2007), p. 323.
7. Colin Gray has himself noted that much work remains to be done on the role of air power in the First World War. See *Strategy for Chaos*, p. 220.
8. An excellent summary of the RFC's role in developing the new artillery techniques is provided in Shelford Bidwell and Dominick Graham, *Firepower: British Army Weapons & Theories of War 1904–1945* (London: Allen and Unwin, 1982).
9. Ibid., p. 101.
10. Ibid., p. 143.

11 Shelford Bidwell, 'After The Wall Came Tumbling Down: A Historical Perspective', *RUSI Journal* 135, 3 (Autumn 1990), pp. 57–9.
12 John Terraine, 'Lessons of Air Warfare', *RUSI Journal* 137, 4 (August 1992), pp. 53–7.
13 H. A. Jones, *The War in the Air, Being the Story of the Part Played in the Great War by the Royal Air Force*, vol. VI (Oxford: Clarendon Press, 1937), appendices XXVI and XXXV.
14 Ibid.
15 Proportion of total strength categorized as 'aircrew' (pilots, observers and air gunners). *Monthly Return of Personnel of the Royal Air Force (Overseas)*, dated 1 November 1918. Air Historical Branch (Royal Air Force).
16 Proportion of Other Ranks classed as 'combatants'. War Office, *Statistics of the Military Effort of the British Empire* (London: HMSO, 1922).
17 John Terraine, *Essays on Leadership and War* (London: Western Front Association, 1998), pp. 27–35.
18 TNA, AIR 1/926/204/5/915, Aeroplane and engine casualties: Return of RFC in France, and TNA, AIR 1/998/204/5/1242 & 1243, Duplicate returns rendered on aircraft, engines and MT. The causes of wastage are summarized in General Brooke-Popham's 1919 lecture to the Royal United Services Institution. Air Commodore Robert. Brooke-Popham, 'The Air Force', *RUSI Journal* 65, 1 (February 1920), pp. 43–70.
19 TNA, AIR 1/1111/204/5/1895, Work summary and statistical returns: 1 and 2 Aircraft Depots.
20 This sort of activity is now described as 'reverse' logistics, to distinguish it from 'traditional' (unidirectional) logistics.
21 TNA, AIR 1/1155/204/5/2428, Quarterly returns of engines and vehicles held by the RAF in the field.
22 TNA, WO 394/20, Summary of statistics, 1914–20.
23 TNA, AIR 1/520/16/12/1 Pt III, Air Policy: Expansion and Organization of the RFC and RAF.
24 TNA, AIR 1/1073/204/5/1655, Weekly returns: Strength of pilots and aeroplanes in the field. This data excludes the Independent Force and No. 5 Group.
25 With this rapid expansion came significant changes in organization, doctrine and capability. The haphazard arrangements of 1914 gave way to standardization in equipment and role specialization – underpinned by the development of supporting technologies and huge improvements in performance.
26 TNA, AIR 1/1073/204/5/1655.
27 TNA, AIR 1/838/204/5/285 and TNA, AIR 1/838/204/5/287, Daily summary of RFC work and operations in France by brigades.
28 TNA, AIR 1/475/15/312/201, Copies of letters from General Salmond to General Trenchard on operations during German offensive. Salmond had taken over as

GOC RFC from Trenchard when the latter took up the new post of Chief of the Air Staff.
29 Christopher Burgess, *Letters of a Fighter Pilot* (Barnsley: Pen and Sword, 2008), p. 180.
30 TNA, AIR 1/475/15/312/201.
31 Ibid.
32 TNA, AIR 1/1019/204/5/1379–1383, Weekly aircraft returns: All RFC units in France, and TNA, AIR 1/951/204/5/1020, Weekly aircraft return: All units, France.
33 TNA, AIR 1/1019/204/5/1379–1383 and TNA, AIR 1/951/204/5/1020.
34 Jeff Jefford, *RAF Squadrons: A Comprehensive Record of the Movement and Equipment of All RAF Squadrons and Their Antecedents since 1912* (Shrewsbury: Airlife, 1988).
35 TNA, AIR 1/686/21/13/2252, Statistical data of the RFC and RAF, contains a detailed breakdown of this analysis.
36 TNA, AIR 1/686/21/13/2252 provides a detailed breakdown of the resources required to support the front line as at October 1918.
37 Martin van Creveld, 'Supplying an Army: An Historical View', *RUSI Journal* 123, 2 (1978), p. 56.
38 G. W. Williamson, 'Some Problems of a Technical Service', *RUSI Journal* 79, 516 (November 1934), pp. 780–800.
39 Peter Dye, 'Logistics and the Battle of Britain', *Air Force Journal of Logistics* XXIV, 4 (2000), pp. 1, 31–9.
40 Quoted in Duffy, *Through German Eyes*, pp. 318–19.

10

The Genesis of Modern Air Power: The RAF in 1918

David Jordan

1918 was not just significant for the development of air power because of the formation of the Royal Air Force (RAF) as an independent service, but because it marked the point at which many of the hard-won lessons about the employment of aircraft in war which had been learned since 1914 were able to be put into practice as British air and land power were integrated in a manner which enhanced the overall fighting efficiency of the British Expeditionary Force (BEF). This chapter examines the way in which air power became a vital, integral part of the way in which the BEF fought its campaigns on the Western Front and the ultimate apotheosis of air-land integration in the fighting of the last 11 months of the war, notably during the German Spring Offensives and the 'Hundred Days' campaign that ended the fighting. In doing so, it traces the ways in which the RAF and its predecessor organizations, the Royal Flying Corps (RFC) and Royal Naval Air Service (RNAS) built a corpus of practical knowledge of how to employ air power to telling effect, and the significance of these developments in the final stages of fighting.

By the end of 1917, the RFC had developed a number of important approaches to the employment of aircraft in support of the BEF; in this it had received no little assistance from the fighter squadrons of the RNAS as the struggle for control of the air reached particularly bitter levels during the Spring and Summer, with the qualitative superiority of German fighters leading to significant British losses during 'Bloody April'. The year was also marked by the momentous decision to create a third service, taking all British air assets away from the Army and Royal Navy and placing them under the control of an independent arm. This decision was driven largely by civilian political requirements; in the aftermath of German fixed wing bombing raids on London during June and July 1917, the government under David Lloyd George had established a committee led by General Jan Christiaan Smuts (erstwhile opponent of the British Empire and now a firm and trusted ally) which was to report on the future of Britain's air services. For all his undoubted intellect, Smuts was not a great exponent of military aeronautics and was given advice by the Director General of Military Aeronautics and General Officer Commanding of the RFC, Lieutenant-General Sir David Henderson. Henderson is very much the forgotten man of British military aviation, despite the fact that he led the subcommittee of the Committee of Imperial Defence whose report led to the formation of the RFC before being appointed to run the subsequent air service. Henderson juggled this not inconsiderable task with commanding the RFC in the field during 1914 and 1915, before he had – slightly reluctantly – returned to the War Office and passed command on to the then-Brigadier-General Hugh Trenchard, the man most often referred to as 'the father of the Royal Air Force'. Henderson's advice to Smuts drew much upon the former's bitter experience of inter-service rivalry, which had, up until 1917, defeated all attempts to draw the aeronautical requirements of the Army and Navy together. When the full picture of rivalry is understood, it is perhaps little surprise that Henderson advised that the obstacles to efficient development of air policy might best be removed by the simple expedient of taking responsibility for air power away from the Royal Navy and the Army and placing it under centralized control.[1] This was an appealing idea for Lloyd George, since it has become clear that he saw the removal of air assets from the direct control of the army, and particularly from Sir Douglas Haig, as being of considerable political benefit in his bid to hamstring Haig's ability to prosecute the war in a manner with which Lloyd George patently disagreed.

This dramatic change to British air power had a number of consequences beyond the formation of a third arm. Trenchard, now the long-standing commander of the RFC in France as a Major-General, was appointed as the first Chief of the Air Staff (CAS) (much to his chagrin), and replaced by his protégé, the 36-year old Major-General John Salmond who had begun the war as a squadron commander.

Trenchard found his lot as CAS less than convivial, and was to submit his resignation from the post less than four months after assuming the role. This led to his replacement by his bitter rival Major-General Frederick Sykes, whose outlook on air power differed from Trenchard's in a number of ways. Sykes, though, was a part-time CAS because of his role with the Inter-Allied

Commission at Versailles, so the change in personnel did little, if anything, to bring about a notable change in the way in which the RFC, and from 1 April 1918, the RAF went about its business. The RAF came into being during one of the most bitter periods of fighting on the Western Front during the war – and, from an Allied perspective, one of the most dangerous periods as well, as the German Spring Offensives appeared to be on the verge of sweeping all before them – in a manner so seamless that it might be said that the change was barely noticed by those in France points to the fact that the development of the fundamental principles of British air power had been well established by this point.

These principles were dominated by the requirement to gain and maintain control of the air. This has often coloured our understanding of air power during the war, since it gave rise to a fascination with the 'aces' and a vision of almost-chivalric air-to-air combat between the participants. This vision was enhanced by flights of rhetoric by the likes of Lloyd George, who observed of aircrew:

> High above the squalor and the mud. . . . they fight out the eternal issues of right and wrong. . . . They are the knighthood of this War without fear and without reproach.[2]

Post-war memoirs and the *Biggles* series of books for boys by Captain W. E. Johns only added to this perception, even though the day-to-day business of the RFC and RAF was the less 'glamorous' task of reconnaissance and artillery spotting. From early 1917, ground attack operations had been formalized, often in support of the advancing infantry, with aircraft attacking trench systems, gun positions and targets that were beyond the range of the artillery. Yet this commitment to the land battle often goes unremarked. A. D. Harvey claims that

> the fact was . . . that aircrew had little real commitment to ground support. The classic image of First World War aviation . . . thrilling acrobatic [sic] dogfights, largely corresponds to the airmen's own ideal.[3]

Such a view is something of a misrepresentation, particularly when one considers Trenchard's advice to Salmond that, as the GOC of the RFC in France, he should

> remember . . . that we are part of the army and that we are not trying to run a separate show at the expense of the army.[4]

This was to prove a source of some irritation to Trenchard later in the war when he found himself commanding the Independent Force, carrying out bombing raids which were held by the Army to divert resources away from the key task of supporting them – a position which Trenchard had done his best to avoid through using the bombers of the Independent Force to attack targets which often appeared to be more relevant to forthcoming BEF operations than to an independent bombing campaign against Germany itself.

In fact, the whole point of air combat was to ensure that the Germans' fighters were unable to interfere with the work of the army co-operation aircraft performing the essential duty of correcting the fire of the artillery which had come to dominate the static battlefields that characterized the Great War. The difficulty, in an era when early warning of the approach of hostile aircraft was dependent upon visual reports from the ground, chance meetings between the opposing sides (who, without radio telephony, were unable to communicate details of these encounters), and signals intelligence information, was that it was relatively simple for enemy aircraft to cross the line. In 1916, Trenchard had noted that enemy aircraft could always penetrate the airspace over British lines 'if they have the initiative and determination to do so', a reasonable enough remark to make given the numbers of fighters available to defend a considerable area.[5] Trenchard's response to this problem was to advocate an incessant offensive, sending fighters well over the German side of the lines in a bid to ensure that they were constrained and forced to engage in combat rather than be in a position to interfere with the work of the artillery observation aircraft.

In many ways, this was successful, since by the end of May 1917, army co-operation squadron losses to enemy fighter aircraft were at an entirely manageable level. The problem with the offensive policy, and the source of much subsequent criticism, lay in the losses that it brought. As well as losses to enemy action, technical problems (particularly engine failures) over German lines meant that many pilots were forced to land and were sent into captivity. The fact that the Germans were able to pick and choose their fights was also a source of frustration, since many offensive patrols failed to encounter the enemy at all. While this could be portrayed as a success of sorts – particularly if the Germans had been dissuaded from taking off and engaging – it did little to boost confidence in the overall wisdom of what appeared to be a rather blunt instrument. Nonetheless, there appeared to be little alternative in the battle for control of the air, and the policy continued until the end of the war.[6]

As noted, though, the most important aspect of the RAF's work was in the form of supporting the BEF through the gathering of information and the direction of artillery shooting. The latter role had been recognized as of great importance even before the war had broken out, and although some senior officers were dubious about the value of artillery observation as late as the Neuve

Chapelle offensive in March 1915, the value of air observation was unquestioned by 1918, not least since it had proven enormously effective in contributing to the destruction and suppression of enemy artillery in the battles of 1917. By the end of that year, there were eight gunners for every ten infantrymen, and any notion that offensive operations could be conducted without the provision of massive artillery support had been consigned to history.[7]

This achievement had not been without cost; the so-called Fokker Scourge of 1915 had a deleterious effect upon the RFC's ability to provide artillery observation, since the lack of effective fighters to counter the combination of the generally mediocre Fokker Eindekker plus synchronized machine gun forced army co-operation machines to fly in formation, reducing the efficacy of their overall efforts and doing little, in fact, to thwart the German aircraft when they were encountered. The provision of better fighters, notably in the form of the DH2, FE2 and the French Nieuport (plus, from 1916, the appearance of the RNAS's Sopwith Pup), removed the Eindekker threat, increasing the opportunities for the effective artillery observation so vital for offensive ground operations.

Artillery spotting was not without its problems, though. The need for rapid reinforcement of squadrons at the front meant that many aircrew were poorly trained when they arrived in their squadrons, and it took time for them to become fully conversant with the skills required for the effective provision of timely and accurate support to the artillery. This prompted a number of concerns in the aftermath of the Battle of the Somme, and while improved training was in fact in hand to address this problem, the end of 1916 and start of 1917 was punctuated by the Germans gaining control of the air once more thanks to the employment of qualitatively better fighter aircraft than those possessed on the British side. The culmination of this came in Bloody April 1917, but yet another transformation occurred with the arrival of new types such as the SE 5a, Sopwith Camel and Sopwith Triplane during the late Spring and early Summer; these regained control of the air from the German air service, in turn enabling the artillery co-operation and reconnaissance machines to gain far greater freedom to operate effectively, the overall quality of support being enhanced by the increasing skills of the aircrew. These were noted during the course of the battles of summer 1917, notably at Messines Ridge and Third Ypres (Passchendaele), and again during the stunning – but temporary – success of operations at Cambrai in November which saw the most effective artillery cooperation of the war to date, as well as successful ground attack operations in support of the British advance. Rather less pleasing for the British was the similar level of success enjoyed by German ground attack squadrons during the enemy counterattack which reversed almost all of the gains of the offensive.

By the end of 1917, there was little doubt among senior Allied commanders that the Germans would exploit the Bolshevik government's decision to cease fighting on the Eastern Front by launching an offensive in the west. This seemed an entirely logical step, since although a significant number of German troops was required in the east, the cessation of fighting meant that the Germans could move a large number of men to the west and attempt to conduct an offensive which could bring about a favourable peace settlement – or perhaps even outright victory – prior to the arrival of American forces; the Germans had already made the gloomy prediction that once the Americans arrived, defeat in the west could only be a matter of time.[8]

As a sign of how integrated air power had become in the British scheme of operations, the documentation illustrating the degree of planning undertaken to meet a possible offensive which had begun prior to Trenchard's reluctant departure for the Air Ministry gives no sense that the RFC was seen as anything other than a significant part of the overall effort. Trenchard produced a long draft memorandum on the subject of air power in defensive operations on 22 December 1917, in which he laid down the way in which he felt that the RFC could be best used in the face of a German assault. As might be expected, he highlighted the importance of effective reconnaissance in gaining intimation of the enemy's plans, noting that this required close co-operation with the intelligence service so as to ascertain the sort of information that was required and the likely places which would require the generation of reconnaissance sorties.[9] This would then be followed by 'sustained bombing attacks designed to interfere with the enemy work'.[10] Although there was much past experience in carrying out preparatory bombing raids – usually in a bid to hamper German defensive efforts prior to Allied offensives – experience demonstrated that a not inconsiderable degree of luck was needed for such raids to have a telling effect. Bombing accuracy was limited, even in a relatively benign environment where control of the air had been obtained, and the destructive power of the largest bombs – usually 230 lb weapons – was not particularly significant. Nonetheless, the potential disruption caused by such attacks was considered worth the effort.

Once the enemy attack was underway, Trenchard highlighted the critical duty for the RFC:

> everything must be subordinated to the duty of keeping artillery machines in the air. Modern artillery plays such an important part in a defensive action that

too much stress cannot be laid on the work of Corps machines. Counter battery work without air observation is . . . of very little value.[11]

Again, past experience informed this particular observation – the Fourth Army's consideration of the Battle of the Somme revealed that without the presence of artillery observation aircraft, the formation's guns had conducted speculative bombardment of likely enemy positions, using twice the amount of ammunition as would normally have been employed with aircraft present, but without any real appreciation of what damage (if any) had been caused by the shells.[12]

This point prompted Trenchard to illustrate a notable concern regarding the attitude of the infantry to the air support that they received. Experience at Third Ypres demonstrated that the infantry would complain about the lack of effort by the flying corps if they did not see friendly aircraft overhead, while the success of German ground attack aircraft during their counter-thrust at Cambrai had given rise to further concern about the morale effect of air attack, a factor in which Trenchard placed great store.[13] This led to Trenchard noting that although it would 'probably not be a popular view', the best employment of the RFC would be to support defensive fireplans for the artillery and then be employed 'with a view to preventing the enemy pressing home the full weight of his attack by delaying the advance of his reinforcements'. This would require attacks against transport hubs and any vehicles found on roads or railways, rather than attacks on enemy front line units. Even so, Trenchard's concern about the attitude of the rest of the army towards his men prompted him to reserve a number of aircraft which would be sent out to attack German troops advancing on the British lines 'in order to encourage our infantry'.[14]

In his response to Trenchard's memorandum on 28 December, Major-General Noel Birch, artillery adviser at GHQ, gave support to Trenchard's encomium on the benefits of supporting the artillery observation machines (perhaps unsurprisingly), suggesting that it might be necessary to abandon notions of interrupting the flow of supplies and providing moral support to the infantry through occasional low-flying attacks. Birch was supported in this view by Brigadier-General John Charteris, the BEF's intelligence chief (albeit not for much longer), who went so far as to suggest that the infantry did not expect the RFC to be seen bombing the enemy's front lines, or to be overhead, since 'they are trained now to deal with low flying enemy aeroplanes by means of machine gun fire'.[15] It is clear that Trenchard's experience of fending off criticism of the apparent lack of effort by the RFC during Third Ypres, and similarly unfavourable comments about the German low-flying attacks at Cambrai, made him much less ready to accept the notion that the infantry could be left to their own devices without the reassurance of seeing at least some friendly aircraft overhead. There was also a decidedly Trenchardian twist to the final version of the policy memorandum, circulated just two days before the end of the year; even though the discussion had been about the provision of effective air power in defence, Trenchard concluded with the following statement:

> The successful performance of the Royal Flying Corps in defence . . . must primarily depend upon its ability to gain and maintain the ascendancy in the air. This can only be done by attacking and defeating the enemy's air forces. The action of the Royal Flying Corps must, therefore, remain essentially offensive.[16]

Although this observation might have seemed somewhat counter-intuitive, it is perhaps worth noting that the value of offensive air operations as part of a wider defensive plan, along with the importance of maintaining control of the air to facilitate both air and land operations has never subsequently been called into question.

It was rather ironic, though, that when the RFC came to be tested by the German attack, weather conditions and the circumstances of the offensives meant that almost all of the planning for the air component contribution to the defence was rendered irrelevant from the outset. By the same token, though, the fact that the RFC (and from 1 April 1918, RAF) was able to play such a significant role in the defence of the Allied lines demonstrated just how significant air power was to British operations, particularly in terms of providing emergency support to hard-pressed infantry units and in causing widespread disruption to German formations whose progress to the front was often slowed by the RFC's attentions, with a concomitant effect upon morale.

The German Spring Offensives opened during a period of particularly bad weather. On 21 March 1918, the first day of the assault, fog was a notable factor across the front. This meant that there was little opportunity for the RFC to conduct reconnaissance sorties or to provide support to the artillery – even if they were able to take off in the dire weather, finding targets was next to impossible. This pattern was to be repeated throughout the early stages of the German attack.[17] This was, though, not the primary problem confronting the artillery. The speed of the German advance was such that the gunners were forced to withdraw rapidly, with some units being compelled to engage approaching enemy troops over open sights. The loss of artillery – either through its hurried departure from the battery sites or by virtue of positions being overrun – meant that targets behind the immediate front line could not be engaged by traditional means, potentially providing the Germans with the ability to maintain the momentum of their assault.

As the fog lifted, John Salmond issued concise orders to the IX Brigade RFC, the formation directly under the command of RFC headquarters:

> Bomb and shoot up everything... very low flying essential. All risks to be taken. Urgent.[18]

Salmond's instructions might, at first sight, appear to smack of complete desperation. In fact, his aircraft had an almost immediate effect. The GSO1 of Fifth Army, Lieutenant-Colonel Percy Beddington, noted that the RFC's efforts in the south of the Fifth Army area had 'frozen up' the German attack, albeit only temporarily.[19] In the circumstances, with Fifth Army being driven back in almost complete confusion, and at an alarming rate, even such small gains in time were of some utility. More telling was the fact that when air power could be brought to bear, it had the ability to impede the efforts of the highly-trained attacking troops who formed the vanguard of the German assault.

On 22 March, the weather improved, and the RFC's attacks increased in number and in their ferocity. In a letter to Trenchard that day, Salmond observed that 'one low-flier thinks he killed 500!' – an observation almost certainly made to highlight the exaggeration in this claim, but perhaps indicative of the success that the pilots thought that they were having – not, as it proved, entirely unreasonably.[20] The most notable effect was that where air attacks were put in against the Germans, their advance was slowed down, buying further time for the allies to regroup. The pace of air operations was little short of frenetic over the next few days, and the German official history of the war offers some rather telling observations about the effect that this had. In its comments about 26 March, the history notes:

> Quite particularly and probably most strongly felt was the shift in the strength ratio [sic] in the air... enemy formation of up to 60 aircraft... pounced on the infantry with great élan and attacked them with bombs and machine gun fire.[21]

By this point, the RFC was roaming over the battlefield with a degree of impunity, and Trenchard's observations about the efficacy of attacks on forces and supplies approaching the battlefield were well-illustrated. Supply columns were severely disrupted, particularly as a result of destroying the surface of metalled roads and by causing horse-drawn transport to scatter by diving upon the columns and panicking the horses.

By 5 April, the Germans had been forced to a halt, with their efforts to break through the Allied lines running into increasing problems. General Erich Ludendorff, commanding the German forces laid the blame for the failure of the offensive squarely upon air power, bitterly commenting upon supply difficulties and the heavy casualties suffered by air attack.[22] The Chief of Staff of Crown Prince Rupprecht's Group of Armies, General Hermann von Kuhl, went even further, making the claim that the 'very disagreeable' air attacks had 'caused about one half of all casualties suffered.'[23] Von Kuhl was not a man given to exaggeration, but even so, it is difficult to accept that this estimate was exact because of the difficulties in ascertaining the exact number of casualties inflicted by air attack and the fact that such a figure would appear to understate the bitterness of the fighting on the ground. Nonetheless, the number of casualties from air attack was clearly significant, and – perhaps almost as importantly – the fact that von Kuhl and countless other German soldiers of all ranks believed that air attack was so deadly had a deleterious effect upon morale, particularly when the negative psychological effect of of air-directed artillery fire upon German troops is also taken into account.

While it would be excessive to claim that the RFC (which became the RAF on 1 April) had been decisive in blunting the German attacks, there is sufficient evidence from both British and German sources to suggest that air power made a major contribution that has perhaps been overlooked for too long – the Spring and early Summer of 1918 illustrated that using aircraft in support of hard-pressed ground units could have a significant effect, preventing the enemy from gaining objectives and buying time for an adequate defence to be mounted. Once the German offensive had been blunted, the Allies were able to move onto the attack. For the RAF and the BEF, the first notable instance of effective air land integration in this phase of the war came at the Battle of Hamel.

The Battle of Hamel has been subject to considerable controversy, often being held as an example of General Sir John Monash's creative thinking in stark contrast to the stubborn blundering of the British high command.[24] Whatever the merits of this particular debate, it sometimes obscures the fact that much of what was achieved in terms of the interaction of air and land forces was nothing more than an evolution of what had gone on before, albeit with some further illustration of the constant innovation that took place. Hamel was notable for the decision to use aircraft to supply machine-gun ammunition to forward troops consolidating their defences in recently-taken positions, and for the first attempts at co-operation between tanks and aircraft.

Once the threat of the German offensives had gone, Tank Corps headquarters examined the matter of co-operation with aircraft, concluding that there was much that could be done to the benefit of the armoured formation, even if there was a serious problem when it came to effective communication between tank and aircraft crew.[25] Although Number 8 Squadron RAF had been tasked with co-operation with tanks, its assignment to this duty came just three days before the Hamel Battle, which required a degree of improvization. As had been suspected, attempting to communicate with individual tanks proved impossible, and 8 Squadron's major contribution came in the form of providing Tank Corps headquarters with information about the position of its units and their progress across the battlefield. They also took to ad hoc attacks against German field guns that had been pressed into use against the advancing tanks, a step that proved effective overall.

The supply of ammunition, using specially-modified bomb-racks and supply boxes equipped with parachutes proved particularly effective, ensuring that machine-gunners in recently-gained positions were quickly supplied with large quantities of ammunition at an early stage, thus allowing them to provide effective defensive fire against German counterattacks. Despite this impressive innovation, it is important to note that once again, the most effective support at Hamel came in the form of ensuring that the accuracy of the artillery was at its peak, enabled by possessing control of the air and denying the Germans the ability to use their aircraft to interfere with the progress of the operation. A similar degree of success was attained on a much larger scale at Amiens on 8 August.

The Amiens operation began the 'Hundred Days' campaign which brought the war to an end, Fourth Army plans envisaged an operation which would be limited in scope, concluding with the seizure of the outer Amiens defences after an advance of some 5,000–6,500 yards.[26] The planning was thorough, albeit marked by some optimistic interventions from Field Marshal Sir Douglas Haig as he attempted to persuade Fourth Army's commander, General Sir Henry Rawlinson, of the merits of an advance to greater depth. Rawlinson ultimately accepted some of Haig's suggestions, but rather unfortunately made clear his alterations to the plan at a conference which was not attended by the commander of V Brigade RAF, who was thus left in the unlucky position of carrying out a plan which in fact supported the original objectives rather than the revised ones.[27] Nevertheless, the overall contribution made by air power to the opening day of the offensive was significant. The level of co-operation with the artillery was at the highest standard yet achieved; by 7 August, 95 per cent of German guns had been located, making it possible for the effective suppression of most of their artillery when the battle opened.[28] Low-flying fighter squadrons tasked with ground attack duties were instructed to target any German artillery that they found in action as a priority, as well as taking on targets of opportunity. Enemy aerodromes were subjected to early morning attacks to ensure that the German squadrons based there would be unable to make any notable contribution to the defence, while bombing of railheads in the German rear areas would begin as 8 August drew to a close in a bid to disrupt the arrival of German reinforcements.

The early morning of 8 August was notable for a heavy mist which prevented much in the way of reconnaissance, and aerodrome attacks produced disappointing results – partly because of the difficulties in locating the targets in the poor weather, but also because a number of the aerodromes turned out to be deserted.[29] Anti-tank guns also began to inflict a toll on the Tank Corps, since it was extremely difficult for 8 Squadron to identify their positions, let alone provide support in the form of attacks against the guns. Nonetheless, the advance proved to be a spectacular success. By noon, the Germans were in disarray and falling back towards the River Somme. The pace of the advance in fact caused confusion among the British high command, as it became clear that objectives were being seized far more quickly than had been expected. The fact that the air support plan had been rendered outdated at such a pace now combined with a temptation to see if the Germans could be trapped with their backs to the Somme and destroyed in detail.[30] The prospects of achieving such a great success led to the unfortunate decision to launch large-scale air attacks against the Somme bridges. Even allowing for the benefits of hindsight, this seems a strange decision, since the weapons available to the attacking aircraft were inadequate for the destruction of the bridges. The possibility that the Germans would appreciate the threat and rush fighters to protect the bridges was ignored, with the end result that much effort was expended to little effect by the RAF, while German fighters were able to inflict a painful toll upon the attacking aircraft. Unfortunately, the possible prize of cutting off the Germans was such as to blind the British commanders to other ways in which their assets might have been used more effectively. German railheads went largely unmolested until 11 August, ensuring that many reinforcements were able to get into the area to shore up the defences as the retreating troops crossed the Somme.

While this marked one of the first occasions where the promise of air power led to wildly optimistic employment of aircraft, the failure of the bridge bombing and the concomitant effects that it had on other air aspects of the Amiens operation should not disguise the fact that the initial air contribution had been notably successful. Even ad hoc attacks against anti-tank guns worked to some extent and the subsequent provision of fighter bomber squadrons tasked with dealing with this threat further enhanced the effectiveness of the Tank Corps as the fighting moved away from static warfare to operations in more open terrain.[31]

The final days of the war were marked by continued success in air-land integration, along with a notable upsurge in ground attack operations as the German air threat all but collapsed after one final attempt to regain control of the air in September.[32] RAF operational reports note the extent of attacks on transport targets behind the German lines, as well as multiple aerodrome attacks to suppress the limited German capability for air operations.[33] Support for the artillery remained impressive in its quality, while the employment of Central Wireless Stations to coordinate artillery and ground attack operations against both fleeting targets and localized areas of resistance proved particularly effective, as did the dissemination of reconnaissance information for exploitation by the Tank Corps.[34] When the Armistice arrived on 11 November, it is not unfair to say that the RAF and BEF were almost seamlessly integrated, with air power making a most significant contribution to the overall effectiveness of Fourth Army's decisive operations.

What, then, are we to make of air operations in 1918? It is not unfair to say that the value of air-land integration had been appreciated long before the final year of the war; nor is it unreasonable to note that many of the tactics and procedures that were employed had their origins in 1914 and 1915. The significance of operations in 1918 lay in the fact that these factors came together, supported by high-quality training and improved technology to the extent that the air effort in support of the land battle reached its highest level of quality. As Gary Sheffield and I have noted elsewhere, the RAF was arguably the most effective tactical air force in the world in 1918, with its example setting the tone for the successes of the German Blitzkrieg in 1939 and 1940, where the exploitation of control of the air for the effective conduct of interdiction and close air support operations brought about stunning levels of success – similar, in fact, to the successes of the Hundred Days campaign.[35] By the end of the First World War, the RAF had developed all the major air power roles that are recognized in doctrine today, demonstrating the vital importance of control of the air and of close air-land cooperation to achieve success. It has been an unfortunate feature of British military history that these lessons have been forgotten all-too frequently and have had to be relearned at some cost.[36] It is, therefore, not stretching the evidence to argue that for the RAF at least, 1918 marked the genesis of modern air power – even if this point has been largely overlooked for more than 90 years, the victim of stereotypes about early air power that have not yet quite been shaken off.

Notes

1. H. A. Jones, *The War in the Air, Being the Story of the Part Played in the Great War by the Royal Air Force*: Appendices (Oxford: Clarendon Press, 1937), pp. 1–8. Also see Malcolm Cooper, *The Birth of Independent Air Power: British Air Policy in the First World War* (London: Allen and Unwin, 1986).
2. *Parliamentary Debates (Hansard), Volume XCVIII*, col. 1, 247.
3. A. D. Harvey, *Collision of Empires: Britain in Three World Wars 1793–1945* (London: Hambledon Continuum, 1994 [1992]), p. 409.
4. Malcolm Cooper, *The Birth of Independent Air Power*, p. 144.
5. *Future Policy in the Air*, 22 September 1916, RAF Museum, Trenchard Papers, MFC73.
6. See Norman Franks, Frank W Bailey and Russell Guest, *Above the Lines: A Complete Record of the Fighter Aces of the German Air Service, Naval Air Service and Flanders Marine Corps 1914–1918* (London: Grub Street, 1993), p. 19 and Oliver Stewart's observations in his review of Trenchard's biography in *The Journal of the Royal Aeronautical Society* 66 (1962), pp. 595–6.
7. Shelford Bidwell and Dominick Graham, *Firepower: British Army Weapons and Theories of War, 1904–1945* (London: Allen and Unwin, 1982), p. 90.
8. See, for instance, Tim Travers, *How the War Was Won: Command and Technology in the British Army on the Western Front 1917–1918* (London: Routledge, 1992), chapters 2 and 3.
9. The National Archives of the UK (hereafter 'TNA'), AIR 1/526/16/12/36.
10. Ibid.
11. Ibid.
12. TNA, WO 95/431, 'Lessons of the Somme'.
13. TNA, Air 1/524/16/12/20; Wilfrid Miles, *Military Operations: France and Belgium 1917*, vol. III – *The Battle of Cambrai* (London: HMSO, 1948), pp. 177, 197, 202; E. R. Hooton, *War Over the Trenches: Air Power and the Western Front Campaigns 1916–1918* (Hersham: Midland Publishing, 2010), pp. 193–4.
14. TNA, Air 1/526/16/12/36.
15. Ibid.
16. Ibid.
17. See for instance, TNA, Air 1/475/15/312/201, Letter, Salmond to Trenchard, 22 March 1918.

18 TNA, Air 1/475/15/312/201.
19 Travers, *How the War Was Won*, p. 86.
20 TNA, Air 1/475/15/312/201. Postscript, letter Salmond to Trenchard, 22 March 1918.
21 S. F. Wise, *Canadian Airmen and the First World War: The Official History of the Royal Canadian Air Force*, vol. I (Toronto: University of Toronto Press, 1980), p. 507.
22 General Erich Ludendorff, *My War Memories, 1914-1918*, vol. II (London: Hutchinson, 1919), pp. 599-601.
23 Wise, *Canadian Airmen*, p. 507.
24 See John Laffin, *British Butchers and Bunglers of World War One* (Stroud: Sutton, 1988), pp. 147-9 and A. J. P. Taylor, *The First World War: An Illustrated* History (London: Penguin, 1966 [1963]), p. 232 for the traditional view of Monash and the correctives by Peter Simkins, 'British Divisions in the Hundred Days, 1918', in Paddy Griffith (ed.), *British Fighting Methods in the Great War* (London: Frank Cass, 1996), pp. 53-4 and J. P. Harris, *Douglas Haig and the First World War* (Cambridge: University of Cambridge Press, 2009 [2008]), pp. 480-1.
25 TNA, WO 95/94, Tank Corps Diaries and Papers.
26 Robin Prior and Trevor Wilson, *Command on the Western Front: The Military Career of Sir Henry Rawlinson, 1914-1918* (Oxford: Blackwell, 1992), pp. 302-3.
27 See *The Haig Papers*, Diary entry for 3 August 1918 (Microfilm copy, University of Birmingham Library) for Haig's intervention; Jonathan Boff, 'Air-Land Integration in the 100 Days: the Case of Third Army', *RAF Air Power Review* 12, 3 (Autumn 2009), pp. 77-88; David Jordan, 'The Royal Air Force and Air Land Integration in the 100 days', *RAF Air Power Review* 11, 2 (Summer 2008), pp. 12-29 for the effect this had on air operations.
28 Prior and Wilson, *Command on the Western Front*, pp. 314-15.
29 Wise, *Canadian Airmen*, p. 526.
30 Ibid.
31 TNA, Air 1/725/97/2, 'Report on Recent Operations' (undated, but clearly late August/early September 1918).
32 Norman Franks, Russell Guest and Frank Bailey, *Bloody April to Black September* (London: Grub Street, 1995) pp. 243-7, 252-3.
33 See, for example, TNA Air 1/1546/204/77/37.
34 Wise, *Canadian Airmen*, p. 560; TNA Air 1/725/97/2; WO 95/94.
35 Gary Sheffield and David Jordan, 'Douglas Haig and Air Power', in P. W. Gray and Sebastian Cox (eds), *Air Power Leadership: Theory and Practice* (London: The Stationary Office, 2002), p. 282.
36 Wing Commander Harv Smyth, 'Re-learning Air Land Co-operation', *RAF Air Power Review* 10, 1 (Spring, 2007), pp. 1-27.

11

The Battle of Amiens: Air-Ground Co-operation and its Implications for Imperial Policing

Simon Coningham

Introduction

This chapter will show that while the main mechanisms of air-ground co-operation were present and in some elements considerably developed by the concluding months of the First World War, the seeds of future discord between the Royal Air Force (RAF) and the Army can be discerned. The implications that this held for imperial policing will also be considered.

On the Western Front, the stalemate in trench warfare had been successfully challenged by Ludendorff's March 1918 offensive, which showed that mobility could be restored to the battlefield, although this offensive had eventually ground to a halt following the exhaustion of participating troops and a failure to move artillery forward.[1] Although further German offensives followed, the Germans lost the strategic initiative at the Second Battle of the Marne (July 1918). This was followed by a major Allied offensive by British Fourth Army and French First Armies near Amiens; the first day of the Battle of Amiens, 8 August 1918, was described by Ludendorff in a phrase that has now become hackneyed, as 'the black day of the German Army in the history of this war'.[2] The offensive proved tactically innovative with some successful co-ordination of infantry, artillery, aircraft and tanks, yet it was flawed in its development over subsequent days. Air-ground co-operation, particularly on the first day of this Battle, which one modern historian has described as 'the black day of the RAF',[3] is the subject of this chapter. Finally, the extent to which the lessons of air-ground co-operation could be carried forward into the interwar period, within the context of the challenges facing the British Empire, will be considered.

The Battle of Amiens

General Sir Henry Rawlinson (General Officer Commanding (GOC) of Fourth Army)'s plan was to free Amiens and its key rail links from German threats by advancing to the old Amiens outer defence line. Haig and Foch, however, extended these objectives more ambitiously further east.[4] Rawlinson's ten divisions were supported by the massive firepower of some 1,400 field guns, 684 heavy artillery pieces, 324 heavy tanks and 96 light Whippet tanks. The Allies had local superiority in manpower: an estimated 75,000 against the 37,000 of the German Second and Eighteenth Armies with their 11 depleted divisions, including reserves.[5] Secrecy was considered fundamental to the success of the attack and an elaborate deception plan was devised to conceal the build up of Allied forces.

800 RAF aircraft were to be deployed in support of the ground attack and with the addition of the French First Army's air arm, the Allies' 1,800 plus planes outnumbered the German Air Force's 365 aircraft, although the Germans could call on a further 850 planes from other fronts.[6] Brigadier-General L. E. O. Charlton, GOC V Brigade, RAF, was to operate under the overall command of Fourth Army, with Major-General John Salmond, GOC, RAF, France responsible for the operational direction of all other RAF elements. V Brigade, RAF's overriding mission was to assist the ground attack: 'more than in any previous battle of the war Amiens was to feature planned co-operation of the closest kind between the air and ground force'.[7] Salmond's plan assumed that enemy ground reserves would not join the battle until the evening of the first day. He therefore ordered that bombing be directed against enemy airfields and only later would local rail centres, billets, road and rail movements be targeted.

On 8 August complete surprise allowed Fourth Army troops to break-in to German defensive lines, with the Australian and Canadian Corps able to advance up to eight miles on a wide front.[8] Before the attack, although low cloud, mist and driving rain made flying hazardous, two Handley Page bombers flew a three hour low level patrol to drown the noise of assembling tanks. At 04.20, assault units moved off the start line following 200 yards behind the creeping barrage with the Germans completely surprised. By 07.15, the two attacking Australian divisions supported by tanks had taken their first objective (green line).[9] Two fresh divisions resumed the attack at 08.20 and little resistance was encountered. Their second objective (red line) was reached by 09.15, overrunning a great deal of German artillery. The final objective (blue line) was reached ahead of schedule.[10] The recently arrived Canadian Corps, unfamiliar with their more difficult terrain, faced a tougher task. Their artillery, only in position for 24 hours, had to register silently, using photographs, maps and calculations. As the mist cleared, the tanks supporting the Canadian advance sustained heavy losses, but the green line was taken only slightly behind schedule. In the face of fierce resistance, two Canadian divisions reached their blue line objective by 17.35. With more difficult terrain to negotiate, and facing fiercer resistance from higher-calibre German troops, the progress of British III Corps north of the Somme was more limited. They took their green line objective, but the important Chipilly Spur remained to threaten the Australian left flank. The French First Army while not reaching their final objectives, performed a valuable function, advancing up to five miles and securing the Canadian right flank.[11]

The RAF's V Brigade machines were unable to participate until 09.00, when the weather cleared. The RAF's battle narrative describes how, for five hours from 09.00, the air above Fourth Army's attacking troops was alive with friendly aircraft bombing and strafing German positions.[12] In the afternoon Salmond radically shifted the centre of air activity. Reports by aircraft indicated that the eight main Somme bridges were swarming with retreating troops and Salmond considered that a sustained disruption of movement would be significant. He cancelled all other bomber and fighter missions of his IX Brigade to focus on destruction of the Somme bridges.[13] By the time the bridge attacks had started, however, German fighter reinforcements were arriving and immediately engaged in ferocious aerial combat. RAF losses were heavy on 8 August; 45 aircraft having failed to return from day missions and a further 52 so damaged as to be written off.[14] By the night of 9/10 August, continuous attacks on the bridges had not been successful and German reinforcements were able to cross them in numbers.[15]

Perhaps complacent following the overall success of Day One, Corps Commanders and the RAF's GOC V Brigade remained uncertain about their future objectives and the attack lost momentum over the next few days.[16] Attacks were still made, the Canadian Corps advanced nearly two miles on Day Two, but these were generally less co-ordinated and by 11 August the battle had ground to a halt. The Germans had lost between 400 and 500 guns, and at least 18,000 prisoners to the British and a further 11,000 to the French, with Fourth Army only losing 4,000 men. The results of the battle massively favoured the Allies and had a serious influence on the morale of the German High Command and on German ground troops. Their only remaining option was a defensive battle.[17]

The mechanics of air-ground co-operation

Amiens demonstrated the characteristic organization of air-ground co-operation, with V Brigade, RAF typically comprising one wing for corps work and one army wing. Corps work was principally reconnaissance, artillery spotting and contact patrols with infantry, tanks and cavalry. Additional support, important at Amiens, included smoke laying and supplying ammunition for machine guns in response to ground requests. The army wing was principally used to support ground attacks, utilizing machine guns and 25 lb bombs. At Amiens, V Brigade, RAF's responsibilities were divided between three areas: Northern in support of III British Corps, Central (Australian Corps) and Southern (Canadian Corps), with squadron allocation as follows:

Squadron Allocation			
	Northern	Central	Southern
Corps work	35	3 AFC	5
Tank co-operation	35	8	8
Cavalry/Armoured Cars	—	—	6
Ammunition Drops	9	9	—
Smoke laying	—	9	5
Ground strafing/bombing	48,80	41,84,201	23,24,605/202

Source: Messenger, *Day We Won*, p. 146.

IX Brigade (HQ), III Brigade and elements of I and X Brigades, all under Salmond's command, were to supply fighter cover and to bomb targets outside the immediate battlefield such as airfields, reserves, dumps and ultimately the Somme bridges.[18]

Balloon companies for static reconnaissance work were attached to forces in the battle.

Reconnaissance

Throughout the First World War the observation role of the RFC/RAF was the most important element in air-ground co-operation.[19] In the words of the RAF's official historians 'its first duty was reconnaissance. All its other and later uses were consequences of this central purpose, and were forced on it by the hard logic of events'.[20] The nature of reconnaissance had developed very considerably by the Battle of Amiens and was the basis of the extensive topographical planning and intelligence used by Fourth Army in its meticulous preparations for the assault. Aircraft were equipped with increasingly sophisticated cameras, enabling map mosaics to be updated on a daily basis and communicated to army command.[21]

In the confusion caused by fast-moving mobile warfare, aerial co-operation, even at the sophisticated level of 1918, often failed to perform its fundamental tasks. At Amiens on 9 August lateral communications between brigades proved difficult because of uncertainty of the locations of headquarters and unit deployments.[22] Certain terrain proved difficult to penetrate, despite greater use of angled cameras and photography from varying heights.[23] Inevitably errors in interpretation caused problems; weather was, however, the major hindrance to all forms of reconnaissance.[24]

There were two categories of reconnaissance. Tactical reconnaissance helped front line forces identify enemy positions and support units, HQs and dumps in the immediate vicinity.[25] Strategic reconnaissance, on the other hand, was wider ranging, covering airfields, communication centres and higher command HQs, longer-range artillery emplacements and road and rail traffic. J. C. Slessor believed that at Amiens insufficient resources were allocated to medium reconnaissance (only one plane/squadron at a time), with the purpose of identifying the origins, pace and likely timings of reinforcements. Little use was made of the massive amount of intelligence, compiled from earlier reconnaissance, to plan the best way to disrupt reinforcements.[26] As a result, fresh German troops were in the line in some quantity during Day One, and particularly so on subsequent days, a major factor in persuading Rawlinson and Haig to call off the attack.

Artillery spotting

In one sense, since artillery was to prove the most potent of weapons in the First World War, artillery spotting represented the peak of air-ground co-operation.[27] Artillery spotting had become vitally important from early in the war for the accurate acquisition of targets and for counter-battery work. The former, after location of the target, required the fall of shell to be observed, corrected and reported back to the battery by wireless transmitter or by phone from a balloon for less distant targets. The latter, the identification of enemy artillery positions for neutralizing fire, was mainly the responsibility of aircraft, with 90 per cent of counter battery observation from 1917 carried out by airmen.[28] Air-to-ground wireless communication, enhanced by the use of coded fire calls (e.g. LL called all available batteries to engage),[29] and by the clock method which enabled targets to be pinpointed,[30] facilitated this process.

At Amiens, aircraft, sound ranging, flash spotting and interpretation of the latest aerial photography had allowed 95 per cent of enemy gun locations to be registered before the attack.[31] After the initial assault, the Germans were forced to take up new gun positions, frequently only visible from the air, and neutralizing fire calls from patrol aircraft proved the best means of engaging them.[32] In addition, many infantry and tanks outran the range of supporting artillery. Artillery patrol aircraft, by facilitating the re-registering of Fourth Army artillery as it moved forward, helped it keep in touch with advancing units.[33] This was achieved by a system whereby aircraft, co-operating with infantry using ground panels to identify the battery, number of guns in action, etc., relayed this back to artillery commanders, who could then co-ordinate the fire and movement of the artillery pieces. This procedure, outlined by Wise, was far from being universally applied; it remained essentially work-in-progress, as gunners and airmen co-operated to solve their problems. On 8 August, 1 Canadian Brigade complained that although field artillery did move up 'There was, however, very little firing and it cannot be said that that our Field Artillery contributed to the advance of the Infantry'.[34] By 9 August the front line had moved so far forward the previous day that much of the heavy artillery could not be put in position and none of these guns had been registered on targets.[35]

Contact patrols

Contact patrols represented an important facet of air-ground co-operation as they were an attempt to fill in the communication gap that often developed on the battlefield. Squadrons kept in touch with advancing troops and tanks, informed commanders of their location and directed ground forces to their targets. This work took airmen close to the battle arena – it was sometimes necessary to descend as low as 800 ft to distinguish friendly troops. Once enemy positions had been identified, aircraft dropped messages to the advancing infantry.[36]

At Amiens, contact patrols experienced difficulty in locating the front positions of their own men, unlike static trench warfare. Contact patrol aircraft often found Allied troops by a dangerous process of elimination, first being fired upon from German-held positions and then circling back until they could identify their own forces. Leigh Mallory's 8 Squadron planes led tanks to their objectives, but problems persisted in communication between tanks and aircraft.[37] The official historian, H. A. Jones, stated that contact patrol work in co-operation with infantry was effective on 8 August, when troops lit flares allowing aircraft to track the advance accurately. Supplies of flares had, however, been exhausted before the end of the day and in any case, troops were reluctant to use them as they marked their positions. Jones also believed that trained observers, with enough experience to understand the ebb and flow of mobile battle, performed best.[38] The location and identification of units at all levels remained a continuing problem.

Ground support

The highest profile form of air-ground co-operation, the provision of ground support, was the last to appear.[39] At Amiens, the fighter squadrons of the Army Wing of V Brigade, RAF, had the major responsibility for providing ground support for the attack. On the first day, as soon as the fog cleared, fighters were despatched in pairs at 30 minute intervals, to attack enemy targets with machine-guns and 25 lb bombs: 'In the confusion caused by the surprise and ferocity of the initial assault . . . the fighters attacked enemy infantry, guns, transport, ammunition dumps, and trains . . . from near ground level'.[40] The Germans were put under tremendous pressure by the fighter squadrons and Slessor maintained that there was 'no question but that the action of the low-flying fighters was a factor of immense importance in the overwhelming success of the initial attack'.[41] Wise quotes from the 5th Battalion Canadian Infantry war diary for 8 August: 'our planes seemed like things possessed . . . the air was thick with them'.[42] While the moral effect of this aircraft activity was pronounced, it must be recognized that, by this stage of the battle, the German line had already been breached almost everywhere, and in many places the move to the red line was well advanced.[43]

Tanks, although highly successful in overrunning German machine-gun nests, proved vulnerable to concealed anti-tank guns. Leigh-Mallory's 8 Squadron supporting the tanks, although having trained in close co-operation with tank regiments, had only limited success in neutralizing these guns. Only 145 tanks out of 415 were still fit for action on 9 August and in his subsequent order of 14 August Charlton emphasized the importance of identifying and destroying anti-tank guns.[44]

Air-ground co-operation clearly improved when both airmen and soldiers not only knew the terrain but had working experience of each other's capabilities and operational limitations.[45] The Australians were familiar with their co-operating tanks and aircraft squadrons having successfully worked with them at Hamel in July 1918; this was not the case with the Canadian Corps deployed to their sector only hours previously. The considerable benefits of co-operative training had been, at least, indicated by Leigh-Mallory's 8 Squadron and later operations in the Hundred Days increasingly saw this recognized.[46] The uneven progress in air-ground co-operation can be partially explained by the fact that it was much more effective when troops and their commanders were receptive of aircraft's potential than when working with conservative, sceptical officers.[47]

Casualties among airmen were high and Sykes reported to the Cabinet that three-quarters of the losses on 8 August were due to ground fire rather than enemy fighter action.[48] Low-flying ground attacks, despite their proven effectiveness against troops in the open, were unpopular with pilots, who regarded them as requiring no special skill and therefore arbitrarily dangerous.[49]

Direct and indirect battlefield support

The RAF helped the army achieve its objectives through both direct and indirect support. Direct support helped troops in the immediate battlefield environment. At Amiens, for instance, for three to four hours after the mist cleared at 09.00, machine-guns holding up infantry, and German artillery further back, were bombed and strafed. German lorries were blown off the road, horse drawn transport stampeded and staff cars shot up, while smoke screens from phosphorus bombs helped infantry and tanks advance in parts of the battlefield beyond field artillery range.[50] These direct methods of helping troops in the immediate battlefield were complemented by more indirect and strategic means to isolate the battlefield. These could range from denying the enemy use of airfields and the destruction or disruption of ammunition dumps, supply lines and balloons, to attacks on lines and centres of communication to prevent reinforcements joining the battle. It was partly for this latter reason that Salmond switched his strategy to the destruction of the Somme bridges.[51]

Local air superiority

The RAF's overall air superiority on the Western Front had enabled it to conceal Fourth Army's preparations and make a major contribution to the surprise element of the attack at Amiens. The RAF needed to preserve its local air superiority over the battlefield in order that assault troops and other arms might carry out their operations more or less unhindered, The Germans also saw this fight for air superiority as the key struggle, which, if won, would allow their reinforcements to join the battle and preserve their lines of communication. The RAF was surprised by the speed with which German fighter reinforcements had arrived in the Somme area and taken up aerial combat.[52] Messenger argues that German operational flexibility prevented the Allies from making best use of their airpower.[53] The Germans, operating from nearby airfields and able to refuel and take off more frequently than British aircraft, found it relatively easy to attack British bombers targeting the Somme bridges, especially during Day One when their fighter escorts were also required to drop bombs. The Germans outmanoeuvred British aircraft by flying under cloud cover to swoop on corps aircraft and those involved in ground attacks.[54]

Various tactical errors took place at Amiens relating to fighter escort procedure and optimal flying heights. Although many of these errors played into the hands of the German Air Force, they can be understood as part of the continuing learning process for the RAF and Army. The fog bank in the early morning had reduced the effectiveness of IX Brigade's attacks on enemy airfields, and in any case the Germans had often already dispersed their aircraft. Continuing disruption of British attacks on the bridges caused by the German Air Force arose partly from neglecting to bomb German airfields when the weather lifted on Day One.[55] The ultimate change in bomber tactics to the targeting of enemy lines of communication was too late to prevent the ground attack from grinding to a halt.[56]

Communications

Communications played a crucial role in air ground co-operation, even though they were always at risk from under-developed technology and the confusion ever present in the fog of war. Communications were not just those between air and ground units, but also involved the identification of both parties to each other: '... each aircraft was to carry distinct markings so that the ground troops could identify its role ...'[57] At Amiens aircraft co-operating with Mark V tanks had a black stripe on either side of the tail plane, while corps squadrons had black squares under the wings. A wide range of signals and message-dropping centres, identified by distinctive markings on the ground, were used while the infantry were instructed to indicate their positions by firing red flares, wearing metal discs and placing rifles in prearranged patterns. Aircraft could call on infantry to indicate their position by firing white Very lights and using klaxons.[58]

Contact patrol work was hindered as visual signals proved of little use in the heat of battle; ground panels also needed to be considerably improved for subsequent battles of the Hundred Days.[59] Amiens proved unsurprisingly to be a battle where practical problems encountered on the spot had to be resolved by participants. Jones pointed out that prearranged signalling locations proved of doubtful value in rapidly changing situations. Dropped messages were adopted as the best method for conveying information to tanks.[60] A useful reminder that carefully prepared battles frequently failed to proceed according to plan is provided by Paul Kennedy: 'advances in combined arms theory were often vitiated by breakdowns in communication during actual battles.'[61] Even the much-vaunted map mosaics did not always reach the sharp end. One pilot recalled that targets were presented to him: 'on maps drawn from memory on an old blue sugar paper bag'.[62]

It was difficult for airmen to appreciate the needs of soldiers and for soldiers to realize both the potential and limitations of aircraft. Progress in this area was slow, but started with the appointment of liaison officers. Their duties included '. . . to find out what the staff wanted done in the way of reconnaissance, counter battery shoots, photography of enemy lines, and contact patrol work: to transmit it to flyers . . . to collect and collate their reports as soon as they landed and to pass it back by reports and telephone-lines as soon as possible . . .'. Corps and Army Commanders had a much better idea of aircraft's potential once there was an air officer on their Staff.[63]

Intelligence

By the time of the battle of Amiens, Intelligence Sections had been established at the HQ of each army wing and corps squadron, consisting of four men, supplying their sponsoring corps with information from observers' reports and air photos. They kept close contact with artillery liaison officers, delivered updates on enemy entrenchments and infrastructure works and disseminated daily interpretation maps during combat.[64] Given the unreliability of other intelligence gathering mechanisms, the Army became ever more reliant on intelligence derived from aerial reconnaissance and photography. There were, of course, many examples where intelligence was incorrect, misinterpreted or not communicated fast enough or at all, but at least the systems to build on this basic precept of air-ground co-operation existed.[65]

Planning

At Amiens the objectives and plans for an all-arms integrated attack on 8 August itself were very clear, even if, as Slessor observed, they lacked objectives for deeper targets behind the battlefield,[66] and that little thought had been given to the concept of how to turn a break-in into a breakthrough.⁶⁷ The objectives for Day Two and later were never clear nor properly put in writing. Monash and Currie, the two principal Corps Commanders, and Charlton issued no advance plans for Day Two.⁶⁸ As a result, although territorial gains were made, the effort was piecemeal with timings dependent on Currie who targeted a late start time of 10.00 because of delays in deployment. Poor and erratic communications hindered the co-ordination of further planned attacks, with intelligence only slowly fed back to Command and confusion continuing as to the actual progress and location of fighting units.⁶⁹ It must be assumed that after years of static warfare, mindsets were dominated by Day One's success and anxiety to consolidate gains before the expected German counter-attacks, which in reality the Germans were in too much chaos to contemplate.⁷⁰ This represented a throw back to the battles of 1916 and 1917 rather than looking forward. There was no clear programme of support for the subsequent days' ground attacks and the ad hoc efforts of RAF ground support aircraft were weakened because insufficient fighter protection led to their being frequently harassed by German fighters.⁷¹ The poor integration of 32nd Division into Canadian plans, following Fourth Army Chief of Staff's initial refusal to release it, which led to continuing confusion about its use and availability, was typical.⁷² The establishment of a Central Intelligence Branch (CIB) later in August was an attempt to resolve these co-ordination problems for subsequent operations.

Command factors

Both Wise and Slessor pointed to the ambiguity in the chain of command at Amiens between GHQ, GOC RAF (Salmond), GOC Fourth Army and GOC V Brigade, RAF (Charlton).⁷³ While there is no actual evidence of misunderstandings, the lack of clarity in the chain of command may have affected events on Days Two, Three and Four. The involvement of air commanders at Fourth Army planning conferences was haphazard and meant that co-operation opportunities were possibly missed – this may have contributed to the confusion concerning objectives.⁷⁴

The effectiveness of air-ground co-operation was limited by a number of factors at Amiens.

Target acquisition

At Amiens low flying ground attacks were generally aimed at targets of opportunity which, while effective when the enemy was retreating, meant that difficult targets such as those blocking troop or tank advances were often missed. There appears to have been no formal brief on likely targets with specific aircraft allocated to attack them.[75] Slessor argued that more effort should have been directed behind the front line in the near to medium battlefield rather than only on ground attack.[76]

Concentration

At Amiens there was no attempt to use the French First Army's large air force in co-ordination with British aerial activities. An indication of French airpower's potential can be seen in two attacks on convoys in the area in and beyond Roye, in one case 68 fighter-escorted bombers dropped 17.5 tonnes of explosives within 30 minutes.[77] Slessor believed that a much greater concentration of the air forces available in all sectors could have assured air superiority at a vital time in order to isolate the battlefield and allow air-ground co-operation to operate unhindered within it.[78] As it was, German aircraft were used expertly to deny the British local air superiority on many crucial occasions.[79]

Non-controllable factors

The weather had prevented corps work and ground attacks being carried out until 09.00 on 8 August. Given the season, this was predictable and certainly had an increasing impact on subsequent battles with the weather worsening as the Hundred Days progressed. While the mist helped the surprise element in the infantry and tank assault on Day One at Amiens, the weather clearly inhibited the planned early attacks on airfields, which seemed later to have been lost sight of as an objective.[80] The impact on the ground assault as a result of the absence of early direct air attacks seems to have been limited, because both Dominion Corps were well advanced towards their objectives by 09.00 when the mist lifted. When direct attack planes did appear, their main role was harassing retreating German forces and attempting to protect tanks from concealed German anti-tank guns. In this context, Slessor's comment about RAF attacks breaking the crust appears questionable.[81] Earlier ground attacks might well have helped British III Corps, which made limited progress in the tougher terrain around the Chipilly Spur.

Failure to isolate the battlefield

At Amiens the decision to try to trap troops as they retreated in disarray, rather than locating and attacking reinforcements further back, was retrograde. Fuller and others had already suggested that more appropriate targets were the enemy's senior HQs in order to disrupt control and communications.[82] Ludendorff actually claimed to have regained control of his forces by mid-afternoon on Day One and was soon overseeing the deployment of reinforcements.[83]

It is important to consider whether the switch in strategy to bombing the Somme bridges was justified. Sykes, Chief of Air Staff, writing at the time, stated that bombing was neither an accurate nor effective method of destroying bridges.[84] As a means of trying to isolate the battlefield the objective was sensible, but after its apparent failure the campaign was too protracted and distracted from other targets. Slessor believed that better use of expertise and intelligence could have been made to identify fewer, but more critical, defiles citing specific villages further back from the Somme which troops would have to pass through and be vulnerable to attack.[85]

The RAF's impact

The Official Historian of the RAF and Slessor concurred that the RAF had little impact on the Battle of Amiens after Day One.[86] The most effective work in support of the army by the RAF was in the preparation/deception period by concealing troop movements and preventing enemy aerial reconnaissance. Corps work was also well executed resulting in excellent artillery communication arrangements.

The weather disrupted this artillery co-operation until 09.00 on 8 August, but artillery spotting then became vital as troops and tanks moved out of gunnery cover. As far as ground attacks by aircraft were concerned, they certainly seem to have been most effective in increasing the panic among German troops already beginning to surrender or retreat in confusion. Jones quotes hundreds of aircraft attacks, but these are hard to quantify as squadrons planned attacks of two aircraft per 30 minutes per squadron.[87] On this basis the number of V Brigade aircraft in the air at any one time was a more modest 18. The apparent exaggeration probably reflects the moral impact of attack aircraft reported by troops from both sides.

Amiens had been innovative for the Allies in several important ways. Complete surprise had been achieved, Fourth Army intelligence had identified a sector of German weakness and tactical opportunity and all-arms had contributed in the battle's execution. Tanks and aircraft both proved to be significant players, the latter not only in the RAF's basic corps work but also in a ground support role even when not achieving anything more than air parity above the battlefield.[88] However both tanks and aircraft showed that they were vulnerable to enemy action, suffering heavy casualties.[89]

The Battle of Amiens set the pattern for the remainder of the Hundred Days offensive.[90] Each of the different British Armies took up the baton in turn and launched successful attacks achieving good results, but then grinding to a halt. Its cumulative effect, however, was to shatter German morale and continue the attrition of German fighting units. The learning process of all arms co-operation would continue with the RAF particularly realizing, after its earlier mistakes, the need to ensure local air superiority and how best to co-ordinate its tactical and strategic efforts to support the Army.[91] Typical of innovation in RAF/Army co-operation was that in later battles the locations of anti-tank guns were predicted and targeted accordingly, improving results.[92] The RAF was to play an increasingly important role in subsequent battles as a valuable constituent, if not yet able to alter the course of a battle on its own. The key impact of air-ground co-operation was in its contribution to the all-arms method, where the total effort multiplied any single arm's contribution.[93]

The extent of the integration of all-arms in the Amiens campaign remains controversial. Messenger recently argued that: 'the attack itself also showed how much the understanding of the all arms battle had evolved. Artillery, tanks, armoured cars, machine guns, trench mortars, infantry and airpower combined as never before.'[94] In fact, as noted the role of the RAF in the initial assault had been limited, the crucial initial breakthroughs being made by the elite Dominion Corps infantry, supported by the massive counter-battery firepower of the artillery and the somewhat more random contribution of the tanks. The RAF was then able to exploit this among panicking German troops in the open. An older view is that of Travers, who took a more cautious view of all arms, describing the tension on the Western Front between the strategy and tactics of mechanical as opposed to traditional manpower warfare. If Amiens represented a victory for the former, he argued that the traditionalists were still influential in the latter stages of the Hundred Days.[95] He believed that the technology of aircraft and tanks was capable of engaging in mechanical warfare but that the: 'tactics, cooperation and protection for these machines of ground and air had not yet been worked out'. This was partly due to the fact that more experience was needed, but also because the emphasis remained with traditional arms.[96] The last word can be left to the most recent of the official historians: 'Amiens . . . was tactically innovative and set the pattern for the remainder of the war. However, despite its initial success, achieved by . . . the effective combination of infantry, cavalry, armour and aircraft, at the operational level Amiens was still a flawed battle.'[97]

The implications for imperial policing

By the end of the First World War it was evident that both the RAF and Army believed in the value of air-ground co-operation. The problem was, however, that this meant different things to each party. As early as July 1917 Trenchard had complained to the RAF Secretary that 'the Army assumption is that the Air Force existed entirely for co-operation with the Army'.[98] The RFC and hence the RAF had derived in large part from the army and its officers and men had mostly served in the army and this was reflected in command and control arrangements. As with other auxiliary arms, brigades, wings and squadrons of the RAF were attached to army formations and were under direct army control. This was logical enough, as the RAF saw its task was to support the army in winning the war.[99] The army was not, however, interested in the wider applications of air power. Taking the vital observation and artillery spotting functions for granted, the army increasingly sought the ultimate in direct air support, the breaking of the crust of enemy positions, thus facilitating a break-in to the enemy's defences by infantry and tanks.[100]

After Amiens, there was a realization by the RAF that it might have operated more strategically. It could have isolated the battlefield by interdicting reserves, lines of movement, reinforcements and supply dumps. The potential for even deeper targets such as communication centres and higher command headquarters was also apparent, if equally neglected.[101]

Amiens had also demonstrated the disadvantages of not involving air commanders in the planning and control of operations. Air staff officers at GHQ and with other commands on the Western Front increasingly felt they might add to the formulation and effectiveness of strategy if they were more fully integrated into the command and control structure.[102] Another of the lessons from Amiens appeared to be the greater flexibility offered by concentrating air assets where and when they could be most effective, and not just frittering them away in small packages, for instance in individual sorties aimed at targets of opportunity.[103] This would not affect the important corps squadron work but would allow other aircraft resources to be better utilized, including the targeting of enemy nerve centres. In due course the RAF, benefiting from its First World War experience, adopted as key principles the concentration of resources, the need for air superiority and an important stake in command and control of the strategic plan in the battlefield, all underpinned by an attitude that the offensive, not the defensive, frame of mind gave the best chance of securing objectives.[104]

These principles, with the possible exception of the need for air superiority, were not compatible with the army's view that the prime task of the RAF was to serve the ground forces, particularly in attacking front line positions wherever and whenever requested. These concerns were not expressed explicitly in 1918 but as the official histories of the Western Front operations imply, fault lines between the services were beginning to appear, as each service took note of the elements of the narrative that suited its own purposes. These disagreements became increasingly pronounced following the end of the war. The RAF was soon to fight not just for its independence but the right to use airpower to its full potential, while the army took a much more limited tactical view.[105]

During the closing stages of the First World War, innovations in air-ground co-operation were rapidly taking place as the British army began to use all the available technologies to the limit of their potential, and to develop tactics that allowed infantry, artillery, armour and aircraft to operate effectively in combination.[106] The whole developmental process of air-ground co-operation and its practice, however, came to an abrupt end after the war. Most noticeably the ground support role 'disappeared completely from the corpus of doctrine upon which RAF procurement and training was based'.[107] It was to remain largely absent from the agendas of both the RAF and Army in Great Britain for the next decade and a half.

The presence of air-ground co-operation in the forces of the British Empire, at least in a rudimentary form, as early as 1919 and 1920, suggests that it still existed in the consciousness of many protagonists who, aware of its benefits in First World War, would look to implement it in the interwar period as circumstances demanded. The majority of improvements in air-ground co-operation during First World War were the result of innovations by airmen and soldiers, building on battlefield experience to solve particular problems.[108] It is a reasonable assumption that this particularly British form of development would be transferred to air-ground practices in imperial policing.

The re-emergence of air-ground co-operation as an operational method in the Empire arose in large measure from the problems and pressures facing Great Britain. It had taken on greatly increased imperial commitments, especially in the Middle East, with the new British mandates requiring protection or pacification. At the same time, all three services were undergoing reductions in establishment numbers and budgets against a background of antagonistic public opinion. Further difficulties arose from the refusal of the Dominions to become involved in imperial defence; the Government of India was similarly reluctant to provide garrison troops.[109] It was clear that in the face of these challenges and increasing indigenous demands for self rule, the British would need to return to their less costly imperial practice of forming governing alliances with elites, which were often corrupt and of dubious legitimacy. They also realized the impossibility of meeting their military commitments both in garrisoning and in countering the inevitable uprisings with reduced manpower and resources. This would mean that drastic and non-conventional solutions taking account of these realities were needed.[110]

Bond has shown that while it is overly simplistic to assume that all elements of the Army were opposed to change, as an organization it was too cautious and inflexible to provide this novel approach.[111] It was top heavy with elderly, senior officers blocking the promotion of war-experienced, reform-minded officers. The Higher Command contained an anti-reform majority, continually opposing innovations such as mechanization while paying lip service to the publicly stated 'all arms' philosophy. The regimental system, admirable in its generation of fighting spirit and camaraderie, was also divisive as it prevented any proper integration of the different units of the army.[112] Significantly, the important Kirke Report on the lessons of the First World War (1932) contained only one anodyne sentence about air support for ground troops; air operations were specifically excluded from the remit of the Kirke Committee.[113] Given the degree of inter-service rivalry and competition for the limited service budgets available, this myopic attitude was scarcely surprising. Indeed the Army remained so obsessively jealous of what it considered any interference by the RAF in its traditional role in imperial policing that it refused, for example, to allow the use of its armoured cars in Iraq.[114]

The RAF with younger senior commanders was characterized by a less deferential system of internal communications, reflecting the democracy among pilots, which made it prepared to examine innovative ideas and technology.[115] Its struggle with the other services, both to define what it believed to be a proper role for airpower and to secure its independent survival, meant that it needed to grasp opportunities not merely on matters such as the air defence of Great Britain and later the strategic bombing strategy but also to play a significant role in imperial policing.[116] For these reasons, despite the concept of air-ground co-operation being largely ignored by both the RAF and the Army in Great Britain, the RAF was flexible and tactically acute enough to resurrect it when necessary to achieve its imperial operational objectives.[117]

In fact, the pressure of events would lead to the full range of the apparently dormant skills of air-ground co-operation being needed to assist British forces in confronting serious problems and defeating insurrections. The earliest instances of air-ground co-operation proved somewhat rudimentary and haphazard, considerably limited by shortages of aircraft. In the Afghan War of 1919 and its later ramifications in Waziristan in 1919–20 and in the Iraqi insurrection of 1920, army and RAF forces co-ordinated their efforts reasonably effectively.[118] Progress would be driven by urgent military necessity. This process might be accelerated by the experience of particular commanders and here it should be noted that many First World War players were to undertake significant roles in imperial policing; Salmond, Borton, Charlton, Ludlow-Hewitt and Ellington were to occupy important command positions and Harris, Slessor, Lee, Coningham, Collishaw and Portal took part at squadron level. As far as the army was concerned, a few effective, experienced reformist leaders such as Wavell, Slim, Auchinleck and Alexander were involved on the North West Frontier of India, and Dill, O'Connor and Montgomery in Palestine.[119]

There was a further learning process as some of the techniques of insurgent control before the war were imported into the newly mandated territories, such as the use of on-the-ground political officers and their police forces for intelligence gathering and dispute resolution. The challenge of imperial policing presented a different sort of warfare which, while not needing combat to achieve air superiority, still required the techniques and skills of air-ground co-operation to be further developed in the face of elusive and effective opponents. New methods of co-operation such as resupplying forces by air, providing air evacuation for casualties and transporting troops to key locations would be developed. Other innovations would build on traditional imperial mechanisms to maintain the peace in troublesome areas, such as extending the effectiveness of the imperial column by means of air patrols after it had withdrawn, thus adding more permanence to its mission.[120]

By 1918, most of the recognized elements of air-ground co-operation had been employed. There had been significant developments in some areas, while other changes merely hinted at future potential. Improvements in communications and air supply, for instance, were limited by the available technology, while reconnaissance, artillery spotting and direct air support had been driven by the urgent need of ground forces. After the war, RAF and Army relationships broke down in Great Britain following disagreements about future strategy, relative shares of a reduced budget and the RAF's continued independence. Imperial policing, in which the RAF had shown itself keen to play an important role despite Army objections, found airmen and ground troops having to work together as they confronted a number of serious insurgencies. There were few differences (except in the availability of air resources) in the level and nature of air-ground co-operation between air control theatres, where the RAF held overall command, and those where the Army was in charge. Confronting insurgencies in Kurdistani Iraq, on the North-West Frontier of India and in Palestine, it is clear that the RAF and troops (whether British, Indian Army or levies) needed to co-operate in order to overcome their skilled and elusive opponents. In these campaigns, developments in air/ground co-operation were not linear. Lessons appear to have needed to be re-learned afresh with each campaign, but a coalition of experience and innovation allowed problems to be recognized and solved and in key areas such as close support, communications, logistics and aerial photography, a considerable level of sophistication had been reached by the late 1930s. This occurred despite continuing attempted interference from the Service Chiefs in Britain.

Notes

1 Gary Sheffield, *Forgotten Victory: The First World War – Myths and Realities* (London: Headline, 2002 [2001]), p. 230.
2 Erich Ludendorff, *My War Memories 1914–1918*, vol. II (London: Hutchinson, 1919), p. 679.
3 Paddy Griffith, *Battle Tactics of the Western Front* (London: Yale University Press, 1994), p. 157.
4 Arguably, Foch's responsibility for extending the objectives has been underestimated. See Gary Sheffield, *The Chief: Douglas Haig and the British Army* (London: Aurum, 2011), pp. 296–7.
5 Robin Prior and Trevor Wilson, *Command and Control on the Western Front: The Military Career of Sir Henry Rawlinson 1914–18* (Barnsley: Pen and Sword, 2004 [1992]), p. 316.
6 S. F. Wise, *Canadian Airmen and the First World War* (Toronto: University of Toronto Press, 1980), pp. 520–1.
7 Ibid., p. 523.
8 Charles Messenger, *The Day We Won The War: Turning Point At Amiens August 1918* (London: Orion, 2008), p. 187.
9 Major-General Sir Archibald Montgomery, *The Story of the Fourth Army in the Battle of the Hundred Days, 8th August to 11th November 1918* (London: Hodder and Stoughton, 1919), pp. 40–1.
10 J. P. Harris with Niall Barr, *Amiens to the Armistice: the BEF in the Hundred Days Campaign 8th August to 11th November 1918* (London: Brassey's, 1998), pp. 91–2.
11 Ibid., pp. 96–9.

12 The National Archives of the UK, [TNA] AIR 1/677/21/13/1887, pp. 118–26.
13 Harris and Barr, *Amiens to the Armistice*, pp. 100–1.
14 H. A. Jones, *The War in the Air: Being the Story of the Part played by the Royal Air Force*, vol. VI (London: Clarendon Press, 1937), p. 445.
15 Ibid., pp. 460–1.
16 C. E. W. Bean, *The Official History of Australia in the War of 1914–18*, vol. VI: *The Australian Imperial Force in France during the Allied Offensive, 1918* (Sydney: Angus and Robertson, 1942), p. 600.
17 J. E. Edmonds, *Military Operations France and Belgium 1918*, vol. IV (London: HMSO, 1947), pp. 154–5.
18 Messenger, *Day We Won*, pp. 147–50.
19 Lee Kennett, *The First Air War* (New York: Simon and Schuster, 1991), p. 40.
20 Sir Walter Raleigh, *The War in the Air: Being the Story of the Part played by the Royal Air Force* (Oxford: Clarendon Press, 1922), vol. I, p. 213.
21 Kennett, *First Air War*, pp. 37–8.
22 Prior and Wilson, *Command*, p. 329.
23 Yigal Sheffy, *British Military Intelligence in the Palestine Campaign* (London: Frank Cass, 1997), p. 306.
24 Wise, *Canadian Airmen*, p. 521.
25 Sheffy, *British Military Intelligence*, pp. 305–7.
26 J. C. Slessor, *Airpower and Armies* (Oxford: Oxford University Press, 1936), pp. 170–1.
27 Kennett, *First Air War*, p. 26.
28 Ibid., pp. 34–5; Shelford Bidwell and Dominick Graham, *Fire-Power: British Army Weapons and Theories of War 1904–45* (London: Allen and Unwin, 1982), p. 143.
29 Ibid., p. 144.
30 Ibid., pp. 101–2.
31 Sheffield, *Forgotten Victory*, p. 314.
32 Wise, *Canadian Airmen*, p. 526; TNA, AIR 1/725/97/21.
33 Wise, *Canadian Airmen*, p. 526.
34 Tim Travers, *How The War Was Won* (Barnsley: Pen and Sword, 2005 [1992]), p. 121.
35 Prior and Wilson, *Command*, p. 327.
36 Kennett, *First Air War*, p. 211.
37 Wise, *Canadian Airmen*, pp. 526–7.
38 Jones, *The War in the Air*, vol. VI, pp. 466–7.
39 Kennett, *First Air War*, p. 221.
40 Wise, *Canadian Airmen*, p. 529.
41 Slessor, *Airpower and Armies*, p. 169.
42 Wise, *Canadian Airmen*, p. 529.
43 Messenger, *Day We Won*, p. 100.

44 Wise, *Canadian Airmen*, p. 527.
45 Jones, *The War in the Air*, vol. VI, pp. 463–7.
46 Harris and Barr, *Amiens to the Armistice*, p. 127.
47 Bidwell and Graham, *Fire-Power*, p. 109.
48 TNA, CAB 23 (20 August 1918), p. 461.
49 Bidwell and Graham, *Fire-Power*, p. 145.
50 Harris and Barr, *Amiens to the Armistice*, p. 100.
51 Wise, *Canadian Airmen*, p. 532; Jones, *The War in the Air*, vol. VI, p. 441.
52 Harris and Barr, *Amiens to the Armistice*, p. 101.
53 Jones, *The War in the Air*, vol. VI, pp. 434–6; AIR 1/1887, pp. 99–104; Messenger, *Day We Won*, p. 230.
54 AIR 1/1887, pp. 127–8; Harris and Barr, *Amiens to the Armistice*, p. 101.
55 Jones, *The War in the Air*, vol. VI, pp. 458–60.
56 Wise, *Canadian Airmen*, pp. 538–9.
57 Messenger, *Day We Won*, p. 147.
58 Kennett, *First Air War*, pp. 33–4.
59 Harris and Barr, *Amiens to the Armistice*, p. 137.
60 Jones, *The War in the Air*, vol. VI, pp. 465–6.
61 Paul Kennedy, 'Britain in the First World War', in Allan R. Millett and Williamson Murray (eds), *Military Effectiveness*, vol. I: *The First World War* (London: Unwin Hyman, 1989 [1988]), p. 51.
62 Nigel Steel and Peter Hart, *Tumult in the Clouds: The British Experience of War in the Air* (London: Hodder and Stoughton, 1997), p. 330.
63 Kennett, *First Air War*, p. 86.
64 Sheffy, *British Military Intelligence*, p. 310.
65 Edmonds, *Military Operations France and Belgium 1918*, vol. IV, p. 157; Messenger, *Day We Won*, p. 231; Harris and Barr, *Amiens to the Armistice*, p. 112.
66 Slessor, *Airpower and Armies*, pp. 165–6.
67 Ibid., pp. 114–5.
68 Wise, *Canadian Airmen*, p. 540.
69 Edmonds, *Military Operations France and Belgium 1918*, vol. IV, p. 114.
70 Ibid., p. 531.
71 Ibid., p. 536.
72 Harris and Barr, *Amiens to the Armistice*, pp. 109–12.
73 Slessor, *Airpower and Armies*, pp. 195–6; Wise, *Canadian Airmen*, p. 524.
74 Slessor, *Airpower and Armies*, p. 151.
75 Wise, *Canadian Airmen*, p. 525.
76 Slessor, *Airpower and Armies*, pp. 168–9.
77 M. Goya, *La Chair et L'Acier: L'invention de la guerre moderne 1914–1918* (Paris: Tallendier Editions, 2004), pp. 410–11.
78 Slessor, *Airpower and Armies*, pp. 183–4.

79 Wise, *Canadian Airmen*, pp. 528–36.
80 Slessor, *Airpower and Armies*, p. 172.
81 Ibid., pp. 101–7.
82 Travers, *How the War*, p. 45.
83 Wise, *Canadian Airmen*, p. 531.
84 Ibid., p. 540.
85 Slessor, *Airpower and Armies*, pp. 173–8.
86 Ibid., p. 164; Wise, *Canadian Airmen*, p. 164.
87 Jones, *The War in the Air*, vol. VI, p. 437; Slessor, *Airpower and Armies*, p. 169.
88 Messenger, *Day We Won*, p. 230; Harris and Barr, *Amiens to the Armistice*, pp. 106–7.
89 Messenger, *Day We Won*, pp. 229–30.
90 Sheffield, *Forgotten Victory*, p. 252.
91 Wise, *Canadian Airmen*, pp. 542–6.
92 Harris and Barr, *Amiens to the Armistice*, p. 127.
93 Wise, *Canadian Airmen*, p. 542.
94 Messenger, *Day We Won*, p. 230.
95 Travers, *How the War*, pp. 48–9.
96 Ibid., p. 130.
97 Wise, *Canadian Airmen*, p. 518.
98 Quoted in Derek Waldie, 'The Third Dimension: A Study of Army-Air Force Relations 1918–1939' (PhD, King's College London, 1980), p. 15.
99 Harris and Barr, *Amiens to the Armistice*, p. 50.
100 David Hall, *Strategy for Victory: the Development of British Tactical Air Power, 1919–1943* (Westport, CT: Praeger, 2008), p. 8.
101 Hall, *Strategy*, p. 8.
102 Ibid., pp. 9–13.
103 Slessor, *Airpower and Armies*, p. 192.
104 Hall, *Strategy*, pp. 14–15.
105 Ibid., p. 25.
106 Harris and Barr, *Amiens to the Armistice*, pp. 296–7.
107 Wise, *Canadian Airmen*, p. 575.
108 Prior and Wilson, *Command*, pp. 307–8.
109 Brian Bond, *British Military Policy between the Two World Wars* (Oxford: Oxford University Press, 1980), p. 1.
110 Keith Jeffery, *The British Army and the Crisis of Empire 1918–1922* (Manchester: Manchester University Press, 1984), pp. 160–2.
111 Bond, *British Military Policy*, p. 71.
112 Ibid., p. 62.
113 Ibid., p. 323; Bidwell and Graham, *Fire-Power*, p. 189. For a rebuttal of the argument that the army made no attempt to analyse the lessons of the war until

the Kirke Committee was set up, see David French, 'Doctrine and Organization in the British Army 1919-1932', *The Historical Journal* 44, 2 (June 2001), pp. 497-515.

114 David Omissi, *Air Power and Colonial Control: The Royal Air Force 1990-1939* (Manchester: Manchester University Press, 1990), p. 61.

115 Neville Parton, 'The Development of Early RAF Doctrine', *Journal of Military History* 72, 4 (2008), p. 1177.

116 Hall, *Strategy*, p. 19.

117 Omissi, *Air Power*, p. 82.

118 Brian Robson, *Crisis on the Frontier: The Third Afghan War and the Campaign in Waziristan 1919-20* (Stroud: Spellmount, 2005), p. 255.

119 Bond, *British Military Policy*, p. 57.

120 Malcolm Smith, *British Air Strategy between the Wars* (Oxford: Clarendon Press, 1984), pp. 29-30.

12

The Battle of Amiens and the Development of British Air-Land Battle, 1918–45

Alistair McCluskey

The Battle of Amiens was one of the most influential battles of the twentieth century. Four days of intense combat from 8–12 August 1918 saw the British Fourth and French First Armies shatter the German Second Army and drive it back, together with the German Eighteenth Army, up to 20 km on a 50 km front between the Oise and the Ancre. In the process the British and French took 30,000 prisoners of war, killed or wounded at least another 13,000 men, and captured almost 500 guns.[1] Although more widely associated with the massed use of tanks, the Battle of Amiens also saw the largest concentration of British airpower for a single operation in the war. Deployed as a separate service for the first time in a major offensive, the Royal Air Force (RAF) played a pivotal role in the combat performance of the Fourth Army. Swarming over the battlefield, its aircraft engaged any German defenders in direct contact with the leading ground troops, harried the retreat of those less resolute and repeatedly drove reinforcements from the road as they struggled forwards in an attempt to avert disaster. In the course of the battle, both the Army and the RAF identified many lessons which they ruthlessly applied during the remainder of the war. As a result they developed a potent Air-Land capability which struck with repeated success at the German Armies in the west and ultimately drove them to request an Armistice.

However, the events at Amiens also provided a critical point of reference that directly influenced the development of British Air-Land battle in the interwar period and its subsequent conduct in the Second World War. In its efforts to maintain its existence as an independent Service in a period of severe economic retrenchment, the RAF used its experiences at Amiens to distance itself from the task of close air support before recasting the role of airpower in the land battle as that of interdiction. Consequently, to a large extent the lessons from Amiens were responsible for the flawed conduct of Air-Land operations in France and Flanders in 1940 and the resultant catastrophic Allied defeat. However, they also provided the intellectual framework around which the British were able to hone the integrated concepts of Air-Land battle with which they took part in the defeat of Hitler's forces in the Mediterranean and North Western Europe between 1942 and 1945.

The drift away from close air support during the interwar period has been analysed in several recent studies. David Hall has argued that the primary cause was the short-sighted and conservative view of airpower held within the War Office. He suggests that the Army, unable to grasp the tenets and potential of air power, made successive attempts to gain command of its own aircraft based on the mistaken belief that the aircraft was a tactical battlefield weapon.[2] This argument contains certain elements of merit, not least in highlighting the consistent and not always helpful calls by the War Office for command of its own air component. However, it glosses over several shortcomings in the analysis of the equally command fixated Air Staff in the interwar period which, as will be seen, led to the dysfunctional conduct of Air-Land operations. These shortcomings are more widely acknowledged by Richard Muller.[3] He too highlights the blight placed on the development of close air support by the ongoing and often vitriolic debate over command and control and concludes that the British lacked an '. . . intellectual [and] practical foundation for using their air force in support of the army'.[4] To analyse these developments, this chapter will discuss the conduct of the air battle at Amiens and how the lessons were utilized in the final months of the War, before analysing its influence on the development of Air-Land battle in the interwar period in detail. Finally, the chapter will analyse the consequence of the interwar developments and the subsequent recovery of Air-Land battle on the battlefields of the Second World War.

The Battle of Amiens took place at a key moment in the history of the RAF. Although it had been an independent Service since 1 April 1918 with elements conducting a strategic air attack on Germany, by far the greatest proportion of its effort was on the Western Front under the overall control of the British Expeditionary Force (BEF). Each BEF Army commanded an RAF Brigade which comprised of a Corps Wing and an Army Wing. The Corps Wing consisted of squadrons whose main tasks were the control of artillery fire and tactical reconnaissance to give formation HQs as clear a picture as possible of the battle situation as it developed. The Army Wing consisted of fighter-reconnaissance, fighter and bomber squadrons whose task it was to take the battle beyond the front line to both protect the Corps Wing from the German Air Force and attack targets in depth. In addition to the Brigades permanently affiliated to the Armies, GHQ commanded IX Brigade RAF which consisted of two 'Army' Wings and a specialist 'Night operations' Wing, but which had no permanent command relationship with any Army HQ, being allocated to the sector of the front where the need was greatest as reinforcement. At Amiens, Fourth Army had V Brigade under command with IX Brigade in direct support and support from III Brigade from Third Army, I Brigade from First Army and X Brigade from Fifth Army available if necessary. Furthermore, V Brigade was reinforced with 8 Squadron, which since 1 July 1918, had been permanently attached to the Tank Corps to develop co-operation techniques between the two nascent arms.[5]

The air plan that the RAF attempted to execute at Amiens was ambitious and strikingly modern in concept, consisting of three broad phases. First, the bomber and fighter squadrons of IX Brigade were to achieve air superiority in the attack sector by destroying the German air units already in the battle area on the ground with a surprise dawn attack. The IX Brigade fighters were then to oppose any German air force reinforcements that attempted to join the battle. Second, the Corps and fighter squadrons of V Brigade were to provide close support to the ground formations of Fourth Army as they punched their way through the German defences and then disrupt any attempts the Germans made to deploy their local reserves. Finally, the bomber squadrons were to launch evening attacks on key railway stations to disrupt the arrival of German strategic reserves attempting to reach the battle area.[6]

The weather disrupted the plan from the outset as thick fog shrouded the battle area preventing IX Brigade from completing its attack on the German aerodromes to full effect. However, from around 09.00 hrs onwards, the clearing conditions allowed V Brigade to increasingly influence the battle. In the thick of the action was 8 Squadron whose aircraft maintained a steady stream of information to the Tank Brigades HQs on the progress of the battle. In addition to this task, by 09.50 hrs, it's aircraft became increasingly involved in the attack on machine guns and field guns being used by German rearguards to hold up the tanks, dropping 81 bombs and firing 6,570 rounds by the close of the day. Alongside 8 Squadron, the fighter squadrons of V Brigade ranged across the battlefield engaging the 'exceptional targets' caused by the confusion within the German lines.[7] Numerous attacks were made both on the line of contact between the ground forces and in depth as the German reserve regiments and battalions attempted to move forward. Among other examples, they disrupted the counter-attacks of 27th and 54th Reserve Divisions at Morlancourt and 109th Division at Harbonnières.[8] Similarly, the 119th Division took over nine hours to travel 15 kilometres by lorry to the front line at Vrély, being forced to halt numerous times by incessant aerial attack.[9] The German Second Army was never allowed to make a coherent response against its assailants.

Whilst V Brigade was completing its mission in support of Fourth Army, the plan for the air battle took a fundamental change of direction. Pilots flying over the battlefield had noticed major traffic congestion around the bridges over the River Somme approximately 15 kilometres behind the front line. Consequently, around midday, Major-General Salmond, GOC RAF, cancelled the planned bombing missions of the railways and redirected IX Brigade to mount attacks, with both bombers and bomb-armed fighters, on the bridges in an attempt to cut the German lines of communication.[10] The attacks met with little success as the bridges proved difficult targets to hit and the bombs that were used lacked the power to cause any major structural damage. Furthermore, the removal of the IX Brigade fighters from their counter air task coincided with the arrival of significant German air reinforcements, in particular the elite air combat specialist *Jagdgeschwader* units flying in from Champagne. The ensuing air battle raged over the next two days as IX Brigade attempted in vain to destroy the bridges. Only on 10 August did the Brigade admit defeat and revert back to the original task of interdicting the railway system.[11]

Analysis of the air Battle at Amiens was swift and, unsurprisingly given the acute need of the BEF to maintain its operational tempo, paid particular attention to the conduct of close air support. The vulnerability of tanks to anti-tank guns once they had outrun their artillery support was of great concern as noted by both the 4 and 5 Tank Brigades.[12] The belief that aircraft could neutralize this threat was one of the primary lessons taken to heart by V Brigade after the battle. On 14 August Brigadier Charlton circulated a memorandum to his squadrons, highlighting the importance of this new task, stating that, '. . . it will be seldom that the duty in which machines are at the moment engaged will not yield in importance to offensive action against the anti tank gun'.[13] His perspective was reinforced by 22nd Wing's report on the close air support given by its fighter squadrons during the battle, submitted on 19 August. One of its key recommendations highlighted the necessity for close liaison with Tank units to optimize the effectiveness of fighter aircraft engaged in attacking anti-tank defences.[14] Action was swift and within two days 73 Squadron, equipped with Sopwith Camels, was removed from IX Brigade and grouped with 8 Squadron in order to specialize in ground attack with single-seat fighters. This small 'group' spent the remainder of the war in permanent support of the Tank Corps, moving flights across the BEF as they followed the tanks. Ground attack also became a higher priority for 8 Squadron as a policy change reduced the number of aircraft allocated to contact patrol work to the minimum necessary, with the remainder diverted to attack anti-tank guns.[15] Furthermore, command and control was improved through the use of wireless telegraphy to enable the engagement of fleeting targets. This system integrated the efforts of the Corps and Army Wings more effectively and provided significant assistance to the later battles at Bapaume (23 August), the Hindenburg Line (27–9 September) and Le Cateau (8 October).[16]

By the time of the Armistice in November 1918, the RAF had become a sophisticated exponent of air power in support of ground forces, complementing its unique roles in the strategic arena. Unfortunately, this situation was not maintained in the interwar period as inter-Service rivalry and senior officer prejudice relegated this capability in importance to the extent that by 1930 it had almost ceased to exist. Only with the rise of the nascent Continental threats in the mid-1930s did the concept of an integrated Air-Land battle re-emerge.

The erosion of Air-Land capability resulted chiefly from two factors; fiscal constraints and inter-Service rivalry. The austere post-war fiscal context ensured that the defence budget was so low that the individual Services struggled to maintain sufficient resources to meet their many requirements. These difficulties were apparent from 1918 onwards as Defence and social reform programmes competed for funds provided by a reduced GDP that was 13 per cent lower in 1921 than it had been in 1913,[17] and undermined by the increased annual cost of servicing the national debt which jumped from £24.5M in 1913 to £344.5M in the 1920s.[18] In such circumstance major economies needed to be made in a significantly restructured national budget. Within a year of the signing of the Armistice the Cabinet instituted the cardinal assumption that Britain would not be engaged in a great war within ten years and that no Expeditionary Force would be required for this role; the so-called Ten Year Rule.[19] This allowed the Treasury to drastically cut the Defence vote from £616M in 1919/20 to £232M in 1920/21. This process was continued by subsequent Governments until 1931/32 when the allocation to defence was £107M.[20]

One of the major consequences of this retrenchment was an increased level of rivalry between the Services. Whereas co-operation had been one of the hallmarks of success in the relatively resource-rich context of 1918, by the early 1920s inter-Service relations became increasingly adversarial. Under the leadership of the Chief of the Air Staff (CAS), Trenchard, the RAF defended itself by claiming that airpower could substitute for the manpower-intensive roles previously conducted by the other Services when Sir Eric Geddes conducted his review of National Expenditure.[21] Alongside the role of 'Air Policing' of the Empire, Trenchard and his staff also developed an embryonic Continental strategy built on the delivery of a strategic air attack on vital centres of production. In this way an enemy nation would be prevented from bringing its potential strength to bear on the battlefield. Although there appears to have been some confusion within the Air Staff as to how this would be achieved, a crucial element of this debate was Trenchard's view that air superiority would be an essential precondition.[22] In the prevailing financial climate, the RAF would not have the resources to fulfil all its potential tasks and in prioritizing its new roles over the old, the RAF's shift away from close support began.

Trenchard's position was articulated in the first formal document to deal with the issue of Air-Land battle, *Confidential Document* (CD) 21, published in June 1921. This document contained a section discussing the tactical roles of aircraft operating in support of the Army, describing an organizational and operational concept identical to that used in November 1918. Unsurprisingly, when discussing the use of aircraft for offensive action the document stated that aircraft were, '... very valuable to silence anti tank guns ...', and that widespread bombing of the battlefield was to be discontinued a few hours after zero in order to '... concentrate on main routes ...'.[23]

However, while this section may have placated the Army, Trenchard's vision was articulated in the following pages. Part II of CD 21 was introduced by the exposition that the primary role of air power was, '... air fighting, air defence against a continental or other threat, [and] aerial bombardment of enemy establishments'.[24] This represented a point of departure from the status quo by the RAF. Although part I described the concept of air support in its established form, the assertion that air power's primary role lay elsewhere would by implication result in the relegation of tasks in support of the other two Services.

The drift away from Army support tasks was even more pronounced in *Confidential Document* 22 (CD22), The Operations Manual RAF, published in 1922. This publication was a much more detailed articulation on how the RAF was to operate on deployment than its predecessor. Although it acknowledged the requirement for co-operation with the Army by including an entire chapter on the subject,[25] the close support role was now formally subordinated to the perceived primacy in the need to gain air superiority.[26] This shift towards the air superiority role had two major implications, both of which undermined the delivery of air support to the Army. First, despite acknowledging the utility of air power in countering anti-tank defences and stating that the best aircraft to undertake this role was the single seat fighter,[27] in order to maintain the flexibility to concentrate forces onto the air superiority task, CD22 also directed that role specialization for these aircraft be minimized.[28] This represented a significant shift away from the combat-proven experience of the air units and formations that fought at Amiens that would almost certainly result in a degradation of close support capability. The second implication was that aircraft earmarked for gaining air superiority were unlikely to be risked on the lower priority task of low-flying attacks which, it was understood, would result in exceedingly high casualties.

The concept that low-flying attacks led to unsustainable casualty rates appears to have become something of an article of faith within the RAF in the interwar period. It was highlighted by Brooke-Popham, who in a lecture to the RAF Staff College in 1924, used the Battle of Amiens to argue that close support with low-flying attacks could not be maintained for more than a few days and was unlikely to be worth the cost, particularly if it compromised air superiority.[29] Likewise, in 1934 the fears associated with low flying were being repeated by the RAF instructor at the Army Staff College in Camberley, Wing Commander John Slessor. Although he highlighted the potential efficacy of low-flying attacks on 'third rate' troops, he again used the example of Amiens, alongside that of Cambrai, to suggest that the cost against a capable enemy would make the task untenable.[30]

Unfortunately, by extending the fairly specific evidence of casualty rates at Amiens, particularly those of 8 August, into deductions with more universal applicability, the Air Staff appear to have been selective in their analysis. Their suggestion that low level attacks were uniformly costly, is not wholly supported by key contemporary documents and nor did they analyse the relative novelty of close support in August 1918. It was not acknowledged that low-level attack in the fluid offensive conditions at Amiens was still an unusual skill for the pilots involved. 8 Squadron had only been operating with the Tank Corps since 1 July 1918, and 73 Squadron was ordered to specialize in this role only after the battle. Had the Air Staff taken the time to analyse air support between 9 August and 11 November 1918, the RAF in general, and these Squadrons in particular, became vastly more effective. On 8 August the ten Squadrons of 22nd Wing flew 261 sorties in support of Fourth Army, dropping 703 25 lb bombs and firing 65,860 rounds of ammunition at ground targets. In the process they suffered 24 casualties of which at least 17 were shot down. The following day 238 sorties were launched dropping 860 bombs and firing 56,290 rounds. This time only 3 aircraft were lost. This dramatic reduction in casualty rates continued through 10 and 11 August where 8 and 5 casualties were sustained from 331 and 282 sorties respectively.[31] This improvement continued into the latter stages of the war as on 10 October, the Wing flew 147 sorties, dropped 458 bombs and fired 39,970 rounds at ground targets without losing an aircraft. The pilots of 22nd Wing clearly learnt from their previous mistakes.

The improvement in performance was even more marked in 8 and 73 Squadrons. Aircraft from these units now refrained from flying indiscriminately at low level in the dangerous airspace over the battlefront, and began to concentrate their efforts on areas where anti-tank defences could be expected to exist. This change in policy seems to have brought about a marked reduction in the number of casualties suffered. At the Battle of Albert, between 22 and 25 August 1918, 8 Squadron dropped 132 bombs and sustained 1 casualty, while 73 Squadron cut its teeth in the close support role by dropping 24 bombs and firing 8,850 rounds of ammunition at ground targets without a single casualty.[32] Furthermore, 73 Squadron is recorded as having given highly effective support to tank units at Ramicourt and Montbrehain on 2–3 October 1918, dropping 94 bombs and firing 7,100 rounds with one wounded pilot being the only casualty.[33] Indeed, from around 1,000 sorties by 8 Squadron aircraft between 8 August and 11 November, a mere five were listed as missing.[34] In contrast, 107 Squadron lost five aircraft from 15 sorties when intercepted by German fighters over the Somme on the morning of 9 August 1918.[35] Whatever the perceived dangers associated with close air support, in the skies over the Western Front there were clearly more dangerous roles.

By misinterpreting the casualty data from low-level attack it would appear that the Air Staff were guilty of the subjective misuse of the evidence of Amiens which created a false perspective of the facts. This may have been inadvertent but in the debate over support to the Army, the RAF was the clear beneficiary. This also contradicts David Hall's belief that the General Staff were to blame for the deterioration in inter-Service relations and the development of tactical airpower; the Air Staff played an equal role at least.

As a consequence of this doctrinal evolution, by the late 1930s the senior echelons of RAF leadership were so far removed from the concept of close support to the Army on the battlefield that they lost the capability in any meaningful sense, particularly with respect to training. As early as 1928 RAF reports were highlighting the fact that fighter squadrons were to be primarily trained to obtain air superiority rather than participate in the ground battle and discouraged ground attack training for the coming year.[36] Although an exceptional exercise was conducted with the Army in 1938 the conclusions it drew were vague and sometimes contradictory.[37] In 1939, while briefing 1 (Bomber) Group for their training support task to the Army, Air Commodore Willock, DSD RAF, stated that, '[w]hat we want to avoid above all for the Army to think that air forces should be diverted from their normal functions or that the potentialities of low flying aircraft should lead to their misuse'.[38] His suggestion that any such aspirations may have resulted in some 'confused thinking' at the War Office may have been correct in certain aspects, but the War Office did not have a monopoly on this vice; the Air Ministry could be equally indulgent. As well as minimizing the necessary training, the Air Staffs lack of appetite for close air support also undermined the requirement for any specialist aircraft. When proposals to this effect were made in 1935 they were rejected by the Air Staff on the grounds that such aircraft were, '…neither in the role of the RAF in war, nor its "imperial police" duties in normal times . . .'[39] despite Deputy Director Plans, Group Captain Arthur Harris, observing, '. . . we shall undoubtedly in the future on occasion wish to exploit this form of attack and there is a danger that this requirement may be overlooked . . .'[40] Without the necessary training or specialist equipment, by 1939 close air support was truly moribund in the RAF.

Despite being partly used to justify the drift away from the task of close air support during the interwar period, consideration of the Battle of Amiens also played a major role in reintegrating the air and land battles through the concept of air interdiction. The key personality in this respect was Slessor.[41] During his time as an instructor at Staff College, in addition to the dangers associated with close air support, he pointed out the potential for air power to influence the land battle by cutting enemy lines of communication in order to isolate the battlefield, the task we now term Air Interdiction.[42] The concepts he developed were refined and eventually published in 1936 in his key book, *Air Power and Armies*. In this he concluded that an enemy's critical vulnerability were his transportation systems in general and his railways in particular.[43] The integrated nature of the railway systems suggested to Slessor that an attack at one point could have a consequence hundreds of miles away due to resultant congestion and delays.[44] This effect became particularly pronounced at junctions where the delays could be simultaneously transmitted along several lines and hinder the use of alternative routes.

Slessor illustrated his conclusions on air interdiction with a lengthy examination of the Battle of Amiens in which he was as excoriating in his criticism of the conduct of the deep battle as he was of close support. Although acknowledging that elements of the air plan were intended to isolate the battlefield, he was extremely deprecating of the attempts to destroy the Somme bridges.[45] In his opinion, not only was this difficult to achieve, it would not realize the desired effect and was therefore a waste of time and resources. In his opinion, far more utility could have been gained by attacking the key rail junctions at Cambrai, Le Cateau, Le Nouvion, Vervins and Laon. By assuming that Rawlinson intended to conduct a deep operation, Slessor suggested that after the successful 'break in' battle, Fourth Army was brought to a halt in by the arrival of 16 German divisions from their strategic reserves. Six of these divisions came from Armies on the northern flank of the German Second Army and passed through the key rail junction of Cambrai over a 48 hour period.[46] Had they been prevented in so doing Slessor concluded that the Second Army would have been hard-pressed to reform an effective defensive line. His vision made its way into official doctrine in both the Air Force and Army operational manuals in the run up to the Second World War. In both the 1932 and 1938 editions of the War Office Manual, *'The Employment of Air Forces with the Army in the Field'* (EAF) and the 1935 edition of *AP1300, RAF War Manual Pt1 – Operations*, advice was given that that the most appropriate target set for bombers employed in support of the Army was the transport system of the enemy.[47]

What Slessor did not consider however was timing of the arrival of these reinforcements and how they influenced the development of the battle. The German troops defeated on the first day were already in place and those defeated on the second day deployed by foot or road vehicle. Only in the evening of 9 August did the Fourth Army run into troops deployed by rail. By this time Fourth Army's artillery target intelligence was greatly reduced from the outset of the battle and very few tanks remained combat ready; the Fourth Army had already shot its bolt.

The Battle of Amiens had a baleful effect on the delivery of an integrated Air-Land battle in the interwar period. Subjective analysis of the close air support delivered by the RAF enabled the Air Staff to overestimate the cost of close air support missions and by extension threaten its ability to attain air superiority. This in turn generated the institutional view that fighters should not be used in the close support role except in dire emergency. Concurrently, doctrinal thought was shifting the efforts of the bombers from attacks on the battlefield to the enemy rear area. Consequently there was little appetite for the task for close air support to troops in contact and little training was conducted. Crucially, this undermined the development of the necessary capability to conduct or control such missions, even if the RAF subsequently chose to do so. Not without reason did an RAF officer point out that in the interwar period, '... the RAF forgot how to support the Army'.[48]

The dysfunctional outlook of the Air Staff in the interwar period had a catastrophic impact on the ability of the RAF to contribute effectively to a land campaign at the outbreak of hostilities. By focussing its fighters on the battle to achieve air superiority it significantly degraded its ability to attack ground targets. Consequently, this task fell to its bomber units which would be forced to survive due to luck rather than judgement if heavy defences existed. This lethal shortcoming was cruelly exposed by the German invasion of France and the Low Countries in May 1940.

Although the rumbling debate over a separate air arm for the Army was reignited by the decision to commit the Army to the Continent in February 1939,[49] the squadrons that deployed to France at the outbreak of hostilities remained firmly under command of the RAF. Although originally deployed in two elements, the Advanced Air Striking Force (AASF) and the Air Component in support of the Army, they were soon unified under Air Marshal Barratt as the British Air Forces in France (BAFF), consisting of 14 squadrons of medium bombers, five and a half fighter squadrons and four reconnaissance squadrons.[50] Unfortunately however, alongside their French allies they were significantly weaker both in quantity and quality than the Luftwaffe, containing many obsolete aircraft.[51] The Nazi invasion on 10 May 1940 pitched these forces into battle and immediately they were found wanting with the crucial engagements taking place over the Meuse crossings.

Following XIX Panzer Corps' establishment of crossing points over the Meuse on 14 May, BAFF joined the French Air Force in attempting to cut the pontoon bridges over which Guderian's troops were trying to deploy.[52] The attacks were disastrous. The 109 British and 43 French bombers supported by 250 fighters, faced 300 German fighters and 303 anti-aircraft guns concentrated over and around the vital bridges. Although the raids rolled on throughout the day, the largest took place between 16.00 and 17.00 hrs when 71 Battle and Blenheim bombers hurled themselves into the fray. Stripped of their weak fighter escort by the German fighters, those flights that got through were hacked apart by the German anti-aircraft gunners. Of the 71 sorties flown, 40 aircraft were shot down;[53] a loss rate that remains the RAFs highest for a comparable mission.

It is of interest to note what may have happened had the RAF's priorities been different. Notwithstanding the additional four fighter squadrons sent to France at the advent of the German assault, 43 remained in the United Kingdom on strategic defence duties.[54] Had a larger proportion of these been deployed to the

Continent and been committed to the battle over Sedan, it is not beyond the bounds of possibility that air parity and maybe even limited superiority may have been gained. XIX Panzer Corps completed its bridges with the 'last yard of available pontoon equipment'.[55] If these had been hit no other equipment was immediately available. The ensuing delay would have brought the German tempo in line with that of the French and enmeshed them in a damaging and potentially fatal battle on the river. The consequences of such a battle will remain in the realm of counter factual speculation, however, as Kershaw has pointed out, support for the Nazi party was to a large extent built on the delivery of stunning and cheap victories that swayed the less belligerent elements of the German population; defeats could have easily taken them in the opposite direction.[56] At the very least, a stalemated Western Front would have denied the Germans the advanced airfields necessary for their single-seat fighters to participate in the Battle of Britain.

Throughout the next two years the War Office continued to agitate for its own resources and the Air Ministry continued to resist. The impasse was broken in the summer of 1942 when two remarkably similar papers were drafted. The first, drafted by the War Office forwarded the suggestion that a new organization, the Army Air Support Group (AAS Gp), be formed consisting of fighters, bombers and reconnaissance aircraft.[57] The intent of the proposal was not dismissed out of hand by the Air Ministry, although they felt unable to give assent to the detail on the grounds that it included permanent decentralization. Instead, they produced a paper of their own written by Slessor that proposed the creation of a similar mixed force to the War Office paper, except this force was to be formed from the existing RAF Fighter, Bomber and Army Co-operation Commands and placed under command of the RAF.[58] Despite a last twitch of resistance from the War Office, the Slessor Plan reflected the advances that had been made in the Desert Air Force that had recently defeated Rommel at El Alamein. Buoyed by this associated success, it received support from Churchill and in early 1943 the Tactical Air Force (TAF) was born.

The TAFs that were prepared for the re-entry into Europe were essential in enabling the RAF and their allies to implement the doctrines of interdiction outlined by Slessor in the 1930s. Equipped with new medium bomber aircraft such as the Boston and Mitchell, and rugged fighter bombers such as the Typhoon, the TAFs possessed the means to strike powerfully at the enemy both at the battlefront and the lines of communication leading to it. However, the path towards interdiction was not always smooth and required assistance from Slessor himself to clear the final obstacles.

Slessor moved to the Mediterranean theatre as Deputy Commander of the Mediterranean Allied Air Forces (MAAF) on 14 January 1944. On arrival he found a debate raging and how the campaign in Italy could be best supported from the air.[59] Slessor conducted a review which articulated for the first time an integrated campaign between the Mediterranean Allied Strategic Air Force (MASAF) and the Mediterranean Allied Tactical Air Force (MATAF). Alongside its strategic role against Germany, the MASAF was to attack the rail network north of the Pisa-Rimini line. South of that line the railways were to come under attack from the MATAF.

In what came to be known as Operation STRANGLE, the medium bombers of the MATAF targeted the marshalling yards while the fighter bombers targeted rail lines and bridges.[60] As a consequence of this assault, by 4 April only 1,357 tons out of the requirement for 2,261 tons per day was getting through to the German front line.[61] Although this campaign was unable to totally isolate the Germans in the Gustav Line, it made the maintenance of their position virtually untenable. As a result, in contrast to the failed ground attacks in February and March, the DIADEM offensive in May shattered the German Tenth Army.

In North West Europe, the air campaign in support of OVERLORD mirrored that in the Mediterranean. The former CO of 8 Squadron, Leigh-Mallory was by this time in command of the Allied Expeditionary Air Force which included the 2nd TAF. In the build up to D-Day, an acrimonious debate broke out between Leigh-Mallory and the strategic air chiefs, Harris and Spaatz over nature of the planned assault.[62] Whereas Harris and Spaatz saw their main effort as the POINTBLANK campaign against strategic targets in Germany, Leigh-Mallory wished to see them utilized against the transport network leading into Normandy. Experience gained in Italy ensured that the debate was decided in favour of Leigh-Mallory. The campaign that followed was perhaps the epitome of an integrated Air-Land battle to date. While Bomber Command and the US VIII Air Force struck at key rail hubs in Western Europe, the final 2 weeks leading up to D-Day saw an intense assault by 2nd TAF and the US IX TAF to isolate the Normandy battlefield. By 5 June all bridges over the Seine downstream from Paris had been cut and such damage done that the German authorities considered the western rail network, '. . . to be completely wrecked'.[63] Nor did the attacks stop on 6 June. The Panzer Lehr Division, in an echo of 119th Division's experience on the Amiens-Roye road in 1918, described the road north from Vire as 'fighter-bomber racecourse'[64] as it came under sustained air attacks losing over 80 combat vehicles in the process. The experience of Panzer Lehr became the norm for the German Armies in Europe from the spring of

1944 until the end of the War. Under savage assaults from the Allied tactical airpower they were never able to concentrate sufficient combat power to mount a realistic challenge to the Allied ground forces and those that they did were destroyed piecemeal.

The application of tactical airpower in Europe between 1943 and 1945 has been the subject of a detailed study by Ian Gooderson. He noted with interest the balance between 2nd TAFs conduct of close air support and interdiction in the guise of 'armed reconnaissance'. His research indicates that armed reconnaissance was by far the more dangerous of the tasks and suggests that mutual support available from ground forces was partly responsible.[65] This is a valid point and may point to the reason why 8 and 73 Squadrons had such low casualty rates in late summer 1918.

In conclusion we can see that the Battle of Amiens played a pivotal role in the development of British Air-Land battle capability between 1918 and 1945 as it provided the 'evidence' which at first separated the RAF from the ground battle before generating its renaissance in a different form. Whereas the response to high casualty levels during the First World War had been to create specialist units in the close air support role and improve command and control measures, the bitter debates in the interwar period had seen this skill wither on the vine. Parsimonious budget allocations exacerbated tensions between the Services. These resulted in acrimonious debates that became increasingly focussed on the sterile issue of command and control of the Air-Land battle rather than its successful prosecution. Rather than produce an objective study of combat experience, the RAF took a subjective view of the losses sustained at Amiens in order to reject participation in the land battle as a profitable task. This took such a deep-rooted hold that the RAF failed to train or equip its personnel for a role that was immediately required once the decision was taken to deploy forces to the Continent in 1939. Notwithstanding the wider shortcomings of the land campaign, the ensuing disaster in 1940 found much at fault in the Air Ministry in the preceding two decades. However, the lessons drawn from the Battle of Amiens also laid the foundations for the rediscovery of Air-Land battle in the latter part of the war. Although the redevelopment of the command and control, and TAF 'hardware', took place independently, the doctrine of air interdiction was rooted in the 1930s analysis of the air battle over Amiens. This provided the final piece in the combat system with which the British and their Western Allies battered the Axis forces into defeat in 1945 and which could trace its heritage to the battlefields of Amiens in 1918.

Notes

1. J. P. Harris with Niall Barr, *Amiens to the Armistice: The BEF in the Hundred Days Campaign, 8 August–11 November1918* (London: Brassey's, 1998), p. 104.
2. David Ian Hall, *Strategy for Victory: The Development of British Tactical Airpower, 1919–1943* (Westport, CT: Praeger, 2008), pp. 153–6.
3. Richard R. Muller, 'Close Air Support: The British, German and American Experience, 1918–1941', in Williamson Murray and Allan R Millet (eds), *Military Innovation in the Interwar Period* (Cambridge: Cambridge University Press, 1996), pp. 163–72.
4. Ibid., p. 172.
5. The National Archives of the UK (TNA), AIR 1/725/97/01, 'History of Tank and Aeroplane Co-operation', 8 Squadron, 31 January 1919.
6. J. E. Edmonds, *Military Operations France and Belgium 1918* vol, IV, *8 August–26 September, The Franco-British Offensive* (London: HMSO, 1947), pp. 557–8. H. A. Jones, *The War in the Air, Being the Story of the Part Played in the Great War by the Royal Air Force*, vol. VI (Oxford: Clarendon Press, 1937), pp. 433–4.
7. Ibid.
8. T. Von Bose, *Die Katastrophe des 8 August 1918* (Berlin: Stalling, 1930), pp. 74, 175.
9. Ibid., p. 192.
10. Jones, *The War in the Air*, vol. VI, p. 441.
11. Ibid., pp. 447–52.
12. Liddell Hart Centre for Military Archives, Fuller Papers, 1/7/1, '4th Tank Bde Reports on Operations 8–11 August 1918'. 1/7/5, '5th Tank Bde Report on Operations with the Australian Corps 8–15 August 1918'.
13. H. A. Jones, *The War in the Air*, Appendices (Oxford: Clarendon Press, 1937), p. 123.
14. Royal Air Force Museum (RAFM), AIR 69/31, 'The Development of Aeroplane co-operation with the Army during the War'.
15. TNA, AIR 1/725/97/01, The History of Tank and Aeroplane Co-operation, 8 Squadron, dated 31 January 1919, p. 8.
16. Jones, *The War in the Air*, vol. VI, pp. 474, 486, 517, 525, 536.
17. G. C. Peden, *Arms, Economics and British Strategy* (Cambridge: Cambridge University Press, 2007), p. 127.
18. Ibid., p. 128.
19. Ibid., p. 98.
20. Ibid., p. 127.
21. Malcolm Smith, *British Air Strategy between the Wars* (Oxford: Clarendon Press, 1984), p. 24.
22. Ibid., pp. 66–8.

23 TNA, AIR 5/168 CD21. Memoranda: The co-operation by aircraft with coastal batteries; The power of the Air Force and the application of this power to hold and police Mesopotamia; Aircraft and the Army, dated June 1921, p. 8.
24 TNA, AIR 5/168 CD21, p. 9.
25 TNA AIR 5/299, CD22. *Operations Manual RAF*, chapter IX, Tactical Co-operation with the Army.
26 TNA AIR 5/299, CD22. Chapter VII, p. 52.
27 TNA AIR 5/299, CD22. Chapter XII, para. 35.
28 TNA AIR 5/299, CD22. Chapter IX, p. 63.
29 RAFM, AIR 69/31, Lecture to 2nd RAF Staff Course, 'The Development of Aeroplane Co-operation with the Army during the War'.
30 TNA, AIR 75/46, Slessor Papers, 'Land Air Warfare', Staff College Lecture, 'The Employment of Bombers and Fighters with an Army in the Field', p. 4.
31 TNA, AIR 1/1811/204/1629, 'Summary of Work 22nd Wing RAF, 2 Dec 1917–15 May 1919'.
32 TNA, AIR 1/2243/209/42/21, 'III Bde War Diary, 1–31 August 1918'.
33 TNA, AIR 1/1596/204/83/38, 'Summary of Work 5 Bde RFC, Aug–Oct 1918'.
34 TNA, AIR 1/1671/204/109/23, '8 Squadron RAF, 'Summary of Casualties, 8 August–11 November 1918'.
35 TNA, AIR 1/1849/204/211/8, '107 Squadron Record Book, 9 August 1918'.
36 TNA, AIR 10/1759, Army Co-operation Report, 1928, pp. 20–1.
37 TNA, AIR 2/1726, 'Low flying attack on enemy troops', 22 Gp Memorandum on Close Support by Aircraft of Land Forces in Europe or the Middle East, dated 5 May 1939.
38 TNA, AIR 2/3030, 'Field Force Bomber Squadrons in co-operation with the Army'. Air Ministry to No.1 (Bomber Group) dated 3 March 1939.
39 TNA, AIR 2/1593. 'Aircraft for Low Flying Attack'. Plans Minute dated 28 February 1935.
40 Ibid.
41 Phillip S. Meilinger, 'John C. Slessor and the Genesis of Aerial Interdiction', in *Airwar: Theory and Practice* (London: Frank Cass, 2003), pp. 64–75.
42 TNA, AIR 75/46, Slessor Papers, Land/Air Warfare, Staff College Lecture, 'The Employment of Bombers and Fighters with an Army in the Field', pp. 8–9.
43 John C. Slessor, *Air Power and Armies* (London: Oxford University Press, 1936), pp. 93, 123.
44 Ibid., p. 123.
45 Ibid., pp. 167–73.
46 Ibid., p. 199.
47 RAFM, AP 1176, *The Employment of Air Forces with the Army in the Field* (London: The Air Ministry, 1932), pp. 18–19; RAFM, *The Employment of Air Forces with the*

48 John Buckley, 'The Air War in France', in Brian Bond and Michael Taylor (eds), *The Battle for France and Flanders Sixty Years On* (Barnsley: Leo Cooper, 2001), p. 120.
49 Hall, *Strategy for Victory*, p. 31.
50 Ibid., p. 50.
51 John Terraine, *The Right of the Line: The Royal Air Force in the European War, 1939-1945* (London: Hodder and Stoughton, 1985), pp. 118-23.
52 Karl-Heinz Frieser, *The Blitzkrieg Legend: The 1940 Campaign in the West* (Annapolis, MD: Naval Institute Press, 2005), pp. 178-82.
53 Terraine, *Right of the Line*, p. 134.
54 Basil Collier, *The Defence of the United Kingdom* (London: HMSO, 1957), p. 108.
55 Frieser, *The Blitzkrieg Legend*, p. 179.
56 Ian Kershaw, *The Hitler Myth; Image and reality in the Third Reich*, Third Edition (Oxford: Oxford University Press, 2001), pp. 151-5.
57 Hall, *Strategy for Victory*, p. 122.
58 Ibid., p. 123.
59 Brigadier C. J. C. Molony, *The Mediterranean and the Middle East*, vol. V (London: HMSO, 1973), pp. 764-7.
60 Ibid., pp. 812-13.
61 Ibid., p. 816.
62 Carlo D'Este, *Decision in Normandy* (London: Harper, 1994 [1983]), pp. 213-17.
63 L. F. Ellis, *Victory in the West*, vol. I (London: HMSO, 1962), p. 111.
64 Ibid., p. 234.
65 Ian Gooderson, *Airpower at the Battlefront: Allied Close Air Support in Europe 1943-45* (London: Frank Cass, 1998), p. 217.

Bibliography

This bibliography is limited to the major studies cited by the contributors in their chapters and does not include references to the numerous national official histories. References to official histories and memoirs/autobiographies can be located in the relevant chapter footnotes.

Books

Abbatiallo, John, *Anti-Submarine Warfare in World War I: British Naval Aviation and the Defeat of the U-Boats* (London: Routledge, 2005).
Allen, H. R., *The Legacy of Lord Trenchard* (London: Cassell, 1972).
Ash, Eric, *Sykes and the Air Revolution, 1912–1918* (London: Frank Cass, 1999).
Asprey, Robert B., *The German High Command at War: Hindenburg and Ludendorff Conduct World War I* (New York, NY: W. Morrow, 1991).
Badsey, Stephen, *Doctrine and Reform in the British Cavalry 1880–1918* (Farnham: Ashgate, 2008).
Bailey, Jonathan, *The First World War and the Birth of the Modern Style of Warfare*, Strategic and Combat Studies Institute Occasional Paper No 22 (Camberley: Combat Studies Institute, 1996).
—, *Field Artillery and Firepower* (Annapolis, MD: Naval Institute Press, 2004).
Beckett, Ian F. W. and Corvi, Steven J. (eds), *Haig's Generals* (Barnsley: Pen and Sword, 2006).
Bellamy, Christopher, *Red God of War: Soviet Artillery and Rocket Forces* (London: Brassey's, 1986).
—, *The Evolution of Modern Land Warfare: Theory and Practice* (London: Routledge, 1990).
Benbow, Tim, *The Magic Bullet? Understanding the Revolution in Military Affairs* (London: Brassey's, 2004).
Bialer, Uri, *The Shadow of the Bomber: The Fear of Air Attack and British Politics 1932–1939* (London: Royal Historical Society, 1980).
Biddle, Tami Davis, *Rhetoric and Reality in Air Warfare: The evolution of British and American Ideas about Strategic Bombing, 1914–1945* (Princeton, NJ: Princeton University Press, 2002).
Bidwell, Shelford and Graham, Dominick, *Firepower: The British Army Weapons and Theories of War 1904–1945* (London: Allen and Unwin, 1982).

Boff, Jonathan, *Winning and Losing on the Western Front: The British Third Army and the Defeat of Germany in 1918* (Cambridge: Cambridge University Press, 2012).

Bond, Brian, *British Military Policy between the Two World Wars* (Oxford: Oxford University Press, 1980).

Bond, Brian and Cave, Nigel (eds), *Haig: A Reappraisal 70 Years On* (Barnsley: Pen and Sword, 1999).

Bond, Brian and Taylor, Michael (eds), *The Battle for France and Flanders Sixty Years On* (Barnsley: Leo Cooper, 2001).

Boyle, Andrew, *Trenchard: Man of Vision* (London: Collins, 1962).

Brooke-Sheperd, Gordon, *November 1918: The Last Act of the Great War* (London: Collins, 1981).

Brown, Ian Malcolm, *British Logistics on the Western Front 1914–1919* (Westport, CT: Greenwood Press, 1998).

British Commission for Military History, *'Look to your Front': Studies in the First World War* (Staplehurst: Spellmount, 1999).

Buckley, John, *Air Power in the Age of Total War* (London: UCL Press, 1999).

Budiansky, Stephen, *Air Power: The Men, Machines, and Ideas that Revolutionized War, from Kitty Hawk to Gulf War II* (New York, NY: Viking, 2004),

Cecil, Hugh and Liddle, Peter (eds), *Facing Armageddon: The First World War Experienced* (London: Pen and Sword, 1996).

Childs, David J., *A Peripheral Weapon?: The Production and Employment of British Tanks in the First World War* (Westport, CT: Greenwood Press, 1999).

Clayton, Anthony, *Paths of Glory: The French Army 1914–18* (London: Cassell, 2005 [2003]).

Cook, Tim, *Shock Troops: Canadians Fighting the Great War, 1917–1918* (Toronto: Penguin, 2008).

Cooper, Malcolm, *The Birth of Independent Air Power: British Air Policy in the First World War* (London: Allen and Unwin, 1986).

Corum, James, *The Luftwaffe: Creating the Operational Air War, 1918–1940* (Lawrence, KS: University Press of Kansas, 1997).

Cox, Sebastian, and Gray, Peter (eds), *Air Power History: Turning Points from Kitty Hawk to Kosovo* (London: Frank Cass, 2002).

Dennis, Peter, and Grey, Jeffrey (eds), *1918: Defining Victory* (Canberra: Army History Unit, 1999).

D'Este, Carlo, *Decision in Normandy* (London: Harper, 1994 [1983]).

Doyle, P. and Bennett, M. R. (eds), *Fields of Battle: Terrain in Military History* (Dordrecht: Kluwer Academic, 2002).

Duffy, Christopher, *Through German Eyes: The British and The Somme 1916* (London: Pheonix, 2007).

Edgerton, David, *England and the Aeroplane: An Essay on a Militant and Technological Nation* (Basingstoke: Palgrave Macmillan, 1991).

Ekins, Ashley (ed.), *1918 Year of Victory: The End of the Great War and the Shaping of History* (Auckland, NZ: Exisle Publishing, 2010).

Ferris, John, *The British Army and Signals Intelligence during the First World War* (Stroud: Sutton Publishing for the Army Records Society, 1992).

Franks, Norman, Bailey, Frank and Guest, Russell, *Above the Lines: A Complete Record of the Fighter Aces of the German Air Service, Naval Air Service and Flanders Marine Corps 1914–1918* (London: Grub Street, 1993).

Fredette, Raymond, *The Sky on Fire: The First Battle of Britain 1917–1918 and the Birth of the Royal Air Force* (London: Cassell, 1966).

French, David, *Military Identities: The Regimental System, the British Army, and the British People, c. 1870–2000* (Oxford: Oxford University Press, 2005).

Frieser, Karl-Heinz, *The Blitzkrieg Legend: The 1940 Campaign in the West* (Annapolis, MD: Naval Institute Press, 2005).

Gollin, Alfred, *The Impact of Air Power on the British People and their Government, 1909–14* (Stanford, CA: Stanford University Press, 1989).

Gooderson, Ian, *Airpower at the Battlefront: Allied Close Air Support in Europe 1943–45* (London: Frank Cass, 1998).

Gray, Colin, *Explorations in Strategy* (Westport, CT: Greenwood Press, 1996)

—, *Modern Strategy* (Oxford: Oxford University Press, 1999).

—, *Strategy for Chaos: Revolutions in Military Affairs and the Evidence of History* (London: Frank Cass, 2002).

Gray, Peter and Cox, Sebastian (eds), *Air Power Leadership: Theory and Practice* (London: The Stationary Office, 2002).

Greenhalgh, Elizabeth, *Victory through Coalition: Britain and France during the First World War* (Cambridge: Cambridge University Press, 2005).

Grey, C. G., *A History of the Air Ministry* (London: George Allen and Unwin, 1940).

Griffith, Paddy, *Battle Tactics of the Western Front: The British Army's Art of Attack 1916–18* (New Haven, CT: Yale University Press, 1994).

Griffith, Paddy (ed.), *British Fighting Methods in the Great War* (London: Frank Cass, 1996).

Groom, Winston, *A Storm in Flanders: The Ypres Salient 1914–1918 – Tragedy and Triumph on the Western Front* (London: Cassell, 2003),

Gudmundsson, Bruce I., *Stormtroop Tactics: Innovation in the German Army, 1914–1918* (New York, NY: Praeger, 1989).

Hall, David Ian, *Strategy for Victory: The Development of British Tactical Airpower, 1919–1943* (Westport, CT: Praeger, 2008).

Hallion, Richard, *Taking Flight: Inventing the Aerial Age from Antiquity through the First World War* (Oxford: Oxford University Press, 2003).

Hammond, Bryn, *Cambrai 1917: The Myth of the First Great Tank Battle* (London: Weidenfeld and Nicholson, 2008).

Hanson, Victor Davis, *The Western Way of War: Infantry Battle in Classical Greece* (Oxford: Oxford University Press, 1989).

Harper, Glyn, *Dark Journey: Three Key New Zealand Battles of the Western Front* (Auckland: HarperCollins, 2007).

Harris, J. P., *Douglas Haig and the First World War* (Cambridge: Cambridge University Press, 2009).

Harris, J. P. with Barr, Niall, *Amiens to the Armistice: The BEF in the Hundred Days Campaign 8 August – 11 November 1918* (London: Brassey's, 1998).

Hart, Peter, *1918: A Very British Victory* (London: Weidenfeld and Nicholson, 2008).

Harvey, A. D., *Collision of Empires: Britain in Three World Wars 1793–1945* (London: Hambledon Continuum, 1992).

Higham, Robin, *100 Years of Air Power and Aviation* (College Station, TX: Texas A&M University Press, 2003).

Holmes, Richard, *Tommy: The British Soldier on the Western Front 1914–1918* (London: Harper Collins, 2005).

Hooton, E. R., *War Over the Trenches: Air Power and the Western Front Campaigns 1916–1918* (Hersham: Midland Publishing, 2010).

Howard, Michael (ed.), *The Theory and Practice of War: Essays Presented to Captain B.H. Liddell Hart on his Seventieth Birthday* (London: Cassell, 1965).

Howard, Michael, *The Causes of War and Other Essays*, 2nd edn (London: Unwin, 1983).

Hughes, Matthew and Seligmann, Matthew (eds), *Leadership in Conflict 1914–1918* (Barnsley: Pen and Sword, 2000).

Hyde, H. Montgomery, *British Air Policy between the Wars, 1918–1939* (London: Heinemann, 1976).

Jackson, Bill and Bramall, Edwin, *The Chiefs: The Story of the United Kingdom Chiefs of Staff* (London: Brassey's, 1992).

Jeffery, Keith, *The British Army and the Crisis of Empire 1918–1922* (Manchester: Manchester University Press, 1984).

Jones, Neville, *The Origins of Strategic Bombing: A Study of the Development of British Air Strategic Thought and Practice up to 1918* (London: Kimber, 1973).

Kaiser, David, *Politics & War: European Conflict from Philip II to Hitler* (Cambridge, MA: Harvard University Press, 1990).

Kennett, Lee, *The First Air War* (New York: Simon and Schuster, 1991).

Kenyon, David, *Horsemen in No Man's Land: British Cavalry and Trench Warfare, 1914–1918* (Barnsley: Pen and Sword, 2011).

Kershaw, Ian, *The Hitler Myth; Image and reality in the Third Reich*, Third Edition (Oxford: Oxford University Press, 2001)

Knox, MacGregor and Murray, Williamson (eds), *The Dynamics of Military Revolution 1300–2050* (Cambridge: Cambridge University Press, 2001).

Laffin, John, *Swifter than Eagles: A Biography of Marshal of the RAF Sir John Salmond* (Edinburgh: William Blackwood and Sons, 1964).

Lindsay, Neville, *Equal to the Task, Volume I. The Royal Australian Army Service Corps* (Kenmore: Historia Productions, 1992).

Lupfer, Timothy T., *The Dynamics of Doctrine: The Change in German Tactical Doctrine during the First World War*, Leavenworth Paper No. 4 (Fort Leavenworth, KS: Combat Studies Institute, 1981).

Lynne, John A. (ed.), *Feeding Mars: Logistics in Western Warfare from the Middle Ages to the Present* (Boulder, CO: Westview Press, 1993).

MacNicoll, R. R., *The Royal Australian Engineers, 1902 to 1919* (Netley: Royal Australian Engineers Corps Committee, 1979).

McWilliams, James and Steel, R. James, *Amiens: Dawn of Victory* (Toronto: Dundurn, 2004).

Marble, Sanders, *'The Infantry cannot do with a Gun Less': The Place of the Artillery in the BEF, 1914–18* (New York, NY: Columbia University Press, Gutenburg ebook, 2007).

Mason, Tony, *Air Power: A Centennial Appraisal* (London: Brassey's, 2001).

Meilinger, Philip S., *Airwar: Theory and Practice* (London: Frank Cass, 2003).

Messenger, Charles, *The Day We Won The War: Turning Point At Amiens August 1918* (London: Orion, 2008).

Millett, Allan R. and Murray, Williamson (eds), *Military Effectiveness: Volume 1 – The First World War* (London: Unwin Hyman, 1989 [1988]).

Morrow Jr., John H., *The Great War in the Air: Military Aviation from 1909 to 1921* (Washington, DC: Smithsonian Institution Press, 1993).

—, *The Great War: An Imperial History* (London: Routledge, 2004).

Murray, J. D., *The Last Waggon. The Final Story of the Royal Canadian Army Service Corps* (Summerside, PE: Williams and Crue, 2001).

Murray, Williamson and Millett, Allan R. (eds), *Military Innovation in the Interwar Period* (Cambridge: Cambridge University Press, 1996).

Murray, Williamson and Knox, MacGregor (eds), *The Dynamics of Military Revolution, 1300–2050* (Cambridge, Cambridge University Press, 2001).

Omissi, David, *Air Power and Colonial Control: The Royal Air Force 1990–1939* (Manchester: Manchester University Press, 1990).

Orange, Vincent, *Slessor: Bomber Champion – The Life of Marshal of the Royal Air Force Sir John Slessor, GCB, DSO, MC* (London: Grub Street, 2006).

Palazzo, Albert, *Seeking Victory on the Western Front: The British Army and Chemical Warfare in World War I* (Lincoln, NE: University of Nebraska Press, 2000).

Paris, Michael, *Winged Warfare: The Literature and Theory of Aerial Warfare in Britain 1859–1917* (Manchester: Manchester University Press, 1992).

Parker, Geoffrey, *The Military Revolution: Military Innovation and the Rise of the West, 1500–1800* (Cambridge: Cambridge University Press, 1988).

Parkinson, Roger, *Tormented Warrior: Ludendorff and the Supreme Command* (London: Hodder and Stoughton, 1978).

Peden, G. C., *Arms, Economics and British Strategy* (Cambridge: Cambridge University Press, 2007).

Philpott, William, *Anglo-French Relations and Strategy on the Western Front, 1914–18* (Basingstoke: Palgrave Macmillan, 1996).

—, *Bloody Victory: The Sacrifice on the Somme and the Making of the Twentieth Century* (London: Little Brown, 2009).

Pidgeon, Trevor, *Tanks on the Somme: From Morval to Beaumont Hamel* (Barnsley: Pen and Sword, 2010).

Powell, Geoffrey, *Plumer: The Soldiers' General: A Biography of Field-Marshal Viscount Plumer of Messines* (London: Leo Cooper, 1990).

Powers, Barry, *Strategy Without Slide-Rule: British Air Strategy 1914-1939* (London: Croom Helm, 1976).

Prior, Robin and Wilson, Trevor, *Command on the Western Front: The Military Career of Sir Henry Rawlinson, 1914-1918* (Oxford: Blackwell, 1992).

Pugsley, Christopher, *The Anzac Experience: New Zealand, Australia and Empire in the First World War* (Auckland: Reed, 2004).

Rawling, Bill, *Surviving Trench Warfare: Technology and the Canadian Corps 1914-1918* (Toronto: University of Toronto Press, 1992).

Reader, W. J., *Architect of Air Power. The Life of the First Viscount Weir of Eastwood* (London: Collins, 1968).

Robbins, Simon, *British Generalship on the Western Front 1914-18: Defeat into Victory* (London: Frank Cass, 2005).

—, *British Generalship in the Great War: The Career of Sir Henry Horne (1861-1929)* (Farnham: Ashgate, 2010)

Robertson, Scot, *The Development of RAF Strategic Bombing Doctrine, 1919-1939* (Westport, CT: Praeger, 1995).

Robson, Brian, *Crisis on the Frontier: The Third Afghan war and the Campaign in Waziristan 1919-20* (Stroud: Spellmount, 2005).

Rothenberg, Gunther, *The Art of Warfare in the Age of Napoleon* (Bloomington, IN: Indiana University Press, 1980).

Rothwell, V. H., *British War Aims and Peace Diplomacy 1914-1918* (Oxford: Clarendon Press, 1971).

Samuels, Martin, *Command or Control? Command, Training and Tactics in the British and German Armies, 1888-1918* (London: Frank Cass, 1995).

Saunders, Hilary St. George, *Per Ardua – The Rise of British Air Power 1911-1939* (London: Oxford University Press, 1945).

Schechter, Damon, *Delivering the Goods. The Art of Managing Your Supply Chain* (New York, NY: John Wiley, 2002).

Schreiber, Shane B., *Shock Army of the British Empire: The Canadian Corps in the Last 100 Days of the Great War* (Greenwood, CT: Praeger, 1997).

Sheffield, Gary, *Leadership in the Trenches: Officer-Man Relations, Morale and Discipline in the British Army in the Era of the First World War* (Basingstoke: Macmillan, 2000).

—, *Forgotten Victory: The First World War: Myths and Realities* (London: Headline, 2001).

—, *The Chief: Douglas Haig and the British Army* (London: Aurum, 2011).

Sheffield, Gary and Bourne, John (eds), *Douglas Haig: War Diaries and Letters 1914–1918* (London: Weidenfeld and Nicholson, 2005).

Sheffield, Gary and Inglis, G. I. S. (eds), *From Vimy Ridge to the Rhine: The Great War Letters of Christopher Stone DSO MC* (Marlborough: Crowood Press, 1989).

Sheffield, Gary and Todman, Dan (eds), *Command and Control on the Western Front: The British Army's Experience 1914–1918* (Staplehurst: Spellmount, 2004).

Sheffy, Yigal, *British Military Intelligence in the Palestine Campaign* (London: Frank Cass, 1998).

Simpson, Andy, *Directing Operations: British Corps Command on the Western Front 1914–18* (Stroud: Spellmount, 2006).

Slessor, Sir John, *Air Power and Armies* (Oxford: Oxford University Press, 1936).

Smith, Malcolm, *British Air Strategy between the Wars* (Oxford: Clarendon Press, 1984).

Smithers, A. J., *A New Excalibur: The Development of the Tank 1909–1939* (London: Leo Cooper, 1986).

Spaight, J. M., *The Beginnings of Organised Air Power: A Historical Study* (London: Longmans, 1927).

Steel, Nigel and Hart, Peter, *Tumult in the Clouds: The British Experience of War in the Air* (London: Hodder and Stoughton, 1997).

Stevenson, David, *1914–1918: The History of The First World War* (London: Penguin, 2004).

Strachan, Hew (ed.), *The Oxford Illustrated History of the First World War* (Oxford: Oxford University Press, 1998).

Strong, Paul and Marble, Sanders, *Artillery in the Great War* (Barnsley: Pen and Sword, 2011).

Sweetman, John, *Cavalry of the Clouds: Air War Over Europe 1914–1918* (Stroud: Spellmount, 2010).

Terraine, John, *To Win a War: 1918 The Year of Victory* (London: Sidgewick Jackson, 1978).

—, *The Right of the Line: The Royal Air Force in the European War, 1939–1945* (London: Hodder and Stoughton, 1985).

—, *White Heat: The New Warfare 1914–18* (London: Leo Cooper, 1992 [1982]).

Thompson, J. Lee, *Northcliffe: Press Baron in Politics 1865–1922* (London: John Murray, 2000).

Thompson, Julian, *Lifeblood of War: Logistics in Armed Conflict* (London: Brassey's, 1991).

Travers, Tim, *The Killing Ground: The British Army, the Western Front and the Emergence of Modern Warfare 1900–1918* (London: Allen and Unwin, 1987).

—, *How the War Was Won: Command and Technology in the British Army on the Western Front 1917–1918* (London: Routledge, 1992).

Van Creveld, Martin, *Supplying War: Logistics from Wallenstein to Patton* (Cambridge: Cambridge University Press, 1977).

Watson, Alexander, *Enduring the Great War: Combat, Morale and Collapse in the German and British Armies, 1914–1918* (Cambridge: Cambridge University Press, 2008).
Williams, George K., *Biplanes and Bombsights: British Bombing in World War I* (Maxwell, AL: Air University Press, 1999).
Winton, Harold, *To Change an Army: General Sir John Burnett-Stuart and British Armored Doctrine, 1927–1938* (Lawrence, KS: University Press of Kansas, 1988).
Woodward, David R., *Lloyd George and the Generals* (Newark, DE: Delaware University Press, 1983).
Zabecki, David T., *Steel Wind: Colonel Georg Bruchmüller and the Birth of Modern Artillery* (Westport, CT: Praeger, 1994).
—, *The German 1918 Offensives: A Case Study in the Operational Level of War* (London: Routledge, 2006).
Zaccaro, Stephen J., *The Nature of Executive Leadership: A Conceptual and Empirical Analysis of Success* (Washington, DC: American Psychological Association, 2001).

Chapters and articles

Ash, Eric, 'Air Power Leadership: A Study of Sykes and Trenchard', in Peter Gray and Sebastian Cox (eds), *Air Power Leadership: Theory and Practice* (London: The Stationary Office, 2002), pp. 160–77.
Badsey, Stephen, 'Cavalry and the Development of Breakthrough Doctrine', in Paddy Griffith (ed.), *British Fighting Methods in the Great War* (London: Frank Cass, 1996), pp. 138–74.
Bailey, Jonathan, 'British Artillery in the Great War', in Paddy Griffith (ed.), *British Fighting Methods in the Great War* (London: Frank Cass, 1996), pp. 23–49.
—, 'The First World War and the Birth of Modern Warfare', in MacGregor Knox and Williamson Murray (eds), *The Dynamics of Military Revolution 1300–2050* (Cambridge: Cambridge University Press, 2001), pp. 132–53.
Biddle, Tami Davis, 'Learning in Real Time: The Development and Implementation of Air Power in the First World War', in Sebastian Cox and Peter Gray (eds), *Air Power History: Turning Points from Kitty Hawk to Kosovo* (London: Frank Cass, 2002), pp. 3–20.
Bidwell, Shelford, 'After The Wall Came Tumbling Down: A Historical Perspective', *RUSI Journal*, Vol. 135, No. 3 (Autumn 1990), pp. 57–61.
Black, Jeremy, 'Was There a Military Revolution in Early Modern Europe?' *History Today*, Vol. 57, No. 8 (July 2008), pp. 34–41.
Boff, Jonathan, 'Air-Land Integration in the 100 Days: the Case of Third Army', *RAF Air Power Review*, Vol. 12, No. 3 (Autumn 2009), pp. 77–88.
—, 'Combined Arms during the Hundred Days Campaign, August–November 1918', *War in History*, Vol. 17, No. 4 (November 2010), pp. 459–78.

Bond, Brian, 'Doctrine and Training in the British Cavalry, 1870-1914', in Michael Howard (ed.), *The Theory and Practice of War: Essays Presented to Captain B.H. Liddell Hart on his Seventieth Birthday* (London: Cassell, 1965), pp. 95-125.

Brown, Ian M., 'Not Glamorous, But Effective: The Canadian Corps and the Set-Piece Attack, 1917-1918', *Journal of Military History*, Vol. 58, No. 3 (July 1994), pp. 421-44.

—, 'Feeding Victory: The Logistic Imperative Behind the Hundred Days', in Peter Dennis and Jeffrey Grey (eds), *1918: Defining Victory* (Canberra: Army History Unit, 1999), pp. 195-202.

Buckley, John, 'The Air War in France', in Bond, Brian and Taylor, Michael (eds), *The Battle for France and Flanders Sixty Years On* (Barnsley: Leo Cooper, 2001), pp. 111-26.

Bushaway, Bob, 'Haig and the Cavalry', *Journal of the Centre for First World War Studies*, Vol. 1, No. 1 (2004).

Cook, George, 'Sir Robert Borden, Lloyd George and British Military Policy, 1917-1918', *The Historical Journal*, Vol. 14, No. 2 (June 1971), pp. 371-95.

Cooper, Malcolm, 'A House Divided: Policy, Rivalry and Administration in Britain's Military Air Command 1914-1918', *Journal of Strategic Studies*, Vol. 3, No. 2 (1980), pp. 178-201.

Deist, Wilhelm, 'The Military Collapse of the German Empire: The Reality Behind the Stab-in-the-Back Myth' (E. J. Feuchtwanger, trans.), *War in* History, Vol. 3, No. 2 (April 1996), pp. 186-201.

Dye, Peter, 'Logistics and the Battle of Britain: Fighter Wastage in the RAF and the Luftwaffe', *Air Force Journal of Logistics*, Vol. 24, No. 4 (2000), pp. 3, 33-42.

Fest, W. B., 'British War Aims and German Peace Feelers during the First World War (December 1916-November 1918)', *The Historical Journal*, Vol. 15, No. 2 (June 1972), pp. 285-308.

Ferris, John, 'Achieving Air Ascendancy: Challenge and Response in British Strategic Air Defence, 1915-1940', in Sebastian Cox and Peter Gray (eds), *Air Power History: Turning Points from Kitty Hawk to Kosovo* (London: Frank Cass, 2002), pp. 21-50.

F.F.G., 'The Royal Air Force: Administration, Organization and Direction', *Journal of Royal United Services Institution*, Vol. 82, No. 525 (1937), pp. 89-102.

French, David, 'Doctrine and Organization in the British Army 1919-1932', *The Historical Journal*, Vol. 44, No. 2 (June 2001), pp. 497-515.

Gardner, Nikolas, 'Julian Byng', in Ian F. W. Beckett and Steven J. Corvi (eds), *Haig's Generals* (Barnsley: Pen and Sword, 2006), pp. 54-74.

Geyer, Michael, 'Insurrectionary Warfare: The German Debate about a Levee en Masse in October 1918', *Journal of Modern History*, Vol. 73, No. 3 (September 2001), pp. 459-527.

Gooch, John, 'The Maurice Debate', *Journal of Contemporary History*, Vol. 3, No. 4 (October 1968), pp. 221-8.

Goulter, Christina, 'The Royal Naval Air Service: A Very Modern Service', in Sebastian Cox, and Peter Gray (eds), *Air Power History: Turning Points from Kitty Hawk to Kosovo* (London: Frank Cass, 2002), pp. 51–65.

Hall, David Ian, 'From Khaki and Light Blue to Purple: The Long and Troubled Development of Army/Air Co-operation in Britain, 1914–1945', *RUSI Journal*, Vol. 147, No. 5 (2002), pp. 78–83.

Holmes, Richard, 'The Last Hurrah: Cavalry on the Western Front, August–September 1914', in Hugh Cecil and Peter Liddle (eds), *Facing Armageddon: The First World War Experienced* (London: Pen and Sword, 1996), pp. 278–94.

Howard, Michael 'The Forgotten Dimensions of Strategy', in *The Causes of War and Other Essays*, 2nd edn (London: Unwin, 1983), pp. 101–15.

Iarocci, Andrew, 'Engines of War: Horsepower in the Canadian Expeditionary Force, 1914–18', *Journal of the Society for Army Historical Research*, Vol. 87, No. 349 (2009), pp. 59–83.

John Lee, 'William Birdwood', in Ian F. W. Beckett and Steven J. Corvi (eds), *Haig's Generals* (Barnsley: Pen and Sword, 2006).

Jones, H. A., 'The Birth of the Royal Air Force', *Journal of Royal United Services Institution*, Vol. 83 (1938), pp. 1–10.

Jordan, David, 'The Battle for the Skies: Sir Hugh Trenchard as Commander of the Royal Flying Corps', in Matthew Hughes and Matthew Seligmann (eds), *Leadership in Conflict 1914–1918* (Barnsley: Pen and Sword, 2000), pp. 68–91.

—, 'The Royal Air Force and Air Land Integration in the 100 days', *RAF Air Power Review*, Vol. 11, No. 2 (Summer 2008), pp. 12–30.

Justice, Simon, 'Behind the Lines: Sir Douglas Haig and the Cavalry Corps, Sep–Oct 1918', *Records: The Journal of the Douglas Haig Fellowship*, Vol. 14 (November 2010), pp. 36–55.

Kennedy, Paul, 'The First World War and the International Power System', *International Security*, Vol. 9, No. 1 (Summer 1984), pp. 7–40.

—, 'Britain in the First World War', in Allan R. Millett and Williamson Murray (eds), *Military Effectiveness: Volume 1 – The First World War* (London: Unwin Hyman, 1989 [1988]), pp. 329–50.

McCarthy, Chris, 'Queen of the Battlefield: The Development of Command, Organisation and Tactics in the British Infantry Battalion during the Great War', in Gary Sheffield and Dan Todman (eds), *Command and Control on the Western Front: The British Army's Experience 1914–1918* (Staplehurst: Spellmount, 2004), pp. 173–94.

Meilinger, Philip S., 'Trenchard and "Morale Bombing": The Evolution of Royal Air Force Doctrine before World War II', *Journal of Military History*, Vol. 60, No. 2. (April 1996), pp. 243–70.

—, 'John C. Slessor and the Genesis of Aerial Interdiction', in *Airwar: Theory and Practice* (London: Frank Cass, 2003), pp. 64–75.

Millett, Allan R., Murray, Williamson and Waltman, Kenneth, 'The Effectiveness of Military Organizations', in Allan R. Millett and Williamson Murray (eds), *Military Effectiveness: Volume I – The First World War* (London: Unwin Hyman, 1988), pp. 1–30.

Millman, Brock, 'A Counsel of Despair: British Strategy and War Aims, 1917–18', *Journal of Contemporary History*, Vol. 36, No. 2. (April 2001), pp. 241–70.

Muller, Richard R., 'Close Air Support: The British, German and American Experience, 1918–1941', in Williamson Murray and Allan R. Millett (eds), *Military Innovation in the Interwar Period* (Cambridge: Cambridge University Press, 1996), pp. 144–90.

Murray, Williamson, 'Thinking about Revolutions in Military Affairs', *Joint Force Quarterly*, No. 16 (Summer 1997), pp. 69–76.

Murray, Williamson and Knox, MacGregor, 'Thinking about Revolutions in Warfare' in Williamson Murray and MacGregor Knox (eds), *The Dynamics of Military Revolution, 1300–2050* (Cambridge, Cambridge University Press, 2001), pp. 1–14.

Northedge, F. S., '1917–1919: The Implications for Britain', *Journal of Contemporary History*, Vol. 3, No. 4 (October 1968), pp. 191–206.

Palazzo, Albert, 'The British Army's Counter Battery Staff Office and Control of the Enemy in World War I', *Journal of Military History*, Vol. 63, No. 1 (January 1999), pp. 55–74.

Parton, Neville, 'The Development of Early RAF Doctrine', *Journal of Military History*, Vol. 72, No. 4 (2008), pp. 1155–78.

Phillips, Gervase, 'The Obsolescence of the *Arme Blanche* and Technological Determinism in British Military History', *War in History*, Vol. 9, No. 1 (2002), pp. 39–59.

—, 'Douglas Haig and the Development of Twentieth-Century Cavalry', *Archives*, Vol. 28, No. 109 (2003), pp. 142–62.

—, 'Scapegoat Arm: Twentieth-Century Cavalry in Anglophone Historiography', *Journal of Military History*, Vol. 71, No. 1 (January 2007), pp. 37–74.

Philpott, William, 'Marshal Foch and Allied Victory', in Matthew Hughes and Matthew Seligmann (eds), *Leadership in Conflict 1914–1918* (Barnsley: Pen and Sword, 2000), pp. 38–53.

Sheffield, Gary, 'The Indispensable Factor: The Performance of British Troops in 1918', in Peter Dennis and Jeffrey Grey (eds), *1918: Defining Victory* (Canberra: Army History Unit, 1999), pp. 72–95.

Sheffield, Gary and Jordan, David, 'Douglas Haig and Air Power', in Peter Gray and Sebastian Cox (eds), *Air Power Leadership: Theory and Practice* (London: The Stationary Office, 2002), pp. 264–82.

Simkins, Peter, 'Co-Stars or Supporting Cast? British Divisions in the "Hundred Days", 1918', in Paddy Griffith (ed.), *British Fighting Methods in the Great War* (London: Frank Cass, 1996), pp. 50–69.

—, 'Haig and the Army Commanders', in Brian Bond and Nigel Cave (eds), *Haig: A Reappraisal 70 Years On* (Barnsley: Pen and Sword, 1999), pp. 78–106.

—, 'Somme Reprise: Reflections on the Fighting for Albert and Bapaume, August 1918', in British Commission for Military History, *'Look to your Front': Studies in the First World War* (Staplehurst: Spellmount, 1999), pp. 147–62.

—, 'For Better or For Worse: Sir Henry Rawlinson and his Allies in 1916 and 1918', in Matthew Hughes and Matthew Seligmann (eds), *Leadership in Conflict 1914–1918* (Barnsley, 2000), pp. 13–37.

—, '"Building Blocks": Aspects of Command and Control at Brigade Level in the BEF's Offensive Operations, 1916–1918', in Gary Sheffield and Dan Todman (eds), *Command and Control on the Western Front: The British Army's Experience 1914–1918* (Staplehurst: Spellmount, 2004), pp. 141–72.

—, 'Herbert Plumer', in Beckett, F. W. Ian and Steven J. Corvi (eds), *Haig's Generals* (Barnsley: Pen and Sworld, 2006), pp. 141–63.

Simpson, Andy, 'British Corps Command on the Western Front, 1914–1918', in Gary Sheffield and Dan Todman (eds), *Command and Control on the Western Front: The British Army's Experience 1914–1918* (Staplehurst: Spellmount, 2004), pp. 97–118.

Smyth, Harv, 'Re-learning Air Land Co-operation', *RAF Air Power Review*, Vol. 10, No. 1 (Spring 2007), pp. 1–27.

Strachan, Hew, 'The Morale of the German Army 1917–18', in Hugh Cecil and Peter Liddle (eds), *Facing Armageddon: The First World War Experienced* (London: Pen and Sword, 1996), pp. 383–98.

Sumida, Jon Tetsuro, 'Forging the Trident: British Naval Industrial Logistics, 1914–1918', in John A. Lynne (ed.), *Feeding Mars: Logistics in Western Warfare from the Middle Ages to the Present* (Boulder, CO: Westview Press, 1993), pp. 217–49.

Sweetman, John, 'The Smuts Report of 1917: Merely Political Window-Dressing?' *Journal of Strategic Studies*, Vol. 4, No. 2 (1981), pp. 152–74.

Terraine, John, 'Passchendaele and Amiens – I', *RUSI Journal*, Vol. 104, No. 614 (May 1959), pp. 173–83.

—, 'Passchendaele and Amiens – II', *RUSI Journal*, Vol. 104, No. 615 (August 1959), pp. 331–40.

—, 'Lessons of Air Warfare', *RUSI Journal*, Vol. 137, No. 4 (August 1992), pp. 53–8.

Thompson, Rob, 'Mud, Blood and Wood: BEF Operational and Combat Logistico-Engineering during the Battle of Third Ypres, 1917', in P. Doyle and M. R. Bennett (eds), *Fields of Battle: Terrain in Military History* (Dordrecht: Kluwer Academic Publishing, 2002), pp. 237–55.

Todman, Dan, 'The Grand Lamasery Revisited: General Headquarters on the Western Front', in Gary Sheffield and Dan Todman (eds), *Command and Control on the Western Front: The British Army's Experience 1914–1918* (Staplehurst: Spellmount, 2004), pp. 39–70.

Todman, Dan and Sheffield, Gary, 'Command and Control in the British Army on the Western Front', in Gary Sheffield and Dan Todman (eds), *Command and Control on the Western Front: The British Army's Experience 1914–1918* (Staplehurst: Spellmount, 2004), pp. 1–12.

Travers, Tim 'The Offensive and the Problem of Innovation in British Military Thought, 1870–1915', *Journal of Contemporary History*, Vol. 13, No. 3 (July 1978), pp. 531–53.
—, 'The Hidden Army: Structural Problems in the British Officer Corps, 1900–1918', *Journal of Contemporary History*, Vol. 17, No. 3 (July 1982), pp. 523–44.
—, 'Could the Tanks of 1918 Have Been War-Winners for the British Expeditionary Force?' *Journal of Contemporary History*, Vol. 27, No. 3 (July 1992), pp. 389–406.
—, 'The Allied Victories 1918', in Hew Strachan (ed.), *The Oxford Illustrated History of the First World War* (Oxford: Oxford University Press, 1998), pp. 278–90.
Van Creveld, Martin, 'Supplying an Army: An Historical View', *RUSI Journal*, Vol. 123, No. 2 (1978), pp. 56–63.
Whitmarsh, Andrew, 'British Army Manoeuvres and the Development of Military Aviation, 1910–13', *War in History*, Vol. 14, No. 3 (2007), pp. 325–46.
Wise, S. F., 'The Black Day of the German Army: Australians and Canadians at Amiens, August 1918', in Peter Dennis and Jeffrey Grey (eds), *1918: Defining Victory* (Canberra: Army History Unit, 1999), pp. 1–32.

Theses and dissertations

Beach, James, 'British Intelligence and the German Army, 1914–1918' (PhD Thesis, University College London, 2004).
Hall, Brian N., 'The British Expeditionary Force and Communications on the Western Front, 1914–1918' (PhD Thesis, University of Salford, 2009).
Hammond, Christopher Brynley, 'The Theory and Practice of Tank Co-Operation with Other Arms on the Western Front during the First World War' (PhD Thesis, University of Birmingham, 2005).
John, V., 'The British Cavalry on the Western Front in 1918' (MA Dissertation, University of Birmingham, 2007).
Jordan, David, 'The Army Co-Operation Missions of the Royal Flying Corps/Royal Air Force, 1914–1918' (PhD Thesis, University of Birmingham, 1998).
Parton, Neville, 'The Evolution and Impact of Royal Air Force Doctrine, 1919–1939' (PhD Thesis, University of Cambridge, 2009).
Pugh, James, 'The Conceptual Origins of Control of the Air: British Military and Naval Aviation, 1911–1918' (PhD Thesis, University of Birmingham, 2012).
Simpson, Andrew, 'The Operational Role of British Corps Command on the Western Front, 1914–1918' (PhD Thesis, University College London, 2001).
Waldie, Derek, 'The Third Dimension: A Study of Army-Air Force Relations 1918–1939' (PhD Thesis King's College London, 1980).

Index

Page numbers in **bold** refer to figures.

Action of Ooteghem, the 103
Action of Tiegham, the 103
Ader, Clement 3
Advanced Air Striking Force (AASF) 241
aerial photography 174
Afghan War of 1919, the 224
Air Board, the 136–7, 157, 160
   becoming Air Ministry 137
Air Council (1916) 184
Air Force (Constitution) Act, the 13
Air Force (Constitution) Bill, The 139, 159
air interdiction 239 *see also* Slessor, John
Air Ministry 11, 12, 13, 137, 138, 153, 158, 160, 161, 162, 184, 196, 239, 242, 244
Air Policy Committee 159
air power,
   evolution of 3–5
      airships, development of 3
      modern airpower, the beginning of 3
      rigid airships, construction of 3
Air Raids Committee 159
Air Reorganization Committee 159
air superiority 15, 45, 89, 151, 173, 175, 186, 214–15, 218, 220, 221, 222, 224, 233, 236, 237, 238, 240, 241
aircraft engine repair,
   aircraft and engine wastage – 1918 **177**
   aircraft salvage – 1918 **177**
Albert, King 97, 102, 104, 106
Alexander, Harold 224
American Civil War, the 2, 3
American Expeditionary Force, the 162
Archibald, Sapper 84
Armée Francaise de Belgique 101
Armistice, the 1, 11, 25, 28, 37, 73, 74, 88, 93, 105, 123, 175, 177, 178, 184, 203, 231, 235

Army Air Parks (AAP) 176, 178, 179
artillery,
   75mm M-1897, introduction of 2
   and aircraft 1
   evolution of 1–3
   as the God of War 2
artillery spotting 15, 211–12
Asquith, Herbert 136, 154
attacking enemy troops 11
Austro-Prussian War of 1866, the 2

Bailey, Jonathan 2, 7, 8, 172, 186
Baird, Brigadier General 30
balloons,
   for bombing 3
   for surviellence 3
Bapaume 22, 29, 235
Barbour, Sapper 86
Barker, Pat 73
   Ghost Road, The 73
Barr, Niall 10, 20, 37, 98
Barratt, Air Marshal 241
Battle of Albert, the 238
Battle of Amiens, the 9, 14, 15, 37, 41, 49, 50, 55, 94, 174, 207–25, 231, 233, 234, 237, 238, 239, 240, 244
   air-ground co-operation, the mechanics of 210–20
      artillery spotting 211–12
      battlefield support, direct and indirect 214
      command factors 217
      communications 215–16
      concentration 218
      contact patrols 212–13
      failure to isolate the battlefield 218–19
      ground support 213–14
      intelligence 216

local air superiority 214–15
non-controllable factors 218
planning 216–17
RAF's impact 219–20
reconnaissance 210–11
target acquisition 217–18
Canadian Corps at, logistics and administration of 37–50
and the development of British Air-Land battle 231–44
imperial policing, the implications for 221–5
Ludendorff's phrasing 207
Battle of Britain, the 143, 171, 186, 242
Battle of Cambrai, the 40, 41, 56, 63, 65
Battle of Courtrai, the 93, 101–3
Battle of Festubert, the 174
Battle of Hamel, the 200, 201
Battle of the Marne, Second 207
Battle of the Sambre, the 10
    BEF at, the 73–90
        bridge, building of the 84
        purposeless loss of lives 85
    Landrecies, the capture of 87
Battle of the Scarpe, the 41
Battle of the Somme, the 173, 180, 186, 195, 197
Battle of Ypres, the 98–100, 100, 180
battlefield support 15
Beaverbrook, Lord 160
Beddington, Lieutenant-Colonel 199
Benbow, Tim 6
Biddle, Tami 149, 150
Bidwell, Shelford 174, 175
Bilton, David 96
Birdwood, General 111
Blériot, Louis 4
*Blitzkrieg,*German 6, 7, 203
Boff, Jonathan 9
Bolshevik government, the 196
Bond, Brian 223
Bourlon village 66
Bramall, Field Marshal 135
Brancker, Major Sefton 4
Britain 2, 4, 12, 98, 105, 150, 152, 154, 155, 156, 184, 192, 222, 223, 224, 225, 235
British Air Forces in France (BAFF) 241
British Air-Land battle (1918–45) 231–44

British Expeditionary Force (BEF), the 4, 9, 10, 11, 19, 37, 39, 40, 41, 43, 44, 47, 49, 93, 111, 150, 171, 176, 179, 191, 194, 197, 200, 203, 232, 234, 235
    technology and tactics post Amiens 55–67
        operational tempo, maintenance of 56–60
        Royal Air Force and the Tank Corps 60–2
        Tank Corps, the 62–6
    see also Canadian Corps
British Second Army, the 93–107
British War Cabinet, the 153
British war policy 155
Brock, Commander 66
Brooke-Popham, 237
Brown, Ian M. 37, 39
    British Logistics on the Western Front 1914-1919 39
Brown, Lt.-Col. 41
Bulgaria 74
Bungo's' force 9
Byng, General Julian 9, 19, 27, 30, 111

Campbell, Major General 30
Canadian Corps, the 41, 42, 50, 208, 209
Canadian Corps General Officer Commanding Artillery (GOCRA) 48
Cavalry Corps, the 111–24
    action between 10 and 16 October 121–2
    action on 9 October 118–21
    appraisals of 115–17
    Edmonds, Haig and 112–13
    improvisation, suggestions for 117–18
    training exercise (17 September 1918) 113–15
Cayley, George 3
Charles, General 87
Charlton, Brigadier-General 208, 213, 224, 234
Charteris, Brigadier-General 197
Churchill, Winston 4, 143, 149, 242
Clausewitz, Carl von 163
Clayton, Anthony 96, 106
Cody, Samuel 5
Cold War, the 172
Collishaw, Raymond 224

command of the air 11
Coningham, Simon 11, 14, 15, 16
contact patrols 15, 212–13
Cooper, Malcolm 143
Courage, Brigadier-General 58
Cowdray, Lord 137
Currie, Arthur 42, 217
Curzon, Lord 136, 137, 139

Daily Mail 136
De Pree, Brigadier-General 28–9
Debeney, General 20
Degoutte, General 94, 98, 99, 100, 101
Dendre river 104, 105
Deverell, Major General 30
Deynze-Ecloo canal 102–3
Dill, John 224
Drews, Dr 74
Duffy, Christopher 173
Dye, Peter 9, 11, 13
Dynamics of Military Revolution, The 8

Eastern Front, the 196
Edmonds, James 20, 112, 123
Eisenhower, Dwight D. 38
Ekins, Ashley 37
Elles, Brigadier-General 60, 61
Ellington, Edward 224
English Channel, the 93
Evans, G. F. 31

Feilding, Major General 30
Field Service Regulations Part I (Operations) 20–1
Field Service Regulations Part II (Organisation and Administration) 21
Findlay, Major 82
First World War 1, 3, 5, 7, 8, 10, 11, 13, 14, 15, 16, 23, 39, 73, 79, 143, 171, 172, 173, 186, 203, 207, 210, 211, 221, 222, 224, 244
flash spotting 174
Foch, Marshal 41, 101, 102, 104, 208
Fokker Scourge 195
Fokkers 135
Fourth Army, the 9
France 1, 12, 46, 57, 60, 61, 87, 96, 98, 137, 140, 141, 142, 150, 151, 158, 160, 175, 176, 192, 193, 232, 241

Franco-Prussian War of 1870–1, the 2, 3
  balloons in 3
Frankland, Noble 143
French Plan XVII, the 150 *see also* German Schlieffen Plan

Geddes, Eric 236
German Air Force, the 208, 215, 233
German Air Service, the 173, 175
German March Offensive, the 182, 183
German Schlieffen Plan, the 150
German Spring Offensive, the 14, 180, 182, 191, 193
Germany 1, 2, 4, 74, 88, 94, 136, 137, 143, 150, 155, 156, 194, 232, 243
Gloucesters, the 86
Gooderson, Ian 244
Gordon, Phillip H. 149
Gough, General Hubert 40
Graham, Dominick 174, 175
Gray, Peter 11, 12
Grey, C. G. 143
Grey, Colin S. 8, 172
Groener, General 74, 88
ground support 15
Groupe d'Armees des Flandres 10, 93
Groves, Percy 161, 162
Guderian, Heinz 38, 241

Haig, Douglas 4, 5, 9, 10, 11, 29, 74, 75, 88, 89, 94, 98, 101, 104, 111, 112, 113, 114, 115, 117, 118, 122, 124, 141, 143, 152, 154, 155, 158, 160, 192, 201, 208, 211
Haldane, Lt. General 22, 23, 30
Hall, Brian 19
Hall, David Ian 15, 232, 238
Hammond, Bryn 9, 10
Harman, Major-General 122, 123
Harper, Lt. General 24
Harris, Arthur 224, 239, 243
Harris, J. P. 20, 25, 37, 98
Hart, Peter 37
Harvey, A. D. 193
Henderson, Brigadier-General 150, 151, 158, 192
Henniker, Colonel 38, 39
Heriot-Maitland, Brigadier General 31
Hermann Position, the 117, 119, 123

Hindenburg, Field Marshal 74
Hindenburg Line, the 19, 21, 22, 26, 58, 74, 113, 117, 118, 235
History of the Corps of Royal Engineers 38
Hitler, Adolf 232
Horne, General 111
Hundred Days campaign, the 19, 111–12, 171, 182, 191, 201, 203, 216, 220
  British Second Army in 93–107
    20 October-11 November 1918 103–5
    battle of Courtrai, the 101–3
    battle of Ypres, the 98–100
    and *Groupe d'Armees des Flandres* 93
  Third Army's operations during 19–31
    attack on the Hindenburg Line 21
    decentralization as a feature 20, 24, 26–7, 31
    delegation, the importance of 21, 31
    vague orders 23

imperial policing 16, 221–5
Imperial War Cabinet, the 153
Independent Force (IF) 12
industrial revolution 1
Infantry Training 1914 21
Inter-Allied Commission 192–3
interdicting supply lines 11
Iraqi insurrection of 1920, the 224
Ironside, Brigadier 22
Israeli-Hezbollah conflict, the 149

Jackson, General 135
Johns, Captain 193
Johnson, Lt. Colonel 57, 82
Jones, H. A. 143, 213, 216, 219
Jordan, David 11, 14, 16
Justice, Simon 11

Karslake, Brigadier-General 61
Kavanagh, Lieutenant-General 113, 114, 115, 118, 120, 121, 123
Kennedy, Paul 216
Kerry, A. J. 39
Kershaw, Ian 242
Kirk, 2nd Lt. 84
  death of, heroic 84
Kirke Committee, the 223

Kirke Report, the 223
Knocker, Guy 181

Lawrence, Lt. General 59, 104
Lawrie, Major General 28, 29
Le Cateau 74, 115, 117, 118, 120, 121, 123, 235, 240
Leigh-Mallory, Major 61, 62, 233, 243
Lilienthal, Otto 3
Lindsay, Neville 39
Lloyd George, David 136, 137, 140, 153, 154, 155, 156, 159, 160, 161, 192, 193
Luck, Chris 11, 13
Ludendorff, General 74, 200, 207, 219
  resignation of 74
Ludlow-Hewitt, Edgar 224
Luftwaffe, the 241
Lynne, John A 39
Lys river 94, 98, 100, 101, 102, 103

McClusky, Alistair 11, 14, 15, 16
McDill, W. A. 39
MacNicoll, R. R. 39
McWilliams, James 37
Marlborough, 1
Marshall, Andrew W. 6
  see also Revolution in Military Affairs
Marshall, Lt. Colonel 83, 84
Matheson, Major General 29, 30
Maxse, Lieutenant-General 113, 115
Mediterranean Allied Air Forces (MAAF) 243
Mediterranean Allied Strategic Air Force (MASAF) 243
Mediterranean Allied Tactical Air Force (MATAF) 243
Milner, Lord 117, 159
mobility 50
modern air power, the genesis of 191–204
modern warfare, genesis of,
  aviation logistics in 171–87
  characteristics of modern warfare 173
Monash, Lt. General 50, 200, 217
Montgolfier, Jacques-Étienne 3
Montgolfier, Joseph-Michel 3
Montgomery, Bernard 224
Mormal Forest 74, 75, 76, 88

Muller, Richard 232
Murray, Williamson 6, 39

Napoleon Bonaparte 1, 3, 7
Napoleonic Wars, the 1
Nazism 162
Neuve Chapelle offensive 194–5
Newall, Colonel 141
Nicholson, Major-General 96, 104
Nicholson, W. N. 38
   Behind the Lines 38
Northcliffe, Lord 4, 136, 159

O'Connor, Richard 224
offensive air power 14
Official History of the New Zealand Engineers... 39
Olliver, G. K. 31
Operation *Desert Storm* 38
Owen, D. C. 30
Owen, Wilfred 10, 73, 84, 89
   death of, the 89

Palazzo, Albert 27, 66
Parker, Geoffrey 172, 173
Pereira, Major General 30
Pilcher, Percy 3
Pinney, Major General 30, 31
Plumer, General Herbert 10, 40, 94, 95, 97, 98, 99, 100, 101, 102, 103, 104, 105, 106, 107, 111
pooling 49
Powell, Colin 38
Prior, Robin 20, 37

Rasch, G. E. 28
Rawlinson, Henry 20, 42, 75, 76, 111, 113, 118, 201, 208, 211, 240
reconnaissance 11, 15, 118, 151, 210–11
   aerial 114, 174, 219
   armed 244
   strategic 211
   tactical 211
Reserve Lorry Parks (RLP) 179
Revolution in Military Affairs (RMA) 5–8, 172
   Benbow's definition of 6
   Marshall's definition of 6
Roberts, Michael 172, 173

Robertson, William 152, 154
Robinson, Captain 47
Rothermere, Lord 12, 140, 159, 160
Royal Air Force (RAF) 8, 12, 13, 14, 15, 60–2, 77, 149, 171, 172, 175, 178, 179, 183, 186, 193, 194, 200, 203, 204, 207, 214, 215, 222, 223, 224, 225, 231, 232, 233, 236, 239, 241
   aircraft serviceability – April-November 1918 **181**
   available aircraft-1918 **180**
   formation of, the 135–44
   inception 135
   as an independent force 140–4
   logistic organization – August 1918 **178**
   supply of aeronautical material – October 1918 **185**
   and the Tank Corps 60–2
Royal Army Service Corps, The 38–9
Royal Artillery, the 3, 5
Royal Engineers, the 77–8, 87, 174
Royal Flying Corps (RFC) 11, 12, 13, 135, 137, 150, 151, 158, 171, 173, 174, 175, 176, 179, 180, 182, 185, 191, 192, 193, 195, 196, 197, 198
   brigade serviceability rates – March 1918 **181**
Royal Horse Artillery (RHA) 116
Royal Naval Air Service (RNAS) 11, 12, 135, 137, 151, 158, 191
Royal Navy, the 4, 136, 191, 192
Rupprecht, Crown Prince 200
Russia 2, 155
Russo-Japanese War of 1904–5, the 2

St. Bénin 123
St Quentin Canal 75
Salmond, Major-General 14, 61, 142, 181, 182, 192, 199, 208, 209, 210, 214, 217, 224, 234
Sambre river, the 75
Sambre-Oise Canal, the 73, 74, 75
Samuels, Martin 20
Schelde river 94
Schreiber, Shane B. 37
Schwarzkopf, Norman 38
Second World War 13, 14, 16, 88, 105, 143, 231, 232, 240
Selle river 112, 123

Shaw, George Bernard 154
Sheffield, Gary 203
Shrapnell, Lt. General 2
Shute, Lt. General 22, 30
Simkins, Peter 95, 106, 111
Simpson, Andy 20, 58
Slessor, John 15, 142, 211, 213, 216, 218, 219, 224, 237
   Air Power and Armies 15, 142, 239
Slessor, Wing Commander 237, 239, 240, 242, 243
Slim, William 224
Smuts, Lt. General 13, 137, 138, 149, 153, 154, 156, 157, 159, 161, 162, 163, 192
Smuts Reports, the 13, 149–63
   German bombing of London and 150
   Second Report 150
Solly-Flood, Major General 23
Somme river 202, 219, 234, 238
sound ranging 174
South African War, the 2
Spaatz, Carl 243
Spaight, J. M. 139
S.S. 135 The Training and Employment of Divisions 20, 21, 22
S.S. 204 Infantry and Tank Co-Operation and Training 56
S.S. 214 Tanks and their Employment in Co-operation with Other Arms 56, 62–3, 66
Stalin, Josef 2
Steel, R. James 37
Strategic Air Offensive against Germany 1939–1945, The 143
Sweetman, John 149
Sykes, Major-General 4, 140, 142, 143, 160, 162, 192, 219

Tactical Air Force (TAF) 242
Tallard, Marshal 1
Tank Corps, the 60–2, 63–7, 202, 203, 235, 237
Terraine, John 37, 175, 176
Third Army, the 9
Thompson, Julian 39
   Fields of Battle 39
Thompson, Rob 9
Thorpe, George Cyrus 38

Times, The 159
Training Note, IGT's 64
Travers, Tim 20, 37
Trenchard, Major-General Hugh 4, 12, 14, 60, 137, 138, 140, 141, 142, 152, 158, 159, 160, 173, 181, 192, 193, 194, 196, 197, 198, 199, 221, 236
Turkey 74

Uniacke, Major-General 115

Van Creveld, Martin 38, 39, 185
Vaughan, L. R. 27
Vaughan, John 122
Von Kuhl, General 200
Von Zeppelin, Ferdinand 4

War Cabinet, the 138–9, 140, 141, 157
War Priorities Committee 159
Wardrop, A. E. 28
Warwicks, the 86
Washington Post 149
Waterloo 1
Waters, Major 84
Wavell, Archibald 224
weapon,
   75mm M-1897 (gun) 2
   breach-loaders 2
      British Armstrong weapon 2
   cylindro-conoidal bullet, the 1
   explosive shell, the 2
   fixed ammunition 2
   rifled musket, the 1
   rifled muzzleloaders 2
      Parrot guns 2
   solid shot 2
Webster, Charles 143
Weekly Tank Notes 66
Weir, William 140, 141, 142, 158, 160
Wellington, Duke of 1
Wells, H. G. 4
   War in the Air, The 4
Western Front, the 5, 7, 8, 19, 38, 40, 55, 56, 73, 74, 88, 93, 94, 101, 111, 150, 152, 153, 154, 157, 158, 171–2, 174, 175, 176, 179, 182, 185, 186, 207, 221, 222, 238, 242
Whigham, Major General 30

Whitmarsh, Andrew 5
Williams, Dennis 10
Willock, Air Commodore 239
Wilson, Henry 111
Wilson, Trevor 20, 37
wireless 19
wireless telegraphy 174
wireless telephony 174
Wise, S. F. 37

Wood, Sergeant 86
Woodcock, General 105
Worcesters, the 86
Wright, Orville 3, 4
Wright, Wilbur 3, 4

Yser river 93, 96

Zeppelins 135, 151

Lightning Source UK Ltd.
Milton Keynes UK
UKOW04f0848080716

277934UK00006B/121/P